Sport Ethics

Sport Ethics

Applications for Fair Play

Third Edition

Angela Lumpkin
Dean, School of Education
The University of Kansas

Sharon Kay Stoll
Director, Center for ETHICS*
University of Idaho

Jennifer M. Beller
Associate Professor of Research/Statistics
Department of Educational Leadership and Counseling Psychology
Washington State University

*With the Endorsement of the
National Association for Sport and Physical Education*

Boston   Burr Ridge, IL   Dubuque, IA   Madison, WI   New York   San Francisco   St. Louis
Bangkok   Bogotá   Caracas   Kuala Lumpur   Lisbon   London   Madrid   Mexico City
Milan   Montreal   New Delhi   Santiago   Seoul   Singapore   Sydney   Taipei   Toronto

McGraw-Hill Higher Education ✖

A Division of The **McGraw-Hill** *Companies*

SPORT ETHICS: APPLICATIONS FOR FAIR PLAY, THIRD EDITION

This book is printed on acid-free paper.

4 5 6 7 8 9 0 DOC/DOC 0 9 8 7 6

ISBN: 978-0-07-246209-8
MHID: 0-07-246209-4

Vice president and editor-in-chief: *Thalia Dorwick*
Publisher: *Jane E. Karpacz*
Executive editor: *Vicki Malinee*
Developmental editor: *Carlotta Seely*
Senior marketing manager: *Pamela S. Cooper*
Senior project manager: *Marilyn Rothenberger*
Production supervisor: *Enboge Chong*
Media technology producer: *Lance Gerhart*
Lead designer: *Matthew Baldwin*
Cover image: © *Getty Images*
Photo research coordinator/Art editor: *Alex Ambrose*
Compositor: *Carlisle Communications, Ltd.*
Typeface: *10/12 Galliard*
Printer: *R. R. Donnelley/Crawfordsville, IN*

NewMedia Inc./CORBIS Chapter 10 opening photo © Reuters
Photos on the following pages are © PhotoDisc
2, 20, 40, 54, 66, 84, 88, 108, 111, 123, 127, 136, 139, 144, 162, 170, 171, 183, 185, 191, 192, 206, 216, 227, 238, 254

Library of Congress Cataloging-in-Publication Data

Lumpkin, Angela
   Sport ethics : applications for fair play / Angela Lumpkin, Sharon Kay Stoll, Jennifer
M. Beller.-- 3rd ed.
      p. cm.
   Includes bibliographical references and index.
   ISBN 0-07-246209-4
   1. Sports--Moral and ethical aspects--United States. I. Stoll, Sharon Kay. II. Beller,
Jennifer Marie. III. Title

GV706.3 .L85 2003
796'.01--dc21   2002070965

Preface

The popularity of competitive sports continues to increase. Other than the media exposés associated with multimillion-dollar salaries for free agents, no subject related to sport seems to command the interest of the media, sport managers, coaches, athletes, and fans more than the erosion of ethical values. Almost daily, another point-shaving incident, bench-clearing brawl, positive result on a drug test, arrest of an athlete for assault or other law-breaking behavior, or athlete failing to maintain academic eligibility brings disgrace or embarrassment to a sport organization.

Some individuals argue that sport ethics has become an oxymoron because of the violations undermining fair play. There are people involved in sport who have lost or never developed the ability to reason morally within a sporting context. Because fair play necessitates that all competitors have the same chance for success, moral knowing, moral valuing, and moral acting are viewed as essential. Too often, though, the quest for winning and gaining awards overshadows individuals' beliefs in sportsmanship and playing within the spirit of the rules.

This text addresses many issues confronting the essence, and possibly even the survival, of competitive sport. We advocate moral reasoning in sport as essential to the attainment of values in sport, such as character development, teamwork, cooperation, and self-discipline. Within these pages, the reader will find philosophic theory that has proven effective in the moral development of athletes. Students preparing for sport management careers will find this book valuable in their exploration of how to preserve ethical values in sport. Regardless of one's role in sport, it is increasingly important to place ethical behaviors in the forefront.

Most people want sport cleansed from corruption and abuse so it will be characterized by fair play and beneficence. The issue remains how to eradicate the problems while preserving what is good in sport. The application of moral reasoning to sport can lead the way.

NEW TO THIS EDITION

Technology Chapter

This new chapter (Chapter 12) highlights ethical issues raised by new developments, such as advanced equipment, that make improved performance possible. It asks the question: Do advanced materials in sport equipment give unfair advantages?

Sport Science Chapter

Chapter 13, a new chapter, focuses on issues related to collegiality, client relationships, commercialization and marketing, athletic training, competency, and codes of ethics and research. Its content is based on the concept of professional responsibility in the workplace.

Updated Content

This new edition has been thoroughly updated, with new or revised content. It features broadened coverage of sport ethics in physical education, sport management, exercise science, health, coaching, and other related fields. In addition, more examples and readings have been added to many chapters.

Rewritten Foundational Chapters

Chapters 1 through 3, which focus on moral reasoning, values and principles, and application and strategy, have been rewritten to make them easier to understand and more appealing to students. With the same important content covered, the overall presentation is less formal than in earlier editions.

CyberSport Boxes

This new feature highlights the many organizations and associations related to sport ethics. These boxes provide Web addresses and brief annotations that invite the student to explore these resources.

PowerWeb

The PowerWeb card packaged with each new copy of this text allows access to a reservoir of course-specific articles and current events. Students can use PowerWeb to take a self-scoring quiz, complete an interactive exercise, click through an interactive glossary, or check the daily news. An expert in each discipline analyzes the day's news to show students how it relates to their field of study.

NEW OR EXPANDED TOPICS

Chapter 1: The Process of Moral Reasoning

- Approaches to the art and practice of moral reasoning.
- Condensed presentation of key concepts.

Chapter 2: Values, Principles, and You

- Increased emphasis on physical education and sport science.
- New scenarios.

Chapter 3: Application and Strategy: Thinking about the Game Plan

- New scenarios.
- Increased emphasis on physical education and sport science.

Chapter 4: Intimidation, Competition, and Sportsmanship

- Updated chapter content.
- Reorganization of selected material.

Chapter 5: Violence in Sport

- Why violent behavior is taught.
- Why and how violence is rewarded.
- More examples used to illustrate key points.

Chapter 6: Eligibility in Sport

- Increased emphasis on research findings and valuing education.
- Updated information on eligibility.

Chapter 7: Sport Elimination

- Homosexuality in sport.
- Sexual harassment of athletes by coaches.

Chapter 8: Commercialized Sport

- Differentiation of commercialized, educational, and recreational sport.
- Recommendations of the Knight Commission on Intercollegiate Athletics.

Chapter 9: Racial Equity: African Americans in Sport

- Historical exclusion of African Americans in sport.
- Discrimination in sport.
- Sport—a reflector or shaper of societal attitudes?

Chapter 10: Gender Equity in Sport

◆ Data on NCAA's gender equity studies.
◆ Revised discussion of recommendations.

Chapter 11: Ergogenic Aids for Sport Performance

◆ Ergogenic aids and health problems.
◆ Impact of ergogenic aids on weight gain or loss.
◆ Changing views on how drugs are viewed in sport.
◆ Information on drug reference guide for athletes.
◆ NCAA study on substance abuse habits of athletes.

Chapter 12: Ethical Considerations of Technology in Sport

◆ Important issues affecting sport, physical education, and athletics.
◆ Advanced materials and their effects on advantage, participation, and physical fitness.
◆ Approaches to distribution of benefits of technology to all sports participants.

Chapter 13: Sport Science, Physical Education, and Research

◆ Professional responsibility in the workplace.
◆ Professional loyalty.
◆ Codes of ethics.
◆ Research issues: human subject review boards, informed consent, scientific integrity and misconduct in research manual.

SPECIAL CONTENT FEATURES

Among the unique features of *Sport Ethics: Applications for Fair Play, Third Edition*, students will find an easy-to-read text, filled with a balanced mixture of theory and application and thought-provoking questions. Through real-life dilemmas that regularly confront athletes, coaches, and sport managers, students are challenged to examine how they would respond to moral issues in sport.

Theoretical Basis for Moral Reasoning in Sport

Chapters 1, 2, and 3 provide an easy-to-read foundation for a philosophic understanding of moral reasoning. Moral character, comprised of moral knowing, moral valuing, and moral acting, requires impartiality, consistency, and reflective judgment. A reasoned moral inquiry based on these three tenets uses individuals' values (both moral and nonmoral) to determine each person's universalizable principles. A consistent value system based on justice, honesty, responsibility, and beneficence leads to a moral standard that will withstand scrutiny.

Thematic Description of the Major Challenges to Morality in Sport

Differing from existing books on sport ethics, this text describes the leading areas threatening the development and application of moral values in sport. Chapters 4 through 10 focus on thematic areas of sport in which individuals are challenged to use moral reasoning to decide how they will respond to ethical dilemmas. These chapters provide historical and sociological perspectives on issues facing all levels of sport. Chapter 4 examines the increasing amount of intimidation and gamesmanship and how these impact sportsmanship, while Chapter 5 describes the pervasiveness of violence in sport. Chapter 6 presents eligibility issues that challenge moral values. In Chapter 7 students look at how sport dropout and burnout may adversely affect athletes. Chapter 8 looks at how commercialized sport has led to an emphasis on the nonmoral value of winning and at all the benefits associated with being "number 1." Chapters 9 and 10 discuss the ethical issues associated with racial and gender equity in sport, respectively. Chapters 11–14 add timely information and raise ethical questions in three current topical areas followed by a concluding epilogue. Chapter 11 raises questions about legitimate and unethical uses of drugs and questions about drug testing. Chapter 12 has been added to address the ethical issues associated with how new technologies have affected and will continue to impact sport as we know it. Chapter 13, another new chapter, expands the discussion of sport ethics into research and sport science settings. Chapter 14 summarizes the importance of applying moral reasoning to sport.

The information in this text leads students to engage in critical and reflective thinking about what values they believe should characterize competitive sports. Students are asked to determine whether the moral values of justice, honesty, responsibility, and beneficence should guide the development and continuation of sports in this country.

Boxes

To provide readers with a more in-depth understanding of moral principles and philosophic theory, Chapters 1 through 11 include numerous boxes. These boxes expand on theory, concepts, and research. By separating this information in boxes, the flow and continuity of the text are preserved. These boxes include knowledge vital to a comprehensive understanding of morality in sport.

Issues and Dilemmas

Students and teachers will value the opportunity to apply moral principles by resolving the *Issues and Dilemmas* in each chapter. Chapters 1 through 3 follow an open-ended discussion format.

The *Issues and Dilemmas* in Chapters 4 through 13 are written in case study format with real-life situations that challenge each student to begin a reasoned inquiry. Follow-up questions conclude each situation so that students can demonstrate their value systems and universalizable principles.

The moral reasoning process requires impartiality, consistency, and reflective judgment in answering each question. The *Issues and Dilemmas* will facilitate an in-depth personal analysis as well as lively student interactions. This feature makes the text come alive with timely applications.

SUCCESSFUL FEATURES

Several pedagogical aids will assist students in benefiting from *Sport Ethics: Applications for Fair Play.*

Chapter Opening Issues

Each chapter begins with a series of questions that introduce the content to follow. The questions are phrased to alert students to significant information, and to get readers to start a reasoned moral inquiry.

Chapter Summaries

The key content areas in each chapter are reemphasized in the summary. By reviewing the summaries, which highlight the main points and reinforce salient concepts, students can solidify their knowledge base and the application of morality in sport.

References

The latest and best documentation provides support for this text. Each source quoted or referred to in the text is cited in full in the reference list.

Additional Readings

Selected readings are provided in each chapter because added resources will guide students in learning more about the topics discussed.

Glossary

A comprehensive glossary at the back of the text reinforces for students the understanding of new terms.

Acknowledgements

We would like to express our gratitude to all those involved in the preparation and development of this book. We particularly appreciate the insights provided by the reviewers' helpful comments. These aided greatly in the development of this edition.

Steve Estes
East Carolina University

Gordon Howell
Rollins College

Donald Melrose
Texas A&M University–Corpus Christi

Paul Wright
University of Illinois at Chicago

Alison Wrynn
California State University–Long Beach

The National Association of Sport and Physical Education (NASPE) endorses this text. We appreciate NASPE's dedication to the field.

Last, we wish to express our appreciation to the McGraw-Hill professionals with whom we worked on this edition. A special "thank you" is extended to our families for their unending support and love.

Angela Lumpkin
Sharon Kay Stoll
Jennifer M. Beller

Contents

Theoretical Framework
for Moral Reasoning

The Process of Moral Reasoning

CHAPTER 1

- What is a value?
- What is a moral value?
- What is an ethos of a game?
- What is character?
- What are the three perspectives necessary to morally reason?

It is never easy to make good ethical decisions about life whether it has to do with working as an educator or sport scientist, being a coach, or playing a good game. Many times, it is difficult because our beliefs and values may disagree with the group, the person in charge, or maybe we just do not know. And, if we are fortunate enough to know how to make an ethical decision, it *seems* that most people don't stand up for what they believe (see Box 1-1). Or perhaps, most people are not quite sure what they believe—or if they believe in anything. Most of us, however, had a mother, father, grandmother, or kindergarten teacher who gave us good advice and shared their wisdom about how to make ethical decisions. "Let your conscience be your guide." However, sometimes we forget what we were taught or our conscience takes a "long hiatus." When we get into the *real* world, we find this advice hard to live by because other folks don't believe or value the same sorts of things that we do.

For example, let's assume that you were taught as a child that it's wrong to tell a lie; however, in the real world just about everyone lies. In fact, many liars get away with it and even seem to get ahead. As one of the current jokes for athletes asks, "How do you know when a recruiting coach is lying?" Response, "Whenever the lips are moving." On television and in the newspapers, it seems everybody lies—from the former president of the United States to professional athletes like Dr. J. And, after all, lying is now cultural entertainment. Hollywood made a successful comedy with Jim Carrey called *Liar, Liar.* So was that childhood advice of "following your conscience" silly? Should we do the right thing, or tell the "truth," or, do we follow what is commonly practiced in society? Everybody else is doing it.

The notion of truth telling is only one of the ethical dilemmas of life in the real world. Our professional world is in constant change and turmoil and what used to be "accepted" as the right thing to do is now "questionable." The rules are changing quickly. How does one decide what is right and what is wrong about such things as respect, fair play, sportsmanship, and responsibility in this cyber-fast world where most decisions about ethics and

BOX 1-1

ETHICS, MORAL—THE TERMS

Etymologically, the word *ethics* is derived from the Greek, *ethiké,* meaning science of morals or character. Typically, the formal study of ethics is concerned with the principles of human duty, or the study of all moral and mental qualities that distinguish an individual or a race relative to other individuals or races. Ethics is an analytical, scientific study of the theoretical bases of moral action. The study of ethics is often categorized according to professions, such as the ethics of law, business ethics, the ethics of medicine, sport ethics, the ethics of teaching, the ethics of coaching, and so forth. Ethics may also be called meta-ethics, analytical ethics, or critical ethics.

In contrast, the word *moral,* from the Latin *mos,* refers to an individual's actual custom or manners. In a technical sense, moral pertains to an individual's *actions* as being right or wrong, virtuous or vicious, or good or bad in relation to the actions, intentions, or character of responsible people carrying out the deed. For example, consider a squash game. We are in the midst of an intense rivalry. You think I have gotten completely out-of-hand. I begin to shove and push. I also have an unnerving habit of hitting the ball directly at myself when you are behind me. This strategy forces you to somehow reach around me, which results in some physical contact. The physical contact gets increasingly worse, and I push you three more times. You finally have had enough, and the next time I push you out of the way for a shot, you "waylay me with a haymaker." Your reaction may seem justified considering the circumstances; however, such retributive actions are suspect. The history of societies tells us that violence begetting violence is a poor solution to a moral dilemma. I might say correctly that "although you are a good person, you acted wrongly—perhaps with good motives and intentions—when you struck me. The consequences were bad even though I provoked you. Surely, there is a better way to solve this problem." Note that in the case of moral action, there is a subtle but important difference between right and wrong and good and bad. "Right and wrong" apply to an individual or agent's acts, whereas "good" and "bad" refer to (1) the person who is the agent of a particular act, (2) the effects of the agent's acts, (3) the agent's motives from which the act was done, and (4) the agent's intention.

morality can occur at nanosecond speed? Isn't this idea of ethical standards rather dated?

For example: What about the traditional notion of fair play? Does it have a place in this new technologically driven society? How would one apply the concept of fair play to—let's say—deciding what is fair or ethical about using more advanced sporting equipment. A silly question? Well, not really. The technological changes in advanced design materials of sporting equipment have radically altered the picture of sport participation and hence changed the perspective of what is acceptable as fair play and what is not. Or, how does one apply fair play and sportsmanship to highly competitive sport? Is it possible or even necessary to play fairly in a sport world where winning drives the perfor-

mance? Does fair play exist for say, a sport scientist? Are their rules or professional codes of conduct that one should follow?

These sorts of questions demand some reflection, some artful soul searching, and some courageous action. The purpose of this book is to offer advice and direction so that as a future sport professional, you will develop a clear vision of what you value. We hope you will be able to evaluate and describe an ethical state of affairs and know how to use systematic reasoning tools to address ethical dilemmas in a thoughtful, reflective manner (see Box 1-2). Hopefully, when we come to the end of our study, we will have made a decision about that childhood advice (letting your conscience be your guide) and have developed a plan of action and a strategy to follow it.

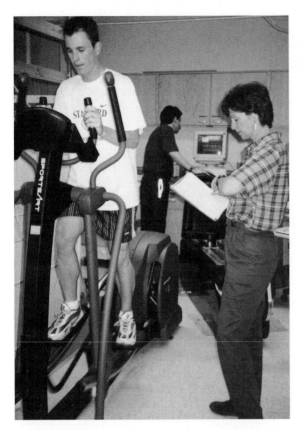

Do ethics and fair play exist for sport scientists and what place do professional codes of conduct play in their professions?

EVERYDAY ETHICAL PROBLEMS IN SPORT

Before we go any further, let us examine the value or the worth of telling the truth. Why is it that as children we were told it was wrong to lie? Isn't it interesting that what we were taught as children, seems not to work very well in the real world. If you think about these questions, it becomes clear that this lying thing is really quite slippery, and that is probably why lying is so common. In fact, lying, except in the courtroom and in a legal document, is the only act of dishonesty that does not have a direct legal result if you get caught. For example, if

you cheat on an exam and you are caught, you fail. If you steal a car and you get caught, you spend time in the legal system. However, if you lie to your friends and you get caught, there is little repercussion. And in many sport situations lying is really quite acceptable—or it seems to be. For example, during a volleyball game, Anne hits the ball over the net. The ball barely grazes off your fingers and lands out of bounds. The referee does not see you touch the ball. **Question 1: Should you tell the referee that you touched the ball? Question 2: If the referee asked, would you say "yes" you touched the ball?**

Any athlete who has played a game in the last 20 years knows the answers—and for them the answer is not about honesty or fair play, it is about strategy and how games are played. The real world of competitive athletics is based on how wins are achieved. Said another way, the ethos, or the character of the game, is about what is commonly practiced and what is commonly valued on the field of play. Most athletes would argue something to the effect as follows.

Question 1: Should Anne tell the referee?

A. "Why should Anne tell the ref? It is the ref's job to catch it."
B. "Why should Anne help the other team? Gaining the advantage is the name of the game."

Question 2: If you were asked, would you say yes?

A. "The referee wouldn't ask—but I wouldn't tell either. It's her job to know what is going on."
B. "All's fair in love, war, and baseball—well volleyball, in this case."

In these responses, lying is accepted or rather the untruth is not considered a lie. The lie is an acceptable deceit. Acceptable because the purpose of the game is about gaining advantage and most conduct is acceptable as long as the athlete isn't caught "fudging" and the win will be assured. It is common and acceptable practice.

TO KNOW, TO VALUE, TO ACT

Lickona (1991) describes the components of good character in his seminal work, *Educating for Character.* Lickona believes that one must have the qualities of moral knowing, moral feeling, and moral action. Each of these components of character have subsets that must be fostered to develop good character. Under the subset of moral knowing, he lists moral awareness, knowing moral values, perspective taking, moral reasoning, decision making, and self-knowledge. Under moral feeling, he lists conscience, self-esteem, empathy, loving the good, self-control, and humility. Under moral action, competence, will, and habit are listed.

Each of the character domains are unequivocally linked. The domains do not function separately; each penetrates and influences in many ways. What we know and feel may affect our behavior and, reciprocally, how we behave may affect how we think and feel. Although we may know what is right and wrong, for many reasons and factors we choose to do wrong. Just knowing does not mean we empathize or have the self-control to follow with moral actions.

The concept of moral reasoning has been challenged by a new breed of moral educators known as the Virtuecrats. Led by Bennett (1993) in his work, *Book of Virtues,* the Virtuecrats argue that moral reasoning has really no place in the development of character. Rather, we learn the basis of good character through reading "good works" and following correct or acceptable behavior. Unfortunately, most ethicists, especially those in the Aristotelian fashion, would argue against such a perspective. Aristotle said that character is the composite of good moral qualities, whereby one shows firmness of belief, resolution, and practice about such moral values as honesty, justice, and respect. He also said that character is right conduct in relation to other persons and to self and that our humanness **resides in our ability and capacity** to reason and virtue results when we use our reasoning ability to control and moderate ourselves. Hence, reading about good virtue—even if the readings are the world's greatest masterpieces—is useless unless we have the capacity to reason and think through our actions.

However, there is another perspective that is more truthful, and based in the ideal notion of fair play. This answer would not be about gaining an advantage, rather, for this athlete the purpose of playing the game is about skill and respect for the rules.[1]

Question 1: Should you tell the referee that you touched the ball?

"Of course, I would tell the referee. Is not the purpose of the game to find out who is the best player, not who has the best eyesight? Or who can outwit the referee?" This answer is based on the notion that the game has merit and value, in and of itself. The win is important and valuable, but only so if the game is played by opponents who want the best play to occur. We respect the rules for what they represent.

Question 2: If the referee asked if you touched the ball, would you say "yes"?

"Yes. I doubt they would ask, because I would probably have beaten them to the punch. I would have called it before the ref asked."

This is a different point of view from what is commonly practiced in sport. In this response, the athlete is more concerned about the performance than the result.[2] The difference in the three re-

---

[1]For a very good discussion of this point of view see Schneider A. and Butcher, R. Fair play as respect for the game, in W. Morgan, K. Meier, and A. Schneider, (2001).

[2]For a very fine discussion of this point of view, see John H. Gibson (1993).

sponses to the question has to do with values. What does the athlete value? Values, however, are rather slippery concepts, too. A value is something that has worth to you. Values tend to be very relativistic—meaning that individuals hold their own set of values. For example, what you value and what I value may be two different things.

There are two types of values: nonmoral values and moral values. You may value Playstation while I value Internet games. You may value rap music while I value classical. These sorts of things are known as nonmoral values, or values about things, places, or events. However, the value of fair play is known as a moral value.

Moral values have to do with how other people value us or how we value people. We might say that Carlos, your teammate, is a good person. We are saying something about Carlos's character, which in this case means what about him? **What is the difference between saying, Carlos is a good person, or Carlos is a good basketball player?** In the former, we are saying something about Carlos's character. We are saying something about how people value Carlos in how he treats others. In the latter, we are saying something about Carlos's ability to do a job or task, which may say a lot about his skill and work ethic but it says little about how Carlos treats others. We will spend more time with this later in our discussion. But suffice it to say, character is a statement of value, and moral values are the relative worth we place on the motives, intentions, and actions of people dealing, working, or playing with other people. That may sound a little jumbled. Let us put moral values into a real-world situation.

Paul Brown, the legendary founder of the Cleveland Browns, began his coaching career at Massillon High School in Massillon, Ohio. In 1928, his high school team was a little slow in the backfield. Being one of the great tacticians of the game, Brown analyzed the constitutive rules (rules directed specifically toward what makes a game a game) to find an advantage.[3] He found one. The

rules made no mention of what a uniform could or should look like, except that there must be a number on the back. Coach Brown seized the opportunity. He took footballs and cut them lengthwise into two halves. He sewed one half on the front jersey of all the backfield players' uniforms. When the quarterback passed off, everyone appeared to have a football. And the ruse worked, the defense was muddled as to who had the real ball, and Brown's team won the game.

Is This a Scenario about Moral Values? Why?

Yes it is, because Brown's tactics had a direct effect on the opposing players, the game of football, his players, and the purpose of high school football. The Federation of State High School Activities Association goes to some great length to discuss the purpose of high school sport, and nowhere in its description is it mentioned, do whatever you've got to do to win. However, an alternative point of view might say, that sure this might be about moral values, but Brown's behavior was not outside the written rules, remember there were no rules against sewing footballs on jerseys; therefore, Brown's behavior was acceptable. Brown's behavior acceptable or not? If no rules exist against a certain action, is that action therefore ethical?

What is your position concerning Coach Brown's behavior? Ask four friends their positions. Do you all agree? Why or why not? You may find that you will not all agree on this scenario. Some people will state emphatically that Brown was cheating. Others will say that he was not cheating. Others will argue that it is perfectly acceptable to do what Coach Brown did and that rules need to be written to address the problem.

How is Brown's ruse a statement of moral value? Is it because Brown's motive, intention, and action directly affected many people? First, what is the purpose of high school football? According to the National Federation of High School Associations, the purpose is to "enhance educational experiences . . .

---

[3]For a very good discussion of constitutive rules see Kathleen Pearson (1995) and Warren Fraleigh's (1995) work.

promote . . . sportsmanship."[4] Did Brown's action here support the purpose of the game? It is rather doubtful that his ruse could support educational experiences and promote sportsmanship. However, his motive was probably good in the sense that he wanted his team to succeed. Winning is desirable. Anyone who says winning is not good or is not the purpose of playing a competitive game, hasn't played a competitive game. If winning is not important, then the purpose of the activity is recreational. When points are kept, games are played to decide a winner and a loser. As competitors, we like to play and we want to stress ourselves to be better. Is wanting to win, immoral?[5] Not hardly. Wanting to win and doing one's best is actually an admirable quality of a competitor. So wanting to win is not an immoral act.[6]

Brown's intention, however, begins to veer from moral value. His intention was not about following the rule book or playing a good game. His intention was to gain an advantage and to place his players' opponents in a position so that they could not play the game. How? They did not know where the ball was and the game had become one of trickery.

The resultant action was deceitful and unfair. The opposing teams were not on a level playing field. They could not play the game as the game was intended to be played. Yes, Brown was resourceful, clever, and witty—it must have been a real chuckle to watch the opposing teams running about chasing and wondering "who had the ball." However, the game had become one of who could confuse the other team quicker with off-the-field antics. Within a few games, as history recounts, every team was sporting the new attire in half footballs. The next year, rules were rather precise about extra adornments on uniforms.

In the Brown scenario, the rules are problematic—if one believes that rules define what is right and wrong. However, being ethical is not just about following rules. An ethical individual in sport follows the rules, values the rules, believes in the rules, and honors the spirit of the rules. In the movie, *Bagger Vance*, the hero, Randolph Junah, played by Matt Damon, is one stroke from winning a golf match when he begins to pick up small sticks around his ball. Junah and two other great golfers, Bobby Jones and Walter Hagen, have waged a great game and somewhere out of guts, desire, or the support of his whole soul Junah is within one stroke of winning the game at dusk. As Junah surveys his ball, he notices small debris of sticks surrounding the ball. When Junah picks away the sticks, the ball inadvertently moves. Only Junah and his caddy, a young boy, see the movement. Junah says, "I have to take a stroke penalty." The caddy responds, "No you don't. Please don't, Junah. It's a stupid rule. It don't mean anything. No one saw it but you and me, and I'll never tell." Junah replies, "I'll know it and so will you." Junah tells the official that he moved the ball. Neither Jones nor Hagen want to win by a rule technicality. They question Junah and state that perhaps the ball really hadn't moved, since the shallows were so long at that time of day. They gave Junah every opportunity to *not* take the penalty. Junah refused and said, "The ball was here and it moved to here (at least 2 inches away)." The penalty was assessed.

Was Junah being heroic? No, he was playing the game by the rules. To him, the rules defined the game and defined who he was. Golf to him was to be valued for the rules and why those rules were developed. The game was not about how well he

---

[4]The mission of the National Federation of State High School Associations (NFHA) is to serve its members and its related professional groups by providing leadership and national coordination for the administration of interscholastic activities which will enhance the educational experiences of high school students and reduce risks of their participation. The NFHA will promote participation and sportsmanship to develop good citizens through interscholastic activities which provide equitable opportunities, positive equitable opportunities, positive recognition, and learning experiences to students while maximizing the achievement of educational goals. (See the NFHA website at http://www.nfhs.org.)

[5]Winning is never an immoral activity. People commit immoral acts when they violate their opponents to get a "win" at any cost.

[6]Alfie Kohn (1986) has written a provocative piece against competition that all competitors should read, *No Contest.* In his work, Kohn argues that the competitive experience is exclusionary and therefore does harm to those who do not win.

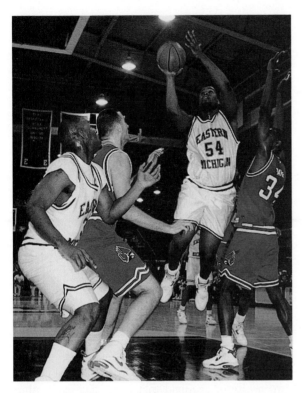

Being ethical has to do with valuing what is important but also valuing one's self and others in relation to that activity.

could use the rules to his advantage or to gain an edge. The rules were there to define the game, and he had a responsibility to the game and the spirit of the rules to play by them.[7]

Being ethical has to do with valuing what is important but also valuing oneself in relation to the activity. Being ethical is not always easy, especially when situations become personal. One of the purposes of this book is to offer some perspectives and give you some tools to use in this sporting situation so that you can make better decisions about the good and the right.

---

[7]*The Legend of Bagger Vance*. A Dreamworks Production, starring Matt Damon, Will Smith, Charlize Theron, and directed by Robert Redford.

A CERTAIN PERSPECTIVE

Philosophers have written for ages about what it takes to be a good thinker. Doing ethics should be about good thinking, though one could be quite ethical without giving it much thought. That is, one could practice ethical action without thinking. These people were raised in a very conservative home where values were taught and rules were to be followed. They have an elevated sense of conscience and appear to have no problems with ethical dilemmas. At the same time, however, even these folks could use some perspective about why something is right and something is wrong. The perspective that benefits ethical thinking has to do with the ability to be impartial, consistent, and reflective.

Impartiality

Being impartial in determining any issue is always difficult and perhaps impossible. Humans tend to seek their own personal pleasure. Our value systems are bombarded with intuition, emotion, and a myriad of values from science, logic, sense experience, and authoritarian perspectives.

What is difficult is quieting our own wants and attempting to develop an impartial reasoning system. To do so means to become concerned with other points of view. This is a tough perspective in sport, where the opponent is often seen as the enemy. When in reality the opponent should be seen as an ally. An ally in trying to obtain the best possible competitive experience. For a game to occur, we must have our opponents. We play the game together. It is said that God is happiest when her children are playing.[8] We all must live in the world with others, we must come to realize that our wants and desires must be tempered by how those wants and desires affect others. In developing a reasoned view, we must grow beyond, "What's in it for me?" Rather, our goal should be to consider our own values and the ramifications of each decision in relation to others who may be affected by our action.

---

[8]*Bagger Vance.*

Interestingly, most of us expect better behavior from our friends. We expect them to be altruistic even when we are not. For example, most of us choose friends who demonstrate certain altruistic virtues (a particular moral excellence that promotes the general good or a special manifestation of specific moral values). That is, we choose friends for certain basic virtues, such as fairness, honesty, and truthfulness, and we usually trust our friends and believe that they will not fail us. Do we choose friends who are known liars, cheats or thieves? Probably not! Though sometimes, you really don't know if they are or not. Of course, the same virtuous traits we find imperative in our friends are traits that we want others to think we demonstrate. Most of us want others to know us as being honest, truthful, responsible, and altruistic, and to think of us as being fair and concerned for others, even if we are not.

To be fair means developing an awareness of others' feelings and needs. Being fair also demands imagining and understanding others' interests and the effect of our actions on their lives. To be otherwise is to risk loss of friendship or companionship and loss of our own civility.

From a moral point of view, being fair or impartial is attempting to be free from bias, fraud, or injustice. Being fair and impartial is trying to be equitable and legitimate, or not taking advantage of others. Such qualities are essential in making decisions about moral issues. Without such qualities, all decisions become biased and centered on the good of one, or what is considered good for one. If you wish to be considered fair, or if you wish to hold traits esteemed by others, you work toward impartiality in your reasoning. Obviously, we will all fail sooner or later because of our own mortality—but the point is to at least try.

Place the concept of impartiality into the volleyball scenario. If you remove yourself from the scenario, does it make a difference in how you answer? In other words, should all volleyball players call an infraction when one occurs? Or should infractions only be called by the referee? This is difficult to answer because the norm today and the rule is to let the referee make all calls. However, you must be careful if the referee is the judge of all behavior. What if the referee does not see all the action? Does the game then become how to outsmart the referee? Should our goal of playing the game rest solely on how good the referee's eyesight is? What exactly is the purpose of the game? How you answer these questions refers directly to what you think is the purpose of the game and the respect you place upon the spirit of the rules.

In the Paul Brown scenario, can you apply the rule of impartiality? For example, should rules be seen only as obstacles that must be overcome? That is, are rules only made so that clever ways can be found to get around them? What exactly is the purpose of the game rules?

Consistency

To reason morally, we must also be logical and consistent. Being logical is the essence of moral reasoning, which involves an exact process. To be consistent when making moral decisions, past and present decisions must be taken into account. If two positions are held that contradict each other, both cannot be truthful or acceptable. For example, suppose that you and Jill are about to play a game of squash. You decide to play by a certain set of rules, whereby you will each call your own errors. You expect each other to follow these rules. Before the game begins, you decide that the serving line is out. If you call an error, then Jill has an obligation to do the same. Suppose though that in the heat of the game, you hit a line shot on the front boundary line. The score is 8-6, your favor; one more point and you win. You have worked hard in this game, and Jill *always* beats you. Jill does not see the line shot. She asks you, "Was it out?" You *saw* it, and you *know* that it was out.

1. What should you say?
2. What would you say?
3. What should you say to be consistent?

In a reasoned sense, Jill expects you to tell the truth, thus you should tell the truth: the ball was out—even though you may want to believe it was in.

In this scenario, you must overcome your own emotional wants and realize that if you hold a different set of standards for yourself than what you expect of others, you are being inconsistent and untruthful to yourself and your opponent. If you truly give your word to follow the rules, then the rules stand for you as well as Jill. In the heat of a close game, if you do not call your serving errors, then you are blatantly lying. Thus you violate two psychological perspectives of moral reasoning, being impartial and being consistent. Apply this reasoning to the volleyball scenario and the story of Paul Brown.

Reflection

We decide our moral and ethical dilemmas through reflective judgment based on clear moral and nonmoral values. Reflective thinking is exercising careful judgment in all moral issues, based on moral and nonmoral values. Unfortunately, few of us exercise reflective thinking. Often, we take a stand on an issue because we are biased by our own cultural, sociological, or biological presuppositions.

For example, the XZY University believes it has gender equity in its distribution of funds for men and women. There are an equal number of sport teams for men as well as women. There are an equal number of coaches. The different mens' teams are football, cross-country, golf, tennis, track and field, and basketball. The women's teams are volleyball, golf, tennis, cross-country, track and field, and basketball. The budget for the mens' program, including football, is approximately three times as large as the women's. However, if figured without football, the budget is approximately equal. Football as the number one revenue sport brings in about 60 percent of the working revenue. Without this revenue there would be no programs for the nonrevenue sports. Therefore XZY University states that equity exists as is.

1. Do you agree?
2. What are the issues in this case?

In traditional ethical inquiry, the emphasis has always been on rationally determining moral issues, which in turn justifies your choices to behave in certain ways. Specifically, critical, reflective thinking is exercising careful judgment or observation about an issue. Critical means to be accurate, exact, and precise about an issue, to take into account all sides of an issue, and to determine its present and future implications. Use critical thinking to examine the different sides of the gender equity issue at XZY.

Case One: Equity exists.
Case Two: Equity does not exist.
Case Three: Equity does not exist, but inequity is acceptable.

Which of the three cases is true? All three cannot be true.

Rebuttal to Case One.   Does equity exist? If equity is defined as equal access to all goods for all people, equity does not appear to exist. If football uses or has access to twice as much funding as the women's programs, equity cannot exist.

Rebuttal to Case Two.   If equity is equated to distribution of funds, equity does not exist, because funds were not distributed equally to both men and women. As with case one, the statement must be true. Equity does not exist.

Rebuttal to Case Three.   Inequity is acceptable in this case, because without football there would be no other programs.

This scenario may be true, or it may not. Put another way, this argument for inequity rests on justification of unequal distribution of goods to men because without men there would be no football and without football there would be no money. Therefore football and more funds for football are acceptable because football funds all programs. This argument is an interesting one that has been raised and supported by many athletic programs and a few academic writings.[9]

---

[9]See James L. Shulman and William G. Bowen (2001), *The Game of Life,* in which Shulman and Bowen argue that the "arms race" has negatively affected the educational values of athletes as well as the purpose of the educational values of the greater institution. Shulman and Bowen are researchers for the Andrew W. Mellon Foundation.

This argument has merit, if the statement "without football there would be no money," is true. Unfortunately, football programs seldom pay for themselves. Even in most competitive Division I athletics, football programs use more funds than they "make."[10] Enough evidence exists to decree that football does not "make" the money.

If, therefore, the statement is untrue, then the argument fails. How then does one justify more funds for some programs than for others? Is this an issue of equity or fairness? The notion of fairness means that both groups receive the exact same distribution of good. In this case, if good is equated to money, then equal amounts of money should be distributed to both groups. However, does this logic hold? Should women receive the same amount of funds?

This argument is a tricky issue, because in the United States we often believe that money determines what is good and right. However, more or less money is really not the issue. Some programs cost more money than others. Some college majors cost more to attain than others. Should all programs have the same access to the same material value? Or should all programs have the same services and facilities? Or is the issue not about the sameness for fairness, but equity. Equity refers to a just distribution of funds. The problem with just distribution of funds and opportunities in American collegiate sport is the problem of very, very expensive sports, that have gotten more expensive because of how the games are played. Recent criticism of collegiate football has recommended that college administrators are responsible for an "arms race" in which competing schools must have the "same" sort of perks and frills. If University A has marble training tables with the school's crest inlaid, then University

Is the issue about funding women's and minor sports, about sameness for fairness, or about equity—just distribution of funds?

B must do the same. If University A's coach has a million dollar plus salary, then University B's coach must also have a million dollars, plus additional perks of country club memberships, retirement IRAs, multiple free cars, and so on, and so on. The critics argue that one way to combat the "arms race" is to return to a football game that is simpler in design, a one-platoon system.[11] One platoon would equate to fewer players, fewer coaches, and less operating funds. Such a concept would radically change what is practiced in American football today. Could this happen? Perhaps, but it is doubtful.

---

[10] To argue that a program must pay for itself seems to be quite antieducation. No academic program must "pay" for itself. Programs are funded by the state, federal government, private funds, and student fees. Athletics should be "educational" and should not be expected to have to pay for itself. At the same time, athletics should be fiscally responsible for whatever funds it earns or is allotted.

---

[11] J. L. Schulman, and W. G. Bowen, (2001), *The Game of Life*.

The counter to this argument is that football would be so radically changed that the revenues would be affected negatively. Without a healthy football program, there would be no funds and therefore no additional support to all of the non-revenue-producing sport programs, that is, tennis, golf, track and field, volleyball, and most of the women's programs. And, would not the radical change advocate the demise of collegiate athletics, period? This may also be true, and it may not be true. Perhaps in the discussion of "funding" the other programs, we must examine how the monies are distributed beyond the "basic needs" of any one given program. For example, the common practice of athletic departments sending their football teams to bowl appearances is to spend every dollar earned and then some on the trip. Most of the central administration, their families, their children (and in some cases the nannies for these children), and other significant individuals receive travel, hotel, and food as well as tickets to the game. In addition, each individual player, coach, and significant others receive warm-ups, gym bags, brief cases, and so forth all emblazoned in team colors, logos, and bowl insignia. It is not uncommon for an athletic department to spend the maximum payout which can be anywhere from $300,000 to millions plus for a one-hour game and overall four-hour event.[12] It is also true that few football programs are financially in the black. Most revenue-producing athletic programs are subsidized by their institutions and spend more than they "make."[13]

The discussion about equity should be directed toward the positive benefits that come from participating in sport. Equity must account for all actions in relation to all individuals involved in the athletic program. Unfortunately, equity has been equated only to funding without realizing that more "of

Equity has been equated only to funding without realizing that "more of what the men have" is not necessarily the best deal for the women.

what the men have" is not necessarily the best deal for the women. Some recent studies show that with increased funding women athletes are suffering the same devaluing of the sport experience in favor of the result.[14] That is, winning becomes the focus and the value of the activity and the value of the educational experience is lost. Women athletes, under the "new" equity model that demands equal funding with the men's programs, are suffering the same

---

[12]See specifically the work of Murray Sperber who has written several different texts on intercollegiate athletic programs and how these programs adversely affect collegiate institutions. His first work was in 1990, *College Sports Inc.*, and in 2001, *Beer and Circuses*.

[13]See J. L. Schulman, and W. G. Bowen (2001), *The Game of Life*.

---

[14]See Stoll and Beller (2001), and see Schulman and Bowen (2001).

erosion of graduation rates and devaluing of educational values. Unfortunately, distribution of funds appears to be "the" way to measure whether programs have equity. And women, often through litigation, are demanding more equity in distribution of funds.

It is certain that distribution of funds will change what sport should be. The change may be good, and it may be bad; however, change will occur. What we do know is that if equity is to occur either belt tightening will happen or administrations will become creative in how to address the problem. Presently many institutions have found solutions to their gender equity dilemma through creative fundraising. The state of Florida legislated a head tax on every game, professional and amateur, played. The tax is directly funneled to girls and women's sport. The University of Michigan as well as many other large Division I schools have found that great amounts of funds exist through merchandising the university's logo. Within just a few years, through controlled licensing of its logo and products, University of Michigan's operating budget is in the +$40 million category with a capital outlay in the hundreds of millions. And even with that, it too has difficulty making ends meet.[15]

Such scrutiny about any difficult issue may or may not bring about new enlightenment. As you can see, we may all agree on the issues after critical reflection, or we may also find that we disagree. It is possible that several different theories may survive the reflective process. You have no guarantee that your means to finding the truth through moral reasoning will support only one view. Even if you do find different views, you will have begun to understand how to defend your moral positions; and you may learn about yourself and your beliefs (see Box 1-3).

---

[15]See the recent work of James Duderstadt (2000), *Intercollegiate athletics and the American university: a university president's perspective*, in which Duderstadt gives a clear vision of the difficulty of even a big-time school—Michigan—to make ends meet. An interesting book with explicit detail on how big money, begets big money, and big deficits.

BOX 1-3

THE STUDY OF MORAL DEVELOPMENT

The study of moral development is concerned with asking how and through what process human beings learn or develop morally and ethically. It is a difficult study; difficult because of the volume and complexity of the material to be studied and because there are opposing views regarding moral development.

The opposing views, or theories, are internalization and constructivist. Internalization models include the (1) psychoanalytic and (2) social learning theories.

Sigmund Freud (1933) in his psychoanalytic theory, which was the first major moral development research, hypothesized that the superego, id, and ego function together to govern aggressive and sexual instincts. He hypothesized that internalization of social norms occurs because of dynamic processes concerning the superego, id, and ego relative to feelings of guilt. Essentially, the superego (an internalization of societal norms and parental values) controls the id (the pleasure seeking/hedonistic instincts) and the ego (personal thoughts and decisions).

In comparison, the social learning theorists (the second internalization model) hold that morality is learned through socialization processes. Moral development is the process by which individuals adopt society's notion of acceptable values and behaviors (Bandura 1977; McGuire and Thomas 1975). Essentially, an individual who consistently internalizes norms is viewed as a greater moral person. Typically, social learning theorists apply the "bag of virtues" approach (Kohlberg 1981). These theorists believe that individuals model their behaviors after others who personify the particular trait, value, or virtue desired. Moral education through this framework uses operant conditioning, reinforcement, and modeling (Bandura 1977; Aronfreed 1968).

Researchers in social learning theory posit that modeling and rewarding of behaviors in particular situations encourage generalization to all areas of life and theorize that throughout an individual's life the same underlying moral processes exist. While social learning theorists posit that moral behavior is the product of social environments, set standards, and the modeling of virtuous behaviors, constructivist theorists concern themselves with cognitive development relative to moral growth (Shields and Bredemeier 1995; Weiss and Bredemeier 1990; Kohlberg 1981). They believe that morality reflects the extent to which individuals use principles to guide moral action. Moral understandings are logically structured and developed through the stages of growth, with reasoning the foundation to moral functioning. Cognitive moral development is based on (1) what is considered right and fair, (2) what are the reasons for doing right, and (3) what are the underlying sociocultural perspectives (Reimer, Paolitto, and Hersh 1990).

Piaget (1932), the first to study moral development from a cognitive moral developmental approach, formulated a model and theory that emphasized cognitive development in children. Morality included the individual's respect for both rules and justice (a concern for reciprocity and equality among individuals). Piaget was concerned with the shift in morality from respect, constraint, and obedience to self-governance and control. He identified two broad moral development categories: (1) heteronomous stage morality of constraint/coercive rules and (2) autonomous stage morality of cooperation/rational rules (Piaget 1932).

Individuals in the heteronomous stage base their moral judgments on unilateral obedience to authority such as parents, adults, and established rules. Because rules are sacred and cannot be altered, individuals feel obligated to comply; right and wrong are usually viewed as black and white, with rightness and wrongness viewed in terms of consequences and punishments. The autonomous stage (morality of cooperation and reciprocity) is characterized by the individual's ability to develop a more subjective sense of autonomy and reciprocity. Right and wrong are situationally dictated, with rules subject to modification, relative to human needs or situational demands. Duty and obligations are relative to social experi-ences, peer expectations, and reversibility (the placing of oneself in another's position). This stage is typified by respect and cooperation with peers, rather than obedience to adult authority. Lawrence Kohlberg (1981) in his work at Yale and Harvard picked up Piaget's banner, expanded it, and spent more than 30 years attempting to make sense of how people learn and develop morality. Kohlberg expanded Piaget's stage theory by positing that moral development follows an invariant, culturally universal, six-stage sequence, organized into the following three levels:

Preconventional
Stage One—Punishment/obedience; avoid punishment.
Stage Two—Follow rules for own interest, others do the same; to serve own needs.

Conventional
Stage Three—Good boy, good girl; reacts to expectations of parents, peers, other authorities.
Stage Four—Social system and conscious maintenance; duty to social order, society.

Postconventional (Principled)
Stage Five—Contract and individual rights.
Stage Six—Universal ethical principles; based on consistent, universal ethical principles.

Kohlberg posited that higher stages require more complex reasoning and that through maturation and education, moral reasoning increases. As individuals interact with people and their environment and are challenged to cognitive dissonance (the questioning of one's values and beliefs), construction and transformation of personal moral understanding occurs. He also hypothesized that moral development could arrest at any stage especially during highly stressful conditions. Although many theoreticians have posited different variations of Piaget's and Kohlberg's models, most have the foundation that moral development is influenced by the following three major factors:

1. Moral education
2. Moral role models
3. Moral environment

THE STUDY OF MORAL DEVELOPMENT—cont'd

By themselves, each is ineffective in developing moral growth, but together they influence and affect moral development.

The passionate controversy between the internalists and constructivists lies in the question of whether moral development can be empirically measured. Internalists believe that morality cannot be measured or *should not* be measured, and they argue that doing so is a dangerous practice because a test cannot be constructed to measure the slippery and complex moral issue in its developmental process. If this is true, they argue, then measuring cognitive

knowledge of morality is impossible. They also typically argue against an empirical measure, in that we know moral value when we see it. Constructivists would argue that the concept of knowing moral value is not true and that a cognitive process (if it can be defined) can be measured, and if measured, can be taught through a cognitive process. (Stoll and Beller, 2001).

It is ironic that both internalists and constructivists are concerned with the same end—better moral growth for all people in the sense of respect and concern for others.

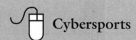 Cybersports

http://www.nd.edu/~cscc

The Mendelson Center for Sport, Character, and Culture views sport as a means of developing and expressing all aspects of human excellence, especially moral character. It offers a broad reassessment of the role of sport in contemporary culture.

www.ets.uidaho.edu/center_for_ethics

The Center for ETHICS,* at the University of Idaho, believes in "teaching the tradition of competitive integrity to inspire leaders of character." Its goal is to improve moral development and character education through intervention, consultation, and leadership in advancing moral education within competitive populations.

www.josephsoninstitute.org

The Josephson Institute of Ethics is a public-benefit, nonpartisan, nonprofit membership organization that advocates principled reasoning and ethical decision making. It conducts

programs and workshops for influential leaders and offers the CHARACTER COUNTS! youth-education initiative.

www.nays.org

The goal of the National Alliance for Youth Sports is to make sports safe and positive for America's youth. The organization emphasizes a positive introduction to youth sports and the proper training of administrators, coaches, and game officials; provides orientation programs for parents; and publishes the *National Standards for Youth Sports.*

www.positivecoach.org

The Positive Coaching Alliance offers a new concept of what it means to be a youth sports coach through its mental model of the positive coach. Starting at the local level, this organization works to transform youth sports groups into outstanding athletic and educational organizations that foster positive character traits in young athletes.

SUMMARY

So, was the childhood advice useful? Should you let your conscience be your guide? The answer, obviously, is dependent on whether you have a conscience or not—and actually there are folks who do not have a conscience—but they are rare. Most of us do have a conscience and learned early that the truth was important and something to be valued.[16] Whether we let our conscience be our guide and whether we value the truth—is up to us. It is easy to ignore one's conscience and even easier to ignore the truth. However, conscience, if it is truly to be effective, should have the support of reasoning skills.

---

[16]In academic terms, this process is known as moral development.

In this chapter we have learned that values have relative worth and that there are two different types of values: moral and nonmoral. Moral values have to do with the importance we place on the motive, intention, and action directed toward others. Motives are the driving force, intentions are how we are going to carry something out, and action—well, is action.

We have also learned that ethics has to do with valuing the right. It is the thoughtful process of thinking about tough issues and being clear about the purpose of an activity and the place of rules within that activity. Rules, in sport and game, are there to give guidelines to the players. Rules are not there to "get around," but are to be valued and supported.

ISSUES AND DILEMMAS

Below find three scenarios about Brent and making decisions about good causes. These are ethical dilemmas because of the good that is being done and a nonmoral value pressing against that moral value.

1. Brent, the newly appointed athletic director at Smalltown U, takes the chair of the local county supervisors on a hunting trip at the expense of the athletic department. While there he tells the supervisors how important it is that environmental restrictions on air quality be enforced gradually at Smalltown gymnasium, to give him and the university time to comply to raise the needed funds for renovation. If Smalltown must comply as stated in the recently adopted policies, the facility will have to be shut down with loss of revenue and student participation.

2. Brent has dedicated his life to helping develop a sports arena for the local high school. Finally, after years of fund-raising, the dream, based on the raising of all the needed funds, has come true. The architectural plans for the arena have been submitted, but recently passed laws require 20 more handicapped parking spaces than originally planned. He offers a friend in the planning department a year's free sports pass if he will make sure the plans are approved as submitted.

3. Brent is the principal of a high school. He accepts an expensive set of golf clubs at Christmas from the sales representative of a large school athletic supply company with which the school does business.

What is the value in each situation and what is the ethical principle being violated.

REFERENCES

Aronfreed, J. 1968. *Conduct and conscience*. New York: Academic Press.

Bandura, A. 1977. *A social learning theory*. Englewood Cliffs, NJ: Prentice Hall.

Bennett, W. 1993. *Book of virtues*. New York: Simon and Schuster.

Duderstadt, J. J. 2000. *Intercollegiate athletics and the American university: A university president's perspective*. Ann Arbor: University of Michigan Press.

Fraleigh, W. (1995). Why the good foul is not good. In Morgan, W. J. and Meier, K. M. Philosophic Inquiry in Sport. Champaign-Urbana, Il., p. 185.

Freud, S. 1932–33. *New introductory lectures on psychoanalysis, XXII*. New York: Morton.

Gibson, J. H. 1993. *Performance versus results*. Albany, NY: SUNY University Press.

Kohlberg, L. 1981. *The philosophy of moral development: Moral stages and the idea of justice*. New York: Harper and Row.

Kohn, A. 1986. *No contest: The case against competition*. Boston: Houghton Mifflin.

Lickona, T. 1991. *Educating for character*. New York: Bantam.

McGuire, J., and M. Thomas. 1975. Effects of sex, competence, and competition on sharing behavior in children. *Journal of Personal and Social Psychology* 32(3): 490–4.

Morgan, W., K. Meier, and A. Schneider. 2001. *Ethics of sport*. Champaign, IL: Human Kinetics Press.

Pearson, K. (1995). Deception, Sportsmanship, and Ethics. Philosophic Inquiry in Sport. William J. Morgan and Klaus v. Miur pp. 183–4.

Piaget, J. 1932. *The moral development of a child*. Glencoe, IL: Free Press.

Reimer, J., D. P. Paolitto, and R. H. Hersh. 1990. *Promoting moral growth: From Piaget to Kohlberg*. Prospect Heights, IL: Waveland Press.

Schulman, J. L., and W. G. Bowen. 2001. *The game of life*. Princeton, NJ: Princeton University Press.

Shields, D. & Bredemeier, B. (1995). Character Development and Physical Activity. Champaign, Il: Human Kinetics.

Sperber, M. 2001. *Beer and circuses*. New York: Holt.

Sperber, M. 1990. *College Sports Inc*. New York: Holt.

Stoll, S., and Beller, J. (2001). Character Education. Moscow, ID: University of Idaho Center for Ethics.

Weiss, M. R., and B. J. Bredemeier. 1990. Moral development in sport. In *Exercise and sport science reviews*. Vol. 18, edited by K. B. Pandolf and J. Holloszy. Baltimore: Williams and Wilkens.

CHAPTER 2

Values, Principles, and You

◆ What is an ethical dilemma?
◆ What is an ethical principle?
◆ What makes a situation ethical?
◆ What is a prime or first principle?
◆ Why are social values questionable when developing ethical principles?

MAKING CHOICES

What Is an Ethical Dilemma?

An ethical dilemma occurs when you are placed in a situation where what you believe is challenged or questioned and you are forced to act. An ethical dilemma involves making choices based on values. For example, let us assume that you are in a class taking a test. You are on your honor (a moral obligation) not to talk to anyone and not to give anyone else your answers. As a student you have committed to a school honor code that lists very clearly your obligation to the rules. Your professor leaves the room. Your best friend asks you for an answer. What do you do? You face an ethical dilemma. You gave your word to follow the honor code, yet you feel a loyalty to your friend. Which is more important? The oath of duty to the rule or the loyalty to your friend.

In this case, you are forced to decide. The friend won't stop asking you, and you have to say something. So, you are now in a situation where you must act and make a choice. In this case your choice

is voluntary behavior. Your choices: You can give your friend the answer. You could leave the room. You could ignore your friend. You could give your friend the wrong answer. You could do all sorts of things because you do have multiple choices. Hard choices are difficult for everyone. Before we go any further, let us talk about the conflicting values in this scenario. We like to call them the tension between social and moral values. As you remember from Chapter 1, a value is something that you think is worthwhile. Values tend to be very relative, meaning that what you value and what I value may be two different things. And most important, we must remember that nonmoral values are different and unique from moral values and that nonmoral values actually drive all moral decision making. It is also true that the decision to choose nonmoral values over moral values defines our own character. Character has both a nonmoral social perspective and a moral value perspective.

We might say, "Carlos, your school team mate, is a good person." We are saying something about Carlos's character, which in this case means what about

21

him? What is the difference between saying, "Carlos is a good person, or Carlos is a good basketball player? If you said that the statement, "Carlos is a good person," is about moral values, then you are correct. However, the statement, "Carlos is a good basketball player," is saying something about a skill that Carlos has. This skill, being a good basketball player, is a nonmoral value. We value the traits and characteristics that it took for Carlos to be good. He may have had some innate gifts, plus he worked hard to accomplish the task. However, Carlos could be a good basketball player and essentially be an immoral person. We use terms like "good" and "successful" to describe hard work, but a "good" person is wholly different than a "good" worker (see Figure 2-1).

Historically, moral values are as old as civilization, law, and governments. Moral values usually have been predicated or based on a belief in a higher power. The world's five major religions—Christianity, Judaism, Islam, Buddhism, and Confucianism—all honor the belief that we, as people, are bound to certain moral values. There is a "universality" about moral values in that certain universal rules exist in doing ethics (see Box 2-1).

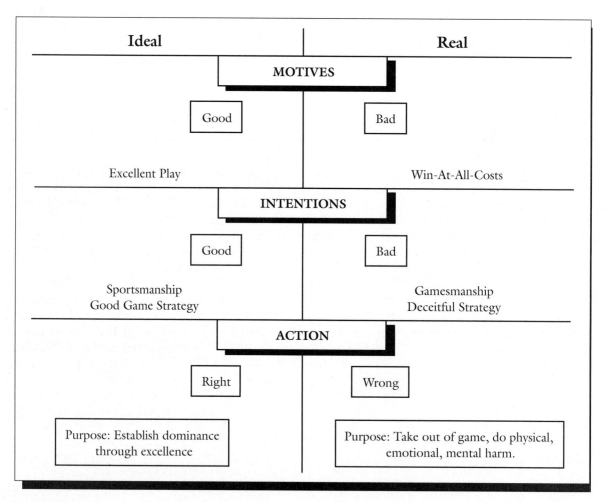

FIGURE 2-1 The perception of sport.

BOX 2-1

KANTIAN ETHICS

We will use the Kantian term, *universality,* meaning applied to all persons the same. Kant stressed two widely accepted principles of morality: (1) that moral judgments must be founded on universal rules, which are applicable to all persons in the same way and (2) that persons must always be treated with respect. His concept of universality requires you to test moral rules by seeing if you can apply them universally in the same way to all persons. His "categorical imperative" stated that duties are prescriptive and independent of consequences. Kantian ethics are widely held today as a standard of reasonableness and rationality.

At the same time people, who are not religious, belong to any church, or perhaps are atheists, believe in the importance of moral values. In fact, anthropologists argue that every society must follow certain codes of moral standards or that society will die.[1] In America, our legal system is based on the moral value of justice. Our government was founded on certain basic moral values that were considered imperative or necessary to the democratic process.

The basic values stated in the Declaration of Independence are life, liberty, and the pursuit of happiness; and from justice: the Constitution of the United States. From our discussion we can state that moral values are necessary for a society to thrive, for a people to live, and for a person to flourish. Take a few minutes and write what moral values you believe are important.

SELECTING VALUES

If you have listed your values. Let us examine whether they can stand alone. If you chose as your primary moral values: honesty (truthfulness), justice (fairness), or responsibility (respect) you have chosen well. Your moral values are prime, meaning they can stand alone. More about this later. However, if you chose what we like to refer to as social values such as: loyalty, commitment, dedication, sacrifice, hard work, determination, cooperation, and friendship, you have chosen values that focus on what the American work ethic finds important. A good worker is loyal. A good worker is committed. A good worker is dedicated. In fact, one probably is not able to be successful in American commerce without these important social values. And when you apply for a position, these values will serve you well in working on the job. These nonprime social values appear to be values of character; however, they can be cruel and hateful if not tempered by prime moral values.

For example, a person could be very loyal, hardworking, dedicated, and committed to being a car thief. A person could be determined, cooperative, and possess a fun personality and still be a liar and a thief. History is full of such personalities. Bormann, Himmler, and Goebbels, Hitler's right-hand men, were entirely dedicated to the genocide of the world's Jewish population. They were totally committed and loyal to Hitler and the cause. They were dutiful sons, husbands, and fathers. However, they had the fatal flaw of being loyal and dedicated to a dishonorable and hateful cause.[2]

These values have moral worth, but have a stronger social value worth. In our American society, loyalty, hard work, dedication, intensity, sacrifice, and so forth, are highly valued. However, we want to be very careful of these nonprime values. Prime values should be about such moral values as honesty, justice, fairness, responsibility, and respect, whereby if we violate any of them, we violate people directly. Social values are positive assets to exhibit but they must be tempered by the prime moral values.

It is true that these social values are admired in our society. One such value that is especially important

---

[1]The myth of amoral practice, especially in business, is highlighted through the work of Richard T. De George (1999).

[2]For an excellent analysis of social values run amok, and the power of personality, see Gitta Sereny (1995).

Loyalty, a social value, is being steadfast, faithful, devoted, or unswerving to a person, organization, or ideal. Loyalty can be dangerous if not tempered by the moral virtues of honesty, responsibility, respect, compassion, and justice.

in any group, whether teenagers, athletics, church organizations, or businesses is loyalty. Loyalty is being steadfast, faithful, devoted, or unswerving to a person, organization, or ideal. Loyalty is an essential value for any group or family to exist. Idealistically, we have many historical examples of people who were loyal to a cause. George Washington was loyal to his country as demonstrated by his service. Abraham Lincoln was loyal to the proposition that all men are created equal. Martin Luther King was loyal to the belief that civil rights are mandated by God. Mother Theresa was loyal to people whom no one else wanted.

In our present day, many coaches and athletes display loyalty, which is to be admired. Pat Summit is loyal to the Lady Volunteers and the State of Tennessee. Dean Smith was and is loyal to the University of North Carolina. Cal Ripken is loyal to the Baltimore Orioles. These individuals have displayed unswerving loyalty to their principles and to the organizations that they lead and serve.

Loyalty, however, can be immoral and dangerous if not tempered by the moral virtues of honesty, justice, respect, and compassion. In 1969, Lt. William Calley, a U.S. army officer in Viet Nam, followed orders to murder and butcher a village of old men, women, and children at Mi Lai.[3] When arrested and tried for his action, his defense was, "I was only following orders." Calley was devoted and loyal to the chain of command. On January 22, 1986, the space shuttle *Challenger* exploded a few moments after launch. In the review of the tragedy, it was found that the Morton Thiokol engineers on the project knew that the O ring that malfunctioned was not developed to stand subzero temperatures. They were almost positively sure that the O ring would fail—though they thought it would be at the launch pad. In reporting the concern, the engineers at the next level of management could not agree. With disparate arguments, upper management decided that too much money was invested and too much country pride was riding on the launch.[4] Management's loyalty was first to finances and politics and then to the astronauts on board. The concerned engineers were overruled. Teacher Christa McAuliffe was to teach from space and President Ronald Reagan would be speaking on the telecast. The O ring malfunctioned and seven astronauts died. Loyalty is dangerous and meaningless without the virtues of honesty, compassion, and respect.

Intellect or coming from a "good home" is also often thought of as an ethical value. If a player is highly intelligent and "field smart," that player has great character and is someone who displays good values. Yet, intellect, in and by itself, is not an ethical value. History is full of brilliant and charismatic leaders who had little moral intelligence. Adolf Hitler was loved for his leadership abilities and his intellect in getting a job done. Numerous writers have noted that he was without comparison in his ability to charm and woo others to follow him, even

---

[3]For an excellent analysis of the problems of duty and orders, see Ronald Hammer (1971).

[4]For an excellent film on group think, see *Groupthink* (1991), Carlsbad, CA: CRM Films.

though he was psychologically evil. Intellect, without being tempered by respect, love, compassion, fairness, and honesty is a demon ready to spring. As Theodore Roosevelt said, "To educate a person in mind and not in morals is to educate a menace to society."[5]

Being from a "good home" does not equal "ethical values." Just because someone is born on the right side of the tracks, does not guarantee good character. Again, history has many ethical heroes who came from disadvantaged backgrounds. Individuals through their character rose from poverty to become world leaders. It is also true that numerous individuals who enjoyed many privileges displayed very poor ethical values.

Therefore, social values like loyalty, charm, personality, sacrifice, hard work, dedication, determination, and economic conditions, a privileged background, or intellectual gifts should not be in our list of ethical values. Our ethical principles should be first principles. Those principles serve as the base for who we are and how we work with other people (see Figure 2-2 and Box 2-2).

---

[5]Thomas Lickona has probably been the single greatest force in this country on the teaching of character. He has been influential in all aspects of the character education movement, which began in the 1980s but did not flourish until the school violence of the late 1990s. Lickona's work, *Educating for Character* (1991), is the bible of character and moral education.

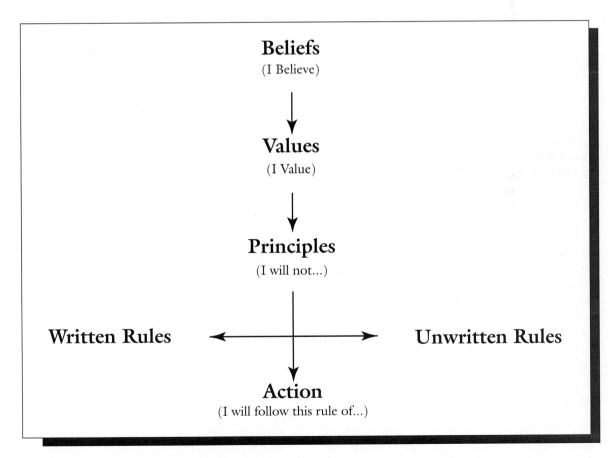

FIGURE 2-2 Paradigm: From beliefs to action.

BOX 2-2

THE NUMBER OF FIRST PRINCIPLES

How many or how few moral values and principles are there? Moral values are varied as we have discussed. Your task is to limit your values so that you can develop a workable set of principles. Too many universalizable values and principles may conflict with each other; however, only one moral value like love and its accompanying principle of "love your fellow human" may be too general, too abstract, or too vague to be useful in making moral determinations. Therefore, more than one is preferable, but more than five is probably ineffective. Writers on the subject of universalizable principles agree somewhat on the content. Most favor principles based on justice, freedom, and beneficence or nonmaleficence. For example, Frankena (1973) reduces the universalizable principles to (1) distributive justice and (2) beneficence. DeMarco and Fox (1990) state that the universalizable principles are (1) Do No Harm, (2) Do Not Be Unfair, and (3) Do Not Violate Another's Freedom. Lickona (1990) calls for only two universal principles of (1) respect for others and (2) responsibility.

DeMarco and Fox (1990) state two general conditions for establishing moral principles, conditions that you can apply to both examining your values and developing principles.

1. Principles must be explicit and simple (no abstraction, just basic concrete statements). In developing principles, simplicity is imperative because difficult moral questions must be easy to understand. Complicated principles affect your efficiency in deliberation and judgment of moral issues; too complicated a principle and you may never resolve the problem.

2. Principles must also be shared, common, and universalizable. (That is, the principles you choose are actually cited by people in many different societies and cultures in various ways.) Common principles are shared by the world's major religions, cultural laws, and knowledge of basic human nature. Because of the universal nature of the principle in relation to other people, the wider the acceptance, the stronger the ability to settle disputes. Realize, however, that universal agreement about a principle is not the complete test. History has shown that some cultures have accepted deviate behavior as the norm. For example, the people of Germany seemed to accept Hitler's genocide of the Jews, which would imply that genocide of Jews was acceptable. Principles must pass various tests of reasonableness and rationality.

The reasonable and rational tests center on: Are your thoughts coherent? Do your thoughts support your convictions? Are you willing to test your reasons by taking others into account? Are you willing to place your principles against the test of impartiality, consistency, and reflection? Can you submit your principles to the scrutiny of others?

Let's now examine first ethical values and see if we can find a flaw in how we use them.

MORAL VALUES

In a moral reasoning process, moral values are usually written down in a special way called principles. Writing about the value and thinking about the language, gives one a better perspective. When we place our stated values into written principles, we have a touchstone that helps give us perspective for making decisions about right and wrong. **Principles** are universal guides that tell which kinds of actions, intentions, and motives are prohibited, obligatory, or permitted in human interactions. Principles should act as "universal rules of con-

Principles are universal guides that tell us which kinds of actions, intentions, and motives are prohibited, obligatory, or permitted in human interactions.

duct," or first rules that identify and define what is valued.

Let us assume that we can write principles that define our values and that by doing so we can understand what we believe. One of the problems with doing this is delimiting our moral values to a workable number. We can get some help in achieving this goal by consulting experts in this sort of thing.[6] Let us also assume that you can limit these first rules to a workable number, like three or four. Why three or four? If we use 5 or 10, it becomes troublesome in deciding which is more important, how they should be ranked, if they mean the same thing, and what the differences between them are. Again, if we consult experts who have invested considerable thought about these things, we might have some direction. In the cases of writing principles, it is argued that certain sorts of principles

seem to be able to stand alone. That is, these principles appear to have theoretical support, they are widely accepted, and are frequently used as a reason for being in sport. Because of their widespread acceptance in sport, these principles have power in arguing that they can be effectively used to solve moral dilemmas. Considering that principles are widely used in moral arguments, and assuming that this is possible, how would you go about selecting four prime values and then expressing them verbally so that they would be useful in everyday experiences.

SELECTING FOUR VALUES

Moral values are numerous and varied, including honesty, honor, truth, respect, sincerity, integrity, justice, duty, cooperation, and so on. How can you select or choose just one or two or three? This is not an easy task, but certain historical guides can help. For example, if we examine certain general, historical, and cultural parameters that can be found in the Bible, the Pali Cannon, the Book of Koran, and most societal ethics, we might find some explicit, simple, common, and shared values. That is, in all of the above cases, four moral values surface: justice, honesty, responsibility, and beneficence. And, in the case of sport, sport science, physical education, recreation, and dance these four values are also commonly supported. For example, fair dealings in the classroom, fair play on the field or the court, fair treatment of clients, and so on; honesty, the absence of lying, cheating, and stealing in class, in work, or at play; responsibility of action, doing what is expected, being accountable for one's action; beneficence, the practice of doing no harm and attempting to do good. These are shared values in our professions and have a universal appeal because they are imperative to human relationships, without which morality can and does not exist.[7]

---

[6]This interpretation comes from the work of Frankena (1973) and DeMarco and Fox (1990).

[7]De George (1999).

Procedural justice (one of four types of justice) is involved when organizations have rule books that state what is considered acceptable and unacceptable on the field of play.

Justice: Moral Value One

The first moral value is justice. Four general types of justice exist: (1) distributive, (2) procedural, (3) retributive, and (4) compensatory. Distributive justice involves the perceived fairness and distributions of benefits and burdens relative to outcomes. Procedural justice involves the perceived fairness of the policies, procedures, and agreements used to determine outcomes. Retributive justice involves the perceived fairness of punishment of a law-breaker or evildoer. Compensatory justice involves the perceived fairness of giving back because of harm or unfairness that a person or persons may have suffered in the past.

Each of these types of justice is inherent in moral reasoning and decision making in sport. For example, organized sport organizations have rule books stating what are considered acceptable and unacceptable actions on the field of play (procedural). If these guidelines or rules are violated, sanctions are imposed in the way of penalty and foul shots, banishments from play, and so forth (retributive). In the most general sense, teams have rules that players must follow in order to participate (procedural) and sanctions if those rules are not followed (retributive).

Distributive justice can also be seen in the passing and implementation of Title IX legislation. The compensatory justice factor is awarding monetary relief or some form of goods for past misconduct. That is, distributive and compensatory justice must be considered in issues of equity, as will be discussed in Chapters 9 and 10. Equity refers to gender and racial opportunity, plus opportunity for persons with disabilities.

We believe justice is also inclusive of what is known as distributive justice, or the equity of treating others, especially competitors, fairly. Theoretically, distributive justice is based on integrity for doing the just and equitable right. Equitable does not necessarily mean being treated equally or the same in this case. Suppose that you and Joe are both swimmers. You swim for health reasons. Joe is an able-bodied swimmer; you, however, are a paraplegic. If you and Joe are treated the same, there would be no special accommodations for you. You would have to access the facility the same way Joe does—no wheelchair ramps and no hydraulic devices to lower you into the pool. In this case it is not fair for you and Joe to be treated the same. "Justice asks us to do something about cases of special need . . . because only with such attention can people have something comparable to an equal chance of enjoying the good life."[8] This does not mean that

---

[8]Frankena (1973).

justice demands that all lives must be equally good in a nonmoral sense; that is, distribution of money, wealth, goods, winning, and success. Rather, it means that justice asks that we treat others equally in the sense that they have the proportionally same contribution to the goodness of their lives, in a moral sense. It does not mean that once a certain minimum has been achieved by all, you must distribute all your goods to help others meet the same standard that you have achieved. To do so would be unproductive and possibly fanatical.

Honesty: Moral Value Two

Honesty is the condition or capacity of being truthful or trustworthy in dealing with others, including competitors. Honesty is dealing fairly and uprightly in speech and action. The moral value of honesty is based on the premise that the actor or agent will not lie, cheat, or steal. (Moral actor or moral agent is common terminology referring to the person who is acting, based on motives and intentions.) For example, honesty refers to the honest person as one who, after accepting the rules and laws as a necessity to playing the game, follows them. If you decide the rules are ineffective, then you must make a decision. You have three choices: (1) accept the supposed flawed rule and play the game; (2) accept the rule as is, but try to change the rules; or (3) refuse to play. Situations 1 and 3 are self-explanatory, but changing the rules may mean open protest and maybe even a rebellion against how the rules were developed. During this rebellion, you have two options, refuse to play by the rules (and accept the fact that the player may not play), or accept the rules as they are until new rules are developed. The conditions stated are such that an honest player is obligated to live within the three situations stated, because an honest player would not covertly violate the rules or cheat.

Responsibility: Moral Value Three

Responsibility is accounting for your actions. Frankena (1973) discusses the three different ways we use the word responsible.

1. Jane is responsible, which says something about Jane's character.
2. Jane was responsible, meaning that Jane is and was responsible for some past action.
3. Jane is responsible for Y (some action), meaning that Jane is responsible for some future action.

Situation 1 concerns moral value. Situation 2 may directly refer to some nonmoral action, such as getting the equipment, or situation 2 may refer to moral action such as blatantly injuring an opponent. Situation 3 has the same possibilities as situation 2, meaning it could refer to either nonmoral or moral values. In sport today the word for responsibility is accountability, meaning both the nonmoral and moral values of situations 1, 2, and 3. Athletes take pride in their accountability to the team, the coach, and the game. Corporate America seeks individuals who have a high sense of accountability for self and the business.

Beneficence: Moral Value Four

Beneficence is the condition of (1) not doing harm, (2) preventing harm, (3) removing harm, and (4) doing good. Considering the perspective of competition in this country, we have taken a moral leap by including this value. In the international sense, beneficence might be called "fair play," the act of giving to another above and beyond the call of game play, or the act of common civility. For example, in the 1952 Olympic Games, the Italian bobsledder, Carlo Monti, was winning the event, with one team to follow. When he heard that the last team had a broken brake, Monti immediately returned to the start and gave the opposing team his brake. The opposing team won, using Monti's brake. The international "fair play" award was given to Monti for his devotion to the concept of fair play.

The following scenario provides an opportunity for showing beneficence to opponents. Assume that you and Josie are playing badminton in the national badminton tournament semifinals. You have played Josie on several different occasions, and you know each other moderately well. You both use the same kind of badminton racquets, with the same hand-grips. You both have identical backup racquets. On the way to the court this morning (a 30-minute drive) the van driver informs Josie that she cannot carry her racquet bag on board. Josie personally places her racquet bag in the rear of the van. When she arrives at the court, Josie discovers that the van driver removed her racquet bag to repack equipment and inadvertently forgot her bag. She asks the driver to return to retrieve her racquet bag. In tournament play a 15-minute forfeit time is allowed before disqualification. The round-trip for the van to the hotel is about 60 minutes. Josie proceeds to the court; by tournament rules, no racquet means a forfeit. If Josie forfeits, you advance to the national championship. Josie checks around and finds you are the only person at the tournament with a backup racquet the same as hers. She explains the circumstances about her racquet and asks to use your backup racquet.

1. Would you give Josie your backup racquet?
2. Would any of the following affect your answer?

   a. You do not especially like Josie.
   b. The winner is guaranteed $1,000, and a forfeit is as good as a win.
   c. What if the prize is $5,000?
   d. The two other players in the semifinals bracket are not of the quality of you or Josie. It is likely that whoever wins this match will win the championship and the $10,000 top prize. Allowing Josie to use your backup racquet may also address other moral values, but essentially this is an issue of beneficence item (4) doing good . The first three conditions, (1) not doing harm, (2) preventing harm, and (3) removing harm, may have already been met; there is no intention here to harm the opponent. No rule requires you to give Josie your backup; however, the final element of beneficence asks you to do good, which in this case may be both moral and nonmoral. Moral good in the sense of treating Josie kindly and nonmoral good in the sense of intrinsic, inherent things. Can you think of any others?

Because doing good plays an important role in sport, it has application in this text on sport ethics. Beneficence passes moral criteria: It is common to the world's religions and cultures and, from a reasoned and rational sense, is paramount to relationships with others. It also supports doing good in the sense of fair play and respect for the game. "Poor racquetless Josie" cannot play without the racquet and if you do not loan her one, you will play a lesser opponent or no opponent.[9] To not play or to play a lesser opponent is to miss the point of competition, which should be to meet the best challenger possible.

WRITING PRINCIPLES

Because we live in a society that believes honor and principles are important (even though sometimes it is hard to find people of principle and value), we need to examine and clarify our values so that they make sense in terms of how we make moral decisions. That is, when we live by our values in our everyday actions toward others, we are demonstrating our principles. Values are usually written in a special way called principles. Principles are guides that tell us what kinds of actions are acceptable in our dealings with other people. We recommend that you write your values in a principled written form by use of the negative, that is, I will not . . .—or—Do not . . . (see Box 2-3). Take a sheet of paper, write your values in the left column and then write the negative in principle form in the right.

Moral Values	Moral Principles
Honesty	I will not . . .

We have stated that we believe there are four universal values: justice, responsibility, honesty, and

---

[9]Critics of the beneficence value, argue that what is needed here is "an appreciation for the rules themselves. Angela Schneider and Robert Butcher have argued that beneficence as well as our other three values is a "bag" of virtues approach—which lacks merit in the logic of playing games. They state that what is needed is a respect for the rules. See R. Butcher, and A. Schneider (2001).

BOX 2-3

WRITING PRINCIPLES

DeMarco and Fox (1990) argue that principles should be written in the negative rather than the positive. Negative principles seem to cover all situations and cases and apply to everybody all the time. The negative seems to be more concrete; we seem to understand the negative more easily. Rules over time have been written from the negative, for example, the Ten Commandments or the National Collegiate Athletic Association's (NCAA) Manual. Positive principles seem to be more abstract. For example, "do not cheat" carries the implication that you should never cheat, under any circumstances; whereas to "play honestly" may not be possible, when out of ignorance you may not be playing honestly. That is, you may be violating a rule because it may be obscure or you do not know the rule exists. Cheating means that you consciously know and covertly act to violate rules; "don't cheat" means that you know the rules and choose to follow them. Negative principles are powerful in that more people can accept them because evils are being avoided. Our negative principles are being stated from a positive value system based on justice, honesty, responsibility, and beneficence.

beneficence. We have tried to apply these values to sport. Now we must develop a set of universal principles by which to lead our sporting lives. A principle is technically a statement written in the negative describing our values and beliefs from which all other rules are developed. For example, I will not lie. Apply the concept of writing in the negative to the four moral values we selected.

Justice: Principle One—Do Not Be Unfair

We mean fair in the sense of treating people by both the same set of standards and the more difficult concepts of distributive justice, procedural justice, compensatory justice, and retributive justice.

This principle simply stands as a measure of fairness. This principle or first rule should be applied to everyone it touches. Such a perspective opens a wide array of questions when dealing with fair play, rule interpretations, and so on.

Honesty: Principle Two—Do Not Lie, Cheat, or Steal

The moral value of honesty is framed within three possible negative precepts of lying, cheating, and stealing. Lying is verbal dishonesty. Cheating is being dishonest in action after giving your word, implicitly or explicitly, to follow some specific rules. Stealing is taking something that belongs to someone else.

Responsibility: Principle Three—Do Not Be Irresponsible

This principle means that you knowingly take your actions into consideration and do what you say you are going to do. You do what you promise to do, and you accept praise or blame for what you have done. You act in such a fashion that others can depend on you to complete what you begin.

Beneficence: Principle Four—Do Not Be Uncivil

We have written this principle to take into consideration the four tenants of beneficence: (1) doing no harm, (2) preventing harm, (3) removing harm, and (4) doing good. We are using this principle as the concept of being civil to others and showing common decency. The concept is that you treat others with a certain sense of decency in which you do no harm, you remove harm, you prevent harm, and you attempt to do good.

QUESTIONING A PRINCIPLE

Writing principles seems easy enough, what happens when we apply these principles to life situations. In other words, are there not times when lying is acceptable?

Let us suppose that you are a Dutch resistance fighter during World War II. You do not believe in Adolph Hitler and you do not believe it is right to take the Jews to concentration camps where you have no idea what will happen to them, though you suspect, they will be killed. You have some dear friends who are Jewish. You hide them in your attic and supply them with food and water. They live there for some time. One day, a Nazi storm trooper stops at your house. When you open the door, he asks, "Do you have any Jews living in your house?" Do you say, "Sure, just pop up the stairs and take them off!" Or, do you tell a lie?

In this case, it is acceptable to lie, because by telling the truth you will surely cause great bodily harm to your friends. To save their lives, lying is acceptable. However, others might argue that it is never acceptable to tell a lie; and the true decision of what happens to your Jewish friends is in the hands of God. These two positions are extreme in how the dilemma is handled. One position says that it is okay to lie; and the other position says that it is not acceptable to lie. Let us examine the argument on both sides.

In Some Extreme Cases, Lying Is Acceptable

The attic scenario is an extreme case, one that obviously does not occur in life very often. In this attic case, two moral principles are placed in jeopardy against each other, that is, two principles are colliding. It is impossible to do one without risking an ethical value. Considering the four ethical values, honesty, justice, responsibility, and beneficence, which values are in jeopardy? Which of the four ethical values is more important in the attic scenario? Why?

Usually, in this case, any reasoned individual would argue that the ethical value of responsibility for human life is more important than honesty. Therefore, to save human life, it is permissible to lie. This practice of weighing moral values, if they are in conflict, is known as (1) stacking and (2) writing exceptions to the ethical values. The term stacking *does* not imply that one is more important than the other in all cases; nor does it imply that we are per-

mitted to stack the values any way we please, whenever we please. Rather, stacking values means that we consider the importance of the values and principles and attempt a rational solution and plan of attack to follow when we are confronted with difficult situations. Stacking the values means that of the four, which is the more important given the existing circumstances? Is honesty more important than responsibility? Is justice more important than honesty? Is beneficence more important than honesty?

Stack your ethical principles from the most important to the least important. State why you stacked your ethical values as you did? On what basis did you decide which was more important?

Our next job is to find any exceptions to our moral principles. In the attic scenario, we found that two principles are in conflict—honesty and responsibility. As you reviewed your stated principles, let us assume that you decided that the most important principle was honesty. In making ethical decisions, a general rule of thumb exists.

General Rule: If and only if, an action violates any of the four prime principles, it is permissible to develop exceptions to the rule.

This means that if one of our principles is being violated, it is good thinking to resolve the problem by considering an exception. That is, in the attic scenario, two principles are colliding: honesty and responsibility. When principles collide and an outside action is questionable and unethical, it is good thinking to reconsider the written principles. The outside questionable action in the attic is the Nazis. Some people would argue, "*If* they are doing wrong, it is okay to lie." However, such reasoning can become very sticky. Do two wrongs make a right? That is, the evil of their actions justifies unethical behavior. Or, is this not a case of situational ethics? If we argue that two wrongs do make a right, then we start a slippery slope of moral justification.[10] Two wrongs do not make a right. If we constantly juggle the practice of two wrongs make a right, each and every time, we become totally in-

---

[10]Albert Bandura (1991).

consistent and liars ourselves. Rather, we wish to consider the consequences of what it means to write an exception to our rules.

When stacking principles, most individuals would choose honesty as the number one principle. If, in fact, honesty is your first most important principle, you will want to consider an "exception" to your principle. It is colliding with responsibility—why? It collides because by telling the truth, we would do great bodily harm to another individual. That is, if honesty is the most important principle, does it continue to be the most important principle if human life is in the balance? Or to put it another way, if honesty is the most important principle, and by being honest we violate another moral principle, should we follow that principle? If you answer, no, then we need to consider "exceptions" to our rules or principles.

What Exceptions Would You Make to Your Moral Principles?

Exceptions to honesty? I will not lie, cheat, nor steal unless. . . .
Exceptions to justice?
Exceptions to responsibility?
Exceptions to beneficence?

We must remember that exceptions should be written with considerable thought. The exceptions should be made only for very important situations. Situations that are serious. Let us also remember that in the attic case, life and death was on the line. Sometimes, folks want to do exceptions for everyday activities. Should we? Should we write exceptions for the dilemmas that we face in our "real-world" lives? What do we do if the situation is not as obviously life threatening as the "attic"? What do we do if the colliding of principles is about some everyday activity?

COLLIDING VALUES IN EVERYDAY LIFE

Delphine is your good friend. You are both competitive dancers. Delphine is always highly sensitive about her clothes; in fact, Delphine is sensitive about everything. You realize this and understand that though Delphine may be too sensitive, she is worth the effort to consider a friend. Delphine buys a new competitive dance costume that is very expensive. She wears the outfit for a special dress rehearsal in which you and she are preparing to compete, though at different levels. She thinks the costume is gorgeous. When Delphine sees you, she tells you about her expensive outfit and how beautiful she thinks it is. In your heart of hearts, you think her choice is just about the ugliest thing you have ever seen. You think it is the wrong style, the wrong color, the wrong length, and the wrong everything for Delphine. There is no malice in your heart. You really care and you really think the dress is ugly. Delphine asks you what you think of the outfit.

Considering the four principles, Delphine is asking you to make a moral decision concerning at least two of them, "Do not be dishonest—and—Do not be unkind." What would you do?

1. Would you tell Delphine the truth, and bear the consequences of her response?
2. Would you tell a little white lie and tell Delphine the outfit is okay?
3. Would your answer be any different if you both were competing in the same event?

If you chose 1, perhaps you believe that the principle of "Do not be dishonest" is more important than "Do not be unkind." In this perspective, you believe that honesty is the most important value. You decide that truth is more important than Delphine's feelings. If you chose 2, then you may think that being kind is more important than being honest. You took into consideration Delphine's sensitivity and think that honesty really is not that important.

Which is the better action, being kind or telling the truth? At this point in our discussion, perhaps neither. Perhaps telling Delphine about her dress is really not an ethical dilemma at all. Rather it is an issue of taste. Just because you do not have the same taste as Delphine, has nothing to do with the problems of telling the truth. Rather the truth is, you have different tastes. So you simply say, "Delphine, I do not have the same taste as you, so it doesn't matter if I like your dress or not." Or, "Delphine, I have poor taste, so you really shouldn't ask me." Therefore a variation, you are not lying but answering truthfully that it is not an issue.

However, such a tactic may be avoiding the problem. You were asked to give a response. Therefore, you are obligated to tell the truth. After you decided the stacking order of your ethical principles, you are bound or obligated to follow this order. Does this mean at all times? Yes, it does unless you can find specific exceptions.

Suppose in this case you argue that "telling the truth" is really hurting Delphine. Should you be so bound to a principle that the principle becomes more important than the person? Perhaps, but principles without context many times cause wrong actions and inconsistencies. In stacking your principles, you need to ask yourself if this moral question is an exception to your principles. If "Do not be dishonest" is your most important principle, does it remain so at all times or does this become an exception? Is telling a friend what you see as the truth about a dance outfit an exception to your principle? Reason and rationality should tell you that to all principles and ordering of principles there must be exceptions. However, what merits an exception? Usually, those exceptions should not be about worrying about hurting someone's feelings. If we worry about hurting feelings—we may never make an ethical decision. However, we do not want to intentionally do damage to Delphine. Let us apply some alternative thinking.

Suppose that in the dance scenario, you chose an alternative approach. Is there a way to address both honesty and beneficence equally? If you can find a way to place both values on an equal plane, this may be an acceptable alternative and a better solution. You are able to take into consideration both principles and may even argue that the principle "Do not be irresponsible" forces you to tell Delphine the truth as kindly as possible. For example, you might say, "Delphine, you are a good friend and I care for you. I wouldn't tell you a lie, therefore, the truth is,

I do not care for your outfit and I think the outfit does nothing for you." (This approach may not work either; Delphine may be so sensitive that whatever you do will hurt her.) If you chose this position, you may have decided that the two principles, "Do not lie" and "Do not be unkind," are at the same level of importance and have no difference in your ordering or stacking of prime principles.

When you order your first principles, you decide which is the most and which is the least important. Notice that we use the word *first* here as another adjective for our most important principles. When conflict arises, ordering or stacking principles will give direction to which *first* principle is more important. You must also take into consideration, when ordering your principles, if an exception exists. This ordering, though, must remain the same and consistent through all situations.

Writing exceptions should be limited to extraneous, difficult, life-threatening situations. I will not lie, cheat, or steal, except and unless human life is in jeopardy. From our Delphine story, we have learned that exceptions must not be written for everyday problems. If they are, our principles are flimsy and our ethics useless.

THE PROBLEM WITH PRINCIPLES— NEVER TELL A LIE

In the Jews in the attic scenario, some ethical and theological purists would argue that it is never acceptable to tell a lie, no matter how difficult the situation. These individuals would argue that when the Nazis came, you were honor bound to tell the truth. If the Nazis hurt the Jews, God's wrath would be on them. Or by telling a lie you would be interfering with God's plan, either God will protect the Jews or God's will would be to let the Jews die. This point of view is difficult to support even if you believe in "evil." That is, if you believe that God or pure good exists, then you must (I think) believe that evil exists. If that is so, do we have a duty to stop evil or attempt to intercede in evil's path? A very difficult question when evil is about us. Martin Niemöller, a Christian who signed a "Declaration

Cheating is violating a promise. Is the common practice of getting an edge cheating? Should we practice getting an edge?

of Guilt" on behalf of the German churches for not opposing Hitler more forcefully, suffered from the same concern. He said, "First they came for the Jews. I was silent. I was not a Jew. Then they came for the Communists. I was silent. I was not a Communist. Then they came for the trade unionists. I was silent. I was not a trade unionist. Then they came for me. There was no one left to speak for me."[11]

The problem then is should we intercede if immorality exists?

A PRINCIPLE AND ITS DEMANDS

As you will recall earlier, we mentioned that the ethical value of honesty should be written in the principle form: I will not lie, cheat, or steal. Honesty can be defined as upright dealings with another person especially in the context of truth telling. This truth telling can exist in three forms: lying, cheating, and stealing. Lying is verbally and intentionally changing what we perceive to be truth. Cheating is violating a promise. That is, I promise to be faithful, or I promise to follow the rules. Stealing is taking another's property. What about a com-

mon practice—getting the edge. Should we practice getting the edge? And does it matter if we cheat a little, lie a little, or steal a little if we win?

Lying, cheating, and stealing is common practice today. All of us have ways to rationalize our behaviors of lying, cheating, and stealing—and worse, few people expect more of us. In the last 10 years, stealing on the job has become a large and real problem in corporate America, including the fitness industry. Companies suffer huge losses from employees stealing all sorts of materials. The theft problem is not limited to the worker on the job taking a bar bell; a large part of the theft comes from the fitness or office worker taking office supplies, for example, pens, pencils, notepads, post-it pads, and then essentially loafing on the job. Workers steal from their employers by not putting in a full day's work. They loaf at the watercooler or write personal notes on e-mail. Not only is the employee not working, but is stealing cyberspace time from his/her employee as well as stealing productivity time. Interestingly, the news is full of violent crime, but more crime occurs in the workplace than ever occurs on the streets.

Lying is so commonplace that most of us think little of telling lies. How often do we lie? Good people lie about four times a day and the more active liars tell that many in an hour and maybe many more. Why do people lie?

We lie because we want something for ourselves. We lie because we want people to think we are bright, or charming, or special in some way. At the same time, we cheat because we want a better grade or a better experience, or we do not want to hurt another's feelings. Sometimes we cheat not for ourselves—or we think not for ourselves—we cheat by helping others cheat. For example, let us review a case we discussed earlier. Let us suppose your friend wants you to give her the answers on a test. What did you say, would you help your friend cheat?

Unfortunately, this sort of cheating pulls at our heart strings. We want to help our friends, because they are our friends. If we analyzed why we do this, it is usually not because we want to help the friend. Rather it's really about wanting our friend to like us or we do not want our friend to be mad at us, or

---

[11]Martin Niemöller (October 14, 1968).

maybe it's just easier to cheat than have an argument with the friend. It is easier to go along than it is to refuse. For whatever reason, either wanting our friend to like us or avoiding a problem, we are really cheating. Yes, we cheat the system and ourselves, and we are cheating our friend. If we truly cared about our friend, we would want her to be responsible and learn the material on her own.

Have you ever thought when you visit your physician how often she or he cheated in school? When your life is in other people's hands and their skills and knowledge are the keys to your living, do you want to think that they cheated in school? Of course, you might argue that this is different; surely the doctor did not cheat on the important stuff.

College students often argue that they may cheat on some classes but they would never cheat in their major classes, because they are the important stuff. The question to pose: "How do you know what is unimportant? Do you have a very special crystal ball that you dial up and that tells you what you need to know—a year from now, or 5 years, or 20 years? How do you know what you do not know?"

Stealing, like cheating and lying, occurs often. Many of us would lie and cheat but, interestingly, would never blatantly steal, like stealing a shirt from the store. In fact, we would be indignant if anyone would ever think that we might blatantly steal—though we tell lies.

What would you do if one of your friends stole from you? Suppose they took your favorite CD? Would the friend still be your friend? Why or why not? Most of us would not tolerate a friend stealing from us. It is rather an interesting double standard. We also expect our parents and grandparents to be honest. We expect our teachers to be honest. We expect our coaches to be honest. But, we do not expect ourselves to be honest. It is also interesting that if we are liars, cheats, or thieves, people measure our character by it. People know if we are liars—maybe not instantly—but usually in time. Which is worse, a cheater, liar, or a thief?

Our goal is to follow a set of principles. In this case, our principle is: Do not lie, cheat, or steal unless by doing so we place another individual in great physical and emotional jeopardy. To do so means that we must remember when we defend a dishonest act and say that we know where the line is or we know when to tell the truth, that we are really dishonest. We are dishonest because it will not be long before we learn to justify every act. We begin to argue that every action has worth. We will begin to argue: Everyone lies, therefore, lying is okay. Everyone cheats, therefore cheating is okay. Everyone steals, therefore, stealing is okay. But is it? Such an argument is faulty thinking. It is easy to lie and it is easy to justify cheating.

A SCENARIO ABOUT CHEATING

Coach Don is the winningest baseball coach in Big City athletics history. At Champion High, he has a 20-year history of coaching the team to beat. Coach Joe is his new assistant and is honored to have the opportunity to work with Coach Don. During pitching drills, Coach Joe notices that Coach Don is showing the star pitcher, James, how to put "goo" clandestinely on the ball. Coach Jo listens to Coach Don's directions and teaching, and waits until Coach Don is by himself. Coach Joe asks, "Coach, isn't it unethical to teach gooing the ball?" Coach Don smiles, "Naw, it's only unethical if you get caught. My kids never get caught. I teach them well. Coach Joe, this is the real world and you have got to learn early what the real world is all about. It ain't about being nice to somebody. It ain't about giving someone a chance—the real world is dog eat dog, and you need to learn that early and well." How would you respond to Coach Don's philosophy? Is this the reality of the world? Coach Don practices "gamesmanship," believing that the real purpose of the game is to push the rules to the limit without being caught. He believes that the purpose of the contest is to figure out ways to gain the advantage.

Rules are there "to get around." Cheating is not cheating. Cheating only exists if you get caught, so do not get caught. The principle: Do not lie, cheat, or steal is hard to follow in the real world of sport. In the real world of sport, winning is important. We play games and we keep score. The end result is important. If you argue that winning is not important and that we shouldn't want to win, then it becomes rather foolish to play any games. Why? Because we keep score in games, and if we keep score, there will be a winner and a loser—or a tie. Games are that way. The nature of the game is to place one's skill against another in competition and take a risk. Now the task gets harder, how do we win if we do not push the rules, if we do not hedge a little? After all, if everybody else is fudging the rules, it becomes questionable to follow the rules.

Such is the case of this true story. Coach Jones is the coach of a little league team. The whole season Coach Jones teaches the importance of following the rules and the importance of the spirit of the rules. The team is not very good, in fact, we could say they were the "cellar dwellers" of the league. The team name sort of said it all: the Squirrels. The season was great; they had a good time, but they did not win many. As luck would have it, the last game of the season was against the best team: the Hawks. The Hawks had never lost a game, *but,* luck was on the side of the Squirrels. The score was 3-2 in favor of the Squirrels. Bottom of the seventh inning (last inning of the game), the Hawks are up to bat with the game-winning run on base. The count was 2-3. The batter hit a long, high fly to right field. As the hit was made, the batter stepped back, bumped the catcher who swung his glove and hit the only umpire in the temple. The umpire fell backward, hit his head, and was knocked unconscious. In the meantime, the Squirrels right fielder, who had caught nothing but a cold all season, ran toward the ball with the glove up. His glasses dangled on his nose, the ball dropped, and he caught it. The Squirrels were jumping for joy; the Hawks were disgusted and dismayed. At this point, the umpire awoke in time to see the right fielder who was running down the baseline, trip, and drop the ball out of bounds. The umpire did not know what happened so he called both coaches to the plate. When the umpire asked the Hawks coach, what happened, his response was, "I do not know, if you didn't see it we have to replay it."

The Squirrels coach gave a play by play but the Hawks coach would not confirm. The umpire, caught in a legal dilemma, only one coach confirmed, called for a replay. The Hawks returned to bat, and this time the Hawks batter got a double and the Hawks won the game.

So what was learned that day? The truth was ignored, the rule was followed, and a cheater won. Unfortunately, both teams learned that the rules are to broken and cheaters sometimes win.

Our task is not to get caught in the cynicism of common practice, but to direct our goal toward the spirit of the rules—to play for the sake of playing, to value the opponent, and to enjoy a great experience. Following principles is not easy. Can we win, and stay within the parameters of the rules and the spirit of the rules? A. Bartlett Giamatti thought so.[12] He argued that competition is a blessed experience. Its purpose is:

> To toughen the body and temper the soul. . . .
> To emphasize integrity and develop courage. . . .
> To be obedient to the letter and spirit of the rules. . . .
> . . . So that winning is sweeter still.

SUMMARY

This chapter focused on examining the differences between social and moral values, selecting four moral values to guide ethical decision making, and then developing written principles. The four values supported in sport are honesty, justice, responsibility, and beneficence. The chapter also reviewed the difficulties in writing principles and the importance of writing exceptions and stacking the principles. Exceptions to principles should be limited to conditions in which harm might be done to another. Stacking principles gives context to how important each principle is and why we should think about these principles in their everyday context. Finally, the principle of honesty was examined and placed in context in real-world sport scenarios.

---

[12]A. Bartlett Giamatti (1989).

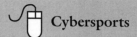

Cybersports

www.nays.org

The National Alliance for Youth Sports is directed toward the goal of making sports safe and positive for America's youth. This site offers information about a positive introduction to youth sports; the training of administrators, coaches, and game officials; the orientation of parents to youth sports; and the *National Standards for Youth Sports*.

www.positivecoach.org

The Positive Coaching Alliance is working to change what it means to be a youth sports coach by offering a mental model of the positive coach. Beginning at the local level, this organization offers a framework for transforming youth sports groups into outstanding athletic and educational organizations that foster positive character traits in young athletes.

www.rohan.sdsu.edu/~thesis/Sportpsy/thiss.htm

This study of moral reasoning focuses on levels of moral reasoning and intentional injurious behavior among female intercollegiate athletes. It argues that moral reasoning outside the sport environment is independent of moral reasoning and aggression within sport.

tigger.uic.edu/~lnucci/MoralEd/Sields.htm

Moral Reasoning in Game Playing offer a provocative look at this issue. Written by the directors of the Mendelson Center for Sport, Character and Culture, this paper highlights the theory of "bracketed morality," which holds that morality is "bracketed off" from everyday life.

REFERENCES

Bandura, A. 1991. Social cognitive theory of morality. In (Eds). *Handbook of moral behavior and development.* Vol. 1, *Theory,* edited by W. M. Kurtines and J. L. Gewirtz, 45–103. Hillsdale, NJ: Erlbaum.

Butcher, R., and A. Schneider. 2001. Fair Play as Respect for the Game. In *Ethics in sport,* edited by W. J. Morgan, K. V. Meier, and A. J. Schneider. Champaign, IL: Human Kinetics Press.

De George, R. T. 1999. *Business ethics.* 6th ed. Englewood Cliffs, NJ: Prentice Hall.

DeMarco, J. P., and R. M. Fox. 1990. *Moral reasoning: A philosophic approach to applied ethics.* New York: Harcourt Brace.

Frankena, W. 1973. *Ethics.* Englewood Cliffs, NJ: Prentice Hall.

Giamatti, A. Bartlett. 1989. *Take time for paradise: Americans and their games.* New York: Simon and Schuster.

Group think (1991). Carlsbad, CA: CRM Films.

Hammer, R. 1971. *The court martial of Lt. Calley.* New York: Coward, McCann, and Geoghegan.

Lickona, T. 1990. *Educating for character.* New York: Bantam.

Niemöller, M. *Congressional Record.* 14 October 1968. Vol. 114, p. 31636.

Sereny, Gitta. 1995. *Albert Speer: His battle with the truth.* New York: Knopf.

ISSUES AND DILEMMAS

In the following scenarios, Carol meets a variety of different ethical dilemmas. In each case, the same moral value comes into jeopardy and it is being "pushed" by a nonmoral value. What is the value, and what nonmoral value is involved? Are any of the scenarios acceptable? Somewhat acceptable? Unacceptable? Somewhat unacceptable? Why? If any are acceptable, give argument as to why the nonmoral value is more important than the moral value? And justify through reasoning.

As athletic director of Largetown University, Carol is constantly barraged with NCAA paperwork—so much so that the job has become tedious. The latest forms require athletes to verify the amount of time spent on practice appear to be more of the same. She decides to kill several birds with one stone—she has all the athletes sign all the season forms at one sitting, whereby she will fill in the appropriate practice times later.

Carol is "laid off" at XYZ Fitness when the local economy has a downswing. She collects the maximum amount of unemployment every two weeks. To do so, she is required to swear that she doesn't have a job and that she has been looking for full-time employment. In fact, however, Carol earns about $200 a month coaching youth sport teams in her local community. She is always paid in cash.

Carol is the owner of a small for-profit, private children's camp, which has no affiliation with any national organization. She learns that she can avoid high property taxes on the camp, which has a religious affiliation. She sends in one dollar and gets a mail-order license as an ordained minister of an unorthodox religious group. She claims her cabin as a church. She holds church each Saturday night with three of her friends on staff, while the campers are visiting family or friends away from camp. During the "service" they play records and talk.

Carol is a highly successful coach at Largetown University, who is well known for her community service. She donates about five hours a week of her personal time to the girls' and boys' club working with handicapped children who like to play ball. At Christmas each year, she gives Largetown athletic passes to the local McDonald's owner so that he in return will give free Happy Meals to the handicapped children with whom she has worked.

Application and Strategy: Thinking about the Game Plan

- ◆ Why follow rules?
- ◆ What are situational ethics?
- ◆ How are rules connected to principles?
- ◆ What are exceptions to principles and rules?

Coach Jones is a loveable individual. He has spent 30 years working with young people at the local high school. Basketball is his passion, but his love is changing the lives of young people. He prides himself on helping the disadvantaged move on to a better life. And for him, that better life is a college scholarship where education can make the difference. Coach is gruff on the exterior but a warm teddy bear at heart. He has been working with Jamal for over two years to win an athletic grant in aid (scholarship) to Big Time U. Big Time U has one of the best and most media visible programs in collegiate basketball. Coach Great at Big Time U knows how to inspire and educate his players. Big Time U is also known for its academic support staff, whereby the majority of men's basketball players graduate. Jamal is probably the greatest basketball player who has ever worn an Inner City High uniform. Jamal is not only a great ball player but is charming and well liked. He has a rather decent academic performance at Inner City High, goes to class, causes no problems, and is basically a good citizen. Coach Jones decided that Jamal appears to have test anxiety in that in the three times he has tried to get a score on the ACT that is high enough to qualify for admission to attend an NCAA school, he has failed. Coach knows that Jamal is intelligent and can do the work, but something psychological is getting in the way. In speaking with his colleagues he also learns that there appears to be an inherent racist design of the ACT. After realizing that the problems with Jamal's test taking may be tied into racist practice, Coach Jones decides its time to "correct" a wrong. He comes up with a clandestine plan to get Jamal a better score. He decides to hire a bright kid, Michael, to take the ACT exam for Jamal. Coach has selected Michael not only for his good academic ability and his looks, which are much like Jamal's, but Michael also owes Coach a "huge" favor. Coach helped pay for medical aid for the young man's grandmother and had secured medical insurance for her, when no one else could. Coach decides to call in the favor and secure Michael's services to take the exam for Jamal. Michael doesn't have to score high on the exam, just enough to make the necessary cut. Coach also knows Mr. Factor, the proctor for the ACT exam. Mr. Factor can be swayed to look the other way when Michael arrives as Jamal. Coach knows such action is unethical and illegal, but morally justifies the action through the amount of good that is being done. His thinking is thus: Jamal is bright and can do the college work. Jamal is a good and decent young man who will make a difference with the college degree and probably will play pro ball someday. The ACT test has racial connotations, which is inherently unfair to the Jamals of the world. Thus Coach reasons that it is acceptable in this case to "get around" the rules and help Jamal get an acceptable score.

The above scenario in some form or another is played out every day in different ways. Good people with a history of strong moral values have a conflict when a rule or law appears to be unjust. The problem is exacerbated when another good moral value seems to be more important. Such is the case of this true moral dilemma. The question becomes, How should one do good, if a "seemingly" bad rule of a large, impersonal institution, lies in the way of progress or betterment for another individual? The rule violates a good and decent person who seems to have shown their merit to attend the institution but is stymied by what appears to be unfair practices. And if the practices are unfair, should not this good and decent person have the chance to succeed? How does one solve this problem? What is the right thing to do and why? In Chapters 1 and 2 we found that, sometimes, principles and rules may clash.

Coach Jones apparently has a very strong, moral value system. He appears to be an honest, caring, and competent individual. He probably has developed these values into principled guidelines such as "Do not be irresponsible," "Do not be dishonest," and "Do not be unkind." In this case, Coach Jones considered whether he should follow the rules or whether he was justified in violating the rules? He decided that "this situation" merited a rethinking of his principles and he placed more weight on Jamal's education and future.

Should Coach Jones be obligated to follow "unfair" rules that appear to violate the potential of another person? What are Coach Jones' obligations in this scenario? In this case, Jones's obligation hinges on (1) obligation to himself, (2) obligation to Jamal, (3) obligation to society and the moral order, and (4) obligation to his own principles (not necessarily in that order).

The difficulty in "living by" good ethics is deciding against "situational ethics." Situational ethics is changing the ethical guidelines whenever a good or better reason exists to change them. That is, if one's brand of ethics does not suit one's needs or wants, then change the ethics. In Jones' case, the nonmoral goods, the possibility that Jamal will (1) attend a university, (2) play on a great basketball team, (3) get the opportunity for an excellent education, (4) have help from a fine academic support service at Big Time U, (5) possibly play in the pros for "big" money, and (6) benefit from all the good that will be transferred down to his immediate family, appear to far outweigh the moral principle of "Do not be dishonest."

If you were Coach Jones, and you were asked to make a decision between the worth of the individual and the rule, how would you decide?

1. Do you follow the rule because you are bound to follow rules, and thus Jamal doesn't go to Big Time U?
2. Do you violate the rule because you believe Jamal is more important than the rule?

It would seem that doing good for Jamal is more important than a rule developed by a "large" seemingly uncompassionate institution,[1] that is, the NCAA. In this case and all cases of conflicting values, there are certain steps that you may follow to help yourself systematically think through a moral problem.

---

[1]Can institutions be compassionate or uncompassionate? Yes. Certain institutions, for example, churches, synagogues, mosques, have a direct compassionate responsibility to serve and care for the sick, the elderly, the needy, those who are discriminated against. Other institutions, for example, stock market companies, have no social responsibility to care for others. Specifically as Milton Friedman said, the only social responsibility of a company is to make money for its shareholders.

STEPS IN THINKING THROUGH A MORAL PROBLEM

Step One: Are Any Moral Principles Violated?

We suggest you choose four moral principles as the basis of your most fundamental obligations to others in sport. When you agree to compete, you agree to apply these moral principles at all times. If you violate any of your principles then you must decide whether this action is an exception to the rule or whether your action is morally unacceptable. How do you know when a principle is violated? The answer lies in knowing what you believe, what you value, and what principles you have developed. If you do not know, you will have continual problems making moral decisions. Your purpose in developing these principles is to outline clearly what you believe as well as give you the necessary tools and skills to support a sport society that is just, honest, responsible, and civil.

In Coach Jones's case, the principle, "Do not be dishonest," is being violated. No matter how we flavor the story or justify the action, Coach Jones is involved in fraud and is attempting to cheat the system through his conspiracy to "get around" the rules. He is promoting a situation where he is also being irresponsible in his action as a moral leader and coach. The question is, How can Jones expect others to be honest and responsible if he himself is not? However, perhaps one can argue that this is an exceptional condition because the rules are "unethical." Should these rules be followed?

Step Two: Are Any Moral Rules Violated?

Numerous moral day-to-day rules follow directly from each principle. These rules govern all behavior in sport settings. These role-specific rules should guide you as you participate; if they do not, you need to address why they are exceptions.

In this case, the rules of the NCAA governing eligibility are clear. The purpose of the rules is fair play and responsibility to the athlete. If an athlete cannot score at a certain level on the ACT or other qualifying exams, the statistical probability of his or her success in the academic environment is questionable. Every individual who works or coaches under the NCAA guidelines has to validate his/her understanding of the process. Coach Jones, however, is not a part of the NCAA, but still is responsible to the system. Basically, Coach Jones is involved in academic fraud. He is the kingpin behind the conspiracy to do "good" for Jamal, when in fact he is planning how to defraud an institution into giving Jamal a scholarship to that institution. If the scholarship is linked to Pell Grants,[2] which many athletic scholarships are, then the conspiracy becomes defrauding the government, which is a federal offense.

Step Three: Is This Case an Exception?

Rules may have exceptions, but the exceptions must be justified. The burden of proof of whether this is an exception means that you must show that there is a good, overriding reason for allowing this exception. For example, you may have an exception if a moral rule is in conflict with a moral principle. Examine a situation involving the moral principle, "Do not be unfair." An athlete has asthma and requires a specific drug to compete at the minimum level. The drug, however, is on the "banned drug" list of the governance body. The "banned drug" is a rule, "Do not use this drug," but the asthmatic athlete cannot compete in a distributive justice sense. This case is an exception. Therefore if you have many of these exceptions, you may need to change the rule to, "Do not use this drug, unless authorized by a physician for medical conditions to meet minimal performance levels."

In Jones's case, the exception may be, "Do not be dishonest, unless the rules are unfair." However, such an exception gets mired in such questions as: Who decides when the rules are unfair? What are the criteria to decide when the rules are unfair? The

---

[2]The purpose of the Pell Grant program from the beginning has been to expand access to universities and colleges, especially for low-income students. Pell Grants have often been used to supplement grants-in-aid to collegiate scholarship athletes.

Sometimes rules are immoral because they arbitrarily harm or are unjust. If the rule violates one of your moral principles, you may truthfully say the rule is morally wrong, even though there appears to be a good reason for the rule.

Jones's exception cannot function because of its slippery slope.[3] If the rules are unfair, then the rules must be changed through the correct procedure. If rules are arbitrarily followed, then the rules have no worth and chaos is the result.

---

[3]A slippery slope is a common philosophic illustration of placing an argument on unsupported facts. One cannot support an argument unless facts are given.

Step Four: Are the Rules Justified?

Sometimes rules are immoral, such as a rule that arbitrarily harms or is unjust. When you apply rules, you must ask whether the rule is a good rule. If the rule violates one of your moral principles, you may truthfully say that it is morally wrong, even though there appears to be a good reason for the rule. Instances of this sort of thinking appears in many bureaucratic institutions. For example, an earlier version of the NCAA Rule Book (1991) stated in section 16.10.2.7, "An institution or its staff member may not provide transportation (e.g., a ride home with a coach) to an enrolled student–athlete even if the student–athlete reimburses the institution or its staff members for the appropriate amount of the gas expense." The purpose of this rule was that a coach or any athletic personnel could not give an athlete a free or reimbursed ride. Its original intent and motive was good to make sure that student athletes do not receive special favors. However, its resultant effect could bring about bad actions. Suppose that coach A is driving through a rainstorm and sees athlete B walking without benefit of umbrella or raincoat. If coach A gives athlete B a ride, she is violating a rule. The NCAA had good reason for the rule, in that the governing organization was trying to keep a rein on unfair inducements or free gifts and benefits. However, the rule in this case was violating two moral principles, "Do not be irresponsible" (letting a human being walk in a rainstorm without benefit of protection, when we have protection to offer) and "Do not be unkind" (offering someone a kind service). The rule in this case violated two basic moral principles; the rule appeared to be in error in its application to this situation, although maybe not under other circumstances. This particular rule has now been remedied because of its inherently unethical position.

In Jones's case, is the rule unjust? The issue of standardized tests for minority populations has been an ethical concern for probably 40 years. The dilemma in solving the problem lies in a valid assessment technique to measure the ability of a potential athlete to perform academically at a university. Unfortunately, validity and reliability seem not to exist in high school grades alone. In Jones's case, the standardized test may be unethical, however, because it is unethical does not warrant a valid argument to "cheat" on the test.

Step Five: How Can the Rules Be Changed?

If the day-to-day rules are your personal rules, you can readily make a change. However, if the changes affect a large social group, such as those made by sport-governing bodies, a change may require political action, a demonstration, or a legislative move. If you cannot morally function within the rules and change cannot be effected, you may even be morally justified in breaking or violating the rule as long as it is done consistently, within the parameters of your moral principles.

If you choose to help Jamal, you might use the following reasoning process.

1. Does your choice violate any of your moral principles? Yes, it does. It violates the principle of justice (following the rules, procedural justice), and the principle of honesty (you implicitly gave your word to follow the rules of the sport organization). Because your choice does violate at least two principles, you may argue that Coach Jones never gave his word to follow the NCAA rules because he is not a coach in the NCAA. However, Coach Jones knows the rules exist and knows that he is being unethical and is probably committing a crime.[4] He may not have given his explicit word, but he does live in a law-governed society of which he is a willing citizen. As such, he has an obligation to follow the rules.

2. Is this case an exception? Yes, you say. The exception becomes, Do not be dishonest except in cases where being dishonest does a greater good.

3. Does the burden of proof state that it is an exception? Can you use this exception in all cases? At this point, you may become hard-pressed to meet the burden of proof. For the burden of proof asks if you can generalize this exception to all cases. Would you want others to follow the same line of reasoning? Would you want other coaches to apply this same exception? What might occur if you do have such an exception to the rules? "Do not be dishonest except in cases where being dishonest does a greater good." Our problem now becomes defining the greater good and controlling the interpretation of the "greater good." If we can make the exception for our earlier condition of the Nazi storm trooper, why not in this case? In this case, Jamal's life is not threatened and assumptions are being made that "bypassing" the rule will bring good—which is not a given.

4. Should the rules be changed? If the exception is strong enough, the rules should be changed. Should the rule now state, "All rules should be followed, except those in which violating the rule might help a player succeed." Or, "All rules should be followed, except those which don't support what an individual wants to do?" Can you write your exception so that it can bear the burden of being universalized to the greater society? Writing exceptions should be limited to those specific cases where "great bodily harm," or "great emotional harm" is done, and only then if no other solution can be found. That is, in Jamal's case, we do not know that attending a junior college to play basketball will do "great" bodily harm. We do not know that getting Jamal help because of his test anxiety would bring "great" bodily harm or emotional harm. In fact, helping Jamal with test anxiety probably is the better course of action, in that he will

---

[4]If Coach Jones's conspiracy works, he is party to defrauding the institution where the ACT scores will be submitted, and as earlier noted, if Jamal receives a Pell Grant, which is a good possibility, Coach Jones is actually committing a federal crime.

need to cope with test anxiety throughout his collegiate career. And, we do not know that gaining a university education is the best course of events for Jamal; perhaps he is better suited to other vocational opportunities. Also, we cannot see into the future and decree that Jamal will play professional ball. We do know that the "chances" for his success are very limited. Hence, we have no basis for our support to "violate" the rule.

OBSTACLES AND FALLACIES IN REASONING

Now that you have an idea of how you can systematically think through a moral problem, what problems will you face in placing your system into action? Because of the very nature of moral reasoning, you will be faced with many personal and social challenges to carry out your game plan of moral reasoning.

To carry out your game plan of moral reasoning, you must first muster the courage (just as we do in competition) to stand for what you value in the face of doubt, ridicule, and misgivings by those around you.

Your first challenge is to muster the courage to stand for what you value in the face of doubt, ridicule, and misgiving by those around you. Many people will not believe that moral values, principles, and rules have any merit. They will set forth various arguments about why moral reasoning is useless, manipulative, and silly. Following are a few of the basic obstacles (a reasoning obstacle is a limited thinking perspective that obscures an enlightened point of view) and fallacies that you will encounter that will work against your moral valuing,[5] which is a subset of moral reasoning.

Skepticism

Some people will show extreme skepticism that any reasoning about moral issues can exist. Skeptics purport that it is not possible to reason about moral judgments. They believe that any determination of morality is simply an expression of feelings or emotion. For example, these skeptics might say, "That act is good only because it is nothing more than a matter of taste such as 'I like that,' 'Well, that's the way I feel about it and that's all there is to it,' 'You are entitled to your feelings and I to mine,' or 'Well, there really isn't a right answer, is there?'" If you examine these statements, you will notice that the skeptics use words such as "simply," "merely," or "nothing more." The study of ethics is complicated, difficult, and hardly, if ever, "nothing but this" or "nothing but that." Morality does involve feelings and emotions, but moral reasoning is more than feelings. Even if moral reasoning were only feelings and emotion, you could still reason about emotions and desires and about how you should or should not morally act. You could still make moral judgments, according to moral rules, principles, and values, on these feelings and emotions. You must keep your mind open to the possibility of solv-

---

[5]Moral knowing, moral valuing, and moral doing are terms used by Thomas Lickona (1990) in his seminal work, *Educating for Character.* According to Lickona, moral reasoning is a process of the moral knowing process.

ing problems by rational means and improve your reasoning, rather than assume you are defeated before you start.

Cultural and Relative Ethics

Relative ethics is a second challenge to your reasoning. All of us have heard others say, "It is all right with me, as long as it does not bother me," "Who am I to judge?" "Everyone has the right to their own beliefs," or "They have a different standard that I have no right to infringe upon." These statements impinge on our ability to address the ethical dilemmas that most of us will face: that moral judgments are judgments with no objective solution and as such are relative. They change by degree as to different times and places. The relativist will use various arguments to show that no standard exists, and any exceptions to a standard prove that it does not exist.

Dogmatism

Dogmatists have all the answers. Because they feel strongly about an issue, they confuse subjective certainty with objective certainty. Obviously, you need strong convictions, but dogmatics refuse the possibility of error or acknowledgment that they may be wrong. "Reasoning is unnecessary because the answer is known; I know and I do not care what anyone says." The dogmatic has a closed mind and refuses to acknowledge any alternative.

One of the aims in moral reasoning is to help straighten out dogmatic thinking. If not, you can oppose yourself in your own thinking, denying responsibility for your own opinions and acts and making it virtually impossible to communicate with others in a rational or coherent way.

False Obstruction of Theory and Practice

Some people believe that ethical theory is after all only a theory and therefore not factual, realistic, or practical. You will hear, "The real world is not like that." You, however, must not reject theories sim-

ply because they are theories. You should only reject theories if evidence shows that they are inadequate. A theory is not inadequate just because it is a theory. All civilized human activity involves theorizing in the sense of generalizing or hypothesizing, and nearly all theories are practical to the extent that they have at least potential applications.

Other Obstacles: Fallacies in Reasoning

As a moral reasoner, you must realize that if you do not follow a standard, logical pattern you may be duped into using fallacious reasoning. If you are very observant, you will notice that most people use psychological, rather than philosophical reasoning. Specifically, the way they use the argument is the strength of the argument. They are highly convincing not because of what they say but how they say it. Such reasoning appeals to things people want to believe or to prejudices they hold.

The Fallacy of Authority

Coach Jones, the commissioner, the official, or God said so, has greater plausibility in that it was said by someone in authority. The fallacy of authority is claiming that something is true simply because someone in authority says it is, rather than because it is supported by evidence.

Ad Hominem Arguments

"You cannot believe a word he said, because he is a jerk." In this fallacy, an opinion or belief is wrong solely because the person saying so is known to be bad or disreputable. Name-calling is difficult to refute and is the most subversive and cowardly method to win an argument. The method is quite effective because it is so vicious. People often try to defeat their opponents by making fun of them. Name-calling also is used in other ways: "Do not believe the coaches' argument that they need more money; they are biased." "Look who is talking" is another variation, suggesting that one flawed person cannot evaluate another.

Misplaced and Improperly Placed Authority

For some reason, you tend to trust experts or people who have professional degrees or important positions. You listen when they have something to say about anything, even when the supposed expert has little experience on that subject. This flawed reasoning is put to capital use when professional athletes endorse and advertise products, and people buy the product because of the athlete's endorsement.

The Appeal to Force

Might makes right, this position supposes that the opinion of the bigger, stronger, greater number is the correct opinion and probably should determine the morally correct position. This position is often thought to be the most realistic conception of ethics because its standard is not some lofty ideal but the real way the world works. Large numbers of people may be very wrong about a moral issue; for example, Nazi Germany was successful for almost 10 years because of its political and military power.

The Appeal to Pity and Ridicule

The appeal to pity threat is typified in, "Woe is me; please help me; I am always wrong; why are you picking on me? You do not like me, nobody likes me."

Begging the Question

This threat is known as a circular argument. Often thought to mean the argument is illogical, rather, it means that the argument is based on incorrect information or the same information again and again. The individual tries to win the argument simply by repeating, insisting, or shouting the same information over and over.

Equivocation

This threat is using words incorrectly or choosing words with the wrong meanings. It also represents arguments in which the words change meanings within the argument. The threat to equivocation is one reason why it is important that we understand ethical terminology.

Psychological Obstacles

The use of psychological obstacles is simply poor reasoning. For various reasons, individuals never learn how to think. They express themselves in slogans or clichés and mimic what Marx called "herd behaviors."

In the case of Coach Jones, and all the other issues discussed thus far, did you fall prey to any of the fallacies and obstacles to moral reasoning? Most of us do. The task is to try to overcome the problem.

A Final Comment on Courage

Even if your moral reasoning does not yield correct answers, the process of moral reasoning may free you from your own prejudices, lead you to discard beliefs based on false premises, and help you to better understand the views of others. If nothing else occurs other than being able to distinguish that moral actions are reasonable or unreasonable, then you have grown in your moral abilities.

Once you have developed the ability to reason morally, you will need the courage to take a stand, because what is morally right is not easy nor oftentimes popular. Courage to act on your moral principles is the only way to address the "new morality."

Finally, once you have developed the ability to reason morally, you will need the spirit and the courage to speak out for what you have reasoned is the right thing to do. Taking a stand for the moral right will not be easy. In fact, you may find that, to paraphrase Robert Frost, it "is the road less traveled." Courage, however, to reason morally and to stand for what is right is the only solution to address "the new morality." A serious examination of morality requires both courage and humility; courage because you may find that others oppose you in your beliefs, and humility because you may need to recognize your own mistakes and limits.

SUMMARY

Let us review the precepts of moral reasoning. Critical inquiry is based on rationally determining moral issues. A critical, reasoned inquiry demands accurate, exact, and precise thinking. A reasoned inquiry also takes into account all sides of an issue in its past, present, and future sense. To reason, then, demands that you follow the three tenets of moral reasoning, that is, to be impartial, consistent, and reflective.

In developing your reasoned inquiry, your personal philosophies also come into play. What you believe and who you are color how you act. That is, your values, both moral and nonmoral, are the de-

ciding factors in your moral inquiry. Values therefore determine your principles and your obligations. If you can reason through your values and determine a consistent value system, you will be on your way to a moral standard that can withstand internal and external scrutiny.

Once you have discovered your values, you then write your universal principles. These first rules should support you in developing your personal and professional rules or guides. You have five steps to follow in using these first rules and numerous obstacles and threats to overcome. Use these tools to examine critical issues in sport today.

REFERENCES

Dubin, C. L. 1990. *Commission of inquiry into the use of drugs and banned practices intended to increase athletic performance.* Ottawa: Canadian Government Publishing Centre.

Fox, R. M., and J. P. DeMarco, 1990. *Moral reasoning: a philosophical approach to applied ethics.* Fort Worth, TX: Holt, Rinehart and Winston.

Frankena, W. K. 1973. *Ethics.* 2d ed., Englewood Cliffs, NJ: Prentice Hall.

Friedman, M. (1980). Free to Choose. N.Y.: Harcourt, Brace, Jovanovich.

Lickona, T. 1990. *Educating for character.* New York: Bantam.

NCAA Manual. 1991. Overland Park, KS: National Collegiate Athletic Association. See also *NCAA Manual.* 2001.

Ross, W. D. 1930. *The right and the good.* Oxford, England: Clarendon Press.

ISSUES AND DILEMMAS

In the following five questions, what threats or fallacies can you find?

1. Look who is calling me a cheater. You are the biggest cheater on the team.
2. Hey, don't pay attention to Smith. He is one of those loud-mouthed know it alls!
3. The commissioner of major league baseball should do away with designated hitters. That's not the way the game was intended to be played.
4. Research shows that football athletes do poorly in college; it is obvious that they are not too bright.
5. You never have liked me, have you? Admit it, that is why you disagree with me.

In the following scenarios. Respond to these questions: What moral value is challenged by what nonmoral value? Are any of the scenarios partially acceptable or acceptable? Which? And Why?

Adam stole $10.00 from Betty's gym bag during lunchtime work-outs at the local gym.

Adam is the athletic director of a small college in which he is in charge of all distribution of funds, including paychecks to part-time coaches. The budget has been tight all year, and every dollar counts. His secretary reports that a part-time coach was shorted $10.00 in the last pay period. She should have received $120.00, but her paycheck was made out to $110.000. Knowing that it will cost over $20.00 to correct the error, Adam takes no action.

Adam is an assistant coach for a large Division I athletic department. All coaches have access to an unlimited amount of snack foods donated by area businesses. The department has decided that a few extra publicity dollars might be made by charging a minimal amount for the donated food—$0.25/bag of snacks which will be donated to the local children's hospital. Last week Adam ate about $10.00 worth of snack foods while he was working without paying for them. He signed a statement when he began working there in which he promised to pay for everything he ate. All of the coaches at one time or another have eaten snacks without paying the money, including the athletic director.

Adam is a recruiting coach for Smalltown University. His budget is somewhat limited but he does have access to unlimited phone usage.

His elderly parents enjoy his phone calls and it makes them feel good that Adam is doing so well. His phone calls to mom and dad cost about $10 a month. He does not report the personal calls, but adds them to this monthly bill. In the following, discuss the issue from two different positions.

Discussion Topic

Athletics at the NCAA Division I level is big business. It brings in millions of dollars in gate receipts, booster fund-raisers, and booster dollars. Even though the NCAA rules state that athletes are limited to 20 hours of practice per week, student athletes in revenue sports typically spend 40 to 60 hours per week preparing for competition. It is time that you recognize that the student athlete is a myth and free yourself from your own hypocrisy. Pay the athletes and establish semipro leagues.

Position A: This question has to do with the purpose of playing games. Exactly why do we have collegiate athletics? If you can answer this question, then you can write reasons for keeping the sport.

Position B: The purpose of athletics is to bring money, fame, and publicity to the university. The athletes know their place in this purpose. The athletes get their pay through the grants-in-aid that they are given. That is all that they need and deserve.

Position C: The purpose of athletes is education. Education for the athlete, education for the community, and education for the university. There is no hypocrisy in having a collegiate athletic program.

The following questions deal with the four principles of

1. Do not be dishonest
2. Do not be unfair
3. Do not be irresponsible
4. Be Beneficent

Which of the scenarios are prohibited by which principle? More than one principle may prohibit an action.

1. Mr. Carlton, director of Small Town Fitness Center, refuses to permit any employee to object to any of his stated policies. He believes objections or criticisms are a sign of disrespect.
2. Bill uses anabolic steroids. He justifies the use by saying that if he wants to compete, he is forced to use them because competitors do.

Application of Moral Reasoning to Sport

PART II

Intimidation, Competition, and Sportsmanship

CHAPTER 4

- ◆ What is intimidation?
- ◆ What is the role of intimidation?
- ◆ Should we want to take out the other player?
- ◆ Can we be intimidating without trying to be?
- ◆ What does it mean to play a good game?

At a recent meeting on sportsmanship, a professional football player was discussing what it meant to be a good sport. He argued that good sportsmanship is linked to how a player treats the opponent before the game, during the timeouts in the game, and after the game. Good sports shake the opponent's hand before and after the game. Good sports help the opposing player up after a good hit; good sports follow the rules; good sports win humbly and lose with little, if any, negative trash talking to the opponent; good sports value the game and what it means to play fair. In contrast to his fair play rhetoric, this specific professional player is portrayed by the media as an "in your face" opponent. When asked what is the place of intimidation in competition his response was, "Hey, I'm a good sport between plays and when the game is over. But the bottom line of my job is to physically, mentally, and spiritually take the opponent out of the game." So then, who would he play? His response, "The second player and then do the same thing to him." When asked: "If this is the case,

why not go into the opponent's locker room before the game and just shoot the opponent? Then, you could play number two, or, on second thought, shoot him too. Maybe shoot them all and then you would win for sure." His response, "I would if it were legal, but it's not. The point is that we want to take the other guy out so that we can win. Football is about life and death, as long as everything is done within the rules."

INTIMIDATION AND ITS ROLE IN COMPETITION

Defining Intimidation

Should intimidation be used as a tool to win sporting events? Should one physically, mentally, and emotionally want to take the opponent out of the game? Should one want to play the second best individual, or perhaps the third best? The answer to these questions lie in one's view and value of intimidation. What then is intimidation?

Intimidation is the act of causing someone to be fearful, withdrawn, or coerced. Intimidation is a polar activity in that it can occur under two cases: purposeful or nonpurposeful intimidation.

Coaching Intimidation: Purposeful

Intentionally intimidating another, either by our actions or words, is a conscious decision. While it has been argued that such behavior is questionable as a moral action, the moral issue will be addressed more in depth later.

Intimidation has long been used as a means to control the behavior of others. Coaches use intimidating practices to motivate athletes to behave in certain ways—to be more aggressive, to do better in classroom performances, or to attend to and meet the responsibilities of being an athlete. The moral agent—in this case, the coach—believes that intimidation will motivate the athlete to act in a certain fashion, through fear of what may occur. Typical methods of intimidation can range from mild tactics like glaring at the athlete or raising the pitch and tone of the voice, to stronger physical and emotional tactics, such as cursing, throwing objects, kicking, berating, grabbing the jersey or face mask, pushing the athlete, or spitting in the opponent's face. In the psychology literature, these forms of motivation are typically called *negative feedback* (Dieffenbach 1998). The constant negative verbal and physical assaults are typically used to "motivate" an athlete to perform to his or her best. Oftentimes, however, these forms of negative feedback set a motivational climate that is outcome/ego oriented. The focus is on the individual in relation to the goal, the win. The focus is not on performance/task/mastery. On the other hand, positive motivation (*positive feedback*) tends to set a climate focused toward the performance/task/mastery environment. Thus, according to researchers, performance is best improved if the motivational climate is set using positive feedback.

The authors once asked a highly intimidating coach why he used such strong negative feedback practices to motivate, considering that most of the psychological research today supports the notion of positive motivational techniques (those that uplift the athlete) rather than negative motivation (those that tear away at the athlete's psyche) (Stoll and Beller 1992). It has long been documented that though both techniques work, positive motivational techniques, in the long run, are better for the athlete, better for the coach, better for the sport, and even better for the fans. The coach responded that although the research might be true, negative motivation gets the job done more quickly and with little investment of his time. We noted that in a baseball game during the seventh-inning stretch, he swore 27 times. What exactly does profanity accomplish? Wouldn't the athletes become immune after about the tenth time? His response, "A coach doesn't have the time or energy to be worried about who needs what form of motivation—positive or negative. Cursing and screaming get the job done quickly so I can spend my time concentrating on strategy." He also noted that his method has been highly successful and is based on the military model. History and tradition were in his favor. He had won numerous local, regional, and even national titles, and several of his athletes have been drafted into the professional leagues. Little doubt

Intimidation can occur with no purposeful motive, intention, or action of the moral agent. Just the demeanor and professional position of many individuals, without any overt decision to be intimidating, may cause others to be intimidated.

VIOLENCE, INTIMIDATION, AND GAMESMANSHIP

Violence means physical force exerted for the purpose of injuring another. Many professional sport administrators have expressed concerns about heightened violence among players, fans in the stands, and city celebrations after the winning of championships. For example, the stabbing of Monica Seles by a crazed fan during a 1993 tennis tournament in Germany illustrates how violence continues to encroach into sport. More prevalent problems, though, may be the dramatic increases in intimidation and gamesmanship displayed by athletes seeking to gain advantages. *Intimidation* is an act intended to frighten or inhibit others or render them too timid to do certain behaviors. *Gamesmanship* refers to pushing the rules to the limit without getting caught, using whatever dubious methods possible to achieve the desired end.

not because of any direct action, but because of the employees' perception of what the supervisors might or might not do. Children may be intimidated by adults, not because of anything the adults do, but because of the adults' size, the depth and strength of their voices, or the manner in which they walk or wear their clothes. Athletes may often be intimidated by a coach because of reputation. The reputation may be the success ratio of wins to losses, or the coach's professional experience, or just being awed and intimidated by the coach's position.

Perception is the key to the problem. The moral agent is perceived as an intimidating individual and thus the moral receiver behaves in a certain way, fears the agent, and may avoid contact with the agent at all costs. If the moral agent has no intention or motivation to intimidate, the resultant perception of the receiver is not the fault of the agent. Though some could argue, *if* the moral agents know that their position, dress, carriage, voice, size, or position intimidates others, then they should seek out different practices. That is, if children are overtly intimidated by the size of the agent, the agent could speak gently to the child, kneel down to speak with the child, or be less brusque in physical actions. However, many times the moral agent has no notion that others are intimidated by them. As such, the moral agent is not responsible for the ensuring intimidation. But remember that each of us perceives our world and the motives and intentions of others differently. What one of us may perceive as intimidating in an individual, another may not. Because perception is an individual view of the world and our perception of another's motives and intentions is unknown, perception cannot be the basis for deciding moral issues.

exists that his technique works; the question is whether positive motivational techniques may be as good, if not more productive, in motivating the athlete (see Box 4-1).

If intimidation is intentionally practiced, then the action becomes a moral issue. If the moral agent has motive and intention to violate another, the agent's action becomes a moral issue. At this point we need to take intimidation and the practice of negative intimidation a step further.

Coaching Intimidation: Nonpurposeful

Intimidation can occur with no purposeful motive, intention, or action of the moral agent. That is, the demeanor and professional position of many individuals, without any overt decision to be intimidating, may cause others to be intimidated. Because of college professors' professional demeanor, professional position, or even professional dress, college students often find their professors intimidating. Employees may be intimidated by their supervisors

Intimidation from the Player's Point of View

Intimidation is also one of the bag of tricks that athletes use to gain an advantage over an opponent. An athlete will argue that if the opponent is intimidated, the feeling of intimidation will psychologically take the opponent out of the game. If the

BOX 4-2

YOU BE THE JUDGE: IS THIS CONDUCT ETHICAL?

1. A lineman or a defensive back is beaten by the opposing lineman or wide receiver, resulting in a big play for the offense. On a subsequent play, the lineman or defensive back takes out his opponent with a vicious blindside hit to the knees meant to cause injury, even though neither player is involved with action near the ball. Is this hit ethical? If not, how should this intimidation be punished? How should the lineman or defensive back be educated? What changes are needed to reduce the potential for injury?

2. In his first at-bat after his grand-slam home run, Mike is prepared for the expected brush-back pitch. He is not ready for the inside fast-ball aimed straight at his head. He attempts to bail out of the batter's box but is hit on the arm. He jumps up and charges the mound, bat in hand, as both benches clear. The ensuing brawl results in the ejection of several players from the game. Why is the brushback pitch seemingly accepted in baseball? Is your justification based on relativism? Why? Does a ball thrown at a batter's head justify his charging the mound? Why are teammates expected to join in the fray? How can these behaviors be changed for the better?

3. The shoving match underneath the basket has escalated without any fouls being called. Finally, Jack has had enough. The next time Pat pushes him to clear the lane, Jack grabs him and refuses to give ground. Pat retaliates by hitting Jack. Before the referees can break the scuffle up, punches from several players have landed. Who is violating sportsmanship rules in this situation? Is the absence of a whistle calling a foul on Jack, Pat, or are both tantamount to condoning their intimidation of each other? Does the failure to penalize minor shoving under the basket ever result in violent assaults? If you were the coach, how would you attempt to change these behaviors, especially if players from opposing teams play this way?

4. Tony is the best player on his ice hockey team, and without him the team does not have a chance to advance in the playoffs. Ray has been given the job of taking Tony out, legally or illegally; that is his role on the team. He must get Tony out of the game by means of penalty or injury. Ray uses his stick to break the arm of an unsuspecting Tony immediately after Tony scores. Ray gets a two-game suspension; Ray's team eliminates Tony because he cannot play with a broken arm. Why have (some) sports moved to the point where opponents are enemies and objects of the other players' physical and psychological abuse? Is the only objective winning, regardless of the method used?

5. The rivalry between East High School and West High School has escalated each year. Three years ago, a few of the West players started a fight late in the game because they felt East players were trying to embarrass them by running up the score. The next year, some of the East and West students in the stands started taunting and cursing each other. Last year had been the worst; the two sides brawled on the field after West pulled out an upset on the final play of the game. As the two undefeated teams prepared to play on Friday, school administrators urged fans and athletes to act responsibly, while arranging for more police officers. Volatile emotions erupted on an official's questionable call in the second period. The fighting on and off the field resulted in cancellation of the game. Is a fight among players in a football game ever justifiable? Do coaches ever use fights among opponents, teammates, and fans as motivational tools? What other strategies do coaches employ to motivate their players? Can the concept of fair play be used to positively motivate athletes? (See Box 4-3.)

SITUATIONAL ETHICS APPLIED TO SPORT

The term *situational ethics* suggests that every ethical or moral decision is made on the spot, with no consistency between acts. People justify their behaviors by stating that nonmoral values, such as money, outweigh moral values. Is any action justifiable because money is riding on the outcome? When played for fun, sport can help teach moral values. But when a sport championship hangs in the balance, is it acceptable to bend the rules? Do individuals' values change because the nonmoral values of fame and fortune increase in importance?

Are moral values for sale? If so, at what price? Non-big-time college and high school sport appears fraught with unethical practices, although little or no money rests on the outcome of contests. Could it be that the imbalanced price of moral values is the inordinate value placed on winning?

In earlier chapters, principles were established on values, rules were developed, and any mitigating circumstances whereby a rule might be violated were taken into consideration. If money and winning cause a change in values, where is the burden of proof about the issues? It is doubtful that anyone would want to reverse or universalize a value that changes when more money is riding on it. Still, in the situations described in Box 4-2, many would endorse the athletes' actions if they were professionals but might not condone them in youth leagues or school programs. Does the skill level or amateur or professional status discount sport rules? Should adherence to ethical principles of conduct apply regardless of the competitive level?

opponent is "cowed", then the athlete or moral agent will have an opportunity to gain the edge and win the game. Intimidation for the player is a double-edged sword as well; it can again be purposeful or nonpurposeful (see Boxes 4-2 and 4-3).

Intimidation by the Athlete: Purposeful

Purposeful intimidation by the athlete is the direct motivation, intention, and action to somehow take the opposing player out of the game. Usually the purposeful activity revolves around psychological tricks such as preening or strutting before, during, or after the game. For example, a gymnast might practice psychological intimidation by purposefully and repeatedly throwing her hardest trick so that the competition will worry about their ability to meet the challenge. Or, a basketball player during warm-ups might make numerous difficult shots and strut his or her stuff, so that opponents will notice.

Generally, intentional psychological intimidation occurs through trash talking. Though outlawed by most amateur sport ruling bodies, trash talking is as common as putting on a game uniform. Trash talking is the verbal act of berating the opponent. The athlete will chide the opponent on his/her lack of skill, physical size, competitive demeanor, or any other attribute that might be in question, "Is that all you got? My Momma plays better than you!" Trash talking exists in youth sports, school sports, collegiate sports, and professional leagues. Women practice it, children practice it, and the fans practice it. The question becomes—if it is common practice, why not let it exist? And, if it is so commonly practiced, is it really a moral issue?

Harrison (1996) argued that trash talking grew from the jive of the intercity playground. Some trace its origin to an inner-city game called "Playing the Dozens," "Basing," or "Jonesing," whereby the goal is to use words and trash talking to put someone else's momma down—often termed their "T Jones." As a cultural practice, trash talking moved from the playground to the court and the playing field. Its purpose may be intimidation but Harrison argued that the trash talking is not about doing any type of physical or emotional damage. Rather, the athlete may use trash talking as a way of bringing the game up to a higher level. Athletes will argue that trash talking makes them more psyched

Usually intentional psychological intimidation occurs through trash talking—the verbal act of berating an opponent. Although common practice, it is outlawed by most amateur sport-governing bodies.

to play the game, and if they are denied the use of trash talking, they will lose a motivational edge. Trash talking, in this sense, may actually be a way of celebrating the very act of competition. Harrison argued that trash talking has been outlawed because of its African American roots and that the outlawing is really a form of racism—denying the worth of a cultural practice. Harrison also noted that trash talking today is definitely not limited in practice to African American players. Larry Bird, while he played the game of basketball, was supposedly the icon of trash talking.

Eassom (1996) noted that name-calling is only what we make of it. He stated that just because a "crazy old man" down the road says nasty things to us, it does not mean that we have to listen, and there's nothing personal meant by it anyway. Just like ignoring the crazy old man, the athlete learns

how to "not listen," to tune out the trash talking that occurs with sport.

In contrast to Harrison's and Eassom's points of view, Dixon (1996) argued that trash talking with all the notion of cultural practice is still words, and "words hurt." He asked, "Have we learned nothing about hurtful words from the history of racism and sexism? Have we not learned that it is hurtful to call women and different ethnic groups names? Have we not learned that words are hurtful? And, have we not as a culture learned that such words can be legally interpreted as sexual and racial harassment? Is it necessary to say hurtful words to play the game and to play it well? Is sport supposed to be about psychological games of hurtful words?"

Rudd argued that trash talking was a moral issue because when trash talking is practiced ". . . individuals . . . show disrespect toward others for their own personal gain" (Rudd 1996, 18). Hence, if the action of trash talking occurs and is purposeful, a moral dilemma occurs. The athlete has a choice, whether to trash talk or not, and if the athlete chooses to trash talk, disrespect does occur.[1]

Physical Intimidation: Purposeful

If an athlete goes onto the court or field and intentionally acts to "take out" the opponent through a physical act, physical intimidation occurs. The direct purpose of physical intimidation may not be long-lasting injury but just enough to make the opponent think twice before acting, to ring his bell hard enough and long enough that fear exists. This issue of physical intimidation becomes cloudy when the practice of sport is about physical aggression, as in ice hockey, lacrosse, football, and today, basketball. The athlete uses the body against an opponent's body to gain the prize. The football player

---

[1]The comments made by sport sociologists and philosophers were made at the 1996 annual meeting of the International Philosophic Society for the Study of Sport (held in Clarkston, Washington). Andrew Rudd gave a paper, "Moral Callousness As Evidenced by Trash Talking," which precipitated the discussion of the topic.

blocks and tackles; ice hockey, lacrosse, and basketball players all "check"—keeping a player from making progress. Players involved in physical contact sports argue that the physical contact and the aggression of the game are what the game is about: "There's nothing better in sport, especially football, than the sound of two bodies hitting as hard as they can." "Lacrosse is about violence." "Wimps don't play ice hockey."

All of these comments may be true, and we do concede that physical aggression and physical contact are part and parcel of contact sports (see Physical Intimidation: Nonpurposeful). However, if the athlete as the moral agent intentionally tries to "take out the opponent," a moral issue is raised. Marten, a former football player, wrestler, and coach said, "If any player goes out intentionally to take out another player, he is a coward. If you aren't willing to put your best against his best, and you have to revert to violence to win, you are a coward. Such is the coward's methods."[2]

Hard words . . . "a coward." Marten's point may seem strong; however, what he says is food for thought. If the intention is to take out the player, who does one play? The second string person, the trainer? Or, is the playing not the point? Therefore, the only purpose at this point would be to increase the chances of a win. If playing games in sport is about using one's mental finesse and physical skills, it is illogical to want to decrease the opportunity to use one's best skills to play the game.

Giamatti, former commissioner of baseball and president of Yale University, wrote a book on baseball, *Take Time for Paradise* (1989). In that text and other works, he noted that the beauty of competition lodges in one's purpose and intention. He wrote:

To toughen the body and temper the soul . . .

To emphasize integrity and develop courage . . .

To be obedient to the letter and spirit of the rules . . .

. . . so winning is sweeter still.

If the intention and motivation is to psychologically and physically take the opponent out of the game, a moral issue arises—because the athlete is neither being just nor responsible in the action toward the opponent. It does not matter what is accepted practice.

Nonpurposeful Psychological and Physiological Intimidation

As in the case of unintentional intimidation by a coach, the same case can and does occur for the athlete. Athletes by their very nature—but without intending to—can intimidate their opponents; that is, their size, their demeanor, and their physical skills may cause the opponent to be intimidated. However, this case is not a moral issue because the athlete is not going about his or her activity with any purposeful negative motive or intention toward the opponent. It is true that the resultant action of a sport practice may intimidate, but in this sense the athlete is not responsible—because it is a matter of perception. Remember, in this case, the moral agent is not responsible for how an athlete interprets the final action. The world would be better if good motives and good intentions were interpreted as right action, but in sports many times they are not.

For example, before a high school gymnastics meet started, the gymnasts from opposing teams warmed up by going through their routines. Coach A watched a particularly talented gymnast from the opposing team. After the young girl dismounted from her beam routine, Coach A told her she had a great routine and wished her team luck. The gymnast never responded but did say to her coach, "What did she mean by that?" Her coach turned toward Coach A and said in disgust, "Ignore them; they're just trying to psyche you out." Coach A had no intention of psyching out the young gymnast.

---

[2]Dwaine Marten and two of the authors were having a discussion one day about the purpose of competition. We were developing our paradigm on the ideal and the real sports contest. As we were discussing the nature of the intentional physical act to take out the other player, Dr. Marten noted that the old-time athletes would consider this nothing more than the act of a coward. His comments are here captured as he made them. Dwaine Marten, Emeriti Professor, University of Idaho.

Coach A enjoyed the routine and truly wished her luck. One of Coach A's athletes, who watched and participated in the drama, had a different perception of the unfolding events. She thought the opposing coach was being rude and obnoxious and said loudly, "Coach, why don't you punch out her lights!" As pedagogists would say, this was a teachable moment, as the situation was discussed; good motives and good intentions are still good no matter how the other individual interprets the final action. Interestingly, the opposing gymnast must have been psyched out, because she was a good practice performer but a poor meet performer. She fell numerous times which she had not done in practice, and her performance doomed her team's chances of success as measured by winning—they lost that day. Perhaps the coach's negative perspective had an influence or perhaps good motives and good intentions had an effect. Perhaps the athlete and her coach had some other psychological performance problem. Coach A and her athlete learned a great deal that day about nonpurposeful intimidation. They had no control over the interpretation of an innocent, supporting remark. In future meets, Coach A was careful not to make any comments to this team or other opponents. She buckled under and played the game with no positive comments, no supporting remarks, and no appreciation for another's skill. Sport took a hit that day. Coach A, her athletes, and opponents were all the worse for it.

Physical Intimidation: Nonpurposeful

Injury and physical harm may occur to an opponent with no intention on the part of the offending athlete; in this case, the same sort of thinking applies that occurs with nonpurposeful intimidation. Injuries do occur. Physical contact does happen. Accidents do occur. However, if the motive and intention is not about causing injury, then the resultant action is not a moral question. Athletes take the risk, the chance, that injury may occur. Sport is not for the faint of heart. Players go out and give it their best shot. They give their all. It is not about half-

hearted activity. If one is blocking in football, one does it with every fiber of his being. If one is blocking a shot in basketball, one does it with the whole self. When activity is physical and opponents are physical, the chance of injury always exists. The injury becomes a moral issue only if the motive and intention of the athlete is to physically harm. Basketball players intentionally use their bodies, arms, and legs to "clear the boards." Football players intentionally use all of their strength, mass, and accumulating force to "hit" as hard as they can. Hockey players "check" with determination and gusto. However, it is a different concept entirely if the athlete does all of the above with "malice afore thought." One can go out to give the hardest hit ever without intentionally thinking about "hurting." Even though the activity might appear brutish, the resultant action may be innocent of intentional moral harm.

Of course, one could always argue that any activity that celebrates aggression is morally questionable. However, such an argument, if supported, would necessitate the end to numerous activities in which physical aggression is necessary to play the game.

Many fans believe that because they bought a ticket they have not only the right, but also the obligation to influence the game through all sorts of intimidating practices such as waving balloons and banners behind the opposing team's basket and having bands play behind opposing team benches during time-outs.

EXTERNAL FORMS OF INTIMIDATION

While intimidation occurs between players, coaches, and referees, a major piece to the puzzle involves external intimidation. In this sense, we mean influences that affect the game, influences which are external to game play itself. Under this category fall the influences and actions of fans, parents, coaches, administrators, media, and others not directly involved in the game play itself. Many believe since they have bought a ticket, they not only have the right but the obligation to their team to influence the game through all sorts of intimidating practices. Mild forms of purposeful intimidation involve such practices as (1) the distribution of various objects to fans so they can wave them behind the basketball goal in an attempt to throw off the shooter's focus or (2) musical bands standing behind opposing players' benches during time-outs and playing loudly. Individuals practicing these actions argue that it is the coach's responsibility to teach his or her players to ignore such actions and that, after all, the opposing team fans have the same opportunity to intimidate. In other words, "All is fair in love, war, and sport."

Although many sport enthusiasts argue that these forms of intimidation are just a natural part of the game, as well as "being a true fan," purposeful intimidation has taken on new detrimental practice lows. For example, in a recent basketball game the student section chanted disparaging remarks targeted at the opposing team. The chant became so loud that the Public Radio station broadcasting the game had to turn down the volume—because they could not broadcast the statements and language on a "family" radio station. The following morning, the local newspaper also carried a column abhorring the student section's actions, claiming the students were worse than the coach in verbal abuse. When administrators, who were in attendance and heard the chants were queried, their response was, "They don't mean it; it's not meant personal; they are just supporting their team." Interestingly though, the tactic appeared to work. The targeted player was held to 18 less points than his season average and his team lost a close game.

External intimidation though is not limited to game time. For example, a high school coach decided that for his team to gain an edge over the cross-town rival team in the district championship game, he needed to intimidate the team. He called a local florist, hired a hearse and driver, and had delivered to each opposing player and coach a wilted, dead rose and a card that said "Wishing you the worst in Saturday's game."

The question then becomes, "What is the purpose of competition?" If the answer is "to win at all costs," then external intimidation is acceptable. However, if the purpose of the competition is about placing an athlete's skills against another athlete's skills, then external intimidation is unacceptable. No self-respecting athlete should want an unfair win. Almost all good athletes are purists—they want fan support, they enjoy spectators, but there is a limit to how far the spectators should be a *part* of the game.

SUMMARY

It appears that the goal today in sport is to take out opponents physically, mentally, and emotionally, to play number two, and thus increase the chances of a win. It also appears that fans and sport enthusiasts, in their attempt to cheer a team, are misguided in their intentions and actions. Although their intentions may be to support their team, the actions (how they carry out their intentions) actually involve an attack on others, which reduces the overall quality of competition. It seems that Giamatti's concept that we need our opponents to play their very best—challenging us to be our very best, thus improving the overall quality of the competitive experience—is lost on players, fans, coaches, and sport enthusiasts today.

What then is the purpose of competition, and what is the role of intimidation in that purpose? The answer lies in the competitor's point of view and his or her value of the game and the competition. Robert Simon (1985) has said that competition should be a "quest for excellence." We agree. Do you?

ISSUES AND DILEMMAS

1. Two rival basketball teams in a conference played a basketball game on team A's court. During the game, team B's star player was consistently heckled whenever she missed a basket, pass, or rebound. In the return game on team B's home court, the home crowd took revenge by heckling team A's players. Such action is fair and acceptable because both crowds have equal opportunity to heckle.

2. Ice hockey is often a violent game. Players get hurt by hitting hard and smashing opponents into the boards. Players A and B are opponents playing in a championship game. While trying to control the puck, player A smashes player B into the boards. Even though the puck is on the opposite side of the arena, player B, a few minutes later, retaliates by smashing player A into the boards. Because "hitting hard" and "smashing players into the boards" are an inherent part of the game, player B's action was acceptable.

3. Yolanda is the best player on XYZ's team. She is a consistently high scorer and when she's on, XYZ wins. Lately, she's been on a lot and XYZ is in the championship game with ABC. ABC is a better team statistically but they are worried about Yolanda. A week before the big championship game, Yolanda's grandmother dies. Yolanda decides to play in the big game, "because MaeMa would have wanted me to." Because of Yolanda's notoriety the whole state knows about "MaeMa." During the championship game, Yolanda performs at the highest quality. ABC decides to revert to serious trash talking. Two players assigned themselves "trash duty." Typical derogatory comments are: "Hey Yo . . . miss MaeMa?" "Yo, drive this way and you'll get to meet MaeMa again." The tactics work and Yolanda is thrown off her game and ABC wins. Is this behavior acceptable or unacceptable? Give reasons why.

4. During a hotly contested women's basketball game, the fans sit directly behind the visiting team. A contest begins to see who can harangue the coach and players more. As the harangue contest between both fan clubs goes to a higher level, the coach and players are not able to communicate during time-outs. The players and coach have to move to the middle of the floor for time-outs. Finally the coach protests to the home team athletic facility manager. His response, "That's the breaks." Every facility has home team advantage. The visiting team does win the contest. Acceptable or unacceptable and why?

5. A field hockey player is permitted to hit the ball hard, providing the ball is not hit purposely at an opponent. Delphine on team A (intently concentrating on the net) hits the ball toward the goal, but unintentionally hits Maria on team B. Maria complains that Delphine purposely hit the ball into her; however, the foul is not called. Down the field, Maria gains possession of the ball, retaliates, and hits Delphine with the ball. Maria's action was deemed acceptable.

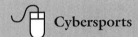 **Cybersports**

www.sportethics.com

Canadians Robert Butcher and Angela Schneider are well versed in the concept of fair play and the positive and negative benefits of intimidation. Dr. Schneider is a former Olympic silver medalist in crew and is currently a consultant with the Canadian Fair Play Commission.

www.vnb.nb.ca/English/Officials/ethics.htm

This is one of many codes of ethics found in the Canadian system that specifically mentions physical and psychological intimidation.

www.nd.edu/~cscc

The Mendelson Center for Sport, Character, and Culture brings these seemingly disparate words together in an effort to promote sport as a means of developing and expressing all facets of human excellence, especially moral character.

www.ets.uidaho.edu/center for ethics

The Center for ETHICS*, at the University of Idaho, believes in "teaching the tradition of competitive integrity to inspire leaders of character." Its goal is to improve moral development and character education through intervention, consultation, and leadership in advancing moral education within competitive populations.

www.josephsoninstitute.org

The Josephson Institute of Ethics was founded to improve the ethical quality of society by advocating principled reasoning and ethical decision making. In addition to conducting programs and workshops for influential leaders, it offers the CHARACTER COUNTS! youth-education initiative.

REFERENCES

Dieffenbach, K. 1998. Letter to author, 23 February.

Dixon, N. 1996. 1996 Meeting of the International Philosophic Society for the Study of Sport. Clarkston, WA.

Eassom, S. 1996. 1996 Meeting of the International Philosophic Society for the Study of Sport, Clarkston, WA.

Giamatti, A. B. 1989. *Take time for paradise: Americans and their games.* New York: Summit Books.

Harrison, K. 1996. Personal communication.

Mihalich, J. C. 1982. *Sports and athletics: Philosophy in action.* Totowa, NJ: Rowman and Littlefield Publishers.

Rudd, Andrew. 1996. Moral callousness as evidence by trash talking tee shirts. Master's thesis, University of Idaho.

Simon, R. 1985. *Sports and social values.* Englewood Cliffs, NJ: Prentice Hall.

Stoll, S. K., and J. M. Beller. 1992. Unpublished raw data.

Violence in Sport

- Were sport rules ever established specifically to attempt to prevent violent behavior and questionable conduct?
- What is violence?
- Does violence include only physical acts, or does it involve psychological ploys, too?
- Why does violence in sport exist, and why is it condoned?
- How did the establishment of sport rules affect the amount and extent of violence in sport?
- How has the emphasis on winning influenced violence in sport?
- What are six categorical imperatives that could present violent behaviors in sport?
- What are several controls that could curtail or prevent violence in sport?

People recognize that bench-clearing brawls in baseball and the exchange of punches in basketball occur outside the rules, although seldom do they classify such behaviors as violence. Fans acknowledge that vicious hits after whistles have sounded in football and hockey sticks used as weapons to cause injuries to knees and heads are malicious, but these occurrences increasingly are accepted in these sports. Many state that physical harm, and even injury, is just a normal part of the game (see Box 5-1).

Some people condone and even applaud behaviors that are psychologically and ethically abusive. Justified on the basis of gaining an advantage, players, fans, and coaches take violence to new heights (or depths).

It has been suggested that violence is so pervasive in sport that some athletes are indifferent when an opponent is injured. In fact, often the intent is to "take out" or debilitate an opponent as a desired goal, all a part of trying to win. Another related

BOX 5-1

MORAL CALLOUSNESS

Kretchmar (1995) discusses to some extent the effect of moral callousness. Kretchmar argues that human beings develop something called moral callouses around our hearts just like we do on our hands. As callouses become so hardened on our hands that we are prevented from feeling what we touch, so moral callouses around our hearts keep us from feeling that actions are morally wrong. To remove the callousness, we must critically examine who we are, what we believe, and how that affects our perspective of the game. Kretchmar says that callouses come with symptoms such as: "everyone else is doing it," if no harm is done or no penalty is assessed, then an action is permissible. Problems arise, however, in distinguishing between what is wrong or right, as well as in understanding the difference between sound strategy and moral trickery.

issue concerns violence to self, as many athletes play with injuries that may permanently debilitate themselves, practice unsafe weight-cutting methods, or subject themselves to harmful drugs.

This chapter suggests that some constitutive, proscriptive, and sportsmanship rules were developed in response to overly aggressive and violent behaviors in sport. Categorical imperatives, or moral principles that underlie these sport rules, are offered as ways to control violence in sport. After discussion of how violence affects sports, why violence is taught, condoned, and rewarded is examined. Recommendations for controls and moral education are suggested.

TYPES AND PURPOSES OF RULES

The absence of standardized rules in sport frees participants to play without constraints, to agree to a few control measures before the game begins, or to devise rules during the competition as the need arises. Although this may seem appropriate for children's games or impromptu contests, organized sport (especially when fans are present and records are maintained) requires rules. Three types of rules—constitutive, proscriptive, and sportsmanship—were developed for sports competitions to standardize play, attempt to prevent harm, and regulate behavior.

Constitutive Rules

Rules that guide play within a specific game are *constitutive rules*. Such regulations developed gradually out of the need to equalize competition, and they govern such areas as length of the game, number of players, eligibility of the participants, and the need to be able to compare team and individual accomplishments. These rules stipulate game-specific skills, strategies and techniques that make football different from basketball and both dissimilar to baseball constitutive rules specify to all players what actions are permissible during games.

Constitutive rules also place boundaries on players' actions. These rules constrain behaviors to those deemed appropriate to the sport. For example, the rules of basketball restrict the amount of permissible contact. Unacceptable touching, hitting, and holding beyond that point are punished with a foul, or for more severe violations, with disqualification. Baseball and softball rules specify when and how one may slide into an opposing player defending a base. In these and other incidents, when players disregard the rules out of ignorance or blatant antipathy to gain advantages, violence occurs, often in retaliation for perceived intent to harm or to gain an unfair edge. Constitutive rules give structure to sport, helping make the contest fair for all. They standardize the playing environment so that each athlete has an equal opportunity to excel.

Rules also regulate such factors as the age, weight, skill level, and maturational status of youth in certain leagues. They stipulate the ages, genders, residences, and academic performances required of school-age athletes. Colleges are constrained by rules governing academic progress, eligibility, recruiting practices, financial aid, and time involvement. Typically, constitutive rules are legislated by sport governing organizations.

Proscriptive Rules

Proscriptive rules expressly forbid specific actions, such as spearing in football and undercutting in basketball, often because of the associated high risk of injury. In some sports, scoring advantages and ultimately winning may be predicated on the utilization of one's body and equipment as weapons against opponents, resulting in pain, serious injury, and even death. Thus proscriptive rules were established to prohibit players from intentionally trying to harm opponents; for example, some rules were legislated after previous incidences of athletes' behaviors were judged as violent.

Many proscriptive rules were enacted in response to stick-wielding hockey players, pitchers throwing at batters' heads, linemen using chop blocks, and bench-clearing brawls. Some proscriptive sport rules governing overly aggressive and violent behaviors

The objective of sport is to play by the rules, not attempt to outwit the referee.

in hockey, basketball, baseball, football, soccer, and other sports are punishable by fines or suspensions by sport governing organizations. For example, the National Basketball Association has an executive whose primary duty is to mete out penalties for violent actions. Had some violent actions occurred outside of sport, they would be punishable by imprisonment or other legal sanctions. Violent behaviors are not restricted to the professional leagues, either; youth, school, and college athletes imitate their heroes' and heroines' violent actions.

Sportsmanship Rules

Another type of rule, *sportsmanship rules,* refers to the inherent quality in playing a game in which one is honor-bound to follow the spirit and letter of the rules. Many of these rules preclude behaviors that place winning above everything else, including opponents' welfare and competition between equitable opponents. Sportsmanship rules are designed to prevent ethically questionable and sometimes violent conduct.

Basketball players, for example, can be charged with an unsportsmanlike conduct foul for arguing with an official or slamming the ball against the floor when whistled for a foul or violation. Soccer officials can give a yellow card (warning) or a red card (ejection) for actions that are unsportsmanlike. In tennis, sportsmanship rules specify that players call their own lines, e.g., for example, indicate that balls are in- or out based on where the ball hit the court regardless if it is to their advantage or disadvantage. A golfer is expected to admit touching or moving a ball when addressing it even though this results in a penalty stroke. In some youth leagues, good sportsmanship is expected, such as shaking opponents' hands before or after a game.

Without rules, the game changes. Rules set parameters while constraining or requiring certain behaviors. Sadly, many existing rules have been established to control or discourage violent behaviors. Yet, the societal emphasis placed on winning has resulted in the blatant disregard for the welfare of opponents in a headlong pursuit of victories.

exist to prevent interference from governmental authorities. Increasingly, sport leagues and governing organizations have imposed rules on their participants to control physically violent actions during competitions—to keep these situations out of the courts. That is, injuries inflicted on opposing players

ETHICAL CONDUCT OR NOT

Some violence in sport occurs because athletes choose to disregard the rules. They participate in and condone ethically questionable conduct to gain an advantage. When an athlete does something that may not break the letter of the rules but certainly is marginally within the spirit of the rules, the opposing player affected may retaliate violently, either through physical attacks or psychological intimidation.

Often, people defend violent and ethically questionable conduct on the premise that "everyone else does it." That is, an athlete may believe a violent behavior is justified if opponents are engaged in violent behavior. Yet, is violence in sport deviant behavior? Many people seem ignorant of the purpose of sport when they say that behaviors they condone and even applaud are not violent but, rather, are used to gain an advantage through craftiness or clever coaching or playing. The rationalization becomes, "Because everyone else is doing it, I must do it, too, or get beaten." Should the fact that everyone commits rule-violating actions make these actions fair, honest, or responsible? Others say that their actions do not directly violate rules. Even if this is the case, does such action infringe on the spirit of the rules? For example, volleyball players often tell officials that they did not touch balls that go out-of-bounds, even when they did. What place, if any, does honesty have in sport?

Sometimes these actions lead to violence when athletes feel that their opponents' behaviors toward them are unfair. Relativism abounds in sport, often with regard to violence. Should the fact that seemingly one's opponent breaks the rules or seeks to intimidate give them license to do likewise? Many athletes state that they choose to initiate rule-violating behavior, hoping that they will not be caught, but that their opponents will retaliate and be penalized.

One additional type of violent behavior in sport, namely hazing, deserves mention. Sometimes in a perverted attempt to build team cohesion coaches and athletes have engaged in hazing even though such behaviors are banned or certainly inappropriate. When athletes are stripped of their clothing by coaches when they miss free throws and forced to run naked, hazing has become disrespectful, if not violent. When older athletes force their new teammates to strip and grasp another person's testicles from behind and walk in a chain, this is bordering on harassment as well as violence. In other cases, athletes have been initiated onto the team through expectations to drink excessive amounts of alcohol, run until they become sick or pass out, or they are even physically beaten, this is not only violence but also illegal behavior. Yet each of these incidents has occurred in sports.

Is Winning the Only Thing?

The cultural imperative of winning directly influences the extent of physical and psychological violence in sport. That is, as winning increases in importance because of financial payouts, status, and symbolic rewards, many players choose to use any means at their disposal, even violence, to attain victory. This phenomenon can easily be seen in an assessment of violent actions at various levels of play. If violence occurs in youth leagues, is it usually associated with adults who have overemphasized winning? Sadly, a few parents have assaulted coaches, officials, and even young athletes in their overzealousness for winning. Thomas Junta certainly acted violently when he fought with the father of an opposing player after his son's ice hockey game. Junta's violent be-

Aggressively attempting to win does not necessitate a disregard for the rules.

haviors that followed some questionable actions during the game resulted in his repeatedly hitting the victim causing his death. Sadly, now both boys are denied their fathers—one dead and another imprisoned for involuntary manslaughter—over actions following what could be called an insignificant game. Violence exhibited by athletes, coaches, parents, and fans in school sports has escalated because of too much pressure to win.

The absence of praise frequently parallels the presence of pressures to win. Not only do some adults model and verbalize the importance placed on winning, they also consider everyone else losers or second best. In a winning-is-the-only-thing world, athletes seldom receive rewards, applause, or positive reinforcement for effort and improvement. Some adults even condition young athletes to rant and rave or throw things when they lose by castigating them for not working hard enough or caring enough.

Since intercollegiate sport in most of the large universities has become business and entertainment, physical and psychological violence have increased. Taunting of opponents leading to fights, circumvention of the rules to gain unfair advantages, and intentional injury of highly skilled opponents are examples of violent behaviors driven by the belief that only winning counts. At the pinnacle of sport, many professionals claim that they are expected to demonstrate violent behaviors, not to care about their opponents, or worry about the consequences of their actions. If they refuse to join in bench-clearing brawls on behalf of teammates or fail to punish, maybe illegally, opponents who sack their quarterback, they may find themselves not playing or cut from the team. The norms of sport, especially when exacerbated by expectations of aggression, seemingly demand increased physical abuse at each higher level of sport.

Some athletes see their opponents as objects rather than people. By objectifying opponents, athletes seemingly feel no remorse in injuring them intentionally. Either take out the opposing player with hard hits, an athlete is taught, or be perceived as weak. The ethos of winning demands unques-tioned loyalty to the team's goal of success by whatever means necessary.

One unconscionable example of objectifying opponents occurred just before the 1994 U.S. Figure Skating Championships when friends of Tonya Harding intentionally injured Nancy Kerrigan. The elimination of Kerrigan from the national championships opened the door for Harding to win the title and qualify for the Olympic Games. The resultant media blitz surrounding the evolving saga included reports of FBI interrogations that implicated Harding as a conspirator, a threatened $25 million lawsuit by Harding against the U.S. Olympic Committee if she was denied the right to skate in the Olympics, shared practice time on the ice with Kerrigan in Lillehammer, Norway, and Kerrigan's silver medal performance surpassing Harding's eighth-place finish. In the quest for a national championship, an opportunity to skate for Olympic gold, and the millions of dollars awaiting the next champion on ice, did an athlete, Harding, choose to eliminate her closest competitor?

A disregard for the rules (constitutive, proscriptive, and sportsmanship) often leads to an objectification of the opponent as an enemy—someone to be overcome physically, mentally, and emotionally. Usually, athletes reveal that they do not wish to inflict career-ending injuries, just injuries that will prevent opponents from competing against them. This permits playing against less-skilled players and enhances the possibility of winning. Protective gear worn by football and ice hockey players may facilitate seeing opponents as objects because so little of the person is seen. Yet other athletes view their opponents, and even their teammates, as objects, too. For example, one collegiate volleyball player stated that she would kick a teammate in the head for telling an official that she had touched a ball before it went out of bounds.

There is a clear connection between the emphasis on winning and a belief in the legitimacy of more aggressive and less sportsmanlike behaviors. Has winning gained predominance because winners receive the trophies, media attention, and popularity, and may continue to advance to higher levels of sport? Because these rewards are valued, and in order to keep them coming, athletes learn to do almost anything, including performing violent acts. Thus, sport perpetuates physical and psychological violence by condoning and rewarding it, especially when it is associated with winning. It seems noteworthy, however, that since violence has been condoned, and even applauded, within sport, incidences have increased.

What is happening in sports when a high school pitcher throws a ball at the head of an on-deck batter? The severe head injury suffered by the on-deck batter ended his promising athletic career, while the pitcher who committed this violent act was unpunished by his coach and advanced into the next level of competition.

Violence was practically nonexistent when sport was played informally without rules or high stakes. As constitutive rules were established to govern competitions, other regulations (proscriptive rules) were enacted to curb actions that could harm opponents. Within structured sport, some players displayed ethically questionable conduct. Sportsmanship rules legislated against this, yet some actions within the letter but outside the spirit of the rules continued. Increases in violence in sport paralleled the emphasis placed on winning and its associated rewards.

CATEGORICAL IMPERATIVES

The pervasiveness of violence in sport calls for establishing categorical imperatives. Needed are moral principles to serve as the basis for disallowing violent acts in sport. A *categorical imperative* is a universally accepted maxim that holds regardless of the situation because it is based on an undeniable moral principle. The following represents a nonexclusive list of some categorical imperatives that, if adhered to, could eliminate, or at least reduce, violence in sport.

1. True sportspersons play to the best of their abilities within the letter and spirit of the rules.

2. Seeking to win is acceptable only if the letter and spirit of the rules are followed.

3. An opponent is not the enemy but a worthy athlete deserving to be treated exactly as everyone would wish to be treated.

4. Retribution is never acceptable regardless of the unfairness or violence of the initial action.

5. Games are not played to intimidate; the ideal purpose is a mutual quest for excellence through equitable and fair competition.

6. Sportsmanship requires modesty and humility in victory, praise for winners, and self-respect in defeat.

HOW VIOLENCE AFFECTS SPORT

Why Violence Exists

Many psychological and sociological theories have been postulated about why violence occurs in sport. One suggests that athletes gravitate to sport because they have aggressive tendencies and need socially acceptable outlets for their release. Another theory suggests that sport nurtures violence through its structure and discipline. That is, only

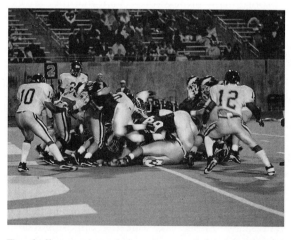

Football sometimes lapses into a violent sport with actions that break the rules to gain an advantage.

those who can submit themselves to an environment that stresses conformity, yet rewards individualistic, hard-hitting, violent behavior, can survive and advance in some sport settings. Last, the social learning theory speculates that violence occurs because it is modeled; that is, people mimic the successful or rewarded behaviors they observe on television or from the stands.

Additionally, societal values have changed markedly. The discipline problems of high school students in the 1940s, such as gum chewing in class and running in the halls, pale in comparison with today's concerns about drugs, guns in schools, teenage pregnancy, and AIDS. In sport, obscene language and gestures, verbal and physical intimidation, vicious hits intended to injure, psychological ploys, strategic advantage, fights and brawls, and gamesmanship are commonplace, although most are of relatively recent vintage. Many coaches and athletes covet the rights and privileges of sport involvement and occasionally stardom but refuse to accept the associated responsibilities of adhering to the categorical imperatives previously presented.

Violence occurs in sport because the rules or the rule enforcers permit it and because players fail to hold themselves accountable to the spirit of the rules. Athletes at all levels quickly learn what they can and cannot do relative to every action. For example, when a football player is not penalized for holding, he is more likely to repeat this action.

Legislating rules to curb and even eliminate violence from sport appears easy, yet many rules elude effective enforcement. Do sport rules exist because people violate others' rights? Do sport rules increase in number because people ingeniously find ways around existing rules? Some coaches and athletes seem to believe only in the letter of the rule, not the spirit. Unless individuals in sport value the welfare of opponents, fair play, and integrity in sport, more and more rules will have to be written and enforced to close the loopholes currently being exploited to someone's advantage.

Given the American addiction for winning at all levels of sport, athletes and coaches spend endless hours developing ways to gain advantages both within and outside the rules. A favorite ploy appears to be trying to see how much one can get away with and not get caught. Rather than matching opponents' talents and strategies, too many games lapse into players and coaches seeking to gain advantages without being penalized. Short of having one official per player and endless whistles, flags, and ejections, can officials, as rule enforcers, prevent increases in violent behaviors?

Should those who write the rules specify the letter of the rule, as well as explain the spirit of the rule? In other words, should the rules include an explanation of why they were developed and how they apply to fair play? This would lead to officials consistently enforcing these rules, with increased and more severe penalties for infractions, and league officials at all levels matching the penalty to the severity of the violation and taking into account prior actions and, possibly, the level of play.

Why Violent Behavior Is Taught

Coaches teach their athletes to act in violent ways in order to gain a competitive edge over opponents. Given the emphasis on winning just described, coaches who emphasize winning over playing the game within the letter and spirit of the rules will succumb to the temptation to gain unfair advantages in any way possible.

Violent behaviors often are learned from and modeled after those seen on the electronic media and praised in videotaped replays during sports reports, on ESPN's Sport Center and other sports highlight shows, and on big screen displays in stadiums and arenas. Young athletes see the aggressive contact without any commentary regarding whether this is appropriate or not. When these athletes are praised, young athletes surmise that such actions are permissible and even expected.

Volunteer, interscholastic, intercollegiate, and professional coaches see these same actions and often model what they teach after these violent actions. Parents and other fans callously perceive that such actions are simply the "way the game is played" and become accepting of violence in sport.

In one despicable act, a high school athlete's father sharpened various aspects of his son's football helmet thus causing cuts and injuries to opponents who were contacted by this helmet. Such behavior, done with the intent to harm, makes one question the extent to which some individuals will go to gain an advantage.

The higher the level of competition the more intense is the pressure exerted by coaches for athletes to perform in violent ways. Professional football players are often drafted and retained on the basis of how aggressively they play. The media praises the aggressive "hurts" put on quarterbacks or receivers by defensive players. Bill Romanowski, linebacker for the Denver Broncos, has received widespread acclaim for his aggressiveness and how destructive he can be on the football field. Some athletes have stated that they take anabolic steroids and amphetamines because these drugs increase their aggressiveness and often lead to out-of-control actions.

Why Violence Is Condoned

Violence continues because some fans enjoy it, the media glamorizes it, and it helps athletes win. Basketball and ice hockey illustrate how fans condone and even encourage violence. Although rule books at every level of play clearly describe basketball as a noncontact sport, this game has increasingly become more physical, even though few of these contacts are penalized. Some fans want the officials to let the athletes play, advocating that pushing and holding are all part of the game. In ice hockey, many fans thrive on the rough and often violent action displayed on the ice. They make heroes out of players whose primary roles are to intimidate and injure opponents.

An unending debate surrounds whether the violence in ice hockey enhances or impedes its growth in popularity. Some claim that the fights heighten the game's appeal, whereas others disdain such violence because it distracts from the skill of the sport. In the past, ice hockey remained content with its image as a violent sport; otherwise, rules preventing some of the violence would have been enforced.

Canada's Fair Play Commission, in conjunction with the International Hockey Program of Canada, offers a glimmer of hope. On the basis of concern about moral education and the image of ice hockey, amateur and professional ice hockey programs are beginning to advertise without the use of violence.

Society reinforces violence in sport. For example, Jack Tatum, a former professional defensive back, received praise for describing in *They Call Me Assassin* his injurious exploits as he continuously intimidated and injured wide receivers. Consider the antics of Dennis Rodman, who many regard as an antihero because of his sometimes violent and offensive behavior on and off the court. Some have posited that the increasing popularity of auto racing is linked to the aggressive driving of its champions, which often results in violent pile-ups such as Dale Earnhardt's crash in 2001. Sport in America rewards the victorious with multimillion-dollar contracts and lucrative endorsements. If violent behaviors help advance an athlete, then these actions will likely be repeated, regardless of who might be harmed in the process.

Do fans condone and thus perpetuate violence in sport by purchasing tickets, watching televised sport, and following their favorite teams in print? Do the electronic and print media glamorize and publicize violence because of its sensationalism? Must fans cease to buy tickets or newspapers to send a clear message that violence is unacceptable? The likelihood of this change remains doubtful because many fans are no more morally educated than most athletes. How can athletes be expected to behave morally when society as a whole fails to do so?

Winning is the chief culprit through which violence continues in sport. With only victories praised and rewarded, too many athletes learn and practice whatever actions, moral or immoral, seem necessary to win. Breaking this cycle will not be easy because sport reflects capitalism and its emphasis on competing to surpass everyone else.

Too often in the professional ranks, sport expectations linked with winning demand that teammates enter the fray in defense of a wronged teammate. Although such behavior may be considered manly, it certainly fails the test of honor. What moral questions arise if an athlete races onto a field or court and swings at people because of team loyalty or affiliation? Teammates may have no idea who threw the first punch or why; some seem not to care—anything for a good fight. Would these actions stop if management dictated that such actions will no longer be tolerated and, furthermore, will be punished?

Competing or striving to perform to the best of one's ability defines sport. However, should an athlete have the right to harm another person or to take an unfair advantage just to win? Many justify such practices, stating that only the winner gets the trophy, the front-page picture, and the chance to advance to the next level of competition.

Why and How Violence Is Rewarded

In addition to violence being taught and condoned, it is also rewarded. Violence pays dividends to those who practice it when it helps in winning games. Aggressive behavior in basketball, for example, intensifies when contact outside the rules is not whistled. Athletes adapt to what officials will permit and usually become as violent as will be allowed. When holding and pushing help athletes play defense more effectively, then opponents score less often. When these actions lead to victories and even championships, recognition and rewards follow.

Oftentimes, violent behavior is used to intimidate. When a defensive back flattens a wide receiver on a crossing pattern and stands over him taunting him, this action seems to say, "come into my space and you will have to pay the price." The aggressive athlete frequently makes the highlight films, gets the endorsement deals, and negotiates a bigger salary. The collegiate athlete who can use violence to his or her advantage too often enjoys perks, such as the adoration of fans and especially females, unearned grades, and under-the-table payments.

The interscholastic athlete who throws at a batter's head after giving up a home run or the runner who attempts to "take out" the second baseman when trying to break up a double play has already

learned that he or she will be rewarded for helping to win in any manner possible. The youth sport athlete who is taught how to verbally intimidate an opponent quickly realizes that aggressive actions are more valued by adults.

Interestingly, sport rules over the years have been liberalized to reward violent behavior. Seldom is a flag thrown for a "roughing the passer" call because quarterbacks are expected to just take the punishment of violent contacts regardless of the number of concussions they may suffer. Increasingly, only a fraction of the holding, pushing, and hacking is whistled in basketball.

Additionally, many individuals involved with competitive sport do not believe that violent behaviors in sport are wrong. They sometimes equivocate winning, which is an amoral value, with the expected norm. Moral reasoning, when focusing on the principles of justice, honesty, responsibility, and beneficence, contradicts this position. When playing fair and demonstrating integrity in all actions, an athlete cannot disregard the rules. Thus, the moral reasoning process suggests that athletes will be governed in their behaviors by the letter and spirit of the rules. Conversely, if athletes believe that lucrative contracts, national acclaim, campus popularity, friendships, and other perks accrue only to the victorious, they may choose to display violent behaviors in order to attain their benefits.

Violent actions are taught, condoned, and rewarded because of the importance placed on winning. The expected norm in sport is to push the rules as far as possible to win because only then will lavish rewards be enjoyed.

The Impact of Violence on Sport

Violence undermines the values that potentially can be learned through sport and make a travesty of the meaning of sport. When permitted, violence threatens to reduce and even eliminate fair play, cooperation, and self-discipline. Antithetical to fair play, violent behaviors are used to gain an advantage outside the letter or spirit of the rules. Contrastingly, fair play demands an adherence to the spirit of the rules to ensure equity for all. Cooperation suggests a willingness to work for the good of the whole, be it the game itself or one's team. Whereas athletes with propensities for violent behaviors primarily care for their personal status and success, the principled player will not inflict injury or harm on an opponent to gain an advantage.

Sport can be defined as games and activities directed toward the play experience in which organization and rules have a significant role. The true meaning of sport requires a fair and just playing field or one on which each opponent has an equitable chance for success. When any individual or team uses violent behaviors, the meaning of sport erodes. For example, is the athlete who holds an opposing player on the line of scrimmage or under the basket cheating and possibly contributing to fisticuffs when this behavior goes unpenalized? Will the values and meaning of sport thrive only when violence and other unethical behaviors are prevented?

In addition to the impact of violence on sport, it should be noted how violent behaviors on the field or court have moved into society. Lawrence Phillips helped his University of Nebraska team win its second straight national championship with his aggressive running style after his coach permitted him to continue on the team after a brief suspension even though he had physically assaulted a female athlete at that university. Although this was one of the most egregious acts of an intercollegiate athlete, sexual assaults, barroom brawls, dorm room fights, and drug-related shootings are among the incidents of violent behaviors of athletes. It appears that the notoriety of some athletes, such as Ray Lewis, may help get them easier treatment from the judicial system. Yet there are numerous cases of athletes of all ages involved with murder, drug dealing, rape, assaults with guns and knives, and other altercations. One wonders if the aggressiveness taught and reinforced through sports makes athletes more likely to engage in such violent actions or whether sport attracts individuals who are inherently more aggressive and violent. It may be, however, that athletes are engaging in violent behaviors less frequently statistically but only that the media chooses to publicize their misbehaviors because of their perceived celebrity status.

RECOMMENDATIONS

Before seeking to control violence, those involved in sport must admit to its pervasiveness. An examination finds parents attacking umpires, other youth players, and coaches; coaches hitting their athletes or verbally abusing them; fans causing riots in the stands and throwing objects at officials or visiting athletes; and athletes intentionally inflicting injuries on opponents.

A myriad of controls are needed to eliminate or at least curb violence in sport. In youth sport, league officials and coaches should teach and enforce sport rules and ethical values. No violations by any player or coach should be tolerated; penalties should be swift and appropriate to the behavior. Any adult—coach, parent, or fan—who engages in violent behavior should be banned permanently from the bench or the stands.

Rules help enhance the quality of play while reducing the likelihood of violence in sport.

Interscholastic sport under the direction of school administrators and coaches should enact similarly stringent rules governing their programs. All sport, league, school, and team rules should be followed and additional ones enacted to prevent violent and unethical behavior. Coaches should be held accountable for teaching these rules and for the skill development of players, not for the number of victories they tally. Parents and fans should be held to a code of conduct that requires them to either behave responsibly or forfeit their right to spectate. Players should comply with constitutive, proscriptive, and sportsmanship rules, including those governing the letter and spirit of the sports they play; if they do not, they should be eliminated from their teams.

Similarly, intercollegiate athletes should be expected to adhere to sport rules and team guidelines for conduct. There should be less emphasis on the winning-at-all-costs attitude that too often leads to rule-breaking behaviors. The college, the athletic department, and the coach should consistently emphasize to athletes that their choice to play or their acceptance of grants-in-aid obligates them only to do the best they can within their abilities, not to resort to violent behavior under the guise of seeking to win.

Colleges should place restraints on boosters and fans who seem to have an insatiable appetite for winning. This is more likely to occur if colleges, rather than independent organizations, govern athletic programs and stipulate that coaches will be evaluated on the basis of players' athletic, academic, and social development, not the number of contests won. In addition, colleges should hold their fans, students, athletic administrators, coaches, and athletes to an ethical code of conduct that prevents violence in and surrounding sport.

Although controls at the professional level are more difficult, they are nonetheless important and possible to implement. Because players' jobs are on the line, league and team management should dictate that violent behavior will not be tolerated and if it occurs will be penalized swiftly and severely. It may take one or two incidents and harsh penalties

to stress the seriousness of the situation, but a clear message will impede the spread of violence. Should Latrell Sprewell have been banned from the NBA after choking Coach P.J. Carlismo? Why are ice hockey players permitted to use their sticks as weapons for violent behavior?

What recourse should a professional football player have against a fan who hit him with a snowball with a rock inside? Fans can be somewhat controlled through the visible use of police officers and through announcements that violators will be removed from the stands. The media should help reeducate fans by ceasing to glamorize and publicize violence in sport. This would be of help at all levels of sport, especially in the professional leagues.

Although these controls may deter some violence in sport, a more effective means for change calls for a comprehensive program in moral education for coaches, athletes, parents, fans, administrators, and the media. This program should focus on values, the recommended categorical imperatives, and moral reasoning. The principles and concepts of moral reasoning would challenge people's values and their commitment to them. As stated in Chapter 2, the moral values that should guide people's actions are justice, honesty, responsibility, and beneficence. The principles based on these values are, respectively—do not be unfair; do not lie, cheat, or steal; do not be irresponsible; and do not be uncivil. Discussions about values and ethics are needed, and everyone involved in sport should commit to these. Such a moral education program should completely refocus people's attention on the values that can be modeled through sport. Perhaps team captains could affirm the following statement on behalf of everyone:

"We are here today to play each other to the best of our ability and not to intentionally harm our opponents. We hope that we are good sports and play by both the letter and the spirit of the rules. We challenge you to help us in this attempt. We ask that you cheer us on to excellence. And, we ask that you neither boo us nor demean our playing in any way. We ask that you help us. Will you be good sports, too?"

SUMMARY

This chapter exposes the ethical problems associated with violence in sport. The development of constitutive, proscriptive, and sportsmanship rules has paralleled growth in incidences of violence. As winning emerged as the most important aspect of sport, rules expanded in an attempt to control violence and other ethically questionable behaviors.

Six categorical imperatives were suggested as the moral principles upon which sport should exist. An examination of sport shows a pervasiveness of violence that undermines these maxims. Possibly understanding why violence exists and is condoned, as well as its impact, will help establish controls to curb or prevent it. Sport managers, officials, coaches, and athletes should reeducate themselves morally if sport is to eliminate violence and replace it with ethical behavior.

 Cybersports

www.sportsethicsinstitute.org

The Sports Ethics Institute examines the ethical standards of conduct that should govern sports.

www.aahperd.org/naspe/position-papers.html

The National Association for Sport and Physical Education provides a "Code of Conduct for Coaches" that describes how coaches should model ethical behavior in sport so that their athletes will perform and act in appropriate ways.

nhl.com/hockeyu/rulebook/rule43.html

The rules of the National Hockey League specify that the intent to cause injury to an opponent is considered violent behavior on the ice.

www.sportinsociety.org/mvp.html

The Mentors in Violence Prevention Program, sponsored by the Center for the Study of Sport in Society, enlists high school, collegiate, and professional athletes in the effort to prevent all forms of men's violence against women.

www.inyouthsoccer.org/iysa/codeofethics.htm

Many sport organizations, such as the Indiana Youth Soccer Association, have developed websites and included their codes of ethics. These codes help guide the behaviors of athletes, coaches, and spectators, such as calling for playing by the spirit of the game as well as the written letter of the rules.

 # ISSUES AND DILEMMAS

CASE 5-1

Peter started playing football when he was eight and had been a linebacker ever since. He loved to make hard tackles and to see the boys he had hit give him looks of respect when they struggled to get up. He always played on championship teams in Pop Warner, junior high, and high school. Coaches loved his aggressive style, which was why he had been recruited to play at the university.

As a freshman, Peter began to learn new techniques for playing his favorite sport. Although in the past his size and strength had enabled him to hit hard, yet cleanly, suddenly everyone vying for a place on the team was at least his six-foot-four and 230 pounds. Peter was coached on how to hold without getting caught, how to fight off blocks using illegal techniques, and how to tackle with the goal of injury, as well as that of stopping an opponent. At first using these maneuvers bothered Peter, but soon he learned that if he did not use them, others who did would get to play, not him. So Peter mastered these and other violent techniques that he could use against opponents to help his team succeed.

The university's team won two major bowl games during Peter's college years, with his play contributing to both victories. It seemed that players at all defensive positions had been taught similar techniques because the Tigers were renowned for their hard hitting, as well as their sometimes unethical techniques. They led the league in penalties but in most defensive categories, too.

1. How is Peter a victim of moral callousness brought on by the game itself?
2. What did his acceptance of and participation in violent behavior indicate about his moral reasoning?
3. What are the ethical ramifications of pushing the rules to the limit and beyond?
4. Given the cultural imperative of winning, how does ethical behavior apply? In what ways is moral behavior contradictory to winning?
5. How could or should have Peter behaved in order to act as a morally responsible person? What would you have done if you had been Peter?

◆ ◆ ◆

CASE 5-2

The Memphis Suns, a Triple A baseball team in the Cardinals organization, were perennial favorites in the Southern Conference. Their nemesis for years had been the Little Rock Stars, who were affiliated with the Braves' minor league system. Although players moved up and down from their parent clubs, the Suns and Stars always managed to vie for the conference title come late August, and 2002 was no exception. As the Suns started the final three-game series in Little Rock Memorial Stadium, they were tied for the league lead with the Stars. Two games later, the situation was the same; either the Suns or the Stars would capture the conference championship in the final game of the season.

The Suns' ace, Carroll Lyttle, held the Stars scoreless through six innings, whereas the Suns had managed to push across two runs. In the bottom of the seventh, the Stars opened with a single by Baylor and a double by Ramsey, with John Miller coming to the plate. Miller hit a line drive to right field, sending Ramsey speeding toward home with the tying run. Because of a misplay by the catcher, Lyttle had to cover home. Although the ball arrived long before Ramsey, he never hesitated as he crashed into the pitcher, who was prepared to tag him out. The six-foot, 195-pound Lyttle crumbled under the impact of the six-foot-six, 249-pound Ramsey and dropped the ball. Instantly, both benches cleared, and the brawl began. Several players were injured by the punches thrown before order was restored, but only Lyttle had to be carried off the field with a broken collarbone.

1. Assuming that the collision at home plate was technically within the rules, how or why is this within the spirit of the rules?
2. Why did the benches clear and a brawl ensue?
3. How would the penalty for participating in this fight affect the possible recurrence of a fight or players' participation in one?
4. Should "taking out" a player covering a base to tag a runner ever be considered violent behavior? Does it violate any constitutive, proscriptive, or sportsmanship rule?
5. If an advantage is gained and the practice is permitted, should the action be questioned on moral principle?

◆ ◆ ◆

CASE 5-3

Mario started playing organized ice hockey when he was six years old. By the time he was 14 he was one of the best junior ice hockey players in New England. Coaches eagerly tried to get him to join their age-group teams because they liked his aggressive style of play, yet were not concerned that he spent several minutes each game in the penalty box for using his stick as a weapon and for fighting.

Mario's team, the Sabres, carried its undefeated record into the league championship game against the Blazers, who had lost only one game against the Sabres. In the final period with the score tied 1–1, the Blazers' star player, Stefan, appeared to break away for a clear shot at the goal. Somehow, Mario managed to catch up with Stefan but only by hitting him on the side of his head with his stick—so hard that Stefan's helmet flew off. This flagrant action was compounded when Stefan's head hit the ice with a thud. Attempts to revive Stefan were unsuccessful, and he was pronounced dead on arrival at the local hospital. Because of a wrongful death lawsuit filed by Stefan's parents, Mario was arrested and charged with manslaughter.

1. Why was Mario allowed to fight and display aggressive behavior as a youth hockey player? Were any of Mario's actions unethical?
2. What values were the coaches who attempted to get Mario to play for their youth hockey team displaying?
3. What values were being shown by Mario's flagrant action against Stefan?
4. How could this unfortunate incident have been avoided?
5. Should Mario have been charged with manslaughter? Why or why not?
6. If Stefan had been injured, instead of killed, should Mario have been charged with assault if he had no intention to harm? Why or why not?
7. In an aggressive game in which bodily contact is part of the strategy, how can aggression be tempered? Can athletes play aggressively in a contact sport and behave in an ethical manner?

◆ ◆ ◆

CASE 5-4

LaShonda and Ramona, the leading players for their teams, kept up a steady barrage of trash talk throughout each of their Women's National Basketball Association (WNBA) games. As they played offense and defense against each other, they traded verbal assaults. Typically, the officials ignored such trash talk, since it was occurring between two of the league's stars.

When their teams met in the WNBA Finals, LaShonda and Ramona significantly increased their attempts to "get inside the head" of the other. But, when LaShonda's language became incessantly vulgar, Ramona asked a referee to intervene before she took matters in her own hands. Observing this plea, LaShonda, convinced that she was winning the psychological battle, escalated the insults she was hurling at Ramona. When the officials seemed unwilling to put an end to LaShonda's vulgar taunting, Ramona punched LaShonda in the face several times before being pulled away.

1. How is psychological intimidation associated with violence in sport?
2. When and how were Ramona and LaShonda guilty of violent behavior?
3. How did the coaches and officials contribute to this violence in sport?

◆ ◆ ◆

CASE 5-5

Mickey by age 17 had developed quite a reputation as a violent wrestler. In age group competitions as well as during his high school years, he had never lost a match. In fact, other boys were afraid of him. Mickey's father, who had wrestled in college and in the Olympics, had taught his son not only advanced techniques at a young age but also several maneuvers that broke the rules because of their violent nature. Several of Mickey's former opponents had broken bones, pinched nerves, and disabling injuries compliments of Mickey. Although he had received numerous warnings, he had never been disqualified despite protests from coaches and parents about his violent actions.

1. What rules, if any, has Mickey broken through his violent behavior?
2. At what point does violent behavior become unethical?
3. What moral or amoral values had Mickey's father taught him?
4. Describe the moral reasoning process that Mickey might use to change his violent behavior as a wrestler.

◆ ◆ ◆

CASE 5-6

John began playing tennis at age four when his mother gave him his first racket. He immediately showed great potential, so much so that he quickly outgrew her instructional ability. John and his mother moved to Florida where he was enrolled in Rod Newcombe's Tennis Academy. John's on-court behavior was characterized by his incessant temper tantrums when line calls did not go his way. He had thrown and broken more rackets by age 12 than most others had ever seen. Neither John's mother nor Coach Newcombe constrained his behavior because they believed that his intensity was one of the primary reasons that led to his championship play. Although they cautioned him to control his racket abuse and, more important, his verbal assaults on linespersons and umpires, John persisted despite being occasionally penalized. John's uncontrolled behavior first demonstrated itself off the court when he started a fight in the locker room with the player who had upset him in the finals of a tournament. Coach Newcombe and John's mother were able to prevent the deserved punishment and to keep this incident out of the media, even though the victim of the assault received a black eye from a punch from John. Even though John's on and off court behaviors became increasingly violent, no one penalized him sufficiently or educated him about behaving in a sportsmanlike manner. After two years of undefeated play, however, John lost in the 18-and-under United States Tennis Association Championship primarily because he was out of control in the final set when he thought a couple of line calls were wrong. That evening, John avenged his loss by beating up and sexually assaulting his girlfriend.

1. What lessons did John learn at an early age regarding violence in sport?
2. Why do you think that John's mother and Coach Newcombe permitted John to throw his racket, argue with officials, and display violent behaviors?
3. What possible actions on the part of John's mother and Coach Newcombe might have prevented John's assault on his girlfriend?
4. Given John's violent behaviors, what should be done to educate him to behave in a morally responsible manner?

REFERENCES

Kretchmar, R. S. 1995. *Practical philosophy of sport.* Champaign–Urbana, IL: Human Kinetics.

ADDITIONAL READINGS

Berger, G. 1990. *Violence and sports.* New York: Franklin Watts.

Fierberg, D. E. 2000. High school, where hazing is amazing. *The Education Digest* 66(4) (December): 48–51.

Jones, J. C. H., K. G. Stewart, and R. Sunderman. 1996. From the arena into the streets: Hockey violence, economic incentives and public policy. *American Journal of Economics & Sociology* 55(2) (April): 231–43.

Leach, R. E. 1997. Violence and sports. *American Journal of Sports Medicine* 25(5) (September): 595.

Leizman, J. 1999. *Let's kill 'em: Understanding and controlling violence in sports.* Lanham, MD: University Press of America.

Leonard, J. 1998. *Smoke and mirrors: Violence, television, and other American cultures.* New York: New Press.

Mertzman, R. 1999. *Violence and aggression in sports and society.* Dubuque, IA: Kendall/Hunt Publishing Company.

Tatum, J. and W. Kushner. 2000. *Final Confessions of NFL Assassin.* C. Al Valley, Il.: Quality Sports Publications. (includes his out-of-print 1980 book *They Call Me Assassin*)

CHAPTER 6

Eligibility in Sport

◆ How do eligibility issues at all levels of sport relate to moral values?

◆ Is it ethical to encourage young athletes to pursue a dream of playing professional sports given the very small number of athletes who attain this level of competition?

◆ Why did the International Olympic Committee eliminate its requirement that Olympic athletes had to be amateurs?

◆ Have eligibility rules developed and expanded because of a distrust of opponents who might not behave ethically?

◆ Why have the number and specificity of eligibility regulations at all competitive levels of sport increased?

◆ Can eligibility regulations legislate moral behavior; does sport mirror society by displaying what is most valued?

◆ How can ethical dilemmas regarding eligibility in all levels of sport be resolved?

Eligibility concerns pervade competitive sports. If the nonmoral outcome of winning exceeds in importance playing the game for the game's sake, competitors will be tempted to do and will often succumb to doing whatever is necessary in order to win. Beginning with early Greek competitors, winners have received lucrative rewards and recognition, whereas nonwinners often are made to feel inferior, as losers. Because athletes vigorously pursue the victors' prizes, eligibility regulations have been and continue to be cleverly and creatively exploited at every level of competitive sport. When seeking to win results in unethical behavior concerning eligibility, the nonmoral value of winning supersedes the moral values of justice, honesty, responsibility, and beneficence.

This chapter begins by examining the major eligibility issues confronting participants in youth, interscholastic, intercollegiate, and Olympic sport.

From historical and sociological perspectives, behaviors manifested by some athletes, coaches, and sport managers indicate that they value winning more than playing fairly, abiding by the rules, and acting responsibly. The reader will be challenged to determine why eligibility rules exist, why they have changed, and how they relate to moral values. Ethical dilemmas associated with these eligibility issues challenge everyone involved in sport to establish a moral reasoning process.

HISTORICAL AND SOCIOLOGICAL PERSPECTIVES

Recreational sports as played by rural youth, urban gentlemen, or upper-class socialites of both genders found no need for eligibility rules. Their games welcomed others like themselves because their purposes included fun, camaraderie, and exercising for health. As winning grew in importance, such as when opponents placed friendly wagers on the outcome, some tried to surreptitiously change the way their games were played.

Amateur baseball in the mid-1800s provides an example of what can happen in sport in the absence of eligibility rules. This sport lacked formalized or consistent rules because these were thought unnecessary for the gentlemen who competed. As winning became more important, though, teams began to recruit and pay the best athletes. Although this did not violate eligibility rules, because there were none, such behavior raised the ire of competitors.

In another example, the Amateur Athletic Union, established in 1879, began sponsoring competition among amateurs who played for fun, not remuneration. Until the late 1970s, this organization controlled many sports—from its age-group events through national championships and Olympic trials—while maintaining an emphasis on amateurism as a prerequisite to eligibility. However, elitist and amateur athletic clubs, in the late 1800s, ceased to sponsor competitions solely between members when these players were replaced by so-called tramp athletes who marketed their skills to the highest bidders. To prevent the appearance of illegitimacy, these lower- and middle-class men were supposedly given memberships in elite clubs in return for their demonstrated prowess; however, these athletes represented the amateur clubs in order to help achieve victories and were not allowed to socially interact with the real club members. Additionally, these athletes were paid lucrative sums and given various gifts. Thus, a model for how to circumvent eligibility rules existed long before sport became organized at different levels.

Youth Sport

Organized sport programs for children began in the 1920s when businesspeople provided the financial resources to sponsor team sport leagues for boys. Although altruistically justified as programs to teach values and to prevent juvenile delinquency, these early sport leagues were characterized by the pervasive advertising of businesses on T-shirts, uniforms, and ballpark signs. As Little League Baseball and Pop Warner Football in the 1930s, and subsequently other leagues, grew in popularity and participation, parents' and coaches' involvement resulted in the formulation of rules to thwart strategies to gain competitive advantages.

Several eligibility problems gradually began to enter youth competitions. These included eligibility issues relative to age, weight, residence, and gender. Today, issues concerning rules against female participation on typically male-dominated youth sport programs have generally been eliminated through court action. Yet issues concerning eligibility and weight, age, and residence still exist. As one way to equalize competition and account for differences that occur because of age and weight, many youth sport leagues separate participants by age. Typically, those of similar age are of approximately the same height and weight, thus helping ensure a more equitable and safe sporting environment. Related to the issue of age and helping ensure that competitors are equitably matched (avoiding the matching of an 80-pound child against a 110-pound child), many youth sport programs, such as football and wrestling, set weight limitations, too.

Issues of eligibility also emerge concerning residency within certain communities or cities. Oftentimes, youth sport programs are sponsored through public recreation departments. The rules of these programs state that those who live within the geographic region financially supporting the program are eligible to participate in the program. Parents sign forms and state that they reside within that particular district, city, or community. These rules exist because families who pay taxes in a particular area support the program and help ensure that players of all skill levels make up each team.

However, because of the drive to win and be number one, even at the youth sport level, eligibility problems arise. Some parents have falsified birth certificates and lied on participation forms concerning residency and legal guardianship. With a falsified birth certificate or age report, a larger, more skilled player plays against a younger, lesser skilled player. For example, in 2001, the father of Danny Almonte falsified his son's birth certificate so that he could compete in a baseball league for younger players. As an investigation revealed, Danny was 14 years old, which made his no-hitter and other pitching achievements more understandable as he led his team to a third-place finish in the Little League World Series. Danny and his teammates had to forfeit all of their year's victories and endure the hurt of becoming pawns maneuvered by the unethical actions of adults. It was unfortunate that the young athletes were victims of cheating instead of beneficiaries of the modeling of honesty and integrity in sport.

Whereas programs such as football restrict players to certain weight classes to limit the injury potential of larger, heavier individuals competing against smaller, lighter players, wrestling raises slightly different eligibility rules. Although scales monitor weights, ethical and health issues surface concerning how athletes attempt to make lower weight classes. In an attempt to make weight, parents, coaches, and others encourage athletes to lose as much weight as possible before the time of weigh-in prior to the actual contest. The quickest ways for children to lose weight in a 12- to 24-hour period is to reduce caloric intake to low levels, exercise in plastic or rubber suits, and/or take diuretics. In an attempt to reduce the injuries and eliminate deaths in wrestling, on all levels of sport, rules have been implemented condemning these practices. Despite the rules, these practices still occur. The potential of serious health problems that could result in death due to dehydration and severe electrolyte imbalance is very real, and these actions violate the rules of most sport-governing organizations. If wrestling in weight classes is about matched competition, what does this say about how we perceive the spirit of the rules and how we value the individual?

Most youth sport programs are loosely organized and rely on voluntary compliance with a philosophy of fun-filled athletic programs for children and adolescents. Yet, the actions of some parents indicate a willingness to do whatever it takes to get and keep their children playing on the best teams. Without a formal enforcement mechanism, usually such actions go unquestioned. Some even praise the crafti-

ness of these individuals. Coaches, like parents seeking ego fulfillment, occasionally violate league rules. Young athletes learn unethical lessons from parents and coaches who irresponsibly demonstrate that eligibility rules are made to be broken rather than followed.

Young athletes are most easily victimized because they often have no choice but to acquiesce to parental dictates whether ethical or not. Seldom are children and adolescents consulted about whether to be held back a grade to give them physical advantages in sport later or about their legal guardian or residence. Even if asked, they probably would agree with actions that could enhance their athletic status, because winning matters the most. Although willing parties in ethically questionable practices at the time, these young athletes later may conclude that they were exploited. Minors cannot be expected to act as moral adults or to be responsible for the immoral actions of their parents.

Interscholastic Sport

Interscholastic sport competitions began in the early 1900s, modeled after those in the colleges. Interscholastic sport had as its main purposes to be an educational extension of the school and to develop character to prepare individuals for life. These contests, which were initially only for boys, became a rallying point for communities. On Friday nights on rural fields and in local gymnasiums, numerous teams and towns vied for bragging rights in football and basketball. Sporadically, abuses crept into school sports when an overemphasis on winning became commonplace (Coakley 2001; Eitzen and Sage 1996). To curb many of the problems that surfaced concerning ineligible players, eligibility rules were enacted by state athletic associations affiliated with the National Federation of High School Associations. These rules addressed age, residence, remuneration, and academics.

Eligibility rules were enacted in interscholastic sport for several reasons. First, because interscholastic sport was formed within the auspices of an educational model with goals, such as the development of cooperation and teamwork, eligibility rules were enacted to help ensure that athletes were enrolled in and making educational progress in classes. Second, eligibility rules existed to help ensure that athletes who resided in a particular geographic area attended schools within the specified region. However, abuses within the system occurred.

Considering that interscholastic sport was developed within an educational context and the education of youth was deemed imperative to society's future, and if, in order to stay eligible, players received credit for courses they did not pass, what did that say about the value of education? If athletes were recruited into districts in order to help win championships, what did this say about the value of matched competition?

Age requirements stipulate both maximal age limits and the number of years a student can compete. To prevent older and more mature students from continuing to play in interscholastic sport, state organizations typically establish age limits for athletes. Unfortunately, falsified birth certificates allow a few athletes to play when they are older than allowed. Another eligibility rule usually specifies that students can compete for only three years between the 10th and 12th grades. Even though state associations have enacted this limitation to prevent parents from holding their children back a year (similar to collegiate redshirting whereby athletes are withheld from competition for a year for developmental or medical reasons), at times parents circumvent this rule by arranging for a child to repeat a grade before high school for athletic reasons.

Most public schools serve a specific geographic area; thus, athletes on school teams must live within a certain district. However, when another school offers what is perceived to be a better opportunity for athletic success, many high school athletes, with their parents' encouragement, have chosen to transfer. Often this is achieved when the legal guardian of the athlete is changed or when the athlete leaves home to live with relatives or friends (sometimes even the coach). Because private and public magnet schools offering unique academic programs have districtwide service areas, many coaches of teams at these institutions openly recruit star athletes. Be-

Sometimes coaches stress their sports so intensely that athletes fail to have the time and energy to achieve success in their academic work.

cause adolescents compete on nonschool teams, regulations limit the benefits they can receive from sport. Normally, this includes competitive expenses, uniforms, and minimal awards for winning or athletic achievements, such as trophies and plaques. When interscholastic athletes who compete during summer receive shoes, warm-ups, bags, and other sport clothing and equipment, they often expect such benefits to continue on interscholastic teams or they are influenced to seek out these benefits, which violate interscholastic sport rules. A few outstanding adolescents accept money and other benefits from sport agents, even though this is in violation of high school and college eligibility rules.

State high school athletic associations regulate the academic eligibility of those youth who represent their schools. One of these regulations, often called **no pass, no play,** helps prevent academic exploitation by requiring that students meet minimal

Too often, athletes in revenue-producing sports make little progress toward their degrees and fail to graduate because of time and effort spent on their sport.

academic standards for eligibility to play on school teams. Under the guise of meeting academic standards, some coaches counsel athletes to take less rigorous technical courses, rather than college preparatory curricula, just to stay eligible for interscholastic sports. Some coaches pressure teachers to give athletes unearned good grades. Is academic eligibility that is achieved in these ways fair and honest? What are these coaches teaching their athletes about acting responsibly?

Intercollegiate Sport

Recreational interclass activities for male collegians were initiated in the late 1800s to offset the rigors of academic work and the perceived oppression of faculty constraints on students' behaviors. As intercollegiate sport developed, became more popular, and expanded in the 20th century, faculties saw a need to exert more institutional control and attempt to integrate athletics with education. Because no regulations or prohibitions had existed, collegians had recruited nonstudents, townspeople, alumni, students from other colleges, and even professional athletes for their teams. Initially, no student or faculty member had considered the need for eligibility standards requiring a minimum time of enrollment at an institution, a certain number of hours enrolled in school or subjects passed, or

progress toward graduation. As a result, the football 11 or the baseball 9 often had a limited relationship to the institution the team supposedly represented. Even though students took no issue with such practices, college presidents and faculty expressed concerns about debasing their institutions' reputations for the sake of victories (Smith and Austin 1993).

The NCAA, regarded by many as the most powerful sport organization in the United States, started in 1906 as the Intercollegiate Athletic Association of the United States. As it grew to nearly a thousand members representing the larger colleges and their conferences, the NCAA depended on institutional control for most eligibility rules. Not until the start of national championships (1920s) and the initiation of college sports on television (1950s) did the NCAA begin to gain leverage over its members. During the 1950s, colleges increasingly agreed to comply with NCAA eligibility rules that governed recruiting and grants-in-aid as long as their opponents would be required to adhere to the same rules. The pursuit of championships and the sharing of television revenue became the lucrative benefits accruing to institutions that complied with the NCAA's extensive eligibility regulations. Banishment from championships, television, and even competition (the death penalty) represented the punishments for noncompliance.

NCAA rules dictate the permitted and the forbidden in amateur sport eligibility in the intercollegiate sport programs of its member institutions. Past rule violations by athletic personnel, especially coaches and individuals interested in promoting a college's athletic program, led to the NCAA's voluminous eligibility regulations. That is, more and more rules were written to explicitly ban wrongful actions performed by coaches and others, who had exploited loopholes in the rules. Essentially, coaches, administrators, athletes, and others regarded ethical conduct as synonymous with only the written rules, meaning that the spirit of the rules did not exist. Specifically, if a particular action was not covered by an explicit rule, it was seemingly acceptable, regardless of whether or not it was ethical.

The eligibility rules broken most often in intercollegiate sport include those governing academic standards, recruiting, and payments to athletes. Falsified transcripts of high school athletes have led to the NCAA rule that prospective student–athletes must be certified by the NCAA Clearinghouse relative to their high school grade-point averages in 13 core subjects and their SAT or ACT scores. The failure of many student–athletes to graduate led the NCAA to require minimum academic loads, progress toward a degree, and declaration of a major before the fifth semester of enrollment.

Academic exploitation, though, continues to characterize some institutions. Some athletes are admitted to colleges even though they are academically unqualified. A few players receive unearned grades, sometimes in courses they never attended. Despite toughened NCAA regulations, some athletes play their four years of eligibility and still find themselves significantly short of earning college degrees because they have performed poorly in their classes or have taken only those courses that will help them maintain eligibility. Often, athletes fail academically because they give priority to sport in their use of time and level of commitment.

Several questions arise whenever these academic abuses occur. If a college gives preferential admittance to college athletes, what effect does that have on students without such treatment? Does the admission of an unqualified student–athlete actually set this person up to fail rather than succeed—even if an academic support system is provided? What ethical obligations does a college have to the student–athlete who, on the basis of standard admission criteria, lacks the ability to succeed academically? (See Box 6-1).

BOX 6-1

COLLEGE SPORTS AND EDUCATIONAL VALUES

Some of the key empirical findings from *The game of life: College sports and educational values* by Shulman and Bowen (2001) follow.

1. Athletes competing on intercollegiate teams constituted a sizable share of the undergraduate student population at many selective colleges and universities, and especially at coed liberal arts colleges and Ivy League universities.
   a. For coed liberal arts colleges, these numbers were 1/3 of the males and 1/5 of the females.
   b. For the Ivy League, these numbers were 1/4 of the males and 15 percent of the females.
2. Athletes who were recruited, and who ended up on the carefully winnowed lists of desired candidates submitted by coaches to the admissions office, enjoyed a very substantial statistical "advantage" in the admission process.
   a. In 1999 for a nonscholarship institution, recruited male athletes enjoyed a 48 percent greater chance of being admitted.
   b. In 1999 for a nonscholarship institution, recruited female athletes enjoyed a 53 percent greater chance of being admitted.
3. One obvious consequence of assigning such a high priority to admitting recruited athletes was that they entered these colleges and universities with considerably lower SAT scores than their classmates.
4. Despite their lower SATs, athletes who attended the selective schools included in this study, along with their classmates who participated in other time-intensive extracurricular activities, graduated at very high rates. When examining grades (rank in class), an entirely different picture emerged. That is, academic standing of athletes, relative to that of their classmates, has deteriorated markedly in recent years.
5. Academic underperformance in college has roots in high school academic performance, in the priority assigned by athletes to academics, and in the "culture of sport."

Some coaches play academic games with their athletes' futures. Coaches seldom lose their jobs for low graduation rates; they are fired for failing to win. In the past, college presidents often turned deaf ears to outcries against coaches who recruited unprepared students or who cared about their athletes only as long as they were eligible to compete. What moral responsibilities do coaches owe their athletes?

If a coach promises an education to a recruit, should this educational opportunity be conditional on a student's esteem for the nonmoral values of effort, self-discipline, and hard work? Often, attaining a degree must include attending summer school and time beyond the four years of playing eligibility. Although college programs serve as training grounds for the few athletes making it into the professional leagues, guaranteeing this advancement in lieu of an education could be considered deceitful, with the percentages of college players who become professional athletes less than 5 percent in football, basketball, and baseball (Coakley 2001).

Athletes are responsible for their actions. Some recruits hear only what they want; others, with visions of professional sport grandeur, make only weak attempts to earn degrees, happily content to "major in eligibility" until they get chances to become professionals. Some athletes refuse to take advantage of tutorial help. A few willingly agree to have substitutes take entrance tests or course examinations. Some colleges hire individuals to walk athletes to class; often even this does not result in athletes taking advantage of their educational opportunities (see Box 6-2). Treating adult athletes like small children, however, fails to teach moral responsibility (see Box 6-3). Should coaches be expected to instruct their athletes in ethical conduct and to demonstrate such behavior themselves? What are some characteristics of ethical conduct relative to eligibility in intercollegiate athletics?

Academic abuses in intercollegiate sport pale in comparison with the rampant violations of recruiting rules, according to various media exposés. Prospective student–athletes who experience impermissible treatment may lose all respect for the

BOX 6-2

VALUING OR DEVALUING EDUCATION

Universities pride themselves on providing academic support programs for their student athletes, often at a cost in the hundreds of thousands of dollars. Plush facilities equipped with the latest technology, paid tutors, and advisers committed to assisting athletes in making progress toward their degrees are among the noteworthy aspects of this service to athletes. Advocates heap praise upon institutions that acknowledge that they owe this academic support to athletes because of the time athletes must spend on the field or court, especially because many recruited athletes are admitted without having met the academic standards for admission. Critics argue that this is yet another illustration of preferential treatment of pampered athletes. These critics also express displeasure that these academic support programs often lapse into violations of intercollegiate athletic association regulations and frequently erode the academic integrity of their institutions. For example, Clem Haskins controlled a tutoring program for his basketball players at the University of Minnesota that was rife with abuses. A person involved with the academic support program at the University of Tennessee alleged numerous improprieties leading to a faculty investigation. In an attempt to ameliorate the criticisms, many universities have moved their programs under faculty control to help ensure that athletes receive only appropriate academic assistance.

integrity of eligibility rules. Most adolescent sport stars know that coaches who offer them financial inducements to sign letters of intent, do so in violation of NCAA rules. Also, by accepting money, sport clothing and equipment, cars, and other financial benefits, athletes become culpable along with these coaches. Individuals representing the sport interests of a college, according to NCAA rules, cannot give gifts or promise money to lure

BOX 6-3

AN EDUCATIONAL FOCUS
FOR INTERCOLLEGIATE ATHLETICS

Research (Byers & Hammer 1995; Duderstadt 2000; Gibson 1993; Sack and Staurowsky 1998; Shulman and Bowen 2001; Sperber 2000; Telander 1995; Thelin 1996) gives rather conclusive proof that if big-time collegiate sport is only about making money, abuses will occur. If coaches' jobs depend on winning, they will be sorely tempted to push all the rules to the limit and maybe beyond. Athletic directors could readily reduce and maybe eliminated violations of eligibility rules driven by a compulsion to win, if they wanted these halted. Possible steps that could be taken to eradicate these violations are quite simple.

1. Make an explicit, public statement about the educational purposes of athletics in higher education.
2. Give a clear pronouncement about the roles and responsibilities of college students who also are athletes.
3. Hire only coaches who have demonstrated commitment to the first two statements.

4. Make it abundantly clear in coaches' contracts that any deviations from the letter and the spirit of the rules provide grounds for contract termination.
5. Make sure all sport managers model the stated rules.
6. Delete any mention of won–lost records in contracts.
7. Set evaluation standards for coaches based on an educational model; for example, athletes' graduation rates and progress toward degrees are most highly valued.
8. Take these action steps to league members; if they cannot or will not accept them for everyone, find a new league with which to affiliate.
9. Encourage and expect athletes to take advantage of their grants-in-aid to grow intellectually; base their continued participation upon this.
10. Withhold grants-in-aid for future athletes until current and previous athletes have earned their degrees.

athletes to their favorite institutions. Athletes become ineligible upon receipt of any of these monetary items, even though frequently these violations are not disclosed until years later, as illustrated by Marcus Camby, professional basketball star, who admitted receiving such benefits while a college athlete at the University of Massachusetts.

Alleged and actual recruiting violations have occurred in luring international athletes to the United States. Sometimes these recruits are elite athletes in their countries who come to a college for the singular purpose of helping win games. For example, Tanya Harding, an outstanding pitcher from Australia, enrolled at UCLA in the spring of 1995 just in time to lead her new softball team to a NCAA championship. Several men's teams, especially in

soccer, track, and tennis, are comprised of more international students than native-born athletes. Some have suggested that many of these international athletes follow a similar pathway to that taken by Tanya, who returned home without a degree soon after accepting the championship trophy. A few of these international athletes view intercollegiate sports as the optimal point of entry into the professional leagues and join their teammates in this singular focus.

Many times payments from coaches, fans, and sport agents to athletes continue after enrollment in a college. Several universities have been given NCAA sanctions for this and other violations. Because NCAA rules restrict financial aid to tuition, fees, and room and board, athletes who receive anything beyond this are in violation of eligibility rules. Some athletes in the major football conferences commonly receive benefits that violate NCAA rules. For example, at many NCAA Division I institutions, athletes have been given money, use of cars, clothing, food, and benefits to family members and friends, such as jobs, homes, and college scholarships, by athletic supporters. Such action was one reason why Southern Methodist University received the "death penalty" from the NCAA.

In trying to equalize competition, the NCAA, the National Association of Intercollegiate Athletics (NAIA), and the National Junior College Athletic Association (NJCAA) specify permissible recruiting practices in minute detail. The legalese used in their policy manuals reflects these organizations' intent to project an image of integrity, although the language used in these manuals to specifically prohibit certain actions may actually contribute to widespread circumventions of the rules.

Some coaches emphasize that no college can fully comply with the myriad eligibility rules because many are too nebulous. The fact that the NCAA primarily sanctions those institutions that repeatedly and flagrantly violate the rules, especially those rules that prohibit giving athletes financial inducements while they are being recruited, reinforces this perception. Thus many coaches and sport managers rationalize that if their actions and institutions are not penalized for noncompliance, then they are by default honest, just, and fair.

Do colleges and universities exist to provide education or to sponsor sport entertainment? In reality, many institutions of higher education in this country enjoy greater status and prestige for their victorious sport teams than for the numbers of athletes who graduate, or for their Nobel Prize laureates or Rhodes scholars. Although academic achievement may not have concerned students who initiated intercollegiate sport, the undermining of educational integrity has always distressed faculties.

The NCAA, NAIA, and NJCAA cannot legislate morality. Rather, these organizations enforce eligibility rules to facilitate equitable competitive opportunities among their member institutions. Small enforcement staffs attempting to investigate compliance by hundreds of coaches, thousands of athletes, and millions of fans can never ensure that everyone plays by the rules. Seldom does an institution self-report a violation and accept the associated penalty. Although many think that if institutions have not been penalized for rule violations they must be in compliance, there remains a good chance that they simply have not been caught.

In a cost-benefit analysis, some coaches may weigh the anticipated results of enticing (through rule-violating actions) the best blue-chip athletes to their institutions against the small likelihood of getting caught and the severity of the possible penalties. The benefits may exceed the low risk of being caught and penalized, such as when a team wins a national championship with illegally recruited players. Many coaches claim that every coach violates some of the rules, as if to justify their similar immoral actions. This rationale of "everyone else does it" in the minds of some seems to justify unethical actions.

Still, ethical issues relative to academic eligibility and recruitment in intercollegiate sport remain (see Box 6-4). If eligibility rules exist to help ensure that athletes have the opportunity to enroll in classes, work toward meaningful degrees, and seek educational attainment, what steps can be taken to reduce eligibility infractions within the explicit rules as well as through the spirit of the rules? If student athletes know that financial inducements are explicitly against the rules, should they lose eligibility to play if they accept these benefits? Because most violations of rules result in sanctions against the entire team and future teams not involved in the violation, what moral issues arise when these teams lose their eligibility for conference and bowl games? If coaches, boosters, and others are involved in eligibility violations both within the explicit rules and the spirit of the rules, what steps can be taken to reduce these types of infractions? And, because many confuse the spirit of eligibility rules with an argument about competition itself ("because everyone else violates eligibility rules, we must too in order to remain competitive"), is anyone morally or ethically bound to follow the rules?

BOX 6-4

QUESTIONS ABOUT ETHICS IN ELIGIBILITY

- Is it ethical to pay an amateur athlete to play a sport? If yes, under what circumstances?
- Why were eligibility rules initially standardized?
- Is it honest to play a nonstudent in an intercollegiate competition?
- When, if ever, does trying to win by any method possible become dishonest?
- Can morality be legislated through rules?
- Does dishonest, unjust, and irresponsible behavior necessitate the establishment of specific rules and regulations governing eligibility? Do such rules and regulations make people honest, just, and responsible?
- Did faculty mandate eligibility regulations concerning academic issues because students were acting unethically?
- Why do some coaches use financial inducements to recruit players?
- Why do some coaches allow and even encourage their athletes to emphasize sport more than earning diplomas or college degrees?
- Are athletes at all levels responsible for making moral decisions?
- Is the lowering of admissions standards for athletes ethical?
- When, if ever, should an athlete's grade be changed to permit eligibility to play?
- Can an interscholastic sport governing organization legislate morality in its competitions?
- Can an intercollegiate sport governing organization legislate morality in sport?
- Why do eligibility regulations in youth sport exist?
- Why do eligibility regulations in interscholastic sport exist?
- Why do eligibility regulations in intercollegiate sport exist?
- Why do eligibility regulations in Olympic sport exist?

- Do eligibility rules result in more honest or dishonest behavior by coaches and athletes?
- Are more and more eligibility rules necessary to prevent coaches, athletes, and sport managers from using every imaginable tactic to try to win? Why or why not?
- Should there be a moral basis for the conduct of sport competitions at all levels? If so, what should it be? Does it vary by level of sport?
- What role, if any, should the media play in promoting a moral basis for the conduct of sport competitions?
- Is it ethical for a college to receive huge revenues and yet not give spending money to the athletes who help earn these revenues?
- What is the ethical difference, if any, between receiving money for agreeing to attend a particular college or university and receiving money for point-shaving?
- What is the moral justification for holding a child back a year in school to gain an advantage in sport?
- Was the IOC dishonest in not declaring athletes ineligible when they received money while claiming to be amateurs?
- Is it ethical for coaches to use athletes for personal gain?
- Is it ethical for parents to use their children for personal gain?
- What are athletes really being told about moral values when they observe adults circumventing eligibility regulations?
- Does the absence of a rule and penalty prohibiting a particular action make that action moral?
- What are the determining factors in making an action moral?
- Is winning a nonmoral value? Why or why not?

Olympic Sport

Eligibility for athletes in the Olympic Games illustrates ethical dilemmas in elite sport. In 1896, the first Olympians in the modern era had to verify their amateur status before they were allowed to compete. Consistent with the British Amateur Sport Ideal as propagated by Baron Pierre de Coubertin, the founder of the Olympic Games, only gentlemen athletes, who played for the love of sport, were eligible. However, it should be noted that while the Olympic Games espoused amateurism, these competitions were also classist and misogynistic for many years.

The International Olympic Committee (IOC), which governs this event, initially prohibited athletes from receiving remuneration and endorsed the ideal that true sportsmen play sport for the game's sake, not for financial gain, thus excluding many athletes from lower socioeconomic levels. However, when athletes received money or other benefits in violation of the amateur rules, the IOC seemed unwilling or unable to enforce its eligibility regulations.

Some national governments, and especially those in the former Soviet and Eastern Bloc, in seeking to promote their ideologies, trained, sponsored, and rewarded Olympic athletes. Under-the-table payments used for training and competitive expenses became commonplace. Some athletes trained for their sports full-time while serving in their nation's military forces. Next came appearance fees as event organizers paid the best athletes to participate in their international competitions. Overt commercialization, such as skiers displaying corporate trademarks on their uniforms or track athletes wearing their sponsors' shoes around their necks on the victory stand, abounded in the 1980s but began much earlier. It appeared that the pursuit of gold medals swept aside ethical concerns about whether athletes met the eligibility regulations for participation.

The Olympic Games have survived numerous barrages directed against their eligibility regulations. Supposedly competitions between amateurs, the Olympic Games have not hosted such idealized events for decades, if ever. While espousing friendship among nations, the Olympic Games grew into opportunities for the promotion of national ideologies. To do so effectively, athletes in many nations were expected to prove their superiority. As a result, the top athletes received funding, preferential treatment, and specialized training to ensure that their national ideology won acclaim. Violations of eligibility regulations, prohibiting athletes from receiving financial rewards for their prowess, continued.

Another issue facing the Olympics is that of determining the eligibility of athletes relative to their nationality. That is, some athletes choose to leave their native-born countries and become nationalized citizens in another country primarily for athletic reasons. Sometimes change enables an athlete to earn a place on his or her country's Olympic team, and at other times an athlete's elite status may result in preferential treatment in obtaining citizenship in another country. The controversy regarding Zola Budd in 1984 was one notable example.

Today, extensive rules unique to each sport specify the monies that Olympic athletes may receive while maintaining their eligibility. For example, Jackie Joyner–Kersee, Olympic gold medalist in track, grossed more than $750,000 in endorsements and stipends in 1992 while being named Amateur Sportswoman of the Year by the Women's Sports Foundation. Most men's and women's basketball Olympians are professionals. Only a few of the Olympic competitors remain amateur athletes.

Sport mirrors society. Values viewed as important in society are transferred into sport settings as highly-regarded outcomes. Rules governing eligibility in sport, regardless of the level, will be followed only if participants respect moral principles. Violations occur because coaches, players, parents, and sport managers esteem the nonmoral value of winning more highly than playing honestly, justly, and responsibly. Eligibility regulations governing youth, school, college, and Olympic sport will be disregarded or violated indiscriminately unless those subject to these rules value them. People who lie, cheat, and deceive to gain competitive advantages do so because they value honesty, justice, responsibility, and beneficence less.

What can lead to an increase in the value of sport rules that govern eligibility? Winning must return to a less dominant place in sport. Traditionally, sportsmanship characterized intercollegiate sport despite occasional scandals, such as those associated with point-shaving and giving unearned grades. Most everyone expected student–athletes to reflect a balance between academics and sports; few recruiting rules existed. Seldom were inducements offered, and athletes usually graduated. Once television revenues, status, and other benefits went to the victorious, some athletes and coaches violated rules to help win. Many argue that NCAA Division III (nonscholarship programs), NAIA, NJCAA, and colleges with a religious mission and focus have kept winning in perspective. Since the financial bonanzas associated with "big-time" sport are not present in most of these institutions, the need to violate eligibility rules to remain highly competitive does not exist. Such is not the case; increasingly athletes in all levels of sport from youth through the Olympics view winning as most important (Beller and Stoll 1995). Many value the nonmoral value of winning as more important than the values of honesty and justice or playing by the spirit of the rules.

ELIGIBILITY AND MORAL REASONING

In order to equalize competition, the essence of sport, eligibility rules govern who can play. At various levels of sport, every athlete desires to compete against opponents who have met the same criteria for playing. Thus eligibility rules govern the age, size, residence, affiliation, academic status, benefits received, and similar qualifications of opponents. Playing fairly, justly, and honestly demands that everyone respects and follows these rules. It also necessitates not cheating or deceiving others.

Athletes are responsible for their on-the-court performances as well as their moral reasoning at all times.

If winning, success, and money become more important than adhering to eligibility rules, then mistreating others to get these nonmoral rewards becomes paramount. Any person who values winning may yield to the temptation of violating ethical principles.

Moral development is learned. Through education and living in a principled environment with honorable role models, individuals learn how to make good decisions. The structure of competitive sport does not always support moral development. For example, when children play on their own, they consider cultural variations and differences in ability without any eligibility rules. Rarely do they argue about who can play. Children understand the meaning of fun. In contrast, when adults make decisions for children, adolescents, and young adults in sports, does this negatively influence how these young people grow morally?

Research (Beller and Stoll 1992, 1995; Beller, Stoll, Burwell, and Cole 1996; Krause and Priest 1993) with more than 35,000 sport participants, from ninth-graders through university students, found that the longer individuals participate in sport, the more morally calloused they become; that is, the less they respect their opponents and teammates or take into account honesty, justice, and the letter and spirit of the rules. Moral callousness is the antithesis of moral reasoning, which challenges individuals to take others' perspectives into consideration when making decisions. The reality of highly-competitive sport today, does not always teach and reinforce the values of responsibility, honesty, fairness, or beneficence.

Young people seldom have to take responsibility for decisions in highly organized sports because adults make all the moral and competitive judgments. When adults make decisions for children, adolescents, and young adults in sports, it negatively influences how these young people grow morally and may stunt the development of their moral reasoning processes. This probably occurs as a direct result of the structure of sport programs at all levels. As noted earlier, moral reasoning is learned. Through education and living in a principled environment with honorable role models, individuals learn how to make good decisions. Unfortunately, at times the structure of competitive sport does not support moral reasoning and, therefore, some athletes do not learn to make good, sound, consistent moral decisions.

Relative to interscholastic and intercollegiate sports, several principles should be considered if moral values are important outcomes of these programs. Should school administrators and coaches make attempts to commercialize interscholastic sport and to thwart violations of eligibility rules? Should college presidents, faculties, and athletic administrators control the existing emphasis on entertainment sports, which often leads to the playing of athletes who are quasi-students? Should educational leaders enforce a defensible standard regarding the academic performance for athletes? Should interscholastic and intercollegiate sport programs increase student involvement in the decision-making process to allow them to mature in their ability to reason morally?

ETHICAL DILEMMAS REGARDING ELIGIBILITY

Issues regarding eligibility challenge individuals involved at all levels of sport. Each person can choose whether to adhere to or disregard the principles of honesty, justice, responsibility, and beneficence. When addressing ethical issues, individuals should begin by establishing the underlying value and then find solutions by determining how chosen actions will affect them and others; every person's actions, it is hoped, will demonstrate consistency and impartiality. Box 6-5 presents challenges relative to moral values and eligibility. Select alternatives from the list on the right side of the box, or suggest others. In responding to these questions, note that the ethical principles in Box 6-6 may guide moral reasoning.

Is moral reasoning a priority in society and in sport? If so, then athletes must be educated about moral responsibility, honesty, justice, and beneficence. Unless those involved with sport value morality, eligibility problems will worsen. Intervention programs that teach athletes how to reason morally are needed because many individuals involved with sport programs do not practice moral reasoning. One teaching method could be discussing sport situations and analyzing how and why athletes would choose to act in certain ways. Through an open forum among teammates assisted by a person who asks probing questions, athletes could begin to question whether their values are being followed or violated in sport. If the latter is found to be the case, then, perhaps change will occur. It takes courage to speak out about one's values and to stand behind them.

In contests between two teams or individuals who previously agreed to conform to established eligibility regulations, when either opponent violates the rules, the equity of the competition is destroyed. Congruency and consistency with the purpose and conditions of sport competitions must exist if fairness counts. Instead of many of the claimed values of sport, lying and other immoral behaviors

BOX 6-5

ETHICAL DILEMMAS: YOU DECIDE

Dilemmas

1. Does the absence of prohibitive rules governing eligibility give moral license to do anything (that is, no rule, no harm)?

2. Are eligibility rules inherently honest?

3. What makes an action such as violating an eligibility rule dishonest?

4. Should youth, scholastic, collegiate, or Olympic athletes who receive money from fans lose their eligibility to compete?

Possible Responses

a) Actions should be based on personal moral values, not rules.

b) This absence of rules gives license to do whatever it takes to win.

c) Adhering to the spirit of the rules and playing in a morally responsible manner should occur regardless of the rules.

a) The existence of a rule does not necessarily make it honest. Civil disobedience calls for violating a rule if it is unjust.

b) Because a rule exists, it is honest and just.

c) Honesty requires compliance only with the letter of the law, not necessarily with the spirit of the law.

d) If a rule exists and everyone agrees to play by that rule, then everyone is obligated to follow it. If anyone disagrees, that person can refuse to play or initiate a movement to get the rule changed.

a) Dishonesty exists only if punishment or penalties result.

b) A fraudulent or dishonest act is immoral, regardless of whether it is penalized.

c) Each situation and the associated circumstances determine independently whether an action is honest or dishonest.

d) Dishonesty is wrong only if a person believes in the value of honesty.

a) Yes, receiving money violates eligibility rules for amateurs.

b) No, rules that prohibit receiving money discriminate against the economically disadvantaged.

c) No, these athletes have earned whatever money they receive on the basis of their athletic achievements.

d) It depends on why the money was accepted; if it is used to fly home to visit a sick parent, it is permissible, but using the money to buy a CD player is not acceptable.

e) Yes, it is immoral to receive money as an amateur athlete.

f) No, athletes are entertainers and should be paid.

g) Yes, these athletes agreed to follow the rules; but, the rules need to be changed.

ETHICAL DILEMMAS: YOU DECIDE—cont'd

Dilemmas

5. Is it ethical to require athletes to achieve at a specified academic level before they are allowed to compete?

6. Are coaches acting honestly when they get athletes promoted or get them unearned passing grades in order to maintain eligibility?

Possible Responses

a) Yes, competition is a privilege, not a right.
b) Yes, schools and colleges exist for the purpose of education, not athletics.
c) No, academic standards discriminate against the academically disadvantaged.
d) No, the system is basically immoral; sport competition remains a right of every student.

a) Yes, athletes deserve preferential treatment because of their contributions to victories, revenues, and institutional prestige.
b) No, athletes should be held accountable for their academic progress.
c) The emphasis on winning has forced coaches to act in this way. It is dishonest only if the athlete does not want this or if the coach is penalized.
d) No, lying or cheating is never morally acceptable.

BOX 6-6

ETHICAL PRINCIPLES FOR RESOLVING ELIGIBILITY ISSUES

1. Keep winning in perspective.
2. Educate coaches, athletes, and sport managers about the basic moral values of honesty, justice, responsibility, and beneficence.
3. Inform athletes, parents, coaches, and sport managers about the importance of the rules and the moral spirit of the rules.
4. Develop and publicize codes of ethical conduct for coaches, parents, athletes, and sport managers and require adherence to them.
5. Penalize consistently every dishonest action by an athlete, a coach, or a sport manager who previously has been educated about moral decision making.
6. Question and change sports rules and policies that are unjust, precipitate dishonest actions, or are irresponsible.
7. Guarantee every athlete an opportunity to get an education and help ensure this with proper advising, tutorial assistance, adequate time to complete academic work, financial aid, and career counseling.
8. Hire and retain coaches on the basis of factors other than their won–lost records.
9. Reward coaches who help their athletes achieve academically.
10. Articulate specific eligibility rules for all levels of sport competition and enforce them consistently and impartially.
11. Recognize and reward athletes, coaches, and sport managers who teach and practice the moral values of honesty, justice, responsibility, and beneficence.

persist to enhance the chance of winning. When a potentially good sport contest is perverted through unethical actions, such as the violation of eligibility rules, the real losers are the athletes.

Ethical conduct is critical to eligibility in sport at all levels. The issues discussed in this chapter can be resolved through moral education, legislation, enforcement, and commitment to playing the game by the letter and the spirit of the rules, not for winning alone.

SUMMARY

Eligibility concerns pervade every level of competitive sport. Typically, eligibility regulations have been violated in order to gain a competitive advantage. Many of these violations have been associated with age, weight, and residency requirements, whereas a large percentage have dealt with aca-

demic abuse. The giving of unearned grades, transcript tampering, and questionable educational progress toward diplomas and degrees head this list. That is, to keep athletes eligible, coaches, teachers, tutors, athletic administrators, and others have undermined the academic integrity of their institutions.

Recruiting continues to be a major area of abuse. Youth, adolescents, and young adults have been lured by and then given monetary and other benefits in direct violation of the eligibility rules of governing associations. These impressionable athletes have learned, thereby, that honesty, trust, and fairness are not valued, and that rules can be blatantly ignored. Amateurism in the Olympics has been cast aside as unenforceable and outdated. Seemingly, with entertainment valued more highly than education in many schools and colleges, the ideals of sport at these levels appear headed in a similar downward spiral.

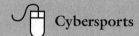 Cybersports

www.ncaa.org

The National Collegiate Athletic Association develops and enforces strict eligibility rules for its athletes to ensure that its amateur code is upheld.

infosports.net/index.html

This site provides information about youth sports opportunities to parents, coaches, and athletes.

www.littleleague.org

Little League Baseball publishes eligibility standards for athletes who play on teams affiliated

with the League in order to ensure equitable competitive opportunities.

www.naia.org/_.htm

The National Association of Intercollegiate Athletics governs intercollegiate competition for more than 300 small colleges in 13 different sports for women and men.

www.njcaa.org

The National Junior College Athletic Association governs the eligibility of the athletes in two-year institutions who play in its competitions.

ISSUES AND DILEMMAS

CASE 6-1

Jerry began wrestling at age eight and quickly developed into a fine athlete in this sport. Wrestling over the years at 55, 64, 70, and 77 pounds, he won or placed high in several local and even state competitions. When he was 11, he began to gain weight, moving up one weight classification and competing against older boys. For several months thereafter, Jerry failed to do well in competitions, usually losing in his first-round matches.

Even though Jerry's weight was average for his age, Coach Miller suggested that he try to lose some weight so that he might wrestle at his previous weight classification of 77 pounds, instead of at 85 pounds. Coach Miller recommended a strict diet with no meats or sweets and daily 2-mile runs in a rubber suit.

Because Jerry loved to wrestle and always tried to do what Coach Miller asked, he strictly followed this training program. Before his next match, Jerry was down to 79, so he still had to wrestle at 85 pounds. Not only did he lose again, but he felt weak during the match.

In the days before the next wrestling event, Jerry ate very little and exercised harder. He believed that all this was worth the effort when he tipped the scales at 77 pounds. At this lower weight classification, Jerry won several matches before losing in the finals.

This near-victory helped motivate Jerry to adhere strictly to his diet and jogging regimen. Although Jerry appeared tired and lethargic, Coach Miller praised his self-discipline and encouraged him to keep his weight at 77 so he could achieve success, which Jerry did.

1. Is Coach Miller violating any ethical principles by instructing Jerry to wrestle at a weight below that at which he would naturally compete? If so, what principles?
2. Is the motivation to succeed influencing Jerry to violate any ethical principles? If so, what principles?
3. Is Jerry cheating by wrestling at an unnatural weight (that is, a more mature athlete taking advantage of a less mature athlete)? Why or why not?
4. How are Coach Miller and Jerry treating the eligibility rule governing weight classifications to equalize competition?
5. What moral lesson is Coach Miller teaching Jerry?

◆ ◆ ◆

CASE 6-2

Lynn, a high school student, has developed a close friendship with James, who is a great athlete, probably one of the best in the history of the school. Besides being a great athlete, James is a good student. If it were not for athletics, James would probably be a straight-A student. But because of the demands of practices, games, and related sport activities, James is doing only above-average work in most classes, except in one, Algebra II, which is causing problems. James's lifelong dream has been to go to college, but this will require better grades in Algebra II. In fact, the final grade must be a C for James to meet the NCAA eligibility requirements. Because the majority of the grade in Algebra II comes from the final exam, if James can make a high grade, a C is a possibility.

Lynn and James stop by the principal's office to ask a question but find no one there, even though the door is unlocked. James sees the final exam for Algebra II lying on the secretary's desk awaiting duplication. James picks it up, walks over to the copy machine, and makes a copy. Lynn says nothing as James leaves with the exam.

1. In this situation, considering the opportunity for a grant-in-aid and a college education, would it be acceptable for James to take the exam?
2. What should Lynn do? (Lynn knows that James must pass this test to go to college. There is no way that James could afford to go any other way than on an athletic grant-in-aid. This may be James's only chance.)
3. If Lynn says nothing, is Lynn being dishonest?
4. Does a friendship take precedence over a moral principle? Does Lynn's loyalty to James come before the rule about honesty?
5. Should Lynn ask James to return the exam?

◆ ◆ ◆

CASE 6-3

Mr. McLendon coaches at Albemarle University, an NCAA member institution. The NCAA requires that he take an examination certifying that he knows and understands the rules, which he has done. One day Marty, who comes from a poor family, stops by his office to talk about strategy for the next game. Marty obviously has a terrible cold. Coach McLendon notices that Marty's coat is too thin for the weather conditions. Marty is not wearing boots. Coach McLendon asks about the coat and boots. Marty replies that he has no money for a better coat or boots. Later that afternoon, weather conditions worsen. On the way home from his office, Coach McLendon passes Marty, who is walking and dripping wet from the sleet. According to NCAA rules, Coach McLendon is not allowed to give Marty a ride or any extra benefits. After picking Marty up, Coach McLendon takes him to a store, where the coach purchases a warm coat and a pair of boots for Marty.

1. Did Coach McLendon knowingly violate a rule?
2. Was Coach McLendon cheating by buying Marty a warm coat and boots?
3. Is it acceptable in this case to violate a rule? Why or why not?
4. If this is an exception, what about the rule? Should the rule be kept or honored if it could violate basic human decency?
5. If you learn about this situation, are you honor-bound to report Coach McLendon's actions to the the athletic director or NCAA?

◆ ◆ ◆

CASE 6-4

After winning several cross-country races and two consecutive NCAA titles, Joan dropped out of college to train for the 2004 Athens Olympic Games. As the United States record holder in the 10,000 meters, she felt confident that concentrated training would help her achieve her life-long dream of winning a gold medal.

Because her parents were unable to help her financially and her training program left time only for a part-time job, Joan depended on her sport successes for money to pay the bills. Her plan worked during the early part of the European track season, until she was injured. Without the guaranteed appearance money, Joan quickly got into a financial bind.

At this time, a sport agent, Edgar Rogers, contacted Joan. He offered her $10,000 to appear in a commercial promoting several types of wine. The contract specified that this television commercial would not appear until after the 2004 Olympic Games because advertisement of alcoholic beverages by athletes would violate the eligibility rules of the International Amateur Athletic Federation (governing organization for track and field). Joan could, however, accept the fee "under the table" immediately.

1. What ethical principle regarding eligibility, if any, would Joan violate if she appeared in the wine commercial?
2. What ethical principle regarding eligibility, if any, would Joan violate if she accepted the fee for doing the commercial?
3. Under what circumstances, if any, would it be ethical for Joan to accept the fee for doing the commercial?

4. Is an eligibility rule unfair and unjust if it prevents an athlete from receiving money to pay the bills for living expenses while training?

5. Does the ultimate objective of winning a gold medal justify breaking an eligibility rule?

◆ ◆ ◆

CASE 6-5

Marlene, the 25-point per game, three-time All-American for South-eastern University (SU), was in serious academic difficulty. Facing final exams in her summer school courses, she knew there was no hope of making the two Bs she needed to remain eligible for her senior year. She realized that, as in most other courses she had taken as a speech communication major, she had put forth little effort. Even though she had been a special admit at SU, she had thus far managed to make minimal progress toward her degree and to achieve the required grade-point average (GPA). But, she had to have Bs in these two courses in her major, or she could not play her senior year.

Coach Harris, who was anticipating his first conference title and NCAA tournament bid, was really upset when he learned that if Marlene was not eligible, it would probably put these two dreams in serious jeopardy. How could she, he asked himself, seemingly have ruined everything? After all, he had managed to get her admitted even though her high school GPA and SAT scores had been significantly below SU's standards. Through a friend, he had helped Marlene's mother get a higher-paying job and qualify for a new home loan. Three times Coach Harris had convinced faculty members to give Marlene special exams or assignments in order to help her raise her grades and stay eligible.

Knowing that no one in the Department of Speech Communication would help Marlene to raise her summer grades after they were recorded, Coach Harris decided to talk with Charlie Stafford, Dean of the College of Arts and Sciences. Since Dean Stafford's daughter was a member of the basketball team, Coach Harris thought that maybe he could get Marlene's grades changed by the Dean.

1. Was it ethical for Coach Harris to get Marlene admitted to SU even though she did not meet the minimal academic standards? Why or why not?

2. Was it ethical for Coach Harris's friend to help Marlene's mother with the new job and home loan? Why or why not?

3. Was it ethical for Coach Harris to get professors to provide special exams or assignments in order to help Marlene maintain her eligibility? Why or why not?

4. Was it ethical for Coach Harris to ask Dean Stafford to change Marlene's grades? Why or why not?
5. What ethical values, if any, had Marlene violated?

◆ ◆ ◆

CASE 6-6

When most people think about interscholastic sports, they assume that these teams are comprised of boys and girls who live in the surrounding school district. Historically, high school coaches could be great coaches but never have truly outstanding athletes attend their schools. In today's world of magnet schools, independent or private schools, charter schools, and summer camps, adolescents are seldom restricted to the local school. Recruiting abounds. Coaches of summer teams influence impressionable adolescents to affiliate with the highest bidder, which could be with a cross-town school, with a team sponsored by a shoe company, or with a coach who can provide national exposure in the media.

1. What factors have contributed to the recruiting of high school–age athletes?
2. What athletic benefits can or should an interscholastic athlete receive?
3. What rules govern the recruiting of high school–age athletes?
4. What ethical values should govern the eligibility rules in interscholastic sports?

◆ ◆ ◆

CASE 6-7

In the wake of media exposés about the academic woes of many college athletes, the NCAA, in recent years, has significantly tightened its academic eligibility rules. The NCAA mandates completion of 13 core courses and a sliding scale of grade-point average (GPA) and SAT/ACT scores in order to qualify through its Clearinghouse for a college grant-in-aid. Once enrolled, a student–athlete must make progress toward a degree and maintain a minimal GPA. Although these higher academic standards have been praised by many, concerns have been raised that these new requirements have disproportionately affected minorities. Recent data have verified that a higher percentage of African American youths have failed to qualify for grants-in-aid or have lost their grants because of academic problems.

1. What are the ethical arguments for raising academic standards regardless of who might be affected?

2. What are the ethical arguments against raising academic standards if they discriminate against a minority group?

3. Assuming that the NCAA academic rules are discriminatory, what is the moral basis for changing this situation?

♦ ♦ ♦

CASE 6-8

Coach Allen had achieved a winning record at Northern High School (NHS), but he had never been able to capture the state 5-A football title. But, when he heard about Nathan Smith's exploits at Central Junior High School, and then observed his bursts through the line and his ability to drag would-be tacklers for yards, Coach Allen was convinced that Nathan could help him attain this elusive championship. This would occur, however, only if he could arrange for Nathan to attend NHS. With the help of some NHS boosters, Coach Allen was able to arrange for Nathan's parents to receive higher-paying jobs and for the family to move into a rent-free apartment located in the NHS district. With the promise of assistance with his academic work and admission into a NCAA Division I university if he had a successful high school career, Nathan was eager to follow whatever guidance Coach Allen provided.

For three straight years, Coach Allen, with Nathan as his team's star, won the state 5-A football title. By the end of his senior year, Nathan had set numerous records including those for yardage gained running and points scored. Nathan was named a High School All-American for two years in a row; many considered him the best high school athlete in the nation. Since all the top universities recruited him so relentlessly, Nathan agreed to let his coach deal with all these coaches. At the recommendation of his coach, and because he had enjoyed his campus visit, Nathan signed with a team that had been ranked in the top five consistently during the past decade. Nathan was especially excited when he learned that Coach Allen would be joining him at the university as the running backs' coach. Only later did he learn that Coach Allen was hired in return for getting Nathan to sign a letter of intent and enroll in the same university. This did not bother Nathan, however, because he was confident that Coach Allen would continue to take care of him relative to providing spending money and getting him whatever help he needed with his academic work.

1. What moral principles, if any, did Coach Allen violate in getting Nathan to attend NHS?

2. What moral principles, if any, did Coach Allen violate in negotiating a package deal of a college coaching position for

himself in exchange for ensuring that Nathan attend the same institution?

3. What moral principles, if any, did Coach Allen violate in "taking care of" Nathan while in high school and potentially in college relative to extra benefits?

4. What are the moral obligations, if any, that Coach Allen owes his athletes and his school?

5. What are the moral obligations, if any, that Nathan owes his coach and his teammates?

6. What eligibility rules may have been violated in this situation and why?

REFERENCES

Beller, J. M., and S. K. Stoll. 1992. A moral reasoning intervention program for student–athletes. *Academic Athletic Journal* (spring): 43–57.

———. 1995. Moral reasoning of high school student–athletes and general students: An empirical study versus personal testimony. *Pediatric Exercise Science* 7(4):352–63.

Beller, J. M., S. K. Stoll, B. Burwell, and J. Cole. 1996. The relationship of competition and a Christian liberal arts education on moral reasoning of college student athletes. *Research on Christian Higher Education* 3: 99–114.

Byers, W., and C. Hammer. 1995. *Unsportsmanlike conduct: Exploiting college athletes*. Ann Arbor: University of Michigan Press.

Coakley, J. J. 2001. *Sport in society: Issues and controversies*. 7th ed. Boston: McGraw-Hill.

Duderstadt, J. J. 2000. *Intercollegiate athletics and the American university—A university president's perspective*. Ann Arbor: University of Michigan Press.

Eitzen, D. S., and G. H. Sage. 1996. *Sociology of North American sport*. 6th ed. New York: WMC/McGraw-Hill.

Gibson, J. H. 1993. *Performance vs. results: A critique of values in contemporary sport*. Albany: State University of New York Press.

Krause, J., and R. F. Priest. 1993. Sport values choices of United States Military Academy cadets—A longitudinal study of the class of 1993. Unpublished manuscript, Office of Institutional Research, United States Military Academy.

Sack, A. L., and E. J. Staurowsky. 1998. *College athletes for hire: The evolution and legacy of the NCAA's amateur myth*. Westport, CO: Praeger.

Shulman, J. L., and W. G. Bowen. 2001. *The game of life: College sports and educational values*. Princeton, NJ: Princeton University Press.

Smith, R. A., and R. Austin. 1993. History of amateurism in men's intercollegiate athletics: The continuance of a 19th-century anachronism in America. *Quest* 45: 430–47.

Sperber, M. 2000. *Beer and circus: How big-time college sports is crippling undergraduate education*. New York: Henry Holt and Company.

Telander, R. 1995. *The hundred yard lie: The corruption of college football and what we can do to stop it*. Champaign: University of Illinois Press.

Thelin, J. R. 1996. *Games colleges play: Scandal and reform in intercollegiate athletics*. Baltimore: Johns Hopkins University Press.

ADDITIONAL READINGS

Bailey, W. S., and T. D. Littleton. 1991. *Athletics and academe: An anatomy of abuses and a prescription for reform*. Phoenix: Oryx Press.

Farrell, C. S., 1995. Report blasts NCAA test score–based sports eligibility. *Black Issues in Higher Education* 11 (January 12): 26–27.

Kirk, S. V., W. D. Kirk, and Richard E. Lapchick, eds. 1993. *Student athletes: Shattering the myths & sharing the realities*. Alexandria, VA: American Counseling Association.

Lapchick, R. E., and Jeffrey R. Benedict, eds. 1995. *Sport in society: Equal opportunity or business as usual?* Thousand Oaks, CA: Sage Publications.

Leonard, W. M. II. 1998. *A sociological perspective of sport*. 5th ed. Boston: Allyn and Bacon.

Sport Elimination

- What are the ethical dilemmas associated with the dropout phenomenon in youth sport?
- What are the ethical dilemmas associated with the dropout phenomenon in interscholastic sport?
- Should youth who lack skills be cut from sport teams?
- How does the emphasis on winning contribute to sport dropout?
- How is sport dropout an ethical issue at the college level?
- What are the moral problems, if any, associated with dropout for elite and professional athletes who have finished their competitive careers?
- Why does physical burnout occur, and what are any moral principles violated in this process?
- What are the ethical issues surrounding psychological burnout?
- What causes social burnout?
- How can sport dropout and sport burnout be prevented, ameliorated, or eliminated?

Millions of people in this country annually participate in, watch, and read about sports. They spend billions of dollars on tickets, signature sports equipment, and team-licensed products and clothing. Few question the pervasiveness of sport in the United States; many individuals plan vacations, special family events, and social gatherings around the in-season sport.

Not everyone, however, is caught up in this sport mania. Millions of nonsport fans and nonparticipants never read newspaper sport sections and sport magazines, do not own a team sweatshirt or autographed racquet, and prefer a movie or video to any televised or live sporting event. Although much has been written about sports fans and participants, the invisible minority (or is it majority?) remains a perceived anomaly. These folks seem totally innocuous

to their self-imposed separation from the most popular coffee club, bar stool, or office topic of conversation—sport. Some of these individuals may have no interest in sport because they dropped out of sport long ago (see Box 7-1).

COMPETITIVE ATHLETICS ARE NOT FOR EVERYONE

In American society, it seems that professional athletes with their multimillion-dollar contracts, college athletes revelling in their championships and media exposure, and high school athletes with visions of achieving what these two groups have attained have become heroes (occasionally heroines) and role models. As the media creates and publicizes these stars, youngsters aspire to "be like Mike"

BOX 7-1

VALUES SOUGHT VERSUS VALUES REALIZED

Dropping out of sport is not inherently an ethical issue. It becomes an issue only if and when certain processes and practices violate the ultimate purpose of the activity. That is, if a sport organization's stated purpose is to provide positive, educational experiences, then the organization and the people involved in the organization are bound to follow the stated purpose or change it. Most educational organizations from youth sport through interscholastic sport to intercollegiate athletics are rooted in the assumption that sport supports the educational mission and goal of the institution. Historically, physical educators advocated sport for all. The traditional triangular approach included instructional physical education and sport for every student (of all ages). Not everyone, but those who wanted to compete participated in intramurals. The most highly skilled became the varsity athletes.

Because educational experiences in this country are predicated on the assumption of fairness, justice, and responsible action, youth sport through intercollegiate athletics are perceived to follow these same ethical tenets. Thus, if an athlete drops out of sport because of practices of the organization or the coach that violate the stated purpose, then dropping out becomes an ethical issue. When coaches are irresponsible in following the educational purposes of an organization or unfair in how they treat athletes, then athletes dropping out becomes an ethical issue. If the organization allows practices that are unfair and irresponsible to the stated mission and goal, then that organization is unethical in its practices.

Parents encourage their children to enter sport because it is believed that they will learn teamwork, fair play, cooperation, discipline, sportsmanship, and self-confidence, values applicable to later life. Youth who play sports want to have fun, participate in exciting games, build new friendships or nurture existing ones, and learn to play better. Dropout at this level occurs when children and adolescents leave sport because it stops being fun, fails to provide positive social interactions with friends, and becomes too stressful. Oftentimes, these negatives occur when adults organize and dominate youth sport programs and lose sight of the stated goals. Adults, thereby, violate their ethical responsibility.

Proponents of interscholastic sport state that these programs positively impact students academically, teach values, develop physical vigor, generate school spirit, and rally community support. Dissenters argue that sports in the schools subvert educational goals by using too many of the limited resources and distracting all students, especially athletes, from their academic work. Dissenters argue further that sports undermine rather than teach moral values. School students usually drop out of sport because they lose the intrinsic motivation to continue, are cut, quit because they do not get to play, want to emphasize academics, or find other interests.

The size of a college or university usually determines whether it sponsors "big-time" athletics or a smaller-scale program. The "big-time" sport programs are operated like entertainment businesses in which the stated purpose of football and men's basketball teams is to earn revenue. All of these programs, with varying degrees of success, claim to provide extracurricular competitive opportunities while stressing academic achievement. Other espoused goals include fitness training, value development, social and psychological enhancement, and preparation for life. Some of the comparatively few high school athletes who play intercollegiate sport drop out of college sport programs because of the lack of playing time, problems with coaches, conflicts between academics and athletics, inadequate time for social relationships or other interests, and excessive pressures to achieve success in sport.

Because professional sport exists to entertain fans, concern for values and individuals has become secondary to economic factors. Athletes as employees exist as expendable commodities given this profit orientation. When athletes drop out because of diminishing skills, recurrent injuries, contract disputes, and a lack of the desire to compete, dozens of others are eager to replace them. Frequently, this dropout is forced when former athletes are released or aspiring ones are cut.

(Michael Jordan, that is) even though the odds are against them. Less than 1 percent of interscholastic athletes will become professional athletes.

Sport elimination, unfortunately, often is an outcome of an overemphasis on competitive athletics. First, not everyone enjoys competition. While competition is valued by the successful, it is avoided by those who do not succeed, in sports and in other activities. The message here is that sports might retain a higher degree of participants if competition and defeating others were not the primary outcomes. Second, athletics, which pit individuals against others and are governed by highly structured rules, do not appeal to or meet the needs of millions. Rather, recreational sports and fitness activities are valued by many for sheer enjoyment, personal development, and social relationships. Millions prefer to avoid competitive sport because of negative experiences or because noncompetitive activity appeals to their interests and meets their needs.

Sport elimination too often occurs because of a loss of fun, a lack of success, and pressures to win. Thus, when faced with the choice between playing competitive athletics or not, the choice often is something else. This chapter begins with an examination of the ethical issues associated with the dropout phenomenon in youth, interscholastic, intercollegiate, and professional sport. Next, the factors that lead to sport burnout at these four levels are analyzed to determine whether any ethical standards are being breached. It is suggested that incidents of dropout and burnout in sport are associated with violations of ethical principles, that is, justice and responsibility, at various competitive levels.

FACTORS LEADING TO SPORT DROPOUT

Numerous factors contribute to the phenomenon of athletes choosing to drop out of sport. Many of these are listed in Box 7-2. **Sport dropout** refers to voluntary or involuntary separation from sport for one or a number of reasons, any of which may be positive or problematic.

Lack of Skills

Children's sports, especially competitive team sports, socialize youth about the cultural values of capitalistic America. Early in life, society encourages boys to engage in sports as a rite of passage and to take pride in their athletic abilities and achievements. Boys learn to link status on the playground with their physical prowess. To a lesser extent, preadolescent girls are reinforced for displaying physical skills but usually only in those sports society deems appropriate for them.

Youth Sport

Youngsters embarking on their first organized sport experience bring few preconceived notions to the field or court. They simply want to play. That is, sport to the young athlete provides the opportunity to enjoy playful experiences on a regular basis. The outcome is secondary to youthful activity. Children prefer playing on losing teams to sitting on the benches of winning teams. Youth believe that their sport participation will help develop their

Too often adults organize school sports programs to such a high degree that youth view sport as important only if they win.

BOX 7-2

REASONS ATHLETES DROP OUT OF SPORT

Youth Sport

- Lack of skills
- Limited opportunities to play
- Cannot play preferred position
- Team cuts
- Loss of enjoyment
- Lack of control over own games
- Lack of intrinsic motivation
- Changing interests
- Pressures from parents and coaches to win
- Lack of positive reinforcement

Interscholastic Sport

- Lack of skills
- Lack of opportunity due to not enough teams or no team in preferred sport
- Team cuts
- Loss of enjoyment
- Lack of intrinsic motivation
- Lack of time because of job
- Changing interests
- Pressures from parents and coaches to win

- Lack of positive reinforcement
- Conflicts with coaches

Intercollegiate Sport

- Lack of skills
- Lack of opportunity because teams are mainly comprised of recruited grant-in-aid athletes
- Loss of enjoyment
- Lack of intrinsic motivation
- Changing interests
- Academic demands
- Pressures from parents and coaches to win
- Conflicts with coaches

Professional Sport

- Released by team management
- Diminishing skills
- Loss of desire to play
- Recurrent injuries
- Pressures from coaches and the media
- Conflicts with coaches and management

---

skills, but they quickly learn that their more skillful teammates play the most in games and at their preferred positions while receiving more praise and attention than those not so skilled. This translates into fewer opportunities to play, a primary reason for dropping out.

The purpose of any youth sport program should be to foster development of physical skills through a positive social and moral environment. Ethical issues arise when the goals of a program are forgotten or displaced in the urgency to become successful as results become more important than performance. If only talented children play while the less talented warm the bench, coaches are openly stating that they think the purpose and goals of the program are wrong. They are demonstrating through their coaching that what is important is winning. That is,

coaches are violating the principles of the program, which they explicitly or implicitly gave their word to follow, and are behaving unethically by focusing on winning. Again, young athletes mostly want to play—because that is what is fun.

Citing lack of money, coaches, and space, many municipalities and leagues set limits on the number of children who can participate on their teams. Instead of making a place for every interested child, after a few days of tryouts coaches post the names of those girls and boys good enough to play. The devastation of being cut as a small child is probably not fully understood by adults. Parents can console and encourage their children to try again next year, but the feelings of inferiority, helplessness, and loss of confidence may be irreparable, especially if it happens multiple times. Some would argue, though, that failure is an important part of growing and living. Is the purpose of youth sport to initiate the development of professional athletes or to maximize participation? If it is the latter, should communities and sponsoring organizations provide all children opportunities to play their favorite sports?

Some children will diligently work on their skills and make the team when a year older and more mature. Others will forget the sport in which they were rejected and channel their energies and interests into different sports. The persistent ones, through whichever sports they are fortunate enough to get to play, will be more likely to lead healthy, active lives as children.

Unfortunately, though, many children will simply never again submit themselves to the humiliation and hurt of not getting selected for a team. These girls and boys may never again attempt to learn the skills and knowledge needed to achieve the healthful benefits of being active in sports. At an early age, they will join the ranks of those who just do not like sports. Thus, at the youth level, one ethical dilemma is whether children should be cut from teams or whether every child should be guaranteed the opportunity to play.

Interscholastic Sport

Many of the reasons that children opt out of sport also characterize explanations given by adolescents. Significant among these, though, may be the fact that schools, like many youth sport programs, limit the numbers of girls and boys allowed to participate on their teams with the justification that this ensures better competition for highly skilled players. Again, limitations in money, coaches, and facilities are cited to rationalize the elimination of dozens of girls and boys who try out for one of the coveted team uniforms. Many others who self-assess that they lack the skills do not even bother to try.

One ethical dilemma at the school level is trying to understand how a public educational institution established for all young people can justify a meritocratic sport program. The ethical issue of justice focuses on the purpose of sport within the school experience. Should a school, whose moral purpose is equitable treatment of all, support a system totally based on a meritocratic philosophy? Is the school being just and fair to all by having such inequities, that is, one program for the elite and none for the rest? This is not to say that elite programs per se are unethical. It is ethically possible and defensible to have elite programs if the stated purpose of the organization provides only for exceptional experiences. That is, it is perfectly acceptable to offer an honors class in chemistry or advanced music classes for exceptional students. Not everyone is talented enough to pass honors chemistry or to sing opera; not everyone should be expected to, and not everyone should be placed in the program.

If funds are available to support the philosophy of an advanced program, then such programs are justified. However, if programs are developed only for the elite with nothing available for the not-so-elite, then such a philosophy violates equitable treatment for all. It is unacceptable to develop an honors chemistry class for advanced students and have no other chemistry class available. It is unacceptable to develop an advanced opera class with no other music classes. So, why is it acceptable to have a varsity athletic program with no other sport experiences available for students not so highly skilled? Do schools have a responsibility to offer intramural or club activities for all students? Should such programs be provided the same financial support and the same level of coaching competencies that exist in the varsity program? If values can be learned through sport, do not all students have the right to learn these principles?

Many schools have increased support for intramural sports for all interested school students, in addition to providing varsity teams for the best athletes. These educators advocate that a combination of interscholastic sports and intramurals focuses on participation and skill improvement for all students, which are appropriate educational objectives.

Intercollegiate Sport

The elimination process in sport continues in college as thousands of former high school athletes suddenly find their skills inferior to those of their peers. With few exceptions, the awarding of grants-in-aid at most colleges and universities automatically dismisses any thought the nonrecruited student may have about trying to gain a place on the team. Some young men, however, searching for team association and the social status of being an athlete, willingly "walk on" and become practice players who never earn varsity letters or compete in a game; a smaller number of women become walk-on athletes as well.

Many former high school athletes become intramural, club, and recreational sport participants in college. Others channel their enthusiasm for sport into the spectator role, even though they are seldom active themselves. Some outgrow sport during their college years as interests change and new talents are discovered. They adopt new interests, deciding that they no longer enjoy sport competitions.

As the pyramid narrows at the top, only the highly skilled become collegiate athletes. Because most of these individuals are heavily recruited, attending a particular institution primarily because of athletics, the regular college student may question the purpose of college and university sport programs. For many institutions, the answer is that intercollegiate athletics exist primarily for entertainment with its possible revenue and only secondarily as a valued extracurricular activity for students.

Professors argue that colleges exist for the purpose of critical inquiry and learning. How, then, can any programs sponsored by universities place entertainment provided by heavily recruited athletes, who may be marginal students, higher in priority than academics? Some would respond that this has occurred because of the lack of institutional control and to appease fans.

If athletics teaches important lessons for life and enhances the collegiate experience, should not every interested student, regardless of skill level, be allowed the opportunity, even encouraged, to participate? However, how can a college or university afford to fund competitive sport opportunities for all who desire them? One way is to use student fees to support intramural and recreational sport programs. Selective systems that separate individuals by ability levels are not inherently wrong. However, some claim that such elitist systems are unethical

when those students who are cut or self-eliminated have few comparable alternatives.

Professional Sport

The less than 1 percent of high school athletes who achieve their goal of playing professionally (Coakley 2001) or reaching the pinnacles of their sport in amateur competition have survived many cuts because of their exceptional sport abilities and dedication (see Box 7-3). Many of these individuals, though, still face the most difficult separation from sport. This final cut traumatizes many athletes because for most of their lives their self-concept has been inextricably linked with sport. That is, many

---

BOX 7-3

THE BUSINESS OF PROFESSIONAL SPORT

Professional sport has quite different ethical dilemmas than does sport at other levels. The purposes of professional sport are entertainment and profits. The athletes who choose to become a part of this system must realize that they chose to be marketed. This is not to say that the professional sport owners and managers do not have to be responsible, fair, and honest in their transactions with athletes. Sport businesses are obligated by law to hold to the same ethical and legal principles that are necessary for any American business. However, it must be remembered that a purpose of professional sport is to make money. Professional sport does not hold to the same equitable, ideal perspectives about the athletic experience that interscholastic and intercollegiate sport do. If an athlete spends three years in the professional arena and then is cut, it is not the professional sport's fault that the athlete is judged to have nothing left to contribute. Many interscholastic and intercollegiate athletes dream of making millions as professional athletes. They want the money and the good life without realizing that huge salaries mean the purpose of the sport experience is no longer fun. However, it cannot be forgotten that the organization's purpose has a direct effect on how it views its moral and ethical responsibilities.

athletes may believe that they are liked, respected, and preferentially treated solely on the basis of their sport achievements; without sport, they will lose the elite status that elevated them above others.

Forced disengagement from sport can be devastating at any age and competitive level, although the longer the personal involvement in sport the harder it may be to cope with the termination of competitive sport. Admitting to diminishing skills when compared with the abilities of youthful stars remains difficult for many professional athletes. A career-ending injury abruptly changes one's life. As a result, some injured athletes totally withdraw from anything associated with the sport experiences they can no longer share.

On average, three to five years after signing a professional contract, winning a gold medal, and reigning as one of the top players in a sport in the world, the dream ends for athletes. The subsequent and often abrupt disengagement from sport traumatizes many athletes conditioned from an early age to singularly focus on sport. They then suddenly find themselves eliminated from sport, often without an education, career counseling, or coping skills for life without sport.

The media has publicized athletes who squandered their professional earnings and ended up destitute, who attempted ill-fated comebacks when life without sport seemed meaningless, and who committed suicide because of depression and other sport-disengagement problems. Did these events occur because the American sport system exploited these athletes by promising fame and fortune, only to forget them as soon as some more highly skilled individuals came along? Does a belief in the worth of the individual sport participant obligate sport managers to educate athletes pragmatically about managing time and stress, coping with and without fame and fortune, and preparing for life after sport?

Not Fun Anymore

Youth Sport

Backyard and playground games, where children make up the rules as they play, have become increasingly hard to find. These spontaneous pastimes ceased to thrive when adults began to impose their rules. Many adults indicate that they organize their children's games because playgrounds have increasingly disappeared as a result of urban sprawl or because crime has made these areas unsafe. Certainly parents want to protect their children, but the question remains, how structured should youth sport be? Because children play sports to have fun and the lack of fun causes many to drop out, should parents provide safe environments and give the games back to the kids? Do youth through sport need to learn how to organize, develop leadership abilities, solve problems, and value fair play? If so, how can adults help facilitate this learning?

By age 12, more than half of all youth already will have opted out of the sport programs in which they previously competed. Many of these girls and boys state that sport is simply not fun anymore, the number one reason for dropping out of sport. Although some may leave sport because of other interests and possibly other sports, what other factors cause early exits from sport?

The most important contributing factor to sports not being fun anymore may be the lack of success. People naturally pursue those activities that provide feelings of accomplishment. Children enjoy receiving praise for their achievements and awards for their physical talents, although adults may have emphasized these extrinsic awards too much. Being successful can be characterized by learning new skills, earning significant playing time, playing a preferred position, achieving status among one's teammates and peers, and avoiding negative reinforcement from parents and coaches. Success does not have to mean being the superstar or the game-winning heroine or hero. However, the lack of positive feedback, whatever the source, can contribute to a young person's conclusion that sport is not fun anymore. A different use of time is thought to be more enjoyable; so they quit.

A contributing factor to the dropout of some athletes may be that instead of sport teaching and reinforcing the moral value of justice, it undermines it. Youth may question whether they are receiving fair treatment when they spend more time on the bench than playing, never get to play their preferred positions, and endure disparaging comments from coaches about their lesser skills. By reducing the fun, does a narrowing of sport opportunities starting at the youth level cast aside those who do not possess sufficient skills?

Many youth sport athletes lose the fun aspect and drop out because the pressures to specialize in only one sport, train year-round, endure pain while playing with an injury, cheat or circumvent rules, and emphasize athletics over academics become too intense and are perceived negatively. See Box 7–4. They also may feel that no one cares about them as individuals. Each athlete weighs the pleasures received in sport against the stressors from any one of these pressures. They continue to participate if sport is personally rewarding.

Interscholastic Sport

Athletes who compete for their school teams usually find their extracurricular sport experiences enjoyable. They achieve a certain status as representatives of their schools and in their hometowns, es-pecially in those towns without college and professional teams. Unfortunately, not all interscholastic sport provides positive reinforcement to its participants. Some coaches take the fun out of sport when they push their athletes too hard in the pursuit of improved physical and skill development. A few coaches, seemingly insensitive to the needs of adolescents, cause their athletes to drop out because sport stops being fun socially and psychologically.

Sport may also stop being fun when schools fail to support it adequately. This may take the form of ill-prepared coaches, schedules that provide no challenge or little hope for success, not enough teams for everyone to get a chance to play, no teams in certain sports, poor facilities, and a lack of general support of athletics by the school. As a result, athletes may adopt a similarly apathetic attitude.

Intercollegiate Sport

Many collegiate athletes who consider practice to be work and certainly not fun have to endure all types of physical, verbal, and emotional abuse just

---

BOX 7-4

MAKING INFORMED DECISIONS

One approach that can help prevent sport elimination is having sufficient information to make sound decisions. In sport, this means that adult athletes and parents of young athletes must be told the risks involved so they can decide whether to participate or not. For example, when an athlete is injured seriously enough to miss a practice or a game, does a physician determine readiness to return to participation? If some type of medication is prescribed and used, have the medical rationales for this treatment as well as any side effects been clearly explained to athletes and parents?

Because athletes learn at an early age that winning is rewarded, they may choose to cover up an injury without realizing that permanent damage may be occurring. The throwing of curve balls by preadolescent pitchers is a classic example. Being informed before being asked for consent allows parents to state that they expect league rules prohibiting the throwing of curves to be enforced. Parents or athletes deserve to know that athletic trainers understand emergency procedures for head and neck injuries. The lack of proper and full information may occur when a professional athlete is not told by a team physician about the severity of an injury, resulting in a permanent disability when the athlete continues to play. So, proper information may help reduce sport elimination. Conversely, experiences at all levels of sport may be shortened when athletes are not allowed to choose when to participate, rest, or heal.

Sometimes coaches expect singular dedication to their sports that athletes stop having fun and drop out.

so they can compete. These individuals suffer through this abuse because they value team and individual achievements and social outcomes as pleasurable enough to overcome the abuse. Others who do not, drop out.

Individuals who choose to quit their collegiate sport teams, even for academic reasons or because of changing interests, are often stigmatized. Sometimes former teammates deride those who quit. Rather than trying to understand why, ex-teammates often impugn the motives of anyone who does not stick with the sport. The negativism associated with quitting increases at higher levels of sport. Males find this especially difficult because their masculinity may be questioned when they do not persevere.

Sport sponsored by educational institutions claims to teach lifelong social, emotional, and ethical values. This societal perception suggests that participation in sport prepares individuals for life in general and specifically for America's capitalistic economy. Because of these firmly held beliefs, those athletes who drop out because they have stopped having fun or for related reasons are thought to be shortchanged in potentially learning and applying these values, and thus are disadvantaged.

Professional Sport

Professional athletes accustomed to starring at lower levels of sport may experience difficulty in adjusting to being substitutes, seldom playing, or losing. This may wreak havoc on their self-confidence, leading to lessened enjoyment. In response, some athletes will work harder to earn a starting position or to improve their abilities; others may become disgruntled or lose interest in playing.

Diminishing skills frequently contribute to professional athletes' loss of enjoyment in their sport. Many find it hard to cope with the reality of being a step slower or of seeing younger athletes surpass them in ability. Many professional athletes choose to retire from sport when they realize that they have played their best, wanting to leave near the peak of their careers. Others remain as role players as long as they have the desire to play or until management releases them.

Sport managers and coaches at all levels should examine whether structural or operational issues based on moral principles cause athletes not to have fun anymore. Do children, adolescents, and young adults have a right to participate in sport competitions that are fun? Is it morally defensible to focus coaching and playing opportunities primarily on those who mature the earliest or possess the greatest physical talents? Can sport programs stress competition while encouraging those less skilled to be physically active through competitions at different levels of play? What changes are needed to ensure fun experiences for all athletes?

Dealing with the Transition Out of Sport

Whether an athlete is 10, 20, or 30, at some point in time she or he will no longer participate in competitive sports, at least not at the same level. Just as corporations help former employees prepare for alternative careers, athletes often need assistance in making a smooth transition into other activities. For children and adolescents, leaving one sport may lead to entering another sport that is more fun and personally rewarding. It may mean substituting recreational activities or other hobbies for competitive sports. Sadly, for many, permanent sport dropout occurs.

Pressures to Win

Youth Sport

The most traumatic and indefensible causal factor in sport dropout include the extreme, sometimes unconscionable, pressure placed on young athletes by some parents, coaches, fans, and the media. Has an emphasis on the nonmoral value of winning emerged as the primary culprit? On manicured fields, with youth-sized uniforms, and in leagues with drafts, play-offs, and championships leading to huge trophies, children and adolescents are coached by individuals who too often mimic the coaches they see on television or read about in the sport pages. As family lives come to revolve around youth league competitions, the importance placed on winning may surmount all else.

Probably most parental involvement with youth sport begins innocently enough as children eagerly choose to join teams. However, some parents burden their children by living vicariously through their offspring. That is, these parents force their children into nonpreferred sports or refuse to let them quit, regardless of the reason. Parental sacrifices of money, time, and team involvement, such as coaching or program leadership, may entrap the young athlete who really does not want to play, or at least does not want to play under the existing circumstances.

Parents who reward and praise winning, while berating or ignoring losing, send clear messages that they value only one outcome. Early in their sport experiences, youth learn how much emphasis their parents place on their scoring, being the game-winning player, and demonstrating superior sport skills. The child or adolescent who lacks self-confidence or places significant importance upon parental approval may be driven to use whatever means available in attempting to achieve the extrinsic rewards and status associated with being a winner. Some parents exacerbate these pressures by withholding love from children who do not win and even physically abusing them. Starting at the youth level, athletes in sport competitions perform under the scrutiny of parents, fans, and the media. Unfortunately, at each advancing level of competition more and more parents, coaches, fans, and teammates begin to expect and even demand victories. Sometimes a young athlete uses pain and injury to escape excessive parental pressures. The pressure to win exists even though most participate in zero-sum games (that is, at least one loser for every winner). Public display of athletes' performances usually intensifies the pressures felt, as does seeking the rewards that primarily accrue to the victorious.

Interscholastic Sport

When parents perceive that their children have been blessed with exceptional sport talents, some increase exponentially the pressures on them to succeed. Youthful pleasures and social relationships often are abandoned in search of greater skill development, often on school teams. Some parents push their children toward professional careers as adolescents or eagerly seek grant-in-aid offers from colleges. Although adolescents may eagerly participate in sport development camps and enjoy specialized coaching, many tire of devoting their lives singularly to one sport. They also grow weary of listening to their parents berate them, their coaches, and sport officials. When many of these athletes become bored, fatigued, or completely fed up, they drop out of sport.

The sport media in various forms contributes to the dropout rate in the most popular sports. An outstanding high school sophomore in the 1980s shot himself. His suicide note conveyed the sobering statement that, after leading his football team to the state championship, he simply could not cope with the pressures of being expected to carry his team to the championship for two more years. An

Pressure to win may adversely affect athlete's performance. (Photo courtesy of the University of Kansas Department of Intercollegiate Athletics.)

age-group tennis champion took her life because she could not handle all the pressures from her parents to keep winning. Certainly other pressures could have played a part in these suicides, but no one will ever know the role that an overemphasis on winning may have had.

Although parents' and coaches' pressures start subtly, the media and fans impose a social responsibility on the teenage sport star. As schools, communities, and states become heavily invested in the sport achievements of young people, these individuals feel increasing pressures to not lose, lest they disappoint their parents, coaches, and fans. Geometric increases in these pressures to win occur as athletes advance up the competitive ladder.

Intercollegiate Sport

Collegiate coaches who lack a balanced perspective about the role of sport may exert even more pressures on athletes. Winning, the driving force at the collegiate level (and increasingly in high schools), becomes essential for maintaining one's job. The status, lucrative salaries, and other benefits accruing to coaches (such as shoe contracts, luxury automobiles, and country club memberships) accrue only to those who win consistently.

Thus, most collegiate coaches expect their athletes to specialize in one sport, condition and train year-round, obey without question all directives, and sometimes even circumvent game rules in pursuit of victories. Fans cheer for and expect such behaviors and the media praise them. Some intercollegiate athletes resent these pressures and disengage.

College coaches exercise control over various academic, social, and psychological aspects of their athletes' lives. Although such domination has been questioned, some coaches continue to dehumanize athletes on the premise of getting them to perform better and to win. A few coaches also have been known to teach their athletes to play unfairly and to take drugs known to enhance performance. Do these pressures from coaches violate athletes' rights?

Some behaviors by coaches occur because of ignorance; other coaches may choose to disregard research or scientific data because these do not concur with their preconceived ideas about or philosophy of coaching. Overall, coaching education remains woefully inadequate, and programs focusing on moral reasoning are nonexistent. Most coaches are good and decent people who may not know what effects they may be having on their athletes psychologically, physiologically, or morally. Fearing for their jobs or their authority, many are unwilling to admit their lack of education or to rectify this situation.

Professional Sport

The pressures to win placed on professional athletes emerge from their roles as entertainers. Fans, through ticket purchases, television viewing, and product purchases pay the salaries and provide the prize money to these athletes, and they expect victories or at least maximal effort. Athletes who intentionally lose or give less than their best efforts can expect boos and derisive comments from the stands and in game coverage by the media.

Conflicts between coaches and athletes can become constant sources of pressure for both. Some conflicts, such as Latrell Sprewell's strangling of his coach, are condemned as unethical because of the physical abuse. But, is a psychological berating by coaches of players unethical, too?

The media derides, questions, and belittles losers, yet praises and rewards winners in big-time college athletics and especially professional sports. Winners advance, and losers go home describes the process to determine who is number one. Fans seem happy only with victories. Athletes must respond to the pressures to win in front of thousands of fans. No wonder individuals who survive the high dropout rate from sport and compete professionally are characterized by a need for achievement and psychological endurance.

Pressures to win can become contradictory to the moral principles of justice, honesty, responsibility, and beneficence. Has winning become the only desired outcome of sport? Should the seeking of victories preclude an ethical approach to sport based on moral principles? The development of the whole person—physically, socially, and psychologically—far exceeds winning in importance because it is lasting; winning is transitory. Should parents, coaches, fans, and the media reevaluate the roles they play in overemphasizing the importance placed on winning?

Two Other Issues

Within sports, rumors abound about homosexual relations among athletes. For example, the media backlash to Billie Jean King's homosexual affair and to Greg Louganis's announcement that he was homosexual seemed to reinforce these suspicions. Even in a time of more liberal attitudes, athletes in the public arena are expected to be heterosexual or to remain "in the closet" regarding their private af-

fairs. Some coaches, especially in women's sports like basketball, may make a point when recruiting young women that allegations about rampant homosexuality were simply untrue. However, some women may have opted out of softball and men out of figure skating because they did not want to be labeled or have people question them.

Parents have expressed concerns when coaches of their children are openly homosexual because these parents do not wish to have impressionable youth exposed to lifestyles with which they do not agree. Coaches who are the same gender as their athletes frequently see their athletes in various stages of dressing and undressing in locker rooms. This may make athletes feel vulnerable because they have no control over the behaviors and thoughts of their coaches. The presence of teammates who are homosexuals also places other athletes into awkward or uncertain situations.

Sexual harassment, unfortunately, occurs in all levels of sport. Some youth sport coaches befriend their athletes with attention and treats such as taking them out to eat or to movies as a way to deceive them and their parents into trusting them. Then these coaches sexually molest these children. Too often, these children have no idea what to do. Some feel shame thinking they caused this to happen; others are psychologically hurt and may need professional counseling to work through the pain and confusion. Sport for fun became an unbelievable nightmare for these youth. Exposés about a male coach of a girls' volleyball team having sexual affairs with his players and a youth ice hockey coach forcing his athletes into sexual relations have frightened many parents and athletes. When a youth sport coach can control the development of girls' or boys' athletic abilities and opportunities, these youngsters are totally vulnerable. The victims of these forced sexual encounters have reported that their unquestioning submission to their coaches had shattered their lives.

With background checks increasingly being required for school employees, some potential promiscuous coaches may be prevented from gaining employment when they have criminal records for child molestation. Some coaches, however, have been and continue to be guilty of sexually harassing their athletes. Inappropriate words and actions can intimidate adolescents when their coaches are the perpetrators. When these adults take advantage of their positions of power over athletes, relative to making the team or gaining playing time, it may cause these young athletes to succumb to sexual advances. These young people may carry the scars from sexual harassment for life, long after dropping out of sports that they perceived as threatening.

Collegiate athletes, even though they are adults, are still vulnerable to manipulation by ill-intentioned coaches. Because coaches control grants-in-aid and thus educational opportunity for many, accommodation to coaches' expectations may be hard to resist. This vulnerability is exacerbated when athletes are physically attracted to their coaches. Even though sexual relations may occur between consenting adults, the power differential between the coach and an athlete, not to mention the adverse effect such an affair may have on a team, makes such relationships sexual harassment and morally inappropriate.

Some, but certainly not all, elite and professional sport organizations prohibit coach–player sexual relations. Federal law prohibits sexual harassment. Yet, both persist at these levels of sport as well. Because some athletes when faced with sexual harassment choose to do nothing except leave their sports, the extent of this problem is unknown. Thus, dropout may occur because of factors having nothing to do directly with sport.

SPORT BURNOUT

To the aspiring athlete, sport should be about skill development and testing oneself, personal growth in areas like cooperation, self-discipline, teamwork, self-control, and intrinsic motivation, and development of social abilities and relationships. Parents who encourage their children to participate in sports seem to believe that these are potential outcomes. Ideally, playing sports, regardless of the final score, should have a positive influence on participants.

Burnout occurs because of too much, too often, and too soon of a supposedly good thing. A parent's purpose is to guide, love, instruct, and care for the child. Coaches essentially have the same purpose to act in the child's best interest. The parents' and coaches' moral and ethical principles should support each child's development. If the motives, intentions, and actions of coaches and parents fail to focus on what is in each child's best interest, then they violate basic moral values. Many people argue that sport specialization is in the child's best interest. Unfortunately, research does not support that position. The data are conclusive: too much, too often, and too soon is not in the best interests of a child. It is the duty of the parent and the coach to stay abreast of the latest information as it impacts programs for their children and athletes. The moral dilemma is how much competition is beneficial, and how much is too much? The answer to these questions should focus on each child's development .

Sport burnout refers to those athletes who demonstrate outstanding sport skills or potential at an early age but drop out of sport before achieving at an elite level. This may occur for physical, psychological, social, or other reasons (see Box 7-5), each taking its toll in different ways. Physical burnout includes the repercussions of overuse, overtraining, and overspecialization. The mental and emotional pressures from demands for improved performances and winning result in psychological burnout. Manifestations of social burnout are the absence of a life outside of sport and the adverse effect on the opportunity to spend time with friends.

Physical Burnout

Youth Sport

The overuse syndrome did not occur in youth sports until programs under adult leaders began to mimic collegiate and professional models, including

BOX 7-5

REASONS ATHLETES BURN OUT IN SPORT

Youth Sport

- ◆ Overuse and fatigue
- ◆ Overtraining
- ◆ Recurrent injuries
- ◆ Overspecialization
- ◆ Poorly qualified coaches
- ◆ Demand for improved performances
- ◆ Overemphasis on winning
- ◆ Loss of intrinsic motivation
- ◆ Changing interests
- ◆ Conflicts in values

Interscholastic Sport

- ◆ Overuse and fatigue
- ◆ Overtraining
- ◆ Recurrent injuries
- ◆ Overspecialization
- ◆ Poorly qualified coaches
- ◆ Demand for improved performances
- ◆ Overemphasis on winning
- ◆ Loss of intrinsic motivation
- ◆ Changing interests
- ◆ Conflicts in values
- ◆ Desire for freedom and independence
- ◆ Loss of friends and social activities

Intercollegiate Sport

- ◆ Overuse and fatigue
- ◆ Overtraining
- ◆ Recurrent injuries
- ◆ Demand for improved performances
- ◆ Overemphasis on winning
- ◆ Loss of intrinsic motivation
- ◆ Conflicts in values
- ◆ Psychological manipulation by coaches
- ◆ Unwillingness to sacrifice physically, psychologically, and academically
- ◆ Desire for more social and extracurricular activities with friends

Professional Sport

- ◆ Recurrent injuries
- ◆ Diminishing skills
- ◆ Loss of desire to play
- ◆ Desire to spend time with family
- ◆ Desire to pursue other personal and business interests

an overemphasis on winning. Children, seeking to become like their favorite athletes, joined competitive leagues that adults organized as miniature versions of professional leagues. The compulsion to develop one's skills was driven by the dream of a professional contract or a gold medal.

Unfortunately, injuries from overuse before maturation plague most children who start their competitive careers early. Many aspiring superstars as youth and adolescents have had their dreams shattered by injuries related to overuse. Young athletes undertaking prolonged and intensive training programs dur-

ing their growth spurt become particularly susceptible to skeletal overuse injuries. Youth baseball leagues had to enact limitations on the number of innings youngsters could pitch because in coaches' overzealousness to win they were overtaxing young athletes' maturing bodies. Sports medicine physicians have found that children and adolescents who compete in organized sport put themselves at risk for musculoskeletal injuries, especially if they fail to participate actively in flexibility and conditioning programs.

Numerous athletes in figure skating, skiing, tennis, ice hockey, and gymnastics have dropped out of

When children begin competitive sports at a young age, they frequently experience injuries from overtraining.

school in order to train with renowned coaches and in locations distant from their families. While Andre Agassi in tennis, Mary Lou Retton in gymnastics, and Michelle Kwan in figure skating have become champions under these circumstances, thousands of other potential stars have flamed out as adolescents. Many of these youngsters showed outstanding ability early, yet their competitors matured, developed their skills, and surpassed those who had defeated them earlier in their careers. These early maturing athletes who find themselves no longer winning oftentimes are unable to cope with being second best or not even that. Pressures to win can be psychologically debilitating to these young athletes who are unable to further extend their skills. As their

dreams seem to fizzle, many of these adolescents become victims of sport burnout.

Overtraining occurs when athletes fail to listen to their bodies and demand too much. Physically immature athletes, in particular, may permanently injure themselves. Prepubescent children, for example, who continually throw curve balls may impede the proper maturation of bones. Many youth sport coaches lack the knowledge to teach sport skills or to pace and sequence them properly. As a result, they often expect too much of their young athletes.

Overspecialization in sport relates to overuse and overtraining. Increasingly, youth sport coaches pressure their young athletes to choose to play only one sport so that they can condition and train year-round. Coaches are entrapped by the belief that more training must be better. These coaches too often are ignorant of appropriate teaching techniques and the latest research, including the value of cross-training and proper rest.

Interscholastic Sport

Overuse and overtraining occur in interscholastic sport, too, even though state athletic associations limit sport seasons. Multisport athletes who never allow their bodies time for rest and recovery may experience fatigue leading to injuries.

Many interscholastic coaches claim that specialization in one sport enhances athletes' skill development and improves their chances of excelling at the next level of sport, including possibly receiving an athletic grant-in-aid. Of course, these more skillful athletes often will help win games for these coaches, too. If later, these athletes become collegiate and professional stars, a few interscholastic coaches enjoy reflected glory and maybe even job advancement.

Parents, too, may encourage their children to focus on one sport. If this sport is chosen by the athlete, no problem exists as long as overtraining and overuse do not occur. But if the parent forces sport specialization, hoping that a grant-in-aid or a lucrative professional career will follow, burnout often occurs, with the athlete lacking interest in and dedication to the imposed sport.

Too often, overspecialization prematurely ends athletes' sport participation. Year-round practices, strength and conditioning programs, and learning of sport skills before the body is mature enough hasten burnout while lessening fun and sport enjoyment. Swimmers serve as good examples of this occurrence. In the past, most swimmers, burned out by twice-a-day practices, stopped competing in their late teens rather than continuing their careers until they had swum their fastest times as adults. Today, older swimmers are setting records through tapered training programs and rest that help them avoid burnout.

Intercollegiate Sport

Recruited collegiate athletes are expected to commit themselves fully to achieving their potential. Whatever training regimen coaches impose must be followed without deviation. Team and individual practices, weight training sessions, film reviews, strategy planning times, and team meetings add up to huge demands on time and the body. The NCAA, in attempting to balance the athletic and academic components of college students' lives, has established a weekly 20-hour limit on the amount of time coaches can involve their athletes in their sport (exclusive of travel time for competitions). Unfortunately, many coaches violate this rule.

Self-imposed or coach-imposed expectations for improved performances, though, may cause athletes to train excessively without proper recovery time. It remains unknown how many athletes push themselves too hard in trying to please coaches who determine whether and how much athletes get to play and whether they receive grants-in-aid annually. Whenever a sport-related goal becomes too important, athletes may train when injured, sick, or fatigued. Eventually, the body refuses to tolerate overtraining and breaks down temporarily or permanently.

Athletes are often taught to be tough and to play through injuries, even though pain indicates a physical problem that needs resolution. Athletes should never be asked whether they want to play while injured, because the answer will invariably be yes. Sometimes well-intentioned coaches push athletes, whom they may categorize as not motivated enough, trying to get more out of them, when in reality these athletes are too injured to compete. Is it ever defensible for coaches to cajole their athletes into playing when hurt? Is it morally acceptable to allow an athlete who was seriously injured to return to practice or competition without a physician's clearance?

Professional Sport

Professional athletes, because they are paid, are typically expected to play while injured, unless the injury is debilitating. Yet sometimes these athletes are lied to or deceived about the seriousness of their injuries so they will choose to compete. Professionals are encouraged to use pain-blocking drugs. Sometimes these athletes become dependent on drugs, even though this practice can result in even more serious injuries or problems. Physicians, not athletes or coaches, should decide whether these athletes can compete, given the possibility of permanent damage to injured areas. Many professional athletes retire, as did quarterback Steve Young, because they are tired of the pain or refuse to risk more severe damage.

Psychological Burnout

Youth Sport

Many young athletes are pressured to improve on their past performances and to win. As these children grow and mature, times run or swum pale in comparison to new expectations placed on them by parents, coaches, fans, and the media. Last year's points per game or batting average seemingly must be surpassed or the athlete is not training, dedicated, or psyched-up enough. Education could help coaches understand and appreciate that more training is not always better. Is attaining and using such knowledge of appropriate training practices a moral obligation?

The appetite for athletes' continual improvement appears insatiable for some youth sport coaches. So, when successive years fail to bring superior performances, athletes are questioned, berated, punished, and pressured. Similarly, athletes and teams who do not finish first are treated with scorn or ignored but seldom praised for their efforts. Too often, such treatment causes athletes to lose their self-confidence, resulting in a downward spiral in athletic accomplishments. A greater realization of the physical and social consequences of intensive training and competition also contribute to psychological burnout.

Interscholastic Sport

Psychological pressures to win may increase when adolescents start representing their schools. Now entire communities, rather than an age-group team and family members, take notice of game results. Sometimes coaches increase the pressure on their athletes because their jobs and status depend on victories. As these pressures compound, some athletes succumb to mental fatigue. When their emotional reserves deplete completely, they become victims of psychological burnout from sport.

Adult-imposed pressures to win and for improved performances can cause teenage athletes to respond in other ways, too. They may replace their intrinsic motivation to compete and train with other, less threatening activities. When adults demand sport involvement, adolescents may seek complete freedom and independence for themselves without any participation in sport.

Intercollegiate Sport

College athletes face increasing pressures to perform at the peak of their abilities; they are recruited and subsidized to do this. "Big-time" sport especially places pressure on athletes because of the fans, media, and money associated with successful programs. These athletes realize that missed free throws, tackles, or pitches may cost their institutions thousands of dollars because the institutions fail to qualify for bowl games or advancement into the next round of tournaments.

Athletes who continually give maximal effort may experience burnout from overtraining or pressures to win. (Photo courtesy of the University of Kansas Department of Intercollegiate Athletics.)

Many universities have hired sport psychologists to assist athletes in handling the mental aspects of their sports and, most important, to enhance performance. For example, a sport psychologist may help the field-goal kicker attain the proper level of arousal to help prevent a game-winning attempt from sailing wide right. Other colleges depend on coaches to artfully provide the appropriate mix of positive feedback and psyching up to prevent psychological burnout from impeding performances.

Professional Sport

Many professional athletes for physical and psychological reasons lose their desires or abilities to play. Upon forced or voluntary retirement, however, some fail to cope with life without sport. Many suffer from health problems such as the aftermath of injuries or heart difficulties associated with weight fluctuations. Many former elite athletes lack the self-discipline to change their eating and activity habits when their careers end, leading to premature death or disability. This leads to the question of whether the cost of shortened lives or impaired quality of life for former stars is too costly just to fulfill Americans' desire for sport spectating.

Disengagement from sport for individuals who have lived sport-centered lives traumatizes many former athletes because their self-image for years has been inextricably linked with sport. Continually, younger and better athletes replace the former stars. In the absence of coping strategies, too many of these athletes may react negatively to the mental and emotional realities of not being special.

Social Burnout

Youth Sport

Early in life, sport plays a minor role in one's life. Weekly practices and competitions consume few hours and seldom detract from schoolwork, family routines, and just being a kid. This all changes whenever children's skills elevate them into the elite leagues or identify them as potentially world class. The social organization of high-performance sport may constrain adolescents' identity development and prevent them from having meaningful control over their lives. Several top-ranked female tennis players have dealt in varied ways with the social and psychological pressures associated with their youthful, yet professional careers. Parents, and especially fathers, have played significant positive and negative roles in their careers.

When sport stops being a pastime and becomes a passion, social burnout often occurs. Many athletes squeeze schoolwork between two-session-a-day training programs. In some sports, athletes like teen gold medalist Tara Lipinski must leave home or the family must move in order to take advantage of top-level coaching. Private coaches spend endless hours perfecting the skills of future gold medalists or number one players. Sport skill development at this level leaves little time for friends and youthful activities and experiences. Social activities are sacrificed for the prospect of future fame and fortune.

Interscholastic Sport

Interscholastic sport stars seldom leave home and must schedule their sport involvement around regular school days. Still, they can become consumed by sport through year-round training and competing. A few become so focused on sport that they abandon their friends, and they practice instead of participating in social activities.

While missing many aspects of the growing-up process, youth and scholastic stars are honing their skills for competing as collegiate athletes or professionals. Besides being adolescents with few if any peer-group friends, these aspiring superstars must cope with the mental and emotional pressures of trying to win. Some handle these pressures well; others do not and burn out. Social isolation traumatizes many young athletes; some quit sport so that they can live like others their ages. The question is whether young athletes should specialize to such an extent that they impede their own social development.

Intercollegiate Sport

Many criticize intercollegiate sport for placing so many athletic demands on players that they have no time left to participate in the extracurricular activities available to other students. These critics claim that because such experiences enrich the college years, all students should be allowed the opportunity to participate in activities such as student government and special-interest groups.

Collegiate athletes, because of their athletic and academic schedules, enjoy few free hours to interact socially, other than with teammates. Some individuals concerned about the emphasis on competitive

Sometimes athletes who have trained intensely to achieve at the highest levels of their sports have difficulty adjusting to life without sport when their competitive careers end.

sport advocate that freshmen should be ineligible so these students may have time to stabilize themselves academically, socially, and extracurricularly before adding athletics to their schedules.

Sometimes collegiate athletes refuse to continue their commitment to their sports because of a desire to participate in more social and extracurricular activities. They determine that these experiences provide more intrinsic rewards than does competing in sports.

Professional Sport

Professional athletes' lives revolve around their training, practice, and competitive schedules. Holiday celebrations, family events such as births and birthdays, and vacations must be arranged around their careers, rescheduled, or missed. When athletes tire of having less control over their lives than desired, many quit. Often, professional athletes cite the desire to spend more time with their families as a primary reason for ending their playing careers. Others add that they want to pursue other personal and business interests not permitted because of their sport careers.

If winning were not so prominent in sports, do you think there would be less burnout? Has the pursuit of handsomely rewarded victories caused an erosion of values? Overuse, overtraining, overspecialization, excessive demands for improved performances and for winning, and overemphasis on sport to the exclusion of a social life threatens the well-being of athletes while displacing the potential for value development.

If coaches and sport managers are behaving responsibly, should they pursue excellence, and even winning, as long as moral values are not compromised? Does honesty demand that athletes have choices, not compulsions? Does justice implore sport managers to treat each athlete fairly so as to not direct him or her along a pathway leading to burnout?

SUMMARY

The dropout and burnout issues raise many questions; resolving these dilemmas may be difficult. Taxpayers' dollars should not be used to support elite competitions until all children have a chance to play sports at the appropriate skill level. Athletes at all levels should be prepared for and provided coping skills for dealing with sport disengagement. Having fun, learning skills, and trying hard should be reinstated as the goals in youth and scholastic programs. Parental, coach, fan, and media pressures to win should be reduced. Performing to one's potential should replace winning as the top priority, even if this means changing the sport rules, banning adults, and losing corporate sponsorships.

Overspecialization has no place in the lives of children; rather, they should be free to play whatever sports they enjoy. Sport managers should ensure that overuse injuries will not occur and that athletes will not be allowed or expected to play while injured or to use pain-blocking drugs. Both dropout and burnout are avoidable. Instead of contributing to these, parents, coaches, and sport managers should recognize and prevent the potential harm, teach and reinforce values, and ensure enjoyable sport experiences for athletes of all ages.

Cybersports

www.fitness.gov

The President's Council on Physical Fitness and Sports promotes appropriate opportunities in sports for all Americans as an alternative to sport burnout and dropout.

www.aausports.org/ysnim/home/aau_index.jsp

The Amateur Athletic Union is the largest, multisport, volunteer sports organization in the United States and promotes amateur sports programs for individuals of all ages.

www.mindtools.com/burnout.html

This site provides strategies for identifying symptoms and tips for avoiding burnout in sport.

www.nfshsa.org

The National Federation of State High School Associations and its affiliated state organizations provide governing leadership and rules to ensure broad participation in interscholastic sports.

 # ISSUES AND DILEMMAS

CASE 7-1

Timothy loved soccer. Since he was six years old, he has played on a youth league team. Although he was never the best or the biggest player, no one played with as much desire and enthusiasm as he did. His parents attended most of his games, encouraging but never pushing him.

Timothy's father sometimes kicked the ball around with him in the yard but did not really have the knowledge to coach him. Each summer, though, Timothy's parents sent him to a soccer camp at State University. There, he was in sheer bliss as he played soccer for hours without ever tiring of the drills and games.

After 10 years of youth soccer, Timothy was confident that he could earn a spot on his high school team as a sophomore. During the three days of tryouts, he tried his hardest and executed all the drills to the best of his ability. It became readily evident, though, that the competition would be tough, with nearly 60 boys trying out for only 22 uniforms. This was not like the youth program where everyone who wanted to play could.

On Thursday morning when the squad list was posted, Timothy scanned the sheet over and over but did not find his name; he had not made the team. He was devastated. How, for the first time in 10 years, could he survive without soccer? It hurt badly that effort and determination seemingly meant nothing as the bigger and more highly skilled boys were selected. When Timothy asked why he was cut, the coach replied that Timothy just was not good enough to play high school soccer.

1. Should high school coaches cut athletes? Is this ethical or unethical? Why or why not?
2. Should schools provide multiple (varsity, junior varsity, A, and B) teams for all interested students who want to compete? Why or why not?
3. What are the financial and moral ramifications of sponsoring multiple school teams of various skill levels?
4. What are Timothy's options now?
5. How should Timothy's parents deal with their son in this situation?
6. Did Timothy learn anything about values through this experience?

◆ ◆ ◆

CASE 7-2

Jane Maxwell began taking gymnastics lessons when she was eight years old. Immediately, her teacher realized that she had the potential to become world-class. So after only one year, during which Jane progressed remarkably in her skills, she changed programs. Her new instructor helped her develop her skills so well that she became a state all-around champion at age 10.

Now Jane and her parents faced a major decision. The best way to ensure that Jane continued to progress was for her to move to Dallas and train in the private gym of Coach Symanski, the national coach. There, she would live with three other gymnasts and a housemother. Between two-hour morning and afternoon workouts, Jane would attend school. The annual cost for this program was $30,000.

Jane's parents could afford to pay for Jane's training in Dallas and urged her to take advantage of this special opportunity to possibly become the top gymnast in the world. Although Jane enjoyed gymnastics because she had always been successful, she was less sure that she wanted to leave her parents and brother to live and train with strangers. This all seemed so frightening to Jane.

Mr. and Mrs. Maxwell stressed to Jane how fortunate she was to have been given so much talent. They promised to visit her every month. Of course, they would attend all of her competitions. With this urging, Jane agreed.

Coach Symanski was a rigid taskmaster, demanding more and more from his young athletes each day. His practices could be called brutal; he pushed his youthful stars hard. As long as Jane progressed, all went well. But when Jane failed to achieve up to his level of expectations, he chastised her, questioning her commitment and talent. Initially, these mind games motivated Jane, but gradually she began to resent his relentless tirades.

In her second year with Coach Symanski, Jane's maturing body began to restrict some of her former skills, and nagging problems became significant injuries. She hid as many of these problems as she could from Coach Symanski because she was afraid that he would harass her about making excuses for not winning. Gymnastics was becoming work instead of being fun.

Besides all this, Jane had become increasingly homesick. She missed her parents, younger brother, and former friends. Although always around people, she felt lonely.

By the time she reached 14, after four years as an elite gymnast, Jane burned out. The physical, psychological, and social stressors had become too burdensome. With great trepidation, she called her parents and said that she was quitting and wanted to come home.

1. What are the ethical issues, if any, associated with starting a highly competitive sport at a young age?
2. Did Mr. and Mrs. Maxwell pressure Jane unduly? If so, why?
3. What are the pros and cons of the sport skills development program operated by Coach Symanski?
4. What types of pressures contributed to Jane's burnout?
5. What ethical dilemmas does this case present for Jane, Mr. and Mrs. Maxwell, and Coach Symanski?
6. If you were Jane's parents would you support her wanting to quit, considering the money invested and the opportunities Jane had to become the best gymnast in the world?

◆ ◆ ◆

CASE 7-3

Virginia Sanborn, although a high school basketball player, was not skilled enough to play for Midwestern State University. Volunteering to serve as manager, Virginia spent four years observing one of the best coaches in the nation. Not only had Coach Turner taken her team to four consecutive NCAA tournaments, but, during Virginia's junior year, the team had advanced into the finals before losing.

Coach Turner stressed fundamentals, teamwork, and never giving up—essentials, in Virginia's opinion, of a quality program. However, Virginia questioned to herself some of Coach Turner's other practices. The coach demanded that team members spend endless hours practicing, even though in excess of the maximum allowed by the NCAA. She seemed to care only that her players stayed academically eligible, never taking an interest in their classes or allowing them to miss practices for academic reasons. She also taught her players how to intentionally violate game rules for their advantage. Coach Turner's methods, to Virginia, emphasized winning as the only important thing.

Virginia was determined to model Coach Turner's positive, but not negative, coaching practices in her first job at Surry High School. Virginia was excited about getting a 4A (competitive division for the largest schools) team to coach, one that had a history of excellent records. She was confident that her emphasis on fundamentals, teamwork, and never giving up would maintain the team's success.

Coach Sanborn quickly earned the respect of her players when they realized that she knew basketball and could teach the skills well. They also really liked her because she seemed to care about them as individuals. Coach Sanborn encouraged them in their classwork, helping if she could or getting them assistance from other teachers if it was needed. Because she always seemed to understand, the players valued her as a confidant whenever they were experiencing family, relationship, or emotional difficulties. The players also learned that Coach Sanborn demonstrated—by her actions, words, and the way she coached—values that emphasized justice, honesty, and civility. She would never allow anyone to be mistreated or a sport rule to be misapplied unfairly in her team's favor.

There was a problem, however. Surry High School's girls' basketball team was not winning most of its games. For two consecutive years, the team finished with about as many wins as losses and did not qualify for the state playoffs—the only times in two decades. Although the girls would have preferred to win, they felt that they were doing their best and certainly were benefiting from their sport experiences.

Shortly after the end of Coach Sanborn's second season, the athletic director, Mr. Ethridge, and the principal, Mr. Farmer, asked her to meet with them. Because Coach Sanborn had developed a good working relationship with both of these individuals, their comments were totally unexpected. Mr. Ethridge commended her on her skill instruction, rapport with the players, and emphasis on academics. But, he said her coaching record was unacceptable at Surry High School. Parents and other fans expected the girls' and the boys' basketball teams to win, not to break even. Mr. Farmer then stated that she had one year to produce a winning girls' team or she would lose her job.

1. Did Virginia Sanborn learn any unethical coaching practices from Coach Turner?
2. Did it take the combination of all of Coach Turner's coaching methods, both ethical and unethical, to build a winning team at Midwestern State University?
3. What were the moral values upheld by Virginia Sanborn as she coached the girls' basketball team and lived her life?

4. How and why did Coach Sanborn earn the respect of her players?
5. Were Mr. Ethridge and Mr. Farmer violating any ethical principles in issuing the ultimatum to Coach Sanborn?
6. What ethical choices does Coach Sanborn have?
7. What would you do if you were in the situation facing Coach Sanborn?
8. Would you quit before sacrificing your principles or would you adopt a different coaching style? Would your answer be different if you were the sole provider for a child?

◆ ◆ ◆

CASE 7-4

Emmitt Larkin was a gifted athlete. In youth sport leagues, junior high school, and high school, he was always the most successful running back and defensive back on his team. He led his teams to numerous championships, including state titles in his junior and senior years. Recruited by every top-ranked Division I university, he chose the University of Michigan, because it was not too far from his hometown of Chicago.

Emmitt was barely eligible for an athletic grant-in-aid, having just qualified with his SAT scores and high school grades. This narrow margin did not concern Emmitt because he had no intention of becoming a serious student. He planned to do the minimal to remain eligible for two seasons of football and then to declare himself eligible for the National Football League (NFL) draft.

Emmitt's phenomenal freshman season seemed to confirm his plans. After his All-American season, however, he did have to attend summer school in order to retain his academic eligibility for his sophomore season. He was even touted as a possible Heisman Trophy candidate in preseason publications.

Disaster struck in the first game of his sophomore season when Emmitt suffered a career-ending injury. While the paralysis slowly dissipated so that he eventually learned to walk again, he would never play football again.

1. Why was Emmitt banking his future on a multimillion-dollar future in the NFL? Was this realistic?
2. What ethical responsibility did Emmitt's coaches have to him relative to academics?
3. What preparation does Emmitt have for a career and life without sport competition?

4.   What should be done to help athletes prepare for an abrupt elimination from sport?

5.   How would you describe what Emmitt valued prior to his injury?

◆ ◆ ◆

CASE 7-5

Lonnie Young had been a Division II baseball player and graduated with a physical education degree. He was hired into a teaching and coaching position at Fulton High School after his first interview for a job. The principal was impressed with the young man's values and his strong letters of reference. While Lonnie might have been able to play minor league baseball, he never seriously considered this, because he wanted to work with adolescents.

In his physical education classes, Lonnie stressed having fun in various sport and fitness activities. He never allowed the lesser-skilled boy or girl to be left out or eliminated. He matched students based on their skill levels to ensure that everyone had the opportunity to feel successful and to enjoy movement experiences.

Coach Young's baseball team reflected the values by which he lived his life. He cared about each player regardless of his skill level. He mandated that everyone be treated with respect and fairly, including opponents and umpires. While striving to win based on extensive conditioning, drills, and strategies, Coach Young placed winning in perspective for his athletes. He gave a uniform to any boy who wanted a spot on the team. While every boy did not play in every game, every player did in most games. Coach Young required all of his athletes to take their studies seriously. They had to pass all of their courses. He provided help to any athlete who was struggling academically.

It took a while for the boys in this urban school to meet Coach Young's expectations, but over the years they continually returned to Fulton High to thank the coach who had taught them how to work hard and enjoy sports. They always told Coach Young that he had helped them become principled athletes and men.

1.   Can a coach stress winning and simultaneously teach moral values? If so, how can this be accomplished?

2.   Why was cutting a boy who wanted to play baseball not an option for Coach Young?

3.   To what, do you think, did these boys attribute their continued love of sport?

4. How do you think Coach Young would have handled a "star athlete" who was disgruntled when he was replaced by a lesser-skilled teammate?

5. How do you think Coach Young would have handled an athlete who cheated, violated a team rule, or displayed unsportsmanlike conduct?

6. How do you think Coach Young would have handled an athlete who did not achieve academically? What if this athlete was the best player on the team?

◆ ◆ ◆

CASE 7-6

Shirley Foster was featured on the cover of *Sports Illustrated* at the age of 16, after she had won every tournament she entered for four years. Coached by her domineering father, she had developed flawless strokes and powerful serves that signaled a bright future. As a pro, she climbed rapidly to the number one spot after winning the United States Singles Tennis Championship. Mr. Foster, who bragged that his daughter would win more Grand Slam events than any other player, managed all aspects of Shirley's career. Her earnings paid all the bills for the family, but she appeared not to mind that her father controlled all aspects of her early tennis career.

Things began to change when Shirley turned 18. With her parents no longer traveling with her, Shirley's interests transitioned to fast cars, partying, and rap music. As she practiced less and less, her game began to erode. When her father attempted to intervene, she got a court order preventing him from seeing her play—alleging that he had physically assaulted her. Her career hit the bottom when she and her friends were arrested after hours of noisy partying that included the use of illegal drugs. Even though she got off without prison time because of some procedural issues, Shirley quit tennis before she reached the age of 20.

1. What are the ethical issues, if any, associated with Shirley's early tennis career?

2. What values did Mr. Foster appear to emphasize during his daughter's tennis career?

3. What factors seem to have been contributors to the changes in priorities when Shirley turned 18?

4. What was Shirley valuing when she made the allegation against her father?

5. How might sport burnout have contributed to the changes in Shirley's approach to tennis?

REFERENCE

Coakley, J. J. 2001. *Sport in society: Issues & controversies.* 7th ed. Boston: McGraw-Hill.

ADDITIONAL READINGS

Engh, F. 1999. *Why Johnny hates sports: Why organized youth sports are failing our children and what we can do about it.* New York: Penguin Putnam.

Hardy, L. 1997. Pay to play. Fees for school sports. *The American School Board Journal* 184 (August): 25–27.

Hirschhorn, D., K. Loughhead, and T. Olisky. 2000. Parental impact on youth participation in sport: The physical educator's role. *Journal of Physical Education, Recreation and Dance* 71(9): 26–29.

Raedeke, T. D. 1997. Is athlete burnout more than just stress? A sport commitment perspective. *Journal of Sport & Exercise Psychology* 19(4) (December): 396–417.

Reeves, K. 1998. Athletic eligibility: Right or privilege? *School Administrator* 55(10) (November): 6–9.

Rotella, R. J., T. Hanson, and R. H. Coop. 1991. Burnout in youth sports. *Elementary School Journal* 91(5) (May): 421–28.

Sandfort, J. A., and G. Linneman. 1992. Athletic values as the value of athletics. *NASSP Bulletin* 76(546) (October): 101–3.

Udry, E., D. Gould, D. Bridges, and S. Tuffey. 1997. People helping people? Examining the social ties of athletes coping with burnout and injury stress. *Journal of Sport & Exercise Psychology* 19(4) (December): 368–95.

Wolff, R. 1996. *Good sports: A parent's guide to competitive youth sports.* Champaign IL: Sagamore Publishing.

Commercialized Sport

- ◆ What ethical issues have emerged because of the increasing commercialization in sport?
- ◆ What are the ethical issues associated with the use of youth, interscholastic, intercollegiate, and professional sport in public relations and promotions?
- ◆ How has commercialized sport exploited athletes at various levels of competition?
- ◆ What moral dilemmas have arisen when sport has become entertainment?
- ◆ Has sport been used to promulgate economic purposes to the detriment of ethical values?
- ◆ What steps could be taken to rectify any erosion of moral values in commercialized sport at all levels of competition?

Sport in the United States supposedly transmits values. Most sports receive praise for promoting character development, dedication, self-control, discipline, fair play, and other virtues. As a result, public officials and school and college administrators have for decades accepted an idyllic image of sport, content to allow sports to regulate themselves, thus remaining relatively free from prescriptive laws and statutes. However, potential revenues (such as from shoe companies), internal conflicts, labor-management disputes, and excessive pressures on coaches and players to win, have tainted the purity of this image. Restrictive policies and rules have been scrutinized, overtly and covertly violated, and sporadically enforced—all because of the tremendous financial and social benefits accruing to winners in many sports. Cheating at all levels of sport is often associated with this compulsion to win or the chance to claim number one status.

Before beginning this discussion, a few definitions could help provide a framework for gaining a better understanding. **Commercialized sport** is comprised of organized competitions that are advertised and promoted for entertainment value and for which the outcome has significance financially and leads to status within the sport context. All professional sports and football and basketball at most of NCAA Division I universities operate their programs as commercialized sport; that is, they are in the entertainment business. **Educational sport** is comprised of competitions between individuals enrolled in schools and colleges that are of interest mostly to the athletes, friends, and family because the outcome, while valued, is secondary to the sporting experience as characterized by behaviors such as fair play, teamwork, and cooperation. **Recreational sport,** which should include youth sport, is comprised of competitions between non-compensated individuals of any age who play sport

BOX 8-1

SHOULD SPORT BE COMMERCIALIZED?

Making money is not immoral; commercialization is not immoral. When sport becomes overly commercialized though, athletes, coaches, and sport managers may be tempted to let a nonmoral value like money, success, or fame influence moral decisions. If these values become the primary foci, will immoral actions such as cheating and a disregard for the welfare of opponents result? The sense that money controls actions may pervade sport. If this occurs, what happens to honesty, justice, responsibility, and civility?

To discuss ethical sport issues in relation to money always raises the question of whether participants and administrators of amateur and educational sport (that is, youth, scholastic, and collegiate) should market their products (the games) as commercial enterprises. Idealists would say that the purpose of sport at these levels is to develop character traits such as dedication, sacrifice, responsibility, and *esprit de corps* (group spirit). If this is true, then commercialization may corrupt the sport experience. As commercialization expands, the purpose of the game becomes selling or marketing the game rather than supporting individual and team spirit. With the emphasis on money, moral values may dissipate. Realists suggest that youth, scholastic, and collegiate sport develop positive character traits, and since the public is supportive of games, why not capitalize on this interest? Charging admission, selling advertisements, and broadcasting competitions on television and radio help defray the costs of these programs. Realists argue that neither money nor commercialization is immoral.

Professional athletes have long acknowledged that they are businessmen (and more recently businesswomen) whose job responsibilities are competing in sport. They realize that their talents are commodities that can be bought, sold, and traded, especially in team sports in which their franchises must invest millions of dollars in order to amass the talent needed to win. Individual athletes realize that they are entrepreneurs whose capital is their ability to win consistently. The economic realities of sport demand that owners and sport managers obtain a consistent

and significant revenue stream from television rights fees, ticket sales, licensing contracts, and league revenue sharing in order to pay the huge salaries of athletes and the costs of conducting business. In addition, title sponsors of sporting events, stadiums, and arenas and advertising revenue are essential to making sport profitable.

The elite intercollegiate athletic programs at the NCAA Division I level have reluctantly admitted that they are commercialized businesses. These multi-million-dollar enterprises depend on the same revenue streams in one or two sports in order to help finance other sports that bring in no revenue. So, in football and/or basketball, athletes and coaches are expected to win because only then will sufficient revenue be produced to keep universities from having to subsidize or eliminate athletic programs. Donations from fans, a unique source of financial support for intercollegiate athletics, have been correlated to the level of success on the field and court. Fans love to be affiliated with winning teams.

A tertiary outcome of the business side of sport is the economic impact on college towns. In some cases, more income from the sale of team-related clothing and paraphernalia, meals, and hotels occurs on game days than at any other time during the year. This is not hard to understand when a capacity football stadium has more people than most towns in a state. To these fans, the game and its outcome are all-important.

The true ethical dilemma in commercialization is not the money or the promotion but what occurs in moral decision making when money and winning become more important than the athletes involved. What occurs is that making more money becomes the goal, and athletes suffer. Sport can be commercial and moral, but sport managers are morally challenged to develop a set of principles and rules to follow when making business decisions. In large athletic departments, the task gets trickier because everyone, including athletes, coaches, and boosters, do not always live by the same set of principles and rules.

for fun, skill development, social interaction, and value development.

Commercialized sport (see Box 8-1) and the associated pressures to win usually affect moral values, often negatively. When sport participants harm opponents physically or psychologically to gain competitive advantages, moral values are sacrificed. This chapter presents an ethical analysis of commercialized sport from the following four perspectives: (1) sport for public relations and promotions; (2) sport as a business; (3) sport as entertainment; and (4) sport as a transmitter of economic values. Each will be examined from the vantage point of various competitive levels.

SPORT FOR PUBLIC RELATIONS AND PROMOTIONS

Even though many think of Greek athletics as the origin of amateur sport, which they were, commercialized sport also began with the Greeks. After centuries of competing with the singular goal of displaying their athletic superiority, the Greeks lapsed into competitions among athletes who were paid for victories and some who even bribed opponents to let them win. Greeks rewarded their native sons with lifelong pensions and other lavish gifts for bringing honor to the city-state as the home of an Olympic winner.

More recently, sport has been used for decades to promote cities, businesses, schools, regions of the country, colleges, and products. Because of their visibility, entertainment value, and association with educational institutions, several sports have historically and socially been publicized as wholesome, worthwhile activities. Affiliation with sport leagues allowed sponsoring groups to gain stature and generate fan interest for their teams, as well as for businesses' services and products. A symbiotic relationship has linked the most popular sports with the print and electronic media. Newspapers and television have promoted sports, and sports in turn have helped sell newspapers, advertisements, and products.

Many towns sponsor youth and school sport teams that help strengthen community pride.

Youth Sport

When towns and businesses began to sponsor youth sport teams in the 1920s, one of the desired outcomes was promotion. That is, while helping youth, businesses could serve their own economic interests, too. At that time, no one questioned this symbiotic relationship; it was small scale. The extent to which it has grown is phenomenal.

Originally, businesspeople furnished equipment, facilities, and T-shirts with the sponsor's name on the back for the boys' teams they subsidized. Minimal adult involvement in these sport leagues led to the claim that these leagues encouraged play and focused on sport skills development. Gradually, though, youth sport programs changed as sponsors sought the publicity associated with winning championships. This resulted in the provision of equipment, facilities, and uniforms modeled after professional leagues, as sponsors tried to outdo competitors.

Today, coaches for many teams sponsored by businesses and towns, in their zeal for success, bid for the best young players in major league-like drafts. Children are traded, benched, berated, and pushed, seemingly unmercifully, to achieve victories. Perhaps city leaders, in attempting to put their towns on the map, and entrepreneurs, in trying to gain a promotional edge for their products, have used children, perhaps unwittingly, for commercial purposes. Techniques frequently implemented include recruiting players from other towns and teams, playing overage youths by falsifying birth certificates, and giving financial inducements such as athletic shoes and clothing to players and their families. Particularly vulnerable are youth from poorer families.

Shoe companies sponsor summer leagues in basketball for youths as young as 12 and feature all-star teams that compete nationally. Many of the top players are enticed to change leagues, and often brands of shoes, with the lure of more free shoes, warm-ups, T-shirts, bags, and all-expense–paid trips to competitions where they can showcase their talents before ever-present college recruiters. Are these young athletes paid performers who already have internalized that success (winning) is most important? Or, are these youths rightfully just benefiting from their athletic talents?

Fun, socialization, and the development of moral values start to erode as young athletes learn that winning-at-all-costs in some leagues is a reality rather than a myth. Outfitted like professional athletes, many young sport participants model the commercialized behavior they view on television or read about in newspapers and magazines. These children grow to expect media coverage and the rewards received by the victorious (for example, playing in the Little League World Series or a Pop Warner National Championship). They also realize that those who do not win receive few benefits. Children also watch as many scholastic, collegiate, and professional athletes successfully exploit sport rules and enjoy winners' awards and acclaim. In what instances, if any, is it acceptable to violate the values of justice, honesty, and responsibility in the name of winning? What instances, if any, exist in which winning justifies whatever is done in order to do this?

Interscholastic Sport

School administrators increasingly face the quandry about whether sport participation at this level is a right or a privilege. If it is a right, then teams must be school-financed and available to all, regardless of gender, race, or skill level. Federal human rights legislation requires that girls and boys and students of all racial, religious, and ethnic backgrounds receive equal access to school athletics. Do the highly skilled, those with average talent, and the differently abled warrant the opportunity to play their favorite sports wearing the uniforms of their schools? Educational administrators and school board members face the challenge of financing all these teams. No longer will support given only to boys with the highest athletic skills comply with federal laws and equity standards. The question, however, is where to find the money to pay for coaching, uniforms, travel, officiating, facilities, and equipment.

Some schools, in addressing this issue, have redefined the opportunity to play interscholastic sports as a privilege rather than a right. With this change has emerged the concept of pay to play. The popularity of this trend increases as schools expect each athlete to pay a fee to defray the cost of personal equipment, the team uniform, and individual travel expenses. Many have supported this alternative in lieu of eliminating varsity teams because of shortfalls in state educational funding. Unfortunately, the economically disadvantaged student may be eliminated from competition because pay to play is possibly an inequitable and unjust standard. In some instances, schools make provisions for these students through funds raised by boosters. For schools that do not, what moral problems surface when students are excluded from play if they cannot pay?

Another method that schools have used to finance interscholastic sport is through booster clubs. Individuals in local communities donate private and business monies and conduct fund-raising activities to help pay the increasing costs of sponsoring athletic teams. Because of their contributions, some boosters may seek to influence decisions (such as who should coach the teams) and to demand winning teams. When schools were paying the bills, school administrators, including athletic directors, seldom experienced interference from outside groups. Now, however, dependent on varying degrees of external revenue sources, educational decision makers often struggle to retain an educational, rather than commercial, focus for their sport programs. Plus, national pride, economic supremacy, and accountability have contributed to the clamor for educational improvement and reform in schools. By comparison, the sponsorship of sport teams appears limited in importance.

The potential for corporate sponsorships and television revenue may be viewed as the panacea for the financial woes of schools. In the struggle to support increased sport opportunities for students, however, schools are faced with difficult decisions. Commercial sponsors, including those selling alcohol, tobacco, and nonnutritional food products, are eager to place advertisements in game programs, on sport facility scoreboards and walls, and on team uniforms. The ethical issue in deciding whether schools should permit advertisements for companies promoting tobacco and alcohol products rests in the question of what the purpose of education is. If the answer involves the importance of health and wellness or social responsibility, then the school has a responsibility to follow tenets that support good health practices. Tobacco use is a known health detriment, alcohol in the hands of children is unacceptable, and misuse of alcohol is illegal. If a school accepts the advertisement of a beer company, it could be argued that the school endorses the use of alcohol. Therefore, the ethical question becomes—is that school being ethically and socially responsible to its mission and educational purpose?

Some sporting goods companies gladly furnish shoes and uniforms to successful teams and pay their coaches. Some boosters and sport agents try to reward the athletic achievements of local stars, despite regulations that prohibit giving these benefits. Who, if anyone, is culpable when these payouts occur? Does acceptance of these monies by athletes or coaches violate any ethical principle?

Because such bonanzas accrue only to the most successful teams and athletes, some coaches may be tempted to use questionable tactics, such as conducting practices outside of the allowable season for a sport, recruiting players from outside a school district, lying about players' ages, arranging for athletes to receive unearned grades to maintain their eligibility, and teaching game techniques for circumventing the rules to achieve victory. What ethical principles are violated when these tactics are used? In addition, school-age athletes are occasionally treated as disposable commodities, of value only in helping improve coaches' and schools' won–lost records. Even at the interscholastic level, commercialization of sport in the quest for revenue may displace educational outcomes, such as the teaching of teamwork, sportsmanship, cooperation, and self-discipline and may lead to unethical actions like cheating.

Intercollegiate Sport

As early as the 1890s, college presidents realized that the popularity of successful football teams could enhance the prestige and external images of their institutions. A century later, numerous universities find that admissions applications grow dramatically after consistent rankings in the top 10 in football or basketball or the winning of national championships. Most fans can name universities that are more nationally acclaimed for winning football or basketball championships than for graduating future Rhodes scholars.

University presidents, who are ultimately responsible for the proper conduct of all programs in their institutions, are often willing to emphasize athletics as the most visible public relations tool at their disposal. Frequently, university administrators nurture alumni involvement through athletic-related social events. It is assumed that alumni and many sport fans who never attended their favorite colleges will donate money both for sports and academic programs; in reality, most contributions from nonalumni fans flow into the athletic coffers. When a university is recognized more for sport

Many colleges promote their women's athletic programs as evidence of equity in sports opportunities. (Photo courtesy of the University of Kansas Department of Intercollegiate athletics.)

achievements than for the quality of its educational programs, is the high visibility of its commercialized athletic program detrimental to its educational mission?

Colleges and universities face ethical challenges relative to commercialization in sport. The four most promising areas for increased income include individual donations, ticket sales, commercial sponsor-ships, and television guarantees, including conference-sharing revenues. Obviously, all are integrally linked with public relations and promotions. People enjoy reflected fame when they affiliate with winning teams. Fans are more likely to give money to teams that win league, conference, and national championships. Joining a booster club named for one's preferred team becomes a status symbol, along with the associated seating, parking, and social affiliation perks.

College booster clubs raise substantial amounts of money, millions of dollars at many NCAA Division I universities. Although most of these monies fund athletic grants-in-aid, some are also used to build or expand athletic facilities and to give performance bonuses to coaches.

The place and purpose of athletic boosters is not an ethical problem if they follow the expressed purpose and goals of higher education. However, an ethical dilemma emerges if boosters violate the stated purposes of athletics within the university. If boosters become a power unto themselves with their own agendas (thus violating the tenets of the university or the NCAA, which the university has pledged to follow), then control of the boosters or even their existence becomes an ethical dilemma. No allied organization or group can be justified if it violates and does not support the mission and goals of the sponsoring entity. Boosters can positively support an athletic program and the university only if they hold to the same set of principles.

Ticket sales often reflect the success of an athletic team. At small colleges, this may mean that only a few dozen, hundred, or thousand attend. Still, collecting these revenues remains critical to the financial viability of many teams. Although "big-time" universities may attract over 50,000 to 100,000 fans to their football stadiums and more than 10,000 spectators to their basketball arenas, oftentimes the size of the crowd does not change the expectation that the number of victories must exceed the number of losses to maintain fan support. Every college and university athletic director will acknowledge that *winning = fans = money = winning = fans = money.* This perpetual cycle brings in much-needed revenue, yet this money must be reinvested to produce more victories. While commercialization predominately affects the revenue-producing sports, commercialization and fund-raising in the so-called non-revenue-producing sports may replicate the problems often associated with the revenue-producing sports. Specifically, if gate receipts are generated or marketing techniques employed successfully, a heightened pressure to "win at all costs" may follow with the potential of compromising educational aims. Are any values violated when the need to make money and gain victories becomes the most important incentive for an athletic department?

Few sport programs could exist without private and commercial sponsorships. Business and corporate advertisements in game programs, on scoreboards, and on uniforms are pervasive. Should an athletic administrator accept the thousands of dollars offered by a beer distributor or a tobacco company for one of these advertisements? If provided sports equipment and clothing and large financial payments, should a university sign an exclusive contract with a company? Do colleges need to establish ethical limits for what components of their sport programs they will market to the highest bidder? Another ethical issue facing universities is deciding whether to sell licensed T-shirts, sweatshirts, and other clothing items with team logos that have been manufactured in international locations where companies are accused of exploiting workers. Because many of these sales are associated with support for athletic teams, especially when teams are successful, and athletic departments are the primary beneficiaries of these revenues, this ethical dilemma faces athletic administrators. That is, should corporations that do not protect the rights of workers be boycotted, even if this means risking a reduction in revenue for the athletic department?

Capitalism, which is neither ethical nor unethical, includes social responsibility tenets such as fair competition and social welfare. Does becoming somewhat subservient to the corporate bottom line lead to compromises in the ethical values of fair play, honesty, and justice?

Television may lead to an erosion in moral values because of the huge potential revenues associated with telecasts. For example, because of the large sums of money that the national, regional, and cable networks wield, will colleges and universities agree to allow their teams to be scheduled at any time, regardless of the effect on their educational programs? Seemingly, the day of the week, the time of day, the place, and the opponent often are dictated by television through the promise of more revenue.

Professional Sport

Professional teams have become extremely important for businesses' public relations. According to many, no city can claim "major league" status unless it serves as home for at least one professional franchise. Witness the willingness of city leaders and prospective owners to pay hundreds of millions of dollars to entice professional leagues to place expansion franchises in their cities.

A vivid example of the tremendous desire to keep a professional team in town was New York City's willingness to refurbish Yankee Stadium at a cost of millions of tax dollars when the city's budget was in deficit. Now the wealthy team owner is asking for a new stadium. In Louisiana, generations will be repaying the debt for construction of the Superdome. Many cities, through public funding, have built massive stadiums and arenas and then rented them for practically nothing to attract and keep professional teams in their cities. St. Louis refused to build a new stadium for its Cardinals (football), then enticed the Rams to move to its city at a huge cost to taxpayers. The justification for using public financing for stadium construction focuses on the economic impact on jobs, taxes, and business profits resulting from the presence of these teams. When municipal revenues go to subsidize professional sports, however, social services may be underfunded, possibly contributing to inner cities being plagued by crime, drug abuse, and deplorable living conditions. When this occurs, what moral values are undermined?

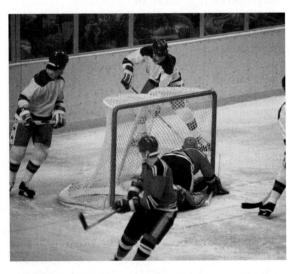

Ice hockey is trying to increase its commercial popularity on television and in southern and western regions of the country.

COMMERCIALIZED SPORT AS A BUSINESS

The media's 24/7 coverage of professional, collegiate, scholastic, and youth teams places sport continuously before the public. Office conversations, game-viewing parties at sport bars, and the popularity of the *USA Today* sports section are three examples illustrating the pervasiveness of sport in our society. Children mimic their favorite sport heroes and heroines. They also imitate the behaviors of antiheroes, resulting in violent behavior, unsportsmanlike conduct, drug abuse, and cheating. Regardless of whether professional athletes want to be role models, they are.

Youth, scholastic, and collegiate stars dream of achieving the fame and fortune enjoyed by many professional athletes shown and discussed during prime time, or 24 hours a day, by corporate sponsors who pay the stars millions of dollars to endorse their products. Companies exploit the popularity of athletes to sell their shoes, food, beverages, pain medicine, and other products. Is honesty an issue when these athletes promote a product for money even though their endorsements about personal usage are fabrications?

Sport permeates the lives of many people. Besides discussing, reading about, and viewing sports, many people promote their favorite teams by proudly wearing licensed merchandise. Professional franchise owners and colleges collect millions of dollars annually from the sale of clothing and team memorabilia. To a lesser extent, youth and scholastic teams garner revenue from the sale of sweatshirts, banners, and caps sporting team logos.

In our capitalistic society, the commercialization of sport remains inescapable. If sponsors pay enough money, they can now rename football bowl games (for example, Tostitos Fiesta Bowl). Television inserts "brought to you by . . ." provide game statistics and replay scoring plays or races; and outstanding player recognitions and championship trophies carry the names of sponsors. Has sport sold out to the highest bidder? Another example of the influence of money can be seen when media representatives from newspapers, magazines, radio, and television receive special perks leading to favorable coverage, which can help attract more fans.

The sport industry is a multibillion-dollar business when its competitive and recreational components are combined. This could be characterized as corporate athleticism. Although recreational sports through their focus on participation may contribute to the development of values such as fair play, self-discipline, and cooperation, the potential to reap financial benefits has changed competitive sport, even at the youngest levels.

The physiological and psychological well-being and personal improvement of each athlete competing in highly structured leagues often are viewed as inferior to an emphasis on winning and on achieving the recognition and rewards given to winners.

Many intercollegiate athletic programs rely on fan support through ticket sales to pay escalating costs.

Most of the increased financing for and commercialization of sport comes from businesses and corporations seeking profits, directly or indirectly, through associations with youth, scholastic, collegiate, and professional teams. Athletic commercialization starts early, for example, through advertising on Little League uniforms and the provision of free shoes and athletic clothing to adolescents.

Youth Sport and Interscholastic Sport

Athletes in youth leagues and on scholastic teams are less likely to experience sport as a business, but at times they do. Early in some of their sport careers, athletes are given lucrative prizes, athletic shoes, clothing, and equipment, even though these young people are amateur competitors. High school athletic associations specify allowable remuneration for students, yet independently organized youth competitions may have no such restrictions. One unfortunate example occurred in 1993. Several male high school basketball players lost their eligibility, were suspended from a few games, or were otherwise penalized when they played in a Nike-sponsored event in violation of state interscholastic sport rules. Using collegiate and professional models, some corporations and youth sport organizations may sponsor competitions without regard for eligibility rules of the athletes in other settings.

Young athletes, as early as four years old, learn that the rewards of victory, such as huge trophies, newspaper publicity, popularity among peers, and preferential treatment, outweigh the few pats on the back for optimal effort in games lost. As these youthful stars mature, become more knowledgeable about the increased value of awards, and experience the stress associated with seeking to gain these lucrative benefits, the pressures to win may lead to ethical dilemmas and unethical actions such as taking performance-enhancing drugs, lying about one's age, and accepting money and other benefits.

Schools, led by the misplaced priorities of coaches and parents, may overemphasize winning for the sake of ego fulfillment. Children's sport successes may enhance parents' status in the community. Stardom in the sport arena also may lead to financial inducements flowing to parents, who it is hoped will persuade their child to attend a certain college. Some youth sport or interscholastic coaches may seek to advance their personal careers through their athletes' achievements.

Intercollegiate Sport

In commercialized intercollegiate athletics (primarily in Division I of the NCAA), there may be many exploited athletes. The greatest travesty ever perpetuated upon this group of people, and especially upon academically marginal students, has been the myth that receiving an athletic grant-in-aid leads to a college degree (see Box 8-2). Most athletes have fulfilled a part of their agreement in

BOX 8-2

ATHLETIC GRANTS-IN-AID: A BUSINESS CONTRACT OR AN EDUCATIONAL OPPORTUNITY?

Perception of right and wrong may become murky for some college coaches and athletic directors who sometimes lose sight of moral values when faced with ethical dilemmas. One ethical issue revolves around whether the purpose of an athletic grant-in-aid is to help an athlete earn a college degree. If the answer is yes, then the athletic portion of the experience is secondary to the educational experience. If the answer is no, then the educational experience becomes secondary.

Ethical dilemmas occur when actions do not match the stated motive and intention. The usual justification for unethical actions when faced with ethical issues and dilemmas is a form of palliative comparison, using business as the backdrop. "Everyone else puts athletics before academics, so we have to do it to stay competitive." For example, if people measure the rightness or wrongness of what they do by what others do, no integrity exists except in relation to the social expectation. Situational ethics becomes the norm.

giving maximally to their sports. Too many colleges, even small-time programs, have failed to adhere to this bargain by withholding financial aid after a year of competition if an athlete does not achieve the expected level of performance or by not helping athletes succeed in the classroom. Many freshmen football and basketball players enter college with the belief that they will earn college degrees, but by the end of their first year, they become more realistic about their meager chances of effectively combining athletics and academics.

Educational exploitation in colleges may take many forms. Lowering admissions standards to allow academically unprepared students into college may set them up for failure. Tutoring, close monitoring of progress, personal advising, and minimal course schedules filled with nonrigorous classes may not bridge the gap for marginally prepared student–athletes. Despite such help, to prevent failure, these students may be tempted to cheat on tests, let others write their papers, or expect good grades to be received because they are athletes. Others may "major in eligibility," with or without their coaches' encouragement, doing whatever it takes to stay eligible to play. Other athletes take full advantage of educational opportunities made possible through their athletic prowess by earning their degrees.

Although the NCAA limits the number of hours in a week that student–athletes can spend practicing and competing in their sports, the time demands on collegiate athletes are extensive. Because compliance with maximal competition and practice time rules is based solely on a program's or coach's integrity to document all hours spent in athletics, many hours go unreported. In some programs, athletes sign blank forms weeks in advance and allow coaches to fill in the maximum allowable times, even though the athletes regularly exceed these hours for practices and competitions. If this rule can be circumvented, can others, too?

Athletic commitments also detract from the opportunities for student–athletes to enlarge their social contacts and participate in other organizations and activities during their years in college. Propo-

Many athletes realize that they are entertainers in commercialized sport.

nents for the ineligibility of freshmen cite the importance of achieving academic success and participating in social and extracurricular activities before allowing athletic competition.

Psychological pressures may exceed academic and social demands. Because most NCAA Division I athletes receive grants-in-aid, they are expected to perform at high levels. Pressures to win, exerted by coaches, fans, teammates, and personally, if allowed to become excessive, may hamper performance. Overemphasis on one's sport may lead to a reduction in social development because no person or thing is as important as winning. Other areas of psychological exploitation include pressures to maintain coach-imposed weights (possibly leading to eating disorders) and the underdevelopment of athletes' decision-making skills and responsibility because of coach domination.

On the financial side, many say that college athletes in Division I programs are exploited. In exchange for grants-in-aid worth between $3,000 and $30,000, depending on the institution, some athletes may help their universities collect millions of dollars in gate receipts, television-rights fees, and NCAA championship revenues. Is this situation an exploitation of athletes? If so, how?

The NCAA also regulates the mobility and duration of collegiate sport careers, collects and distributes profits (to and from its members), and polices its members by levying penalties as it deems appropriate. For example, if an athlete signs a letter of intent with a particular college and later decides to transfer to another institution for academic or athletic reasons, the athlete is not allowed to compete for one year at the new institution. Does this rule violate the moral principle of justice? In contrast, a coach can drop or reduce an athlete's grant-in-aid at will with no due process accorded the athlete. Have the moral principles of honesty and beneficence been violated in this action? Moreover, coaches can break their contracts and move to colleges offering more lucrative benefit packages without penalty. How is this behavior honest, or is it?

Professional Sport

Professional athletes realize that they are paid to entertain. Yet they question whether they must endure physical exploitation. Playing while injured may be the standard in the professional leagues, but is coercing athletes to endanger their postcareer well-being defensible? Some athletes have been subjected to improper treatments for injuries and incomplete diagnoses resulting in chronic and career-ending disabilities. One example of a continuing controversy focuses on whether playing on artificial turf, which is more cost-effective for stadium owners, actually causes many athletes to suffer debilitating injuries. Lowered life expectancies and mobility limitations are among the realities facing many former pros.

Regardless of the level of sport, exploitation occurs when winning surpasses more important outcomes such as obtaining an education and value development. Exploitation is felt when athletes are manipulated and used for the benefit of others, usually with no regard for the welfare of those inte-

grally involved. What is the moral effect on sport when winning and gaining financial benefit become all-important?

SPORT AS ENTERTAINMENT

One moral dilemma of sport as entertainment centers around whether this role of sport threatens the educational mission of schools and colleges. Educational institutions exist to help students learn, thus preparing them for life experiences and making contributions to society. Universities seek to create and disseminate knowledge. Critical thinking, learning, and the pursuit of knowledge are the goals of education. Can sport as entertainment coexist with these purposes? Have moral dilemmas become commonplace because the concept of sport as entertainment within educational institutions is inherently contradictory?

Youth and Interscholastic Sport

Although modeled after collegiate and professional programs, sport for young athletes remains somewhat insulated from the seamier side of entertainment. Lesser-skilled athletes attract fewer spectators and associated problems. Still, though, parents and overly enthusiastic fans may expect or even demand adult-level entertainment from children and adolescents. Pressures to succeed, usually self-imposed, have led some youth sport coaches to use overage players or to recruit athletes from other towns or programs.

A handful or a few hundred fans may boo and berate adolescent athletes who do not win championships. Other adults may heap bountiful recognition and rewards on the winners. Family, school, and town pride may rest on the narrow shoulders of adolescents who feel heavy burdens both to entertain and to win. When the pressures become too intense, youthful athletes may cheat and violate rules to win games, praise, and awards. If sport spectators pay, do they expect to be entertained, even when the athletes are in miniature? No doubt the higher the skill level, the greater the expectation for entertainment. Failure to perform up to the standard demanded may lead to disparaging comments and abandonment of support.

Intercollegiate Sport

The president of the University of San Francisco eliminated the men's basketball program during the 1980s because of NCAA sanctions for abuses. He questioned how educational institutions could allow their principles, integrity, and students to be prostituted for the purposes of winning and achieving ill-gotten recognition and income. Does sport as entertainment cause newspapers to print point spreads used by gamblers? Do the huge amounts of money bet on college sports contribute to athletes' accepting money to intentionally lose games or "cover the spread"? Universities today face an ethical quandry of trying to preserve their academic credibility when their highly visible athletic programs are multimillion-dollar entertainment businesses. The tough question remains: Should universities and colleges sponsor athletic teams that are commercialized businesses more than they are educational programs? Does the fact that these programs have existed for decades automatically exclude them from scrutiny?

The extent to which coaches, sport managers, and even presidents may use sport as entertainment to promote themselves, their universities, and their teams is not known. However, the monetary stakes are huge. Perhaps no ethical boundaries exist for sport used as entertainment, at least not as long as sanctions are ineffective deterrents. This is even more true when we realize that many interpret the rules to their institutions' benefit and push the rules to the limit. Whether athletic programs are conducted honestly, justly, responsibly, and beneficently depends on the ethical values of those in charge and on their application of moral principles.

Although presidential and institutional control are pivotal factors that can lead to reforms in intercollegiate athletics, athletic departments' multimillion-dollar budgets are primarily financed by gate receipts, television appearance guarantees, and conference-sharing agreements (from bowl games and television packages). Many university presidents have found out the hard way that controlling the policies, personnel decisions, and actions of those administering athletics on their campuses is difficult. One question often asked is whether integrity is compatible with sports as entertainment.

The NCAA and its Division I member institutions are in the entertainment business. Fans value, as indicated by their willingness to purchase tickets, the entertainment provided by collegiate athletes. The fact that these athletes are students is secondary in importance, if relevant at all. The coach has one primary responsibility—to provide the most enjoyable entertainment possible, which is usually defined to include winning (see Box 8-3).

Professional Sport

Athletes in the professional leagues realize that they are expendable commodities in a continual process of providing entertainment while making money. Players are bought, sold, and traded either to enhance chances of winning or to save money. In a time when a World Series title could be bought (like the 1997 Florida Marlins) or a championship team sold (the 1998 Florida Marlins), fan loyalty to identifiable players on their favorite teams eroded as free agency blossomed.

Professional athletes with their multimillion-dollar contracts are the beneficiaries of huge television revenues and high ticket prices because fans are willing to pay to be entertained. They revere Cal Ripken who will sign autographs endlessly. They will wait for hours to have Peyton Manning sign a football and proudly wear a Shaquille O'Neal jersey because the electronic media has shown their heroics time and again. While having heroes is positive, should most children name sports stars, rather than parents, teachers, and community or national leaders, as their heroes? What is being valued in these choices?

THE KNIGHT FOUNDATION COMMISSION
ON INTERCOLLEGIATE ATHLETICS

Keeping the Faith with the Student Athlete— a New Model for Intercollegiate Athletics (March 1991)

In 1989, the Trustees of the Knight Foundation created this commission and asked it to propose a reform agenda for intercollegiate athletics because abuses associated with athletics threatened the integrity of higher education. Through receipt of input from experts in the field, public meetings, and debate among themselves, the 22-member commission identified problems in the areas of recruiting, unending efforts to maximize revenue to and renown for the university, and an overemphasis on entertainment. The ascendancy of these "ends" that have outweighed the "means" were found to be deep-rooted and long-standing by the commission, thus resulting in a loss of focus on the reason intercollegiate athletics should exist, for example, for the students and their educational development. The commission recommended a "one-plus-three" model for reform, with the key (the one) being presidential control. Academic integrity, financial integrity, and certification (the three) were essential to return intercollegiate athletics to a proper balance for student–athletes, their sports, and higher education.

A Solid Start—a Report on Reform of Intercollegiate Athletics (March 1992)

In the midst of increasing expressions that intercollegiate athletics were out of control, including concern expressed by the Presidents' Commission of the NCAA, the commission reconvened to assess what progress had been achieved. Changes in NCAA rules during the 1992 NCAA Convention, as proposed by the Presidents' Commission, led to significantly higher academic standards for student–athletes and other actions that reflected a willingness to make intercollegiate athletics more equitable, less costly, and more focused on integrity.

A Call to Action—Reconnecting College Sports and Higher Education (June 2001)

According to the third Knight Commission report, despite reform efforts during the 1990s, the problems in big-time college sports have grown rather than diminished. Because of academic abuses, a financial arms race, and commercialization, the chasm between educational values and intercollegiate sports at the highest level has worsened. An overemphasis on winning, permitting potential revenue sources such as television and corporate interests to dictate actions, illicit payments to athletes, sport for entertainment and gambling, and the denigration of the ideals of higher education litter the landscape of major college sport in the 21st century. The good news, however, is that despite this disgraceful environment, some major colleges operate their programs without sacrificing their academic integrity and ethical standards.

The commission's latest report did not paint a pretty picture when it characterized intercollegiate sport as corrupt, thoroughly professionalized and commercialized, and replete with deplorable sportsmanship and misconduct. Some former university presidents, such as A. Bart Giametti and James Duderstadt, told the commission that unchecked intercollegiate athletics damage the reputation of colleges by having the sideshow of sport engulf higher education and displace its academic integrity. The commission also heard from James Shulman and William Bowen, authors of *The Game of Life,* who reported that even in academically selective institutions core educational values are being threatened by intercollegiate athletics. The commission concluded by recommending academic reforms, a deescalation in the athletics arms race, and a deemphasis of the commercialization of intercollegiate athletics as well as a restoration of athletics to a balanced part of the academic mission of colleges.

SPORT AS A TRANSMITTER OF ECONOMIC VALUES

Early in an athlete's career, economic values may exceed ethical values because the former are rewarded while the latter may be faintly praised. Financial benefits are so important that most people have redefined sportsmanship as "pushing the rules to the limit without getting caught." For example, athletes of all ages too often are rewarded for throwing at a batter's head, taking out a player with an illegal block, or holding an opponent on a rebound attempt. It is difficult for athletes to see the difference (is there one?) between shaving points in basketball games and receiving money as inducements to get them to attend particular universities.

Economic Concerns and Rule Violations

Sport competitions require rules and participants' respect for them. A direct result of the importance of economic values occurs when the "spirit of the rules" dies. Constitutive rules (see Chapter 5) give boundaries to sport. If a player commits an act outside these boundaries, then a violation has occurred. Sometimes players violate rules unwittingly; other times they do so intentionally to help win and attain the associated benefits. Two kinds of intentional violations are frequently observed. First, a player may consciously violate a rule expecting to be caught, yet willingly accept the penalty in order to attain some tactical advantage that the violation affords. Second, a player may intentionally violate a rule, hoping to avoid getting caught and benefiting from breaking a rule.

Penalties for intentional fouls are stated in basketball rules because players have violated rules to gain advantages. Faking an injury in football to stop the clock and thus allowing the field goal kicker onto the field may be within the letter of the rules, but some would argue that it violates the spirit of the rules. Do these rule violations or circumventions occur because the economic rewards for winning outweigh ethical behavior such as honesty and development of values such as sportsmanship?

Youth Sport

In some situations, youth ice hockey teaches and rewards rule infractions. In fact, instead of being taught formally and systematically the normative rules of the game, some are taught how to perform illegitimate acts and how to avoid detection. Since the use of illegitimate tactics is considered strategically important by some coaches, players may believe that disobedience to game rules is important to the coach. That is, rules should be violated if this helps win. These same behaviors also characterize some in youth football as players are coached how to hold without getting caught. In youth volleyball, players are coached not to say they touched balls tipped out of bounds on a block attempt.

Intercollegiate Sport

Some common myths surround the economics of "big-time" college sports. Box 8-4 lists some of these myths and the realities found in some programs. At times, media exposés claim that the intercollegiate athletic system is morally bankrupt. Some sportswriters argue that the NCAA and many of its member institutions value economic, not ethical, outcomes. For example, coaches and sport managers apparently feel no ethical trepidation about pocketing annual salaries in excess of $100,000 while some of their athletes have no spending money because of the limits placed on grants-in-aid.

A more realistic argument places the responsibility for the commercialization of intercollegiate athletes on the shoulders of administrators and coaches. Each university votes to enact the regulations that make the NCAA heavily reliant on voluminous rules. Often, these rules have been legislated as knee-jerk responses to the behaviors, usually perceived as unethical, of NCAA members. Member institutions of the NCAA have perpetuated economic (not ethical) outcomes and only they can change this spiral of moral bankruptcy.

Gambling (see Box 8-5) provides a graphic example of how sport can be used and abused economically. Sport and gambling, although inseparable in

BOX 8-4

MYTHS AND REALITIES IN
COMMERCIALIZED INTERCOLLEGIATE SPORT

Myth

1. Intercollegiate athletics is part of the educational mission of all American colleges and universities.
2. The alumni demand large and successful intercollegiate sports programs—rather than strong academic programs—in their alma maters.

3. Intercollegiate athletics is incredibly profitable, earning huge sums of money for American colleges and universities.
4. Universities receive millions of dollars when their teams play in football bowl games.
5. The money earned from intercollegiate athletics helps support other parts of the university.

6. Coaches in colleges deserve high annual incomes because they generate huge profits for their athletic programs.
7. Intercollegiate athletic programs provide a wonderful opportunity for black coaches.
8. Intercollegiate athletic programs provide a wonderful opportunity for women coaches.
9. Intercollegiate athletics provides an excellent opportunity for black youngsters to get out of the ghetto, earn a degree, and contribute to American society.
10. For collegiate athletes, the opportunity for a university education is as important as playing intercollegiate sports.

Reality

1. The main purpose of NCAA Division I sports is commercialized entertainment.
2. Many alumni contribute to the academic units of their colleges and universities. Other research indicates that many major donors to athletic programs actually are boosters, people who never attended the school, who give money to the athletic department only in proportion to its team's success on the field or court, and who do not contribute to the institution's academic programs.
3. Most intercollegiate athletic programs expend more money than they earn in revenues.
4. After expenses and conference sharing, most universities participating in bowl games do not make money and may even run a deficit.
5. Because athletic department expenses usually exceed revenues, most money earned by collegiate sport teams stays in the athletic department. There are, however, a few notable examples of athletic departments using revenues for nonathletic scholarships, library support, or other university-wide purposes.
6. The vast majority of coaches direct programs that lose money for their institutions. Market factors and past winning records lead to high salaries.
7. White athletic directors mostly hire individuals who look like them.
8. The percentage of women coaches in colleges has decreased significantly and steadily in the past 25 years.
9. Some athletic programs recruit black athletes primarily to play sports, even though they are ill-prepared for the academic demands of college.
10. Many collegiate athletes in "big-time" programs hope to play their sports at the professional or Olympic level and regard college as their pathway to the pros or the national team.

BOX 8-5

IS GAMBLING AN ETHICAL ISSUE IN SPORT?

Gambling may or may not be a moral issue. Gambling can be defined as one person placing a wager (stakes) on whether a future event will occur. The ethical dilemma of gambling occurs when individual principles such as honesty, responsibility, and justice are violated and others suffer because of the act. The dilemma really exists outside of the issue of legality because in most states government-supported gambling, such as a lottery, flourishes. Legally, gambling may be judged moral because governmental agencies benefit. However, even legalized gambling may become a moral issue if the gambling violates responsible decision making. In the case of sport gambling, the gambling is not the issue; rather the issue is the effect of the gambling on the individual and the integrity of the game. Because people are highly affected by the power of money, and gambling usually uses money as the stakes, gambling becomes questionable moral behavior. Most sport leagues do not permit gambling by their athletes.

In recent years, several incidents of gambling by college athletes have led to heated discussions about whether the Congress should legislate that gambling on college sports is illegal even though the number of legal sports bets in Nevada and via the Internet pale in comparison to the wagers among friends and on the office pools during March Madness. Point spreads in newspapers appear to legitimize gambling in sport at the NCAA Division I level as well as on professional games. It is easy to see how athletes could rationalize that they should not be penalized for doing what thousands of others do. Yet two questions remain: Should athletes be permitted to bet on the outcome or point spread of a game in which they could have an influence on its outcome or score? If athletes choose to place a bet on these games, are these actions unethical?

the minds of many, continue to tarnish the image of sport as a builder of values. To heighten interest, thousands of people wager millions of dollars annually on collegiate and professional sport. Although such gambling is illegal, except in a few locations such as Nevada, newspapers persist in publishing point spreads that encourage sport betting. Point-shaving scandals in the past 50 years, especially in college basketball, and millions of dollars of friendly wagers, may have been fostered by these printed point spreads. Some players have justified shaving points because of the money they received as long as the outcome was not affected, especially because newspapers indirectly abetted in breaking the law. Is sport gambling unethical? Should athletes be allowed to place bets on their teams?

Sport potentially can teach teamwork, yet many young athletes injure themselves through overuse while their teammates languish on the bench. Sport potentially can teach self-control; still, basketball coaches and players are cited for technical fouls, abusive language, and on-the-court fighting. Sport potentially can teach discipline; however, college and professional athletes are repeatedly arrested for driving while intoxicated, using illegal drugs, and assault. Sometimes, coaches and sport managers disregard these behaviors as frivolous or mischievous; sometimes, these athletes are aided in avoiding arrest and punishment for their actions. Sport potentially can teach fair play, but athletes are often taught how to obey the letter of the (sport) law but not the spirit. Sport potentially can teach that the athlete's well-being as a person is foremost, but many coaches treat athletes as expendable commodities. Has the pursuit of profits resulted in a widespread erosion of ethical values? Are sport actions and behaviors influenced by how they will benefit a team or individual, regardless of right and wrong, or potential harm to others? Have economic values replaced ethical values?

ETHICAL DILEMMAS RELATIVE TO COMMERCIALIZATION

Commercialization affects sport at all levels, although the ethical issues vary. Each athlete, coach, and sport manager must choose repeatedly whether public relations, entertainment, and economic values supersede an emphasis on the ethical values of justice, honesty, responsibility, and beneficence. Box 8-6 uses questions to challenge one's thinking about the ethical dilemmas associated with commercialization. Alternatives are suggested, although anyone may have a better resolution.

BOX 8-6

ETHICAL DILEMMAS IN COMMERCIALIZED SPORT

Dilemma	Alternative Resolutions
1. Is a primary purpose of sport the promotion of a city, educational institution, or product?	a) Yes, this is acceptable whenever any of these entities provides funding for sport. b) No, cities large or small should not use sport to "put themselves on the map." c) Sport is an extracurricular activity, not the reason why educational institutions should exist. d) Because corporations pay so much to fund sporting activities, they deserve any and all associated promotional benefits.
2. Should sport be used for public relations purposes?	a) No, educational institutions should build their reputations and status on academic, not athletic, programs. b) Yes, educational institutions should seek to benefit from the popularity and success of their sport teams. c) Yes, having a professional team franchise makes a city "big league."
3. Does the winning-at-all-costs mentality in sport lead to the exploitation of athletes?	a) Yes, but it is permissible to cheat as long as no one is hurt. b) Yes, it is permissible to cheat as long as one does not get caught. c) Yes, it is acceptable to put maintaining eligibility ahead of rule adherence to win. d) Yes, coaches have the right to use their athletes in any way necessary to help win (and possibly save their jobs). e) No, winning is never more important than the physical, psychological, emotional, social, and academic well-being of athletes. f) Yes, often athletes are exploited and ethical principles violated under the guise of winning.

Continued

BOX 8-6

ETHICAL DILEMMAS IN COMMERCIALIZED SPORT—cont'd

Dilemma	Alternative Resolutions
4. When should sports exist for the entertainment of fans?	a) Never for youth sports because the purposes should be fun and sport skill development.
	b) Not in interscholastic sports because these should be extracurricular activities that teach educational values.
	c) Most intercollegiate athletic programs provide competitive activities that enrich the collegiate experiences of participants, not entertainment.
	d) Because football and men's basketball teams at many universities attract huge crowds, these programs are and should be in the entertainment business.
	e) Professional sports exist for the purpose of entertainment.
5. Do economic values and ethical values conflict in sport?	a) Yes, when money and other financial inducements become paramount, ethical values often are violated.
	b) Young athletes never have to choose between these (that is, no conflict exists).
	c) Seldom are scholastic athletes lured by money or other benefits to break sport rules.
	d) Only males in the major football and basketball programs are faced with ethical dilemmas with regard to economic issues.
	e) No conflicts between money and moral principles exist in professional sports.
6. How has increasing commercialization impacted sport?	a) Positively, because athletes at all levels are treated better through higher salaries, more grants-in-aid, better facilities, and increased media coverage.
	b) Negatively, because money influences so much that happens in sport such as when, where, and who to play.
	c) Positively, because sport has become more important in the lives of most Americans.
	d) Negatively, because getting more money has replaced the teaching and reinforcing of values as primary outcomes.

SUMMARY

Corporate athleticism exists today. The abuses in intercollegiate athletics prevalent in previous years have only expanded, spreading downward into youth programs as well as pervading up through the professional leagues. Through televised sport, a college or city can promote itself, but such exposure expands only for those who win. The cycle of *winning = fans = money = winning = fans = money* perpetuates itself. Exploitation occurs when what is best for the athlete physically, educationally, and psychologically is replaced by what has to be done to win. Too many seem to believe that it is permissible to break any rule necessary to ensure victory. Winning and money are not the villains; the actions of people are suspect. Sport participants can win and still be moral. The challenge is how to subordinate winning and gaining lucrative benefits while treating others morally and playing fairly.

Athletes learn early in their careers that they are entertainers. Professional athletes openly acknowledge this, while the colleges still hide behind the myth of the student–athlete. For younger athletes, the higher they climb on the elite sport ladder, the more they realize that they may become pawns used for promotions and the entertainment of others. As a result, sport at many levels has become a business and a transmitter of economic, not ethical, values. Although sport can teach values, such as loyalty, dedication, sacrifice, and teamwork, moral values such as justice, honesty, responsibility, and beneficence are often compromised when people value more highly making money through sport. Today, commercialized sport has become a powerful and an influential force permeating all competitive levels.

Cybersports

www.olympic-usa.org

The United States Olympic Committee, which governs the athletes and the activities involved with the Olympics for this country, is highly commercialized because it must raise funds to support teams and individuals in the Olympic Games.

www.nfl.com

The National Football League promotes its teams and seeks to maintain its high level of popularity and entertainment value.

www.ncaachampionships.com

The commercial profitability of the Men's Basketball Tournament, or March Madness, brings in millions of dollars that help pay the costs of less profitable championships in other sports.

www.majorleaguebaseball.com

Major League Baseball officials claim that the economics of its sport are so crushing that some teams should be eliminated while at the same time superstars are receiving skyrocketing salaries and fans are being priced out of attending games.

www.nba.com

Given its small number of players, the National Basketball Association has a recent history of promoting its superstars, such as Larry Bird, Magic Johnson, Michael Jordan, Shaquille O'Neal, Kobe Bryant, and Allen Iverson, in order to lure new and continuing fans to its games.

www.dickbutkus.com/dbfn/popwarner

Pop Warner, the largest youth football and cheerleading and dance organization in the United States, provides competitions sponsored by local organizations through age-group national championships. One of its leading promotional features is that it is the only national youth sports organizations that requires youth to maintain satisfactory academic progress as a condition for participation.

ISSUES AND DILEMMAS

CASE 8-1

Midwest State University (MSU) annually hosts Parents' Day on a fall weekend that includes an evening home football game. Lectures, exhibitions, and social activities scheduled months in advance allow parents and their children to spend an educational and enjoyable time together on campus. Early in the week before Parents' Day, the national television network planning to broadcast the MSU football game contacted the athletic director asking to change the starting time for the game from 7 P.M. to 11 A.M. A larger viewing audience and an additional revenue of $500,000 was promised to both the host university and the opposing institution, which was ranked in the top five nationally. Each member of the host institution's conference would also receive $100,000 if the game time were changed.

1. Are there any ethical issues involved? If so, what are they and how should they be addressed?
2. Who, if any, should be consulted by the athletic director before making a decision about whether to change the game time?
3. Should MSU change the starting time of the football game?
4. What would be the justification for changing the starting time? For not changing it?
5. What is the purpose of intercollegiate athletics in relation to the rest of the institution?

◆ ◆ ◆

CASE 8-2

Lamont Adair is a talented age-group tennis champion, having already won the United States Tennis Association's 12-and-under and 14-and-under titles twice each. Lamont's parents provide their precocious child with private tennis lessons daily with one of the best pros in the country. By age 15, Lamont is entering and winning an average of 30 local, state, regional, national, and international tennis tournaments annually. Because Lamont, an only child, misses so many classes while traveling to tennis tournaments, his mother has started home-schooling him. Lamont's father handles all tournament arrangements, serves as hitting partner before competitions, and acts as coach during events.

Lamont has won many professional qualifying tournaments and progressed into the late rounds of several tour events. Because of his potential, a sports agent has contacted the family about a variety of endorsement opportunities when Lamont becomes a professional. Lamont is considering becoming a professional soon, and Mr. Adair debates whether to quit his job to manage Lamont's professional career.

1. What are the moral and ethical issues in this case?
2. What are the advantages of a 16-year-old becoming a professional tennis player? What, if any, ethical issues are involved?
3. What are the disadvantages of a 16-year-old becoming a professional tennis player? Do any of these involve ethical issues?
4. What are the moral dilemmas, if any, associated with adolescents dropping out of high school in pursuit of professional tennis careers?
5. Are Mr. and Mrs. Adair acting responsibly if they decide to let their 16-year-old son support the family financially? Why or why not?
6. What are the pressures placed on Lamont? Should a 16-year-old have such pressure to succeed?

◆ ◆ ◆

CASE 8-3

Danny Washington's outstanding performances as the freshman center for the University of Western California (UWC) Cougars carried his team to its first Sweet Sixteen appearance in the NCAA Division I men's basketball tournament. As a sophomore, Danny led the nation in scoring (26.2 points) and rebounding (15.5) while helping the Cougars make it to the Final Four. Although his team did not win, everyone knew that Danny's next court appearance would be in the pros.

Even when he was a schoolboy star, Danny and his family had benefited from his All-American status. Danny's room overflowed with basketball shoes, athletic clothing, and sport bags as he profited from switching summer league teams each of his last three years of play. His father got a higher-paying job, and the family moved into a bigger house through the help of friends of the various teams on which Danny starred. Other influential friends made sure that Danny received passing grades in classes that he seldom attended, provided him with a car and spending money, and intervened on his behalf when he had problems with the police for traffic violations, an assault charge, and marijuana use.

When the college recruiting wars intensified, the Washingtons simply stated their price and waited for someone to pay it. While most institutions refused, UWC agreed to the $100,000 payout, which was cleverly deferred until after Danny signed with the Miami Heat. The following year UWC was placed on probation by the NCAA, but UWC Coach Charlie Wilson and Danny Washington had already advanced their careers at the expense of the university.

As a collegian, Danny experienced additional academic and legal problems. He allowed athletic personnel to arrange his classes and grades as long as they maintained his eligibility. Charges of driving while under the influence of alcohol, for assault and battery, and of rape were kept out of the media by powerful UWC supporters. Danny never faced the consequences of his actions because of his "big man on campus" status; he believed that enough money could fix any problem. As a professional, Danny openly marketed his remarkable talent, his dashing good looks, and his charismatic smile. His 12-year, $500 million contract soon paled in comparison to the endorsement deals he signed with 20 corporate sponsors. Within a year, he surged into the top 10 in non-sport endorsement income.

Danny's on-the-court performances and likable personality added to his popularity with the fans. Affectionately lauded as "King Danny," he began to rule the "paint" in NBA battles against other centers. Not only was he named NBA Rookie of the Year; he also captured Player of the Year honors in his first year as a pro.

Danny had a reckless lifestyle that included fast cars, plenty of alcohol, occasional drug use, and women whenever he wanted them. He bought everything his heart desired and believed that money could prevent any legal problems. A similar attitude also characterized Danny's play as he expected (and often received) preferential treatment from the officials. Seemingly, they allowed him to hold, push, and play more physically than the other athletes because of his premier status.

1. What ethical values, if any, did Danny violate in summer league play?
2. What ethical values, if any, did Danny violate while in high school?
3. What ethical values, if any, did Danny violate as a collegiate athlete?
4. What ethical values, if any, did Danny violate as a professional athlete?
5. Are the moral principles applicable to sport always the same, or should they vary by level of competition?
6. How did the economic values learned in his earlier years affect Danny's behaviors as a professional athlete?

◆ ◆ ◆

CASE 8-4

Voters in San Jose would soon decide the fate of professional sports in their city possibly for decades to come. The fate of the funding for the proposed football stadium rested with individuals who had been exposed to a barrage from print and electronic media that sought to win advocates for or against the bond referendum. Proponents argued that the only way that San Jose could become a "big-league" city was to have a team that played in the National Football League (NFL) or the National Basketball Association (NBA) or was a major league baseball team. As the National Hockey League's Sharks had attempted to show, San Jose's economy would benefit as would its national stature by having professional sports teams. Opponents argued that only the wealthy would benefit from hotel and restaurant revenues, purchases from other businesses, and corporate executives who could afford to use luxury suites for business purposes. Because of skyrocketing ticket prices in all professional sports, it also was argued that most people in San Jose would not be able to afford to attend an NFL game.

1. What are the ethical issues, if any, associated with the vote on the bond referendum to publicly fund a football stadium?
2. Should all citizens pay for a football stadium? Why or why not?
3. Is it unethical for a city to build a football stadium so that a team owner can profit from its use? Why or why not?
4. What are the ethical issues, if any, when the revenues from a professional team go mostly to the wealthy?
5. What are the ethical issues, if any, associated with the increased cost of ticket prices for professional sport events?

◆ ◆ ◆

CASE 8-5

Southwestern University was facing a budget crisis. For the past three years, its NCAA Division I football and men's basketball teams had lost more games than they had won. Even though the university had received over $2 million from the Mid-South Conference because of the successes of other teams, it still faced a $1.5 million deficit. Given the fact that Southwestern had to increase funding for its women's programs because of a pending lawsuit claiming that the university was in violation of Title IX, Athletic Director Andrew Fleming knew that his program was in dire straits and needed a miracle.

The phone call from Michael Zemski appeared to be just such a miracle. After months of negotiation, Zemski confirmed that his chain of chicken restaurants would pay the Southwestern Athletic Department $2 million immediately and another $1 million annually for 20 years if the university would do the following:

◆   Name its football stadium in honor of Zemski's father.
◆   Place patches with his corporate logo and name on team uniforms.
◆   Paint his corporate logo and name on the floor of the basketball arena.
◆   Appoint him permanently to the Board of Directors of the Athletic Council.

1. What ethical issues, if any, were presented regarding Southwestern University's budget deficit?
2. Is violating Title IX unethical? If so, why?
3. Who should decide whether or not to accept Zemski's offer with its conditions as stated or after additional negotiations?
4. What would have been the ethical issues, if any, if Zemski's corporation were in the alcohol or tobacco business?
5. Would there have been any ethical dilemmas if Zemski had stated publicly that as soon as he became a member of the Board of Directors of the Athletic Council he would lead the effort to fire John Lewis, the football coach?
6. What are the major ethical issues facing Division I sport programs that seem to be in the entertainment business?

◆ ◆ ◆

CASE 8-6

Coach Palmer knew that if he could not win more games than he lost in the upcoming season he would be fired, even though he had two years left on his contract. Even though he had been a successful head coach at another college, tough competition in this conference had resulted in five consecutive losing seasons. Off the field and in the classroom, his players had maintained eligibility and graduated at the highest levels ever for the university. Not a single incidence of misbehavior leading to legal action had occurred under this watch. As a result of the losing seasons, attendance in the 60,000-seat stadium had dropped precipitously leading to athletic department deficits.

A few athletic boosters approached Coach Palmer and offered to help. They believed in Coach Palmer's ability to coach, but they said he just needed better athletes. They offered to assist with recruiting as long as Coach Palmer agreed not to interfere.

The university had its most successful year ever attracting high school All-Americans and other talent from throughout the country. Excitement was so high in anticipation of a turnaround in the program that almost 50,000 tickets were sold for the first game of the season. Playing seven freshmen as starters, including the highly recruited Darryl Chambers at quarterback, the team's record was 6-5 for the season. The following year, with the enrollment of another great freshman class of football players, the team finished 9-2 and attended its first bowl game in 20 years. Coach Palmer's contract was renewed for five years as the athletic department finished in the black for the first time in two decades.

1. What values are emphasized when winning games is more important than the educational progress of athletes?
2. What was being valued (and why) by Coach Palmer and the athletic boosters by their agreement and subsequent actions?
3. What was the relative value placed on winning in this situation if it is assumed that not all NCAA recruiting rules were followed?
4. What values were the highly recruited athletes learning if they were being enticed by benefits not allowed by NCAA rules?

ADDITIONAL READINGS

Byers, W., and C. Hammer. 1995. *Unsportsmanlike conduct: Exploiting college athletes.* Ann Arbor: University of Michigan Press.

A Call to Action—Reconnecting college sports and higher education. 2001. Charlotte, NC: Knight Foundation.

Coakley, J. J. 2001. *Sport in society: Issues & controversies.* 7th ed. Dubuque, IA: McGraw-Hill.

Duderstadt, J. J. 2000. *Intercollegiate athletics and the American university—A university president's perspective.* Ann Arbor: University of Michigan Press.

Engh, F. 1999. *Why Johnny hates sports: Why organized youth sports are failing our children and what we can do about it.* New York: Penguin Putnam.

Hall, L. 2001. *Just let the kids play: How to stop other adults from ruining your children's joy and success in youth sports.* Deerfield Beach, FL: Health Communications.

Keeping the faith with the student athlete—A new model for intercollegiate athletics. 1991. Charlotte, NC: Knight Foundation.

Murphy, S. M. 1999. *The cheers and the tears: A healthy alternative to the dark side of youth sports today.* San Francisco: Jossey-Bass.

Quirk, J. P., and R. D. Fort. 1999. *Hard ball: The perilous future of pro team sports.* Princeton, NJ: Princeton University Press.

Perrin, D. 2000. *American fan: Sports mania and the culture that feeds it.* New York: Morrow/Avon.

Sack, A. L., and E. J. Staurowsky. 1998. *College athletes for hire: The evolution and legacy of the NCAA's amateur myth.* Westport, CT: Greenwood Publishing Group.

Shulman, J. L., and W. G. Bowen. 2001. *The game of life: College sports and educational values.* Princeton, NJ: Princeton University Press.

A solid start—A report on reform of intercollegiate athletics. 1992. Charlotte, NC: Knight Foundation.

Sperber, M. 2000. *Beer and circus: How big-time college sports is crippling undergraduate education.* New York: Holt.

Zimbalist, A. 2001. *Unpaid professionals: Commercialism and conflict in big-time college sports.* Princeton, NJ: Princeton University Press.

Racial Equity:
African Americans in Sport

- What effects has school integration had on African American athletes and coaches? Were all of these effects ethical?
- Have African Americans been exploited academically?
- What is "stacking," and how has it affected African Americans in sport?
- What has been the media's portrayal of African American athletes? Why?
- What are the myths and realities about upward mobility through sport for African American athletes?
- Why are African Americans largely excluded from management positions in sport?
- What are the ethical and moral issues associated with racial equity in sport for African Americans?
- How can the ethical and moral issues associated with racial equity in sport for African Americans be ameliorated?

Sport fans as recently as a few decades ago would have seen only white male athletes performing in the major sports, and most print media publicized their sport achievements to the virtual exclusion of reporting on the sporting achievements of African Americans. Discriminatory practices and written and unwritten agreements prevented African Americans from competing against and with the supposed dominant Caucasian race. White males dominated sport because of moral ignorance supported by racist educational and social systems. The exclusion of African Americans continued because many whites truly believed that their attitudes, beliefs, and values were proper.

The predominance accorded whites in sport reflected the power and control positions they held in government, education, business, and religion since the founding of this country. Such dominance signaled a lack of justice, honesty, responsibility, and beneficence toward all other groups. For example, the privilege of voting was not extended to African Americans by constitutional amendment until 1865 and, in actual practice for all, not until much later. Whites governed at all levels, dominated education (although separate but unequal schools and colleges existed for African Americans), managed almost all commercial enterprises, and perpetuated the status quo through social mores proclaimed from pulpits. Firmly entrenched in positions of power, most whites accepted and acted upon the belief that everyone else was inherently inferior and undeserving of equitable treatment. Educational, job, and social discrimination was perceived as morally defensible on the basis of one's heritage.

Reflecting white males' dominant place in society, sport included both *de jure* (legal) and *de facto* (existing) segregation.

Ethical concerns emerged because of discriminatory treatment based on preconceived ideas, unfounded prejudices, and widespread biases. Some athletes claimed physical and intellectual superiority over African Americans, Hispanics, Jews, Irish, and Italians. Lest this superiority be disproved, most white sport leaders and athletes simply refused to allow African Americans, and sometimes other minorities, to join their leagues. When a few tried to break this barrier, they were verbally and physically assaulted. Without the economic power to challenge such exclusion, African Americans formed separate teams and competed among themselves, usually under austere conditions. For example, Negro League stars like Cool Papa Bell and John Henry Lloyd were never allowed to compete in Major League Baseball, although their talents equaled or surpassed the talents of contemporaries like Ty Cobb and Rogers Hornsby.

Discriminatory practices and segregation in sport set the stage for an examination of the many inequities endured by African American athletes. Historical, organizational, and societal events and perspectives in this chapter describe how such treatment has violated ethical principles. Although the situation has been ameliorated somewhat to yield something approximating equity, several recommendations for improvement are provided.

HISTORICAL PERSPECTIVE OF RACIAL INEQUITY IN SPORT

In the 21st century, it is sometimes difficult to imagine the racial discrimination experienced by African Americans in this country. African Americans were excluded from social interaction with whites including their games. Segregated swimming pools, competitions between educational institutions that admitted only one race, and the "whites only" policies in Major League Baseball and the United States Lawn Tennis Association are illustrative of this shameful snubbing.

Sadly, most sports fans are unaware of the remarkable sports achievements of Paul Robeson (football), Ora Washington (tennis and basketball), and Josh Gibson (baseball). Yet, these African Americans were as good as, if not better than, their white contemporaries. Only on the pages of African American newspapers, however, were the outstanding performances of these and other athletes recognized. To most whites, these African American athletes were ignored or worse.

Before the middle of the 20th century, African Americans seldom attained economic power; most suffered the ignominy of slavery or the remnants of this subservience. Enduring separate housing, menial labor, and often inferior educational opportunities, African Americans were forced by society to accept such discriminatory treatment. A few challenged the status quo, usually with harsh repercussions. Did the exclusion of African Americans from all levels of sport violate any moral values? Did white sport leaders fail to reason morally and thus act in an unethical manner?

From Exclusion to Opportunities Limited by Economic Realities

The sons and daughters of African Americans suffered the same exclusionary ignominy their parents did as recreation departments, private organizations, and country clubs excluded them from their sport programs. The limited number and power of African Americans relegated them to forming competitions for their children or having them be denied sport opportunities.

Because African Americans lacked the financial resources to purchase expensive sports equipment and clothing, pay for sports instruction or coaching, and fund travel expenses, their children never got the chance to play golf, to swim, or to attend a sports camp. Children who never had learned to ski, fence, play tennis or field hockey, or row were unlikely to develop strong skills in these. Even in recent decades, few African American children are members of swimming, tennis, and golf clubs or gymnastics teams. Tiger Woods in golf and Arthur

Ashe in tennis are notable exceptions to the typical dearth of African Americans in these sports.

Youth sport opportunities historically and today have differed in urban, suburban, and rural areas. Basketball, for example, has been touted as the ultimate urban sport based on the limited equipment and space required and has been characterized by individualized moves and a fast-paced style of play associated with the playground. Basketball also is sometimes characterized as the spot shooting game of choice of boys in rural settings, and especially in Kansas, Kentucky, and Indiana.

Suburban sports for youth reflect the higher economic status of the families that reside there. Public and private sport organizations offer numerous football, baseball, and more recently soccer leagues. Golf, tennis, swimming, and other individual sports are more likely to be available for the children in suburban locations because their parents can afford the associated costs.

School Segregation Gives Way to Integration

Within their segregated world, African Americans managed to offer their children limited sport opportunities in schools, albeit with few of the amenities enjoyed by the more economically blessed. In all-black schools, judged by the Supreme Court in the 1954 case *Brown* v. *Board of Education* as unequal, African American boys competed in football, basketball, baseball, and track. Although segregated schooling became illegal and civil rights legislation starting in the 1960s guaranteed everyone's rights, only gradually did integration in educational institutions occur. Subsequently, school consolidation and court-ordered busing forever changed the face of public education.

A significant consequence of integration was the closing of many former African American schools. Would a more reasoned approach have been to promote cultural diversity by placing students of all races in both former all-white and all-black schools, rather than usually uprooting African American students? As a result of consolidation and the closing

of many formerly all-black schools, numerous African American coaches lost their jobs; almost all white coaches at the traditionally all-white schools retained their coaching jobs. As the movie *Remember the Titans* poignantly depicted, acceptance of African American coaches was begrudging and often volatile.

Court-ordered busing sought to adjust the racial mix in schools, thus affecting athletic teams. Sometimes, African American males were not chosen for sport teams or not given the playing time they deserved by white coaches, though most coaches put racial biases aside and simply played the athletes who could help win. Through support for football, basketball, and baseball in these integrated schools, many African American students enjoyed better facilities, equipment, and competitive opportunities than they had previously.

As competition for places on baseball, football, and basketball teams increased, fewer white athletes saw these teams as their only sport options because often their family circumstances allowed them to pursue sports such as swimming, tennis, and golf that were often associated with private lessons and facilities. As a result of increased numbers of African Americans in team sports and some whites selecting other (individual) sports, many school teams began to separate largely on color, depending on the sport. Today, many football and basketball teams have a much higher percentage of African Americans than do the schools' student bodies. What are the ethical issues associated with this phenomenon?

Integration of Intercollegiate Sport

In colleges where only African Americans enrolled, men proved that they possessed the physical and intellectual abilities to become top athletes and play all positions. Although a few earned spots on Olympic teams, primarily in track, seldom did this Olympic competition, or even Olympic victories, change their plight back home. Jesse Owens, winner of four gold medals in the 1936 Berlin Olympics, personified this fate. Occasionally, when African Americans did get to play on a northern college's athletic team, they suffered mistreatment from teammates, had to sleep and eat in segregated facilities, endured physical and verbal abuse from opponents and fans, and often did not get to play when teams from the South refused to compete against them. Even if African Americans were allowed to compete, they often suffered from the indignities of segregated housing and food service. Did coaches' or athletes' discriminatory practices retard their moral development?

Colleges began to recruit African American athletes to help win, even though these individuals formerly were barred from admission and remained nonrepresentative of the student body. The classic example of this shift in recruiting strategy occurred after the all-white University of Kentucky basketball team lost to the predominantly African American Texas Western at El Paso team in the 1966 NCAA championship game.

African American men traditionally have been expected to be star players; otherwise, they would not have received grants-in-aid. They were not to date white women, even though few African American women were to be found on campus; they were to accept without retaliation or comment racial slurs and segregated living and travel accommodations (see Box 9-1). Seldom did anyone assist them if they were not developmentally prepared for their academic work. Did college coaches care more about these athletes' physical talents than about them personally? Did coaches, teammates, and fans, in a reflection of their value systems, show empathy for the plight of these African American athletes?

While traditional white colleges enjoyed the contributions of these African American athletes, historically black colleges saw their best talent lured away by the larger, supposedly prestigious, colleges that promised glamour, media exposure, and potential professional contracts. Usually, these historically black colleges did not have the grant-in-aid budgets, facilities, and other amenities to compete in recruiting the best African American athletes.

For years, no African Americans were hired to coach by the mostly white athletic directors in the

---

BOX 9-1

DID THIS REALLY HAPPEN?

Mitchell Tatum, the only African American on the team, was the star halfback of Midwestern University having gained a conference record of 1,572 yards rushing during his senior season. While earning All-America honors individually, he also led his team to the conference title and an invitation to play in the Sugar Bowl. Mitchell was a solid B student in his music major.

When the team bus arrived from the airport, Mitchell's coach pulled him aside and introduced him to the music director (Dr. Cooper) of the famed Southern College (a historically black college) band. Dr. Cooper talked briefly with Mitchell before inviting him to his home for dinner and to show him his famous instrument and music collections. Mitchell's coach gave his approval, and off they went to Dr. Cooper's house. After a delicious dinner and

hours of conversation about music, Dr. Cooper invited Mitchell to spend the night since his coach had told him this would be okay. After a hearty breakfast, Dr. Cooper drove Mitchell back to the team hotel just as the bus arrived to transport the team to the field.

Mitchell was really pleased with his 104 yards rushing in the Sugar Bowl but disappointed with his team's loss. In reflecting on his experiences, which were even more memorable because of the time he spent with Dr. Cooper, he wondered why not a single teammate had asked him about his absence at team meals or at the hotel. Then Mitchell realized that his coaches had arranged his time with Dr. Cooper so the team, including him, would have no problems. That is, the team hotel refused to serve and house African Americans.

NCAA Division I level, despite the fact that the percentage of African American athletes far exceeded the number of coaches of their race. The few African American head and assistant coaches today have at least overcome some of the discriminatory hiring practices of the past (see www.sportinsociety.org for the racial report card from the Center for the Study of Sport in Society). Because their numbers remain low, many of these individuals serving as assistant coaches on otherwise all-white staffs are viewed as tokens hired primarily to recruit African American athletes. In the aftermath of racist statements or actions by coaches or racial turmoil on campus, some institutions have used the hiring of African American coaches to show that they do not discriminate.

Professional Sport

Although Jackie Robinson is credited with opening the door for African Americans in professional sport in modern times (1947), he was preceded without significant notice by Kenny Washington, Woody Strode, Bill Willis, and Marion Motley in the NFL in 1946. Yet only slowly did prejudicial attitudes and behaviors dissipate and change, even though the professional leagues in football and baseball today comprise approximately 65 percent and 15 percent African Americans, respectively. Although superstar African Americans like Shaquille O'Neal, Marshall Faulk, and Sammy Sosa, have signed huge professional contracts, many African Americans receive lower salaries than comparably skilled white athletes; proportionately fewer substitutes of color ride the bench. Some have conjectured that the presence of white substitutes helps appease predominantly white fans, especially in basketball, where color is so visible.

In the early years of integration in the professional leagues, African Americans (as notable as Willie Mays) often lived and ate together, socially segregated from their white teammates. Like Jackie Robinson, they were told to passively endure physical and verbal abuse from opponents and fans if they wanted to keep their jobs. They were told to

not expect teammates or management to intervene on their behalf. Until recently, no African American, not even stars like Hank Aaron, Julius Erving, and Jim Brown, could expect to earn endorsement and appearance income to match that available to the star white athletes. Michael Jordan and Tiger Woods have far exceeded (by millions of dollars) the endorsement earnings of most professional athletes, regardless of their race. As the dominant athletes in their sports, they also have carefully managed their positive images, thus making them desirable spokespeople for numerous products. However, up until recent years, African Americans were unlikely to have the opportunity to earn nonsport revenue because of discriminatory practices in society.

For decades, African Americans knew better than to expect to be hired as coaches and front-office administrators in professional sport. To date, only a small number of African Americans have been hired in these positions. Also, seldom have they been rehired by another team if they were fired, although whites are. Biases have led those hiring to secretly profess or demonstrate by their practices that African Americans are not intellectually capable of coaching or administering a sport. Although Al Campanis lost his job as vice president for player personnel for the Los Angeles Dodgers because of his racist statement reflecting this perspective, African Americans have achieved limited advances into professional sport management positions.

Those in control of programs at all levels are increasingly being held responsible for treating all athletes alike, regardless of color. Can whites honestly hide behind their prejudices and biases? Does beneficence call for administrators, coaches, teammates, opponents, and fans to treat all athletes equitably? How can moral knowing and moral valuing bring about greater equity in sport for African Americans?

SOCIETAL ATTITUDES

Many racial biases are associated with class issues. The socioeconomic status of minority athletes today is probably more of a limiting factor regarding sport opportunities than is race. Some sociologists have suggested that what sports African American athletes choose to participate in are a direct result of what they can afford. Private lessons in ice skating or gymnastics are impossible when a family is on welfare. Sport teams offered by public agencies and schools, such as basketball and track, are much more likely to have African American athletes, whereas sports teams with associated high costs are not. In addition, in order to play soccer or tennis, children must have transportation to practices, lessons, and competitions as well as the funds to cover the associated costs. So, with only a few exceptions, socioeconomic status determines sport choice.

Individual and group attitudes are difficult to alter because society has reinforced maintenance of the status quo. Racial discrimination, once a way of life in this country, has resisted elimination. Many have lauded sport as a leader in integration of the races; in reality, sport reflects society. Most of the first African Americans in sport, law, medicine, business, and education suffered through harsh name-calling, physical abuse, and psychological badgering. Only gradually, and in the face of grudging changes in attitudes, did African Americans achieve more equal status in these and other careers.

Although some individuals from other races gained acceptance because they did not disclose their heritage, skin color stereotyped most African Americans regardless of their abilities. Because of a few courageous forebearers, federal laws, and the desire to win and make more money, today, athletic talent counts more than race, nationality, or any other personal characteristic. In an increasingly diverse culture, acceptance slowly is being based on a belief in equality of all, rather than on some externally mandated opinion (see Box 9-2).

The key to equity is education. Today, societal leaders urge everyone to accept cultural diversity on the moral principle that learning about different cultures will lead to greater appreciation and acceptance. Can people value different cultures, sharing commonalities such as respect for self, respect for others, and respect for private property while accepting varying perspectives? Establishing mutual values appears to be an appropriate framework in which to work for the elimination of injustices, but this framework may be doomed without an educational program to support these values. Also, people need to develop principles and rules to live by and the ability to critique what they have established.

BOX 9-2

SPORT—A REFLECTION OR LEADER
OF SOCIETAL ATTITUDES

Reflection

Discriminatory practices and exclusion characterized all aspects of society.

Society historically viewed African Americans as inferior, less intelligent, and stereotypically.

Laws mandated equitable treatment in all aspect of society.

Role models of successful African Americans came from throughout society.

Leader

Sport eliminated racial discrimination before society accepted integration.

Sport allowed African American athletes equitable opportunities to prove their merit and skill before society treated African Americans fairly.

Coaches, white athletes, and athletic administrators accepted African Americans as equals long before society did.

African American athletes served as role models for success long before African Americans achieved this level of stature in society.

ARE ORGANIZATIONAL POLICIES AFFECTING AFRICAN AMERICANS DISPROPORTIONATELY?

The NCAA, NAIA, NJCAA, and National Federation of State High School Associations (NFSHSA) did not overtly discriminate against African Americans. Although their rules and regulations were established to facilitate competitions among their members, they failed to prevent or remove harm. Thus, it could be argued that the application of these policies has differentially disadvantaged African Americans, primarily in the area of academics.

Most states require minimal academic achievement for continued participation in interscholastic sports. These **no pass, no play** directives have disqualified more African Americans than whites, more as a result of socioeconomic than racial factors. That is, students raised in disadvantaged circumstances often do not have educational encouragement and learning materials such as books and computers. These circumstances can retard students' readiness academically and cause them to fall farther behind each year. When athletes, including many African Americans, subsequently are given unearned good grades for the sake of maintaining eligibility, are they being deprived of an education? Are they being taught to value athletics more than academics? Worst of all, are they being taught dishonesty?

Highly skilled high school athletes dream of earning college grants-in-aid and playing professionally, although meeting admissions criteria required by the governing collegiate associations makes the first dream an illusion for many and the second available only to the very best. For example, the NCAA currently mandates that a prospective student-athlete must score at least 820 on the SAT or 68 on the ACT with a high school grade-point average of 2.5 in 13 specific core courses. A sliding scale allows a student to be eligible for intercollegiate competition by raising either the test score or the grade-point average to compensate for a lower score on the other.

Some African American coaches have protested that these academic standards discriminate against people of color, limiting the number of African American athletes qualifying for grants-in-aid. Some African American leaders have argued that academic standards remain too low, suggesting that if requirements were raised, athletes would meet them. Although a higher percentage of African Americans have been denied grants-in-aid and eligibility to compete for NCAA member institutions because of these academic eligibility requirements, college presidents and athletic administrators claim that higher standards have been enacted to improve the image and integrity of intercollegiate athletics, not to discriminate against African Americans.

ROLE MODELS

African American culture disproportionately rewards the athletic prowess of its sport heroes and heroines, who are more likely to be role models than are doctors, lawyers, or business executives. African American males may practice their sport skills more diligently because they are rewarded with status and because they see sport as a ticket to a better way of life. The dream of a sport career is dashed for the 99 percent of high school athletes of all races who never sign professional contracts. Those, however, who do achieve their dream, on average three to five years later, find themselves out of jobs and, too often, poorly educated.

The importance of having role models starts at a young age. Adults encourage or discourage children in almost self-fulfilling prophecies as they overtly or subtly tell them about their opportunities in life. Boys growing up in families without fathers at home may seek male role models at school, who are frequently coaches. The bond that develops between the coach, usually white, and the athlete, often African American, may lead to a singular emphasis on sport, unless the coach encourages a balance between academics and athletics. The athlete may want to become a coach, but more often the goal is to earn a college grant-in-aid and play in the pros.

During their school years, students choose heroes and heroines, usually of the same race, in their preferred sports. These individuals serve as powerful role models of behavior, both moral and immoral. Also, each person assimilates the values of the group with which the most time is spent. Although parents and families may teach and model morally acceptable behavior, coaches or teammates might not. It is often coaches and teammates whom the athletes imitate. Does the nonmoral value of winning ever displace moral actions because those involved with sport fail to address the issues facing them in moral terms?

Modeling also occurs in position selection in sport. Do few African American boys aspire to become quarterbacks because they subconsciously believe that this is traditionally a white man's position? Have coaches urged African Americans, even though they possessed the requisite skills and leadership for quarterback, to play other positions? Often athletes self-select by modeling their heroes who have historically played in positions requiring speed and reaction time rather than decision making and centrality to the action. This phenomenon has been called **stacking.**

STACKING AND A QUOTA SYSTEM

Position allocation, or stacking, refers to a disproportionate concentration of African Americans in specific positions. African American athletes still predominate in certain positions but seldom play in others. There are several possible explanations for stacking: (1) racist stereotypes about the physical, social, and personality attributes of athletes; (2) racial discrimination that keeps some athletes from leadership, responsibility, and authority roles; (3) an economic assumption that athletes of color from lower socioeconomic groups do not have access to training and facilities needed to develop certain position-related skills; (4) self-selection by athletes of color into positions in which they perceive they have the greatest chance to achieve success; (5) the possibility that athletes of color choose to emulate those of their race, who have historically played only in certain positions; and (6) a residual prejudicial attitude that African Americans excel

African Americans have too often been limited to certain positions (such as tailback) and not allowed to play other positions (such as quarterback).

only at reactive positions. Because of one or more of these circumstances, African Americans have often competed against themselves, not against whites, for some positions and opportunities to play.

Historically a **quota system,** whereby only a limited number of minorities could play at one time, has also restricted sport opportunities for African Americans at interscholastic, intercollegiate, and professional levels. Additionally, African American athletes in schools and colleges acknowledge that the odds of retaining a place on the roster with only average talent tip heavily in favor of whites. The injustices endured by African Americans serve as a chronicle of the discriminatory practices of coaches and sport managers. Has the idolizing of men of their race who have become pros led many African Americans down a dead-end road? Has accepting position shifts and enduring quota systems damaged African American athletes' self-esteem and limited their options? Have coaches treated these athletes dishonestly? Does ethical behavior demand that team selection, opportunities to play any position, and hiring be based on documented abilities, not the color of one's skin?

AFRICAN AMERICAN ATHLETES AS PORTRAYED IN THE MEDIA

Until recently, the media condoned and perpetuated a second-class status for African Americans in sport. The African American press proclaimed the achievements of Buck Leonard and Ora Washington, but most whites knew little about these outstanding athletes. The white print media praised Joe Louis, who fit its image of a modest champion, while detesting Jack Johnson, who refused to behave demurely, flaunting his wealth earned as the heavyweight boxing title holder. When Hank Aaron became the greatest home-run hitter of all time, many in the media refused to lavish upon him superstar status, and racists sent him death threats.

In sport, African Americans were conditioned to passively take orders from white coaches as the media praised those who "knew their place." Boston Celtics star and one-time NBA coach Bill Russell suffered verbal attacks and criticism at the hands of sportswriters and broadcasters because he outspokenly lambasted prejudicial attitudes and behaviors. Tennis champion Arthur Ashe spoke out against apartheid in South Africa and racism in the United States.

Has the media perpetuated prejudice against and stereotyping of African Americans? What values have been reinforced by how the media has portrayed African American athletes? Can the media help make an athlete a star or preclude this based on the amount and type of exposure it provides? Does the media influence whether athletes attain celebrity status, which often translates into endorsement and appearance income? Does race influence how athletes are portrayed by the media? Is there a lack of equity in sport reporting?

African American athletes have achieved at high levels of success in sports like track.

DISPELLING MYTHS

Society has perpetuated several racial myths that need to be examined and dispelled before sport will equitably accept African Americans.

Myth 1: *African Americans are physiologically superior (that is, they can run faster and jump higher).* In reality, the research is inconclusive. Questions have been raised about the appropriateness of statistical design, validity, and sampling techniques in some studies that seem to indicate such superiority. Knowledgeable people continue to disagree about whether genetics gives African Americans physical advantages in sport. Are the high numbers of African Americans in interscholastic football, basketball, baseball, and track programs related more to opportunities than to genetics? Contrastingly, do few African Americans participate and excel in golf, tennis, swimming, figure skating, and gymnastics because the cost of private lessons, club memberships, and expensive equipment and facilities bars those from lower socioeconomic levels? Although certain bodily measures have shown differences between black and white athletes in areas such as mesomorphy and vital lung capacity, it has not been proved that these variations directly affect athletic performance.

Myth 2: *African Americans are intellectually inferior and thus not qualified for coaching or team management positions.* In reality, the "good old boys'" network led to the hiring of coaches, scouts, general managers, and sport officials who were also white. Maybe those in the power positions feel better about hiring someone known, someone like themselves, rather than an unknown person who is different. If athletic managers use objective criteria and open job searches, will qualified African Americans continue to largely be excluded? Are there any ethical issues or moral values involved in traditional hiring practices?

Myth 3: *African American athletes use sport as a vehicle for upward mobility.* In reality, African Americans and whites on the playground have about a one-in-a-million chance of becoming a professional athlete, with an average career of less than five years. While chasing the elusive media image of the superstar, too many youths squander educational opportunities. Because of differential socioeconomic opportunities, however, the African American seems disproportionately affected.

Football coach Joe Paterno, former tennis champion Arthur Ashe, and many others have argued that the myth of upward mobility for African Americans has channeled these youths into viewing a sport career as the only goal worth pursuing, even though most do not achieve it. Without a professional contract or a degree, the stark reality of a limited future hits abruptly and harshly. Parents and coaches should emphasize education to youth over sport at all competitive levels.

Myth 4: *African American athletes are treated as equals of their white teammates.* In reality, compared with white athletes, African American athletes on average earn lower salaries, receive fewer and smaller endorsement opportunities and less media exposure, and seldom are retained if they are marginal players or substitutes. However, it should be noted that the star African American athletes have reached the pinnacles of their sports. Fame and fortune was and is enjoyed by Michael Jordan, Reggie White, Ken Griffey, Jr., and Tiger Woods. Do white teammates, coaches, sportswriters, announcers, owners, and members of teams' management staffs ever utter racist comments? Do whites resist consciously or unconsciously any loss of power or dominance over African Americans? Does justice and beneficence require that all athletes receive equitable opportunities and treatment?

Myth 5: *African American athletes have the ability to play only reactive, rather than decision-making or leadership, positions.* In reality, African Americans have historically been restricted to reaction-time positions such as defensive back, outfielder, or power forward. Position shifting by coaches or self-selection by athletes was attributable to role modeling and a perception that African Americans will be allowed to succeed only in certain positions. Such stacking has retarded opportunities to develop the leadership skills needed to play quarterback, catcher, or point guard. Although African Americans have demonstrated the skills required to play every position in football, baseball, and basketball, their percentages in the so-called thinking positions consistently remain less than their overall participation numbers.

Racist behavior, founded on myths and prejudices, can be traced to a lack of moral valuing and reasoning and an insufficient determination to change. Most people in sport simply have not been educated for social responsibility. Values do not come to sport managers and athletes—or to anyone—through osmosis; values must be taught and learned. Moral valuing and reasoning and appreciation and understanding of social responsibility evolve only through concerted efforts to instill these values in participants.

RECOMMENDATIONS

As discussed in the first three chapters, the moral values of justice, honesty, responsibility, and beneficence should guide the attitudes and behaviors of individuals involved with sport. Racial discrimination and inequity are antithetical to each of these. Does justice demand that African Americans: (1) receive equal opportunities to play every team position; (2) be hired for coaching and management positions on the basis of their qualifications; (3) receive salaries, endorsements, and media exposure on the basis of merit; and (4) earn degrees even when this necessitates remedial academic support?

Should whites honestly admit to past and present discriminatory treatment of African Americans while seeking to eliminate such treatment? An honest appraisal of interscholastic, intercollegiate, and professional sport reveals that equal employment opportunities and affirmative action directives have failed to permeate whites' stronghold in athletics. Has this occurred because these directives may not have been valued by those who could make a difference?

Honesty also enters the recruiting picture. Given the past exploitation of African American athletes, should recruiters honestly assess young athletes' potential for professional careers, as well as their ability to successfully earn degrees? False promises lead to broken dreams and continued exploitation of athletes' physical talents. If a recruiter pledges an opportunity for a degree, does the institution have a moral obligation to provide the support services that achieving this level of success requires?

Responsibility encompasses an ethical accountability for the care and welfare of another, thus countervailing discrimination. Responsibility includes providing education, at all levels of sport, directed at understanding and appreciating universal values and principles. Will the responsible sport manager treat every African American athlete in the same way as white athletes? Can those who act irresponsibly by making racial slurs, exploiting the athletic talents of African Americans, or discriminating in sport personnel decisions be reeducated?

Beneficence goes beyond treating others fairly. Beneficence means showing kindness. The belief of treating another as one wishes to be treated knows no color. Will the beneficent person in sport oppose intentional and unintentional words or actions that cause hurt or harm? The beneficent person does no harm, removes harm, prevents harm, and does good because doing good is right.

Racial discrimination and inequities cannot coexist with justice, honesty, responsibility, and beneficence. When those in positions of power understand, appreciate, and act on the basis of these four moral values, sport will harbor no color barriers. Consider the following questions in reflecting on racial equity in sport: (1) What do you believe about equitable treatment of African Americans in sport? (2) Could you change your response to the first question and be able to live with it if you were an African American? (3) Could you universalize your beliefs to all people in all races and ethnic backgrounds? (4) Are there any exceptions to your belief statements?

SUMMARY

This chapter provides an overview of some of the past and present inequities suffered by African Americans in sport. Historically, African Americans have been excluded from competition with white athletes because of the color of their skin and because of ignorance on the part of whites concerning fair and just treatment. African Americans' physical abilities often have been discounted as inherited, rather than developed through hard work, and they have been accused of being intellectually inferior without any basis other than racial bias. The media often has ridiculed, stereotyped, omitted, or shortchanged the achievements of African American athletes. African Americans have achieved only slight movement into the management positions controlling athletics.

Cybersports

www.sportinsociety.org/rgrc2001.html

The Center for the Study of Sport in Society at Northeastern University has provided a racial and gender report card which documents that opportunities continue to be limited for non-white males and females in sport.

www.ed.gov/databases/ERIC_Digests/ ed416268.html

This article on the Department of Education's website describes the athletic experiences of ethnically diverse girls.

www.sbpweb.com/noGoldenAge.asp

The author of this article questions the claim that African Americans had a golden age of

sports by suggesting that these minority athletes have taken one step forward and two steps backward in dealing with the social, political, and economic complexities of their chances as African American athletes.

www.ibcsports.com/ and http://blackcollegesports.org

These websites provide up-to-date reports on the accomplishments of African Americans at historically black colleges.

Significant progress has been noted, however, in the many sport achievements of African Americans. No longer must they endure blatant discrimination in and exclusion from sport. Certainly, African American superstars enjoy huge salaries and the adoration of millions of fans. Yet few would agree that African Americans below this top level of professional sport have achieved equity in sport. Success will occur only when hiring decisions, team selection, media coverage, and other benefits associated with sport are equitable for all, regardless of race.

Although this chapter focuses on the discriminatory treatment experienced by African Americans and their progress toward racial equity in sport, it does not address the fact that many other minorities are involved in sport. Historically, ethnic groups including the Irish, Italians, and Jews have used sports such as boxing for upward mobility. Many Latinos have contributed their talents in baseball, soccer, and other sports. These groups plus Asians, Native Americans, Hispanics, and others have had to combat subtle and overt racism and inequitable treatment. With changing social attitudes and renewed

emphasis on moral values, the future could be bright. It is hoped that all ethnic groups will soon compete side by side and against one another, with all individuals having the opportunity to display their athletic prowess while playing the game justly, honestly, responsibly, and beneficently.

ADDITIONAL READINGS

Aaseng, N. 1993. *The locker room mirror: How sports reflect society.* New York: Walker and Company.

Coakley, J. J. 2001. *Sport in society: Issues and controversies.* 7th ed. Boston: McGraw-Hill.

Hoose, P. M. 1989. *Necessities: Racial barriers in American sports.* New York: Random House.

Lapchick, R. E. 2001. *Smashing barriers: Race and sports in the new millennium.* Lanham, MD: Madison Books.

Lapchick, R. E. 1991. *Five minutes to midnight: Race and sport in the 1990s.* Lanham, MD: Madison Books.

Lapchick, R. E., and Jeffrey R. Benedict, eds. 1995. *Sport in society: Equal opportunity or business as usual?* Thousand Oaks, CA: Sage Publications.

Minority hiring not making the grade in collegiate sports. 1998. *Black Issues in Higher Education* 15(2) (March 19): 6.

Shropshire, K. L. 1998. *In black and white: Race and sports in America.* New York: New York University Press.

ISSUES AND DILEMMAS

CASE 9-1

Myron Atkinson played basketball on the courts a couple of blocks from his tenement apartment in Newark, New Jersey, every chance he got. Everybody chose him as a teammate whenever possible because Myron's shooting, passing, rebounding, and defensive skills were the best in the neighborhood. On the courts, he could forget about the loss of his father in a drug-related shooting and about how tired his mother always was from working two jobs to provide for him and his three sisters.

Besides being the star in pickup games, Myron, who was six-foot-five, dominated play on his West Side High School team. For the second straight year with his 23.5-point scoring average and 10.7 rebounds per game, he was named All-State. As he approached his senior year, he was already being recruited by dozens of colleges, including Duke, Kansas, and Kentucky.

Coach McPherson had always ensured that Myron could focus on basketball by getting the teachers at West Side to give him and many of his teammates passing grades. Because Myron respected his coach so highly, he never questioned how or why his white coach managed to keep the best athletes—most of whom like Myron were African Americans—eligible. Myron did not dislike school and always attended classes; it was just easier and more fun to play basketball than to study. Besides, why study when his grades would be taken care of?

At the start of his senior year, Myron learned about the requirements for eligibility to play on an NCAA Division I team. Myron's dream of starring in college and later in the NBA suddenly evaporated. His 625 on the SAT the preceding year and his marginal grades in mostly non-college preparatory courses left him woefully short of qualifying. Myron questioned Coach McPherson about why he had never explained these requirements and about what Myron could do. Coach McPherson told Myron that staying eligible for the West Side team, which had a good chance of winning the state championship that season, was more important than academics now or later. Coach McPherson told Myron that he would continue to help him academically as a senior, but only if Myron continued to take technical-type courses in which teachers would take care of athletes.

1. What moral values or principles are in jeopardy in this situation?
2. What are the ethical issues, if any, in Myron's situation?
3. Has Coach McPherson treated Myron unethically? If so, how?

4. Who is culpable in this situation, and why?
5. If you were Myron, what would you do?
6. What role did the teachers who gave athletes unearned grades play in this situation?
7. Is it possible that Coach McPherson had good intentions? How and why?
8. If Coach McPherson was in error, what could be done to change his value system?

◆ ◆ ◆

CASE 9-2

Dr. William Simmons wanted only the best for his son and daughter. He especially encouraged them in tennis, his favorite sport, although basketball had paid his way through college and his premedicine studies. Frequently, the entire Simmons family played mixed doubles, various combinations of singles, or just hit for fun at the Forest Hills Country Club.

As the years passed, young Billy became a repeat age-group winner and then the club champion. Because the Simmonses were the only African American members of the Club, Billy had always competed against whites, where skill, not color, determined the outcome of matches. In United States Tennis Association sanctioned tournaments, however, he learned that some people could be racist and unethical. He heard his first racial slurs uttered by parents of the boys he played. He also realized at a young age that some opponents will cheat on line calls to gain unfair advantages. When he first experienced these incidents, his level of play dropped dramatically. Seemingly, the more these comments and behaviors affected him, the more frequently they occurred.

After a long talk with his father, during which he learned about the many abuses Dr. Simmons had suffered while playing intercollegiate basketball, Billy determined that he would block out others' statements and actions. With a greater focus, Billy's game soared as he led his high school team to two consecutive state titles and achieved a top 10 ranking in the 18-and-under competitions in Georgia.

On the basis of his record, Billy expected to be recruited by the University of Southern Georgia (USG), which had a top-rated tennis program. Although he received numerous athletic grant-in-aid offers to attend less prestigious institutions, Billy chose to attend USG on an academic scholarship. He was sure he could earn a place on the tennis team.

It did not take Billy long to learn why Coach Vines had not recruited him. He was told that Coach Vines had never had an African American tennis player, and some had heard him make disparaging remarks about

African Americans when his team played them. Despite learning all this, Billy really wanted to play tennis for USG.

On the first day of practice, Billy arrived at the courts early. Coach Vines first ignored him and then asked him what he wanted. Billy simply asked for a chance to make the team. On the basis of the week-long tryouts, including the matches played, Billy was clearly one of the best players. But the team roster posted the next day did not include the name Billy Simmons. Upset, Billy called his father. After assessing the situation from Billy's perspective and talking with Coach Vines, Dr. Simmons scheduled a meeting with USG Athletic Director Bruce Holcombe.

Dr. Simmons stated the facts as he viewed them, indicating that he believed his son had been discriminated against because of his race. He asked Holcombe to investigate the situation immediately and intervene, if appropriate.

1. What principles or moral values are in jeopardy?
2. Is this a moral issue, and why?
3. What questionably moral actions are occurring, and why?
4. How had Billy been treated during his early years of playing tennis? What does this tell you about the values of the individuals he played at his club?
5. What were the conflicts Billy experienced in competitions outside his club?
6. On what values did Coach Vines base his recruiting and team selection decisions?
7. What legal and moral values, if any, were violated by Coach Vines in not selecting Billy for the tennis team?
8. What action should Athletic Director Holcombe take if he finds that Coach Vines has discriminated against Billy?

◆ ◆ ◆

CASE 9-3

The Miller boys and their father loved football. Regardless of the season, as soon as Mr. Miller got home from work, Wayne, Robin, Eric, and Jeremy urged him to play with them. All of the boys enjoyed catching their father's accurate spirals. The Miller boys admired their father for all the trophies he had won in football and especially for his all-star performances at Grambling State University, where he had played quarterback.

When Wayne, Robin, and Eric got old enough to join youth football leagues, first Wayne and then Robin and Eric wanted to play wide receiver. As experienced recipients of their father's passes, they earned starting positions and did well each year. Jeremy was different; he wanted to be a quarterback just like his father. Each year he tried out for quarterback, and each time the white coach told him that his skills were more appropriate for a wide receiver or running back. Although Jeremy accepted this decision initially, he began to question it when some of his African American teammates hinted that he would never get to play quarterback as long as a white boy wanted to play that position. Mr. Miller encouraged Jeremy to try his hardest in whatever position he was assigned while coaching him at home on how to play quarterback.

When Jeremy tried out for the high school team, on which Eric played wide receiver, he was eager to play quarterback. The neighborhood Miller-to-Miller combination was unbeatable because the two boys had played together so much. Jeremy was told by the white coach that he was good enough to earn a spot on the team but that he would not get to play quarterback. Again, it seemed to him that skin color, not skill, was the determining factor in who was selected to play quarterback.

Mrs. Miller, a teacher at the high school her sons attended, began to inquire about why Jeremy was not allowed to play quarterback, especially because the three white boys who attempted to lead the team had been doing poorly. When Coach Dobbins heard about Mrs. Miller's questions, he informed her that African Americans possessed physical traits such as the ability to run faster and jump higher that enabled them to be superior wide receivers and defensive backs. African Americans, he added, were better at these reactive positions but less adept at thinking positions such as quarterback and linebacker. Everyone who knew football, he assured her, understood that this was a fact based on racial genetics.

1. What, if any, moral values or principles are involved in this case?
2. Is this a moral issue and, if so, why?
3. What morally questionable actions are occurring, and why?
4. What effect, if any, did role modeling have on the football positions that the Miller boys chose to play?
5. Did the Miller boys experience any discriminatory treatment while playing in youth football leagues? If so, what was it?
6. Were the beliefs expressed by Coach Dobbins based on fact or myth, and was he behaving morally by espousing them?
7. Did the position shifting of Jeremy by his white coaches violate any moral principles?
8. What action if any, should Mr. and Mrs. Miller take if they believe that Jeremy has been discriminated against because of his race?

◆ ◆ ◆

CASE 9-4

Marilyn Scott fell in love with ice skating when she was seven years old. Although she was the only African American child skating at the rink, she was used to this since she attended a mostly white private school in Boston. Every afternoon, Marilyn joined a small group of aspiring figure skaters for the three hours of practice. Marilyn's talent surfaced quickly so that by age 11 she competed for the junior national title. For the next three years, Marilyn continued to improve dramatically, but each time she fell short of winning the championship. By that time, her mother was convinced that Marilyn was the victim of racial discrimination. Several people and even one judge had hinted that if Marilyn had been a blue-eyed blonde she would have won the past two years.

1. Historically, why have some sports been categorized as "white sports" while others have been associated more with African American athletes? Are there any ethical issues involved in this?
2. How are championships selected in figure skating, and how could this process have been impacted by discrimination?
3. What recourse, if any, do Marilyn and her mother have?

◆ ◆ ◆

CASE 9-5

Nicole spent the first 14 years of her life in a predominately African American and poor section of Atlanta living at times with her mother, grandmother, and aunt. She and her five half-brothers were never quite sure when they would see their mother given her history of drug and alcohol abuse. School was never a favorite with Nicole, especially after she joined a gang and started getting into serious academic and behavioral problems. After Nicole barely avoided being sent to a juvenile detention center for her role in a gang-related robbery, she was placed into the foster care system.

Mr. and Mrs. Foster gave Nicole a stable home life for the first time and imposed discipline that she initially resisted and begrudgingly accepted, but only because Mr. Foster refused to let her play softball unless she complied with family rules. Although Nicole had occasionally played softball at the Boys and Girls Club in Atlanta, she became one of the best players at Marietta's East High School.

As one of the two African Americans on the team, however, Nicole sometimes felt that Coach Smith treated her unfairly. Coach Smith was hard on all the girls but seemed to constantly yell at Nicole. On more than one occasion, Coach Smith called her actions niggardly and said that she was too dumb to play softball when she mistakenly threw the ball to the incorrect base. But Nicole endured his tirades and racist comments because she loved to hit. With her .432 batting average and .798 slugging percentage, she finally had achieved some degree of self-esteem. Unfortunately, not all of her teammates liked her increasing celebrity status, and she had heard that some were calling her hateful names behind her back. Such jealousies really hurt Nicole and caused her to think that her teammates were racist.

1. What values were being displayed by Nicole that may have contributed to her educational and behavioral problems in school?
2. What values were Mr. and Mrs. Foster teaching Nicole?
3. What values were being modeled by Coach Smith?
4. What values were being displayed by Nicole's teammates?
5. What role should Coach Smith have played relative to more positive player-to-player interactions?

◆ ◆ ◆

CASE 9-6

Grant Brown was an outstanding three-sport athlete at Southern High School. His athletic prowess resulted in grant-in-aid offers from NCAA Division I institutions in all three sports. Because he felt like his best possibility of becoming a professional was as a baseball pitcher, he accepted the offer to play for the Eastern State University Tigers. Grant was red-shirted his first year in college so that he could mature physically and because the Tigers had a large number of outstanding pitchers. Grant did notice, however, that all the pitchers, except for him, were white. Although Grant pitched effectively in practice, in his first year of varsity competition, he never got to pitch in a game. Grant seriously considered transferring after thinking that as an African American he never would get a fair chance to show his ability.

The following year, Grant started six games and compiled a 3-1 record, including one complete game. The next year Grant achieved a 10-2 record with a .242 earned run average. Unfortunately, in the conference championship game, he hurt his pitching arm. While this injury eliminated him from the pro draft that year, Grant was hopeful that the doctors were wrong and that he would be able to pitch again. Months of therapy and rehabilitation failed to restore his ability to pitch.

Since he had graduated, Grant asked his coach for a graduate assistant's position with the baseball team, but a former white player from another team was selected. After several negative responses, Grant was able to get an assistantship at a Division II college, where he worked with the baseball team for two years while completing his master's degree.

During the next 20 years, Grant was never able to achieve his dream of becoming a head coach at a Division I institution despite the winning records he compiled in high school and five small colleges. He had several interviews for head coach positions that gave him the opportunity to discuss his well-deserved reputation as a very good on-field coach and a person committed to helping his athletes achieve in the classroom. But, in every case a white man was hired.

Following his 12th failure in landing a Division I head coach's position, Grant concluded that he was the victim of racist hiring practices, especially after another coach told him that many white athletic directors had never hired a head coach of color. Although Grant was hurt and angry, he knew that to make an allegation of racism or to take any legal action would be disastrous because the baseball fraternity was small and individuals who were perceived to be problems were quickly blackballed.

1.   What concerns did Grant have with his college coach, and how could any of his actions have been perceived by him as racially motivated?
2.   What values were being displayed by Grant in how he dealt with his college experiences?
3.   Grant demonstrated as a coach what values?
4.   What values were being displayed by the athletic directors who refused to hire African Americans as head coaches?

◆ ◆ ◆

CASE 9-7

Historically, most public schools have offered football, basketball, and baseball for boys and basketball, if anything, for girls. Only in recent decades have opportunities expanded to include sports such as tennis, track and field, swimming, wrestling (for boys), and volleyball and softball (for girls).

An interesting phenomenon in sport participation appears to have occurred concurrently. Many African Americans, prior to and following public school integration, chose football, basketball, and track. Simultaneously, more and more whites opted out of sport or chose tennis, swimming, golf, and soccer as their sports. As a result, many high school sports are nearly segregated by race.

1.   What have been the contributing factors to this near separation of the races by sport?
2.   What role have nonschool sport opportunities played in this phenomenon?
3.   What role has economics played in the selection of sport by race?
4.   Are there any ethical issues involved in this near separation of the races by sport?

Gender Equity in Sport

◆ How have societal attitudes influenced females' participation in athletics, and have these attitudes related to any ethical issues?

◆ What has been the impact of Title IX on the sport opportunities of female athletes, coaches, and administrators?

◆ What was the educational model of the Association for Intercollegiate Athletics for Women, and why did it cease to exist?

◆ What did the NCAA do to change the governance of women's intercollegiate athletics, and why?

◆ Why are females largely excluded from management positions in athletics?

◆ What are the ethical and moral issues associated with gender equity in sport?

◆ In what ways can greater gender equity in sport be achieved through the resolution of ethical dilemmas?

Societal expectations about appropriate feminine behavior and gender-bound roles curtailed women's active participation in sport until relatively recent times. This country's early laws, such as those prohibiting women from owning property or operating businesses, verified the dominant position of males, leaving females with few rights. Not until 1920, for example, did all women receive, through constitutional amendment, the right to vote. Most females were illiterate until a few in the upper class began to attend private women's colleges in the 1800s. Although only a few pursued careers outside the home, these women threatened the status quo of a woman's "true calling" as wife and mother.

Historically, men have been able to engage in sporting activities but women have been excluded. In some cases, females were permitted and occasionally encouraged to watch, while in other instances they were explicitly banned from any involvement in sports. During the past century, a few women disregarded disparaging comments and competed in various sports. Notable among these have been Eleonora Sears (tennis, squash, walking, polo), Babe Didrikson (track and field, basketball, baseball, golf), Billie Jean King (baseball, tennis), Joan Joyce (softball, golf), and Jackie Joyner–Kersee (basketball, track).

HISTORICAL PERSPECTIVES

Some women, dressed in restrictive feminine attire, engaged in sports such as golf, tennis, and figure skating that emphasized gracefulness rather than assertiveness. However, when female participation in sport increased, especially by the upper class, these women were heavily influenced by a staunchly held belief in Victorianism. This dominant societal perspective dictated the boundaries of propriety in a woman's dress and behavior. She was never to be seen sweating (women at the time were supposed only to "glow"), her interest in sport remained frivolous, and social encounters in sporting events always surpassed victories in importance.

During the latter years of the 19th century and well into the 20th century, upper-class women in golf, tennis, archery, and equestrian events invariably stayed within societal norms. Society applauded, albeit briefly, that Gertrude Ederle accomplished the unthinkable for a woman by swimming the English Channel plus shattering the record set by a man. Helen Wills, Glenda Collett Vare, and Gertrude Ederle, although a part of the 1920s Golden Age of Sport, were probably more accepted for their participation in the traditional women's sports of tennis, golf, and swimming, respectively, than for their outstanding sport achievements. The All-American Girls Baseball League (1943 to 1954) and Hazel Walker's Arkansas Travelers professional basketball team (1949 to 1966) were always concerned about the feminine dress and behavior of their athletes, especially in these traditionally male sports.

The clothing worn by female athletes has constantly been a concern because of the fear that these garments would reveal too much flesh. Athletic attire has been transformed, albeit gradually, from long dresses including yards of petticoats and corsets to bikinis for beach volleyball. The latter outfit is believed to appeal to male fans more so than worn to enhance performances. Bloomers for basketball gave way to the "scandalous" shiny, short uniforms of the Golden Cyclones (Amateur Athletic Union basketball champions led by Babe Didrikson).

Even with the dramatic growth in sport opportunities for females in the past two decades, many males still devalue females' athletic prowess, and the media largely ignores most of their accomplishments. Until 1997 with the Women's National Basketball Association, repeated attempts to start women's professional basketball leagues had failed because of lack of fan support. Radio and television mention girls' and women's game scores infrequently, with the exception of premier golf and tennis events and a few glamorous Olympic sports like figure skating and gymnastics.

It should be noted, however, that males (with some females concurring) have truly believed their attitudes and actions to be proper and appropriate. As protectors of their wives and daughters, most men believed that it was their responsibility to shield girls and women from physical harm, including that in sport. At the time, no moral dissonance even hinted at the issue of gender equity. Quite the contrary, moral education based on unenlightened beliefs or an ignorant cultural heritage yielded a sexist social system and structure that largely went unquestioned.

Given the legal, educational, and social model that restricted women's potential involvement in many facets of life, as well as sport, how and why moral change has occurred is the focus of this chapter. This examination includes how and why discriminatory treatment historically, organizationally, and societally has violated ethical standards. Although greater gender equity has been achieved, full acceptance of sportswomen has yet to be achieved.

GENDER INEQUITY IN SPORT

Sport has traditionally been a man's world. Males competed, coached, organized, publicized, owned, announced, wagered on, and watched sport in virtual exclusion from females. Religious, medical, and societal beliefs relegated women to their homes as wives and mothers, or possibly allowed them to watch or lead cheers while men competed. Assertiveness, dominance, toughness, tenacity, and leadership were viewed as masculine traits, inappropriate for women. Many characterized females as too frail, slow, short, or weak to become anything more than recreational players in any sport.

History reveals, though, that these attitudes about excluding women from sport grew out of ignorance or preconceived ideas and medical myths of the time. For example, physicians claimed that

"Women's insides will fall out through excessive jumping and running," "Women will become sterile if they participate in vigorous sport," and "Women have limited energy resources that if used up in sport will leave them helpless when they must endure the demands of childbearing." People may have suffered from a lack of reasoned thinking if they believed these myths.

Sometimes by fiat, but mostly by societal constraints, girls learned early in lives that their brothers and male classmates were encouraged, while they were discouraged, to play sports. Toys directed boys into assertive, vigorous, and competitive activities; girls' toys reinforced passive, cooperative, and domestic play. Sometimes girls, disenchanted with inactivity, joined the boys in their games and occasionally surpassed them in skills. Yet, around puberty, most girls faced self-imposed, parentally imposed, or societally imposed choices. Many dropped out of competitive sport, perhaps continuing as fans or cheerleaders. Others continued participation in a more acceptable sport for females, such as tennis or golf, even though they might have preferred baseball. The choice of actively participating in one's favorite sport carried the risk of being labeled a tomboy or having one's femininity questioned.

What seems remarkable in retrospect is that few people questioned this status quo. It seemed as if males possessed some genetic or physiological right to sport that females lacked. Given the valued outcomes thought to be associated with competitive sport, such as teamwork, fair play, cooperation, discipline, and self-control, how could society advocate the development of these desirable outcomes for only males? Did this societal exclusion of most girls from sport violate the moral principles of justice, honesty, responsibility, and beneficence?

Limited Opportunities

Medical opinion contributed to the perception that females were incapable of taxing their bodies as males did. Many women physical educators in the early decades of the 1900s reinforced the notion that females should be encouraged to play, not

Historically, girls have been excluded from sports such as baseball.

compete, because moderate activity was healthy. Competition was considered unbecoming to a lady and potentially dangerous.

Before the 1970s, few youth sport programs offered the same competitive opportunities to girls that they did to boys because parents, peers, and societal attitudes failed to encourage most girls to develop their sport skills. Maybe these girls lacked interest, were disadvantaged physiologically compared with the boys, or realized that competitions did not exist at higher levels and became discouraged about developing skills that they would have limited opportunities to use. The few girls who successfully became youth sport athletes, usually in sports deemed appropriate for them, demonstrated self-confidence and determination in surmounting others' discouraging statements and actions.

A lack of opportunities for girls certainly characterized interscholastic sport until the 1970s. Before this time, other than a small percentage of girls who played basketball, usually in rural small-town settings, most girls were considered not to be interested in or skilled enough to become serious athletes.

Similarly, few competitive sport opportunities existed for college women. Most female physical educators staunchly opposed the male model of highly competitive, commercialized intercollegiate athletics. Instead, they claimed that women's activity needs were best met through instructional physical education programs, intramurals, and occasional play days or sports days (where social interaction surpassed friendly competition in importance). Gradually, however, in the 1960s, it became clear that women with higher levels of athletic skills wanted to compete. Within a decade, a new model for intercollegiate athletics for women, different from the men's, would begin to challenge the exclusiveness of sport as society questioned the moral basis for excluding females from sport competitions.

Governing Organizations and Policies for Women's Intercollegiate Athletics

Building on efforts of preceding organizations, by 1971 the Association for Intercollegiate Athletics for Women (AIAW) emerged as the governing organization over women's sport competition in colleges. Founded on the principle of an educational model that served women athletes, the AIAW grew to offer 41 national championships in 19 sports for its nearly 1,000 member institutions. Competitive opportunities for women at the state and regional qualifying levels skyrocketed, too.

Most collegiate sport programs for women, however, operated on shoestring budgets. Coaches initially volunteered their services, and players bought their own uniforms and equipment. Teams traveled in cars and vans, ate at fast-food restaurants, and stayed four to a room just so they could compete. Because they loved competitive sport, they endured difficulties in scheduling facilities, little to no access to athletic trainers, sports information personnel, and weight-training equipment; and few opportunities to receive grants-in-aid.

Title IX

The landmark event in equal opportunity for girls and women in sport occurred in 1972 when Congress passed the Education Amendments Act.

Title IX helped increase competitive opportunities for females.

Title IX of this legislation stipulated that schools and colleges could not discriminate in their educational programs, including athletics.

The NCAA opposed Title IX vigorously from the outset, lobbying against the initial passage of the legislation and repeatedly attempting to limit the scope of Title IX's application. Nonetheless, through the issuance of "Title IX of the Education Amendments of 1972; a Policy Interpretation; Title IX and Intercollegiate Athletics" in December 1979, the Department of Health, Education, and Welfare (HEW) explained the scope and application of this legislation. To clarify the meaning of "equal opportunity," HEW required that compliance was required in these three areas: (1) financial assistance (scholarships) based on athletic ability must be available on a substantially proportional basis to the number of male and female participants in each institution's athletics program; (2) program support areas for males and females must receive equivalent treatment, benefits, and opportunities in equipment and supplies, games and practice times, travel and per diem, coaching and academic tutoring, assignment and compensation of coaches and tutors, locker rooms, practice and competitive facilities, medical and training facilities, housing and dining facilities, publicity, recruitment, and support services; and (3) the interests and abilities of male and female students must be equally effectively accommodated. Possibly because of the money involved or the extent of male dominance, many colleges resisted complying with Title IX.

On behalf of its member institutions, the NCAA claimed that equal sharing of athletic monies, facilities, and services would threaten the viability of the revenue-producing sports. That is, only an unequal distribution of goods would enable men's revenue-producing sports to earn the capital to support both men's and women's sports. This argument seems flawed because the potential to earn revenue should not justify a moral injustice. No one knows what would happen with complete equity because in the over quarter of a century since Title IX was passed, it has not been achieved. Distributive justice dictates that inequality can never be legitimately defended or justified on the basis of scarcity of goods or an entitlement for those who earn revenues. The question becomes one of whether monies, facilities, and services are more important than people and how they treat each other.

After the NCAA failed to get athletics exempted from the requirements of Title IX, most colleges and universities began to provide more money for women's athletics. Administrators in institutions that expanded their women's athletic programs stated that their actions were based more on a moral obligation than fear of losing federal funding for noncompliance. Many of the larger universities excluded football from their gender comparisons when reporting on progress in complying with Ti-

tle IX, even though this violated the law. Others slowly and grudgingly provided more equitable support for women's teams to avoid costly legal battles or negative publicity. Some complied only under the threat of lawsuits alleging discrimination. Interestingly, these same responses continue to characterize strategies for partial compliance with Title IX today. Some women resorted to legal recourse whenever they believed that decision makers in athletics (largely men) violated moral principles.

A few institutions refused to change. One college claimed that Title IX did not apply to athletics because this program received no direct federal funding. The Supreme Court in 1984 agreed in the *Grove City College* v. *Bell* case. In effect, this ruling eliminated the application of Title IX to athletics, resulting in the withdrawal of, or the Office of Civil Right's suspension of, dozens of cases involving college athletics. Discrimination against women in intercollegiate athletics continued to exist, and in certain instances increased until 1988 when the Civil Rights Restoration Act reapplied Title IX to all institutions receiving any federal funds.

In 1992, the Supreme Court in *Franklin* v. *Gwinnett County Public Schools* strengthened the importance of Title IX by ruling that individuals discriminated against could receive punitive damages. The moral issue, though, is why are congressional action, judicial rulings, and the threat of financial losses required before athletic administrators will treat female athletes equitably?

Some advocate that the NCAA's decision to compete directly with AIAW championships in 1981–1982 was a power move. Given the AIAW's weak financial status and the NCAA's offer to provide more than $3 million in expense reimbursements to competing institutions, the struggle was short-lived. After the defection of 20 percent of its members during the 1981–1982 season, in 1982 the AIAW ceased to exist.

Conversely the NCAA claimed to offer women's athletes greater opportunity through expanded programs, more financial support, and television coverage. Rather than seeing the end of the AIAW as an aggressive takeover, the NCAA viewed its actions positively and in the best interests of women's sports in its member institutions. The NCAA alleged that Title IX required it to sponsor women's championships.

According to legal cases, most notably the 1996 Supreme Court decision not to hear *Cohen* v. *Brown University,* to comply with Title IX, an institution must meet at least one of the criteria of the three-part test: (1) participation opportunities are substantially proportionate to the undergraduate enrollment of females and males; (2) if members of one gender have historically been underrepresented among intercollegiate athletes, then there must have been a continuing practice of program expansion to meet the interests and abilities of this group; and (3) in the absence of number 2, an institution must demonstrate that the interests and abilities of this gender must have been fully and effectively accommodated. The first of these, called the proportionality test, has three possible issues associated with it. First, gender discrimination could persist if an institution cuts men's teams because no additional opportunities for females have been added (greater proportionality may have been achieved, but such action is judged insufficient to meet Title IX requirements). Second, colleges have been expected to achieve proportional progress even though other organizations or schools may not be providing equal opportunities for younger females. Third, just achieving proportionality does not exempt schools and colleges from the moral obligation to eliminate gender discrimination.

Outcomes of Change

With the NCAA in control of women's and men's athletics, males today are primarily the coaches and administrators for women's programs partially due to an increase in the number of teams and partially because of males hiring males to coach. Since 1972, there has been a drop from more than 90 percent to less than 50 percent in the number of women's teams coached by women (see Table 10-1). Similar findings are reported for NAIA institutions and in high schools. The number of females involved in intercollegiate athletic administration has dropped dramatically, too (see Table 10-2).

Women athletes today specialize in one sport, train year-round, and sometimes prioritize athletics over academics, as do their male peers. Sport has been found to negatively influence females' moral reasoning levels in comparison with those of nonathletes. Although female athletes' moral reasoning and development is significantly higher than that of male athletes, females' moral reasoning levels decrease the longer they participate in sport.

Recent incidents of the elimination of women's sport teams at many institutions countervail the requirements of Title IX. Sometimes, cuts that are made to save money include a similar number of men's teams slated for elimination. In most cases, the institutions have reinstated the women's teams because of public outcry or legal mandates.

Of significant note, however, has been the argument that the only way women's teams can be added or increased support provided is to eliminate men's teams. This pitting of the men against the women leads to the question, what is the ethical basis for simultaneously doing good and doing harm?

Interscholastic Sport Changes for Girls

The National Federation of State High School Associations and its member (state) organizations traditionally ignored girls' sport. By assuming a lack of interest or skill in females, administrators in most high schools disregarded the activity and competitive needs of half of their students. The 1970s ushered in a new era in the treatment of aspiring female athletes in schools.

The impact of Title IX, although gradual, was dramatic in most schools. Girls and boys in the 1980s began to share more equitably the use of practice and competitive facilities, athletic trainers, and weight rooms. Some school administrators, however, have resisted treating all athletes fairly and justly. Credentials and experiences usually govern coaches' stipends in the schools, rather than the gender of the coach of the team. However, some

TABLE 10-1

Trends in the Gender of Coaches of Women's Teams in National Collegiate Athletic Association Member Institutions

Year	Female Head Coaches (%)	Division I	Division II	Division III
2000	45.6	46.0	39.4	48.4
1999	46.3	46.5	40.0	49.5
1998	47.4	46.2	41.7	50.7
1997	47.4	46.7	42.3	50.8
1996	47.7	47.5	41.9	51.3
1995	48.3	47.7	43.2	51.3
1994	49.4	46.9	45.4	53.6
1993	48.1	45.5	44.1	52.3
1992	48.3	46.6	42.3	52.6
1991	47.7	45.9	42.1	51.7
1990	47.3	44.2	44.0	51.8
1989	47.7	—	—	—
1988	48.3	43.8	45.7	53.3
1987	48.8	—	—	—
1986	50.6	45.5	46.8	57.2
1985	50.7	—	—	—
1984	53.8	49.9	52.2	58.8
1983	56.2	—	—	—
1982	52.4	—	—	—
1981	54.6	—	—	—
1980	54.2	—	—	—
1979	56.1	—	—	—
1978	58.2	—	—	—
1972	90.0+	—	—	—

Available from R. V., Acosta, and L. J. Carpenter: *Women in intercollegiate sport: A longitudinal study: Twenty-three year update 1977–2000*, P.O. Box 42, West Brookfield, MA 01585.

schools pay higher salaries to coaches for boys' teams in football, basketball, and other sports.

Teams for girls have proliferated since the 1970s with the number of girls competing increasing by the hundreds of thousands. Because of a lack of enough females prepared for or interested in coaching, the increased number of teams, greater equity in coaching stipends, and male athletic directors hiring coaches for girls' teams, more and more men were hired. Some women eager to coach competitively in the 1970s found that they did not enjoy the pressures of coaching and quit. Others burned out because of multiple team assignments combined with family responsibilities. This trend of men

TABLE 10-2				

Trends in Females in Athletic Administration in National Collegiate Athletic Association Member Institutions

Year	%*	Division I	Division II	Division III
2000	17.8	8.5	17.4	25.6
1998	19.4	9.9	18.6	29.4
1996	18.5	8.8	16.7	27.9
1994	21.0	—	—	—
1992	16.8	8.6	15.0	24.8
1990	15.9	7.0	15.2	24.8
1988	16.1	8.4	14.6	23.0
1986	15.2	9.4	15.2	20.4
1984	17.0	10.0	15.9	21.2
1980	20.0	—	—	—
1972	90.0+	—	—	—

*Percentage of female head athletic directors of women's programs.

Source: Available from R. V. Acosta, and L. J. Carpenter: *Women in intercollegiate sport: a longitudinal study: Twenty-three year update 1977–2000,* P.O. Box 42, West Brookfield, MA 01585.

coaching girls' teams has continued to expand to more than 50 percent today. These hiring practices may be attributable in part to the fact that most high school athletic directors have been and continue to be men, who frequently consider men more qualified to coach than women.

The importance of Title IX, along with the Civil Rights Restoration Act, to girls and women is unquestionably critical in the elimination of gender-based discrimination in sport. Would this federal legislation have been unnecessary had people truly valued females' participation in sport? Why did decision makers value the educational experiences of sport for males but not for females? Was it fair and just to refuse to fund competitive opportunities for females? Why did the legal system have to mandate compliance and threaten with financial losses those who refused?

Did the possible loss of federal funding and the negative media attention lead to greater compliance than did the belief that gender equity in sport is a moral issue? The establishment and growth of the AIAW primed the pump, encouraging women to develop their sports skills. Title IX's mandate for the elimination of inequities in financial support, access to facilities, and overall athletic opportunities, has led to significant increases in the quality and quantity of sport programs for girls and women.

SOCIETAL ATTITUDES

As discussed in the historical section, societal attitudes have hampered sport opportunities for females. Society teaches girls to not be assertive, independent, or tough, although success in sport demands each of these traits, as well as other so-called masculine characteristics. Society heaps praise and rewards on boys and men who achieve in sport. To a much lesser extent, girls and women receive accolades, trophies, and other awards for their sport achievements. Does the media largely ignore sportswomen, giving most of its print and broadcast coverage to males? Often when sportswomen's accomplishments are publicized, the media depicts

Females today are more eager to test their physical skills against males in sports such as basketball.

them in sexist ways that undermine their seriousness as athletes. Does the media's image of female professional athletes trivialize their accomplishments as athletes? Do male tennis stars receive praise for their physical prowess and skillful performances, while the coverage of female tennis players emphasizes clothing, hair styles, and mannerisms?

Although males in general possess physical advantages in sport, whenever females succeed in competing on equal terms with males—that is, at similar elite levels or as opponents—often their femininity is questioned or they are derided as somewhat less of a woman. Babe Didrikson, the Associated Press' greatest female athlete of the first half of the 20th century, had to endure numerous disparaging comments because of her multisport prowess. Female athletes have been exposed to

stereotypical statements and prejudicial treatments whenever they step outside others' perceived boundaries of propriety.

These societal attitudes may result from ignorance of physiological facts about women moving and competing. The discrimination that has occurred will change only if values are challenged through education, dialogue, and debate. Reasoning must center on challenging those in charge who hold to unfair practices.

Another illustration of societal or psychological pressure placed on females is the emphasis on participating in acceptable sports. Supposedly, women should not play baseball or football, box, race cars or horses, play rugby, pole vault, wrestle, or ride rodeo bulls. It is permissible to play basketball, softball, volleyball, soccer, or even to run track but with some risk about how others view these athletes' femininity. Those who opt for tennis, golf, swimming, figure skating, and gymnastics are more likely to receive media attention and societal approval.

Homophobia, a fear of those who choose partners of the same sex, has become a major issue in sport, and especially women's sport. Coaches and athletic administrators seek to ensure that their programs are never accused of condoning homosexual behaviors among their athletes. They believe that such allegations would harm recruiting and reputations.

In 1993, the NCAA's Gender Equity Task Force released its first status report on women's intercollegiate athletic programs. Some advances were reported in the 1997–1998 report from this same task force.

Funding Category	1993	1997–1998
Participation in varsity athletics	35%	40%
Grants-in-aid received	30%	40%
Recruiting	17%	About 33%
Operating expenses	23%	31%

The question remains, Do these data indicate full compliance with Title IX regulations? It has been strongly suggested that when the participants in both men's and women's sports programs would accept as fair and equitable the overall program support of the other gender, then equity has been achieved. Given the fact that this does not exist on most school and college campuses, the struggle to achieve full equal opportunity continues.

A few strategies to help in these efforts might be to (1) urge the federal government to strictly enforce Title IX; (2) reduce unnecessary expenses associated with men's revenue-producing sports, reallocate these monies to women's sports, and aggressively seek new dollars to be used to eliminate gender discrimination in sports; (3) adopt the NCAA Division III non-grant-in-aid model with athletics conducted within a primarily academic, noncommercialized framework; and most important, (4) accept the moral responsibility to treat males and females equitably by making athletics "gender-blind."

Despite Title IX, in many competitive situations males continue to receive better equipment, facilities, coaching, awards, and other program support because those in management positions believe that male athletes deserve preferential treatment. If people acted justly, would they demand that all athletes receive equal benefits? In NCAA institutions, male athletes receive 60 percent of the monies available for grants-in-aid, an amount disproportionate to their enrollment numbers and to the number of athletes by gender. With the occasional exception of tennis, there is a disparity between men's and women's prize winnings. Is this because corporations provide more sponsorship dollars to men's events or because women's sports do not have a large spectator following? Can sport managers develop their moral reasoning leading to gender equity in sport?

CONTINUING QUESTIONS

Girls and women do not suffer from total exclusion from sport or have to endure many of the discriminatory practices of the past. But, even though over three decades have passed since Title IX banned gender discrimination in educational institutions that receive federal funding, equity for girls

Female athletes want to develop their abilities to the highest extent possible.

and women in sport remains elusive. Insidious discrimination, advancements occurring only because of threats of lawsuits, and continued underrepresentation of females in coaching, athletic training, officiating, athletic administration, and sport media persist. Several problem areas are identified below, with alternatives to consider about each.

Issue 1: *Who should coach the teams of girls and women, and who should administer these programs?*

Discussion: It is revealing that if the question were asked about who should coach and administer boys' and men's sport teams that the nearly 100 percent response would be males, of course. But, relative to the gender of the coach or administrator for females' teams of all ages, opinions are sharply divided. This ongoing issue is based on the hegemonic status of males in their domination of sports based on their physical superiority. Societal restrictions on the proper roles of females also has certainly affected the acceptance of males as predominant on the fields of play and competition. Arguments persist that males know more about sports and thereby are better qualified than females to coach and lead athletic programs. So, as the number of teams for females at all competitive levels increased along with increased salaries for the coaches of these teams, more and more males chose to coach females, especially when it was easier to get this position than one coaching males. These males were also more likely to be hired by the male athletic directors.

Lacking female role models, many females, even those with highly successful playing experiences, opted not to become coaches. A lack of sufficient female applicants made it easier for males to hire males. Societal attitudes continue to dictate that females carry a disproportionate level of responsibilities for home and family, thus making it more challenging for females to balance these responsibilities with the long hours and travel demands of coaching. The supportive spouse of the female coach is the exception, whereas the long-suffering spouse of the male coach is expected and applauded.

Does society (specifically, competitive sport) value and appreciate females as coaches and athletic administrators? To facilitate a change in attitudes, women need a mentoring system to provide these individuals opportunities to develop the knowledge and skills for success. Because role modeling helps teach values and develop a moral reasoning process, administrators should hire female coaches to provide their athletes with these same-gender teachers of ethical principles. Perhaps because of the current predominance of males in sport there remains the perception that male coaches are better. The challenge is to encourage women to pursue careers in coaching and to educate young athletes to value women coaches.

Issue 2: *Does financial support for sport programs at all levels of competition inequitably favor males? If so, how can this be changed?*

Discussion: Although equal opportunity, as required by Title IX, does not stipulate the expenditure of equal dollars for male and female teams, it does mandate equity. Despite repeated threatened and actual lawsuits during the past three decades, the treatment of female athletes, while significantly enhanced, has yet to fully equal that enjoyed by males. Certainly in some situations, females enjoy equitable funding for grants-in-aid, operating expenses, number of teams, and even the salaries paid coaches. More than half the students in colleges are females, yet they receive 40 percent or less of the athletic departments' financial resources. Most colleges expend huge sums of money on their football programs, regardless of whether they are revenue producing or not, and then claim that equity exists in their athletic programs as long as football is omitted from any comparisons. Another example of inequity often seen is providing an excellent baseball stadium for male athletes, and promising year after year (as soon as the money becomes available) a new field for the female softball team.

Decison makers in sport should allocate proportionate and equitable funding for males and females on the basis of participation numbers. A quota system is not necessarily fair because it assumes that a 50/50 split is the answer to a problem that cannot be addressed so simplistically. Such an arbitrary decision, alleging required by Title IX, could be unfair to males. [see Jessica Gavora (2001) and Christina Sommers (2000)]. Moral reasoning demands that one examines what is just, honest, responsible, and beneficent when determining the treatment of others. For example, is it honest to claim that men's football finances all other sports and thus that this team deserves a larger budget, when in reality most football teams lose money? Is it just to perpetuate traditional practices of preferentially treating men's programs? Is it responsible to provide men's teams with better facilities, certified athletic trainers, plush travel accommodations, and highly qualified coaches while women's teams experience few of these program support services? Is it beneficent to fail to promote, fund, or expand women's competitive opportunities? Greater opportunities for females demand increased funding. If males should not receive special treatment, as reasoned thinking should lead one to conclude, people should eliminate those benefits that cannot be justified and redistribute these resources to women's programs. Another alternative obligates administrators to raise more money.

Issue: *Should more college grants-in-aid be awarded to male athletes?*

Discussion: An argument for favoring males in the awarding of grants-in-aid is that males are more highly skilled and more interested in sports and thus willing to work harder to enhance their skills. But the most vocal advocates for this position simply state that male athletes bring in the revenue, and thus it should be theirs to receive or allocate as they choose. Conversely, those who support the equitable distribution of grant-in-aid funds state that discriminating against females is illegal and immoral. Once funds are available in athletic departments, each student athlete should be treated the same. Providing financial assistance to only males or only males playing in revenue-producing sports denies females opportunities to improve their skills and engage in school- or college-sponsored extracurricular activities. Moral reasoning calls for a distribution of grants-in-aid in ways that are ethically defensible. That is, what is fair?

Issue: *Should males have a greater number of participation opportunities than females at all levels of sport?*

Discussion: Society traditionally has encouraged boys to engage in sports while providing less encouragement to girls. As a result, many more teams were available for boys and men while some teams for females could not even be formed because of lack of interest. Although in recent years more and more females have been eagerly seeking out teams to join, they are not always welcome, such as on baseball, wrestling, or football teams. It is unknown to what level of interest female participation on sport teams will grow. The important decision that recreation departments, private clubs, schools, colleges, professional leagues, and the public must

make is to what degree to finance teams for females. Decision makers must determine whether to permit teams of girls and boys, how many different competitive levels of teams can be financed, and what sports should be offered. The challenge is to ensure that every child, student, and adult has the opportunity in sport that she and he deserves and desires.

Issue: *Should men control all levels of sport, with only a few women holding administrative positions in sport?*

Discussion: Those who hire athletic directors and their assistants, sports information and promotions directors, athletic trainers, and other administrative personnel should seek qualified women for these jobs. They also should actively seek women for internships and assistants' positions to prepare them to become coaches and administrators because of the unique skills, perspectives, and styles these females would contribute to athletics. No longer will only the autocratic, task-oriented, structuring management style of the ex-coach work in athletics. Rather, the building of relationships through encouragement, flexibility, delegation, and nurturing—traits more characteristic of females—will enhance performance in the sport setting as they have in the corporate world.

MORAL EDUCATION

An overarching resolution to each of these issues can be classified as moral education. Athletic leaders need to understand how their personal values and beliefs relate to personal and professional relations. An athletic department's mission statement and purposes, as reflective of its staff's values and beliefs, should match a philosophy that encompasses moral knowing, moral valuing, and moral acting.

The ethical issues pervading gender equity in sport remain, as does the importance of justice, honesty, responsibility, and beneficence. Justice requires that female athletes receive fair treatment. This encompasses all the financially supported services associated with athletics. Is it just to fly the men's basketball team to a competition 250 miles away while expecting the women's basketball team to ride in vans or a bus? Would you reverse your response if you were a member of the women's basketball team? Does distributive justice demand equitable treatment regardless of skill level or fan popularity?

Are athletic directors, who are mostly men, honest when they state or demonstrate through their hiring practices that women are not interested in or qualified for coaching or athletic administrative positions? Admitting to past discriminatory hiring practices and aggressively seeking to rectify them verifies that one values and believes in women serving as leaders in sport. Given the discussion about moral reasoning and moral development in the preceding chapters, it appears that one effective strategy could be an educational intervention that helps individuals analyze what they value and why.

Responsibility governs how sport leaders and athletes deal with each other. Both should demonstrate a commitment to making things work for the greater good. If administrators act responsibly on the basis of their beliefs and values, can the existing system enact change and promote gender equity in sport?

Based on this historical, organizational, and societal analysis of women in sport, have the characteristics of beneficence been achieved? If people truly believed in beneficence, would they work tirelessly to remove and prevent sexism in sport? Beneficence leads to kind words and deeds. Athletic administrators and media personnel should stop demeaning, stereotyping, or ignoring female athletes. Kindness will lead to acceptance of females as equals in management positions in sport. Beneficent individuals will encourage females to achieve their athletic potentials through increased participation and competitive opportunities in the absence of discriminatory treatment.

SUMMARY

Gender equity in sport has yet to be achieved. Historically, females' opportunities have been limited because of societal perceptions of their lack of interest and ability, physiological myths, and discriminatory exclusion. Many women lack the physiological skills to compete equally with most men. Yet, it can be argued that women have sold out to

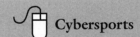 Cybersports

http://bailiwick.lib.uiowa.edu/ge

This site at the University of Iowa provides information about gender equity issues in intercollegiate sports.

www.ed.gov/pubs/TitleIX

At this site can be found a review of the 25 years of progress since the passage of the 1972 Education Amendments.

www.edc.org/WomensEquity/resource/title9

The Equity Resource Center established through the Women's Educational Equity Act has helped build a gender-equity infrastructure that supports Title IX and creates models of gender-fair education.

www.aahperd.org/nagws/nagws_main.html

The National Association for Girls and Women in Sport advocates for equity issues in sport programs.

www.nacwaa.org

The National Association for Collegiate Women Athletic Administrators has as its goals the enhancement of athletic and administrative opportunities for women and promotion of positive attitudes toward women in sports.

www.gslis.utexas.edu/~lewisa/womsprt.html

The site provides links to general and sport-specific pages on the Web for girls and women.

men by not celebrating their biological differences. Instead of playing men's games by men's rules, maybe women should develop their own games that highlight their unique physical talents.

Women's athletic programs remain unequal, even after being combined with existing men's governance structures. Title IX helped females achieve greater equity, but full equality remains elusive because too many people still do not value the right of women to equitable treatment within sport. Females have not achieved significant movement into the power positions controlling sport. However, each new female head coach or athletic director hired signals another victory in the battle for gender equity in sport. Many more are needed, along with equitable treatment, before discrimination is eradicated.

 # ISSUES AND DILEMMAS

CASE 10-1

Lisa Whitley grew up playing baseball. Despite her mother's attitude that sports were unfeminine and inappropriate for her daughter, Lisa shared her father's love of baseball. He played with her, taught her the basic skills, and coached her teams. By age 12, Lisa demonstrated the best baseball skills of any youth sport athlete in Southern California. Although her team lost in the finals of the Little League regional qualifying tournament, Lisa's .495 batting average for the year was the main reason the team advanced so far.

Although she had encountered occasional sexist remarks and disparaging comments about a girl playing with the boys, Lisa disregarded them. She just wanted to play baseball. Unfortunately, the baseball league for boys 12 to 15 years of age did not want her to play. She and her father were told that only under court order would a girl be allowed to participate in the league.

Because Lisa's family did not have the money to hire a lawyer and file a lawsuit, she was forced to quit organized baseball. Because the local school had just started a softball team for girls, Mr. Whitley urged Lisa to redirect her talents into this sport.

At first, Lisa was despondent and unwilling to play what she perceived to be a less challenging sport. Finally, Lisa's competitive spirit prevailed as she enthusiastically embraced softball, especially the opportunity to pitch. Through long hours of practice during her middle school and high school years, Lisa became an outstanding pitcher. She finished with a high school record of 75-2, with an earned run average of 1.31. She led the nation with a .453 batting average.

Lisa chose to attend Southeastern California College (SCC) on a partial softball grant-in-aid because its team had done well in the preceding year's NCAA tournament and her father could attend her games.

Once enrolled, Lisa learned that the college only marginally supported softball. The coach was part-time, the budget limited, and the institutional support services for female athletes quite different from those offered for male athletes.

Lisa questioned the situation because, in high school, the girls' softball and boys' baseball teams had been treated equitably. She learned that Mr. Riddick, the athletic director and former baseball coach, had resented the establishment of the softball team. He often stated that women had no business playing this sport, especially because money for softball in his opinion could be better spent on baseball. But because Dr. Whitmire, President of SCC, in the face of a threatened Title IX–based lawsuit, mandated having a softball team, one was established. Despite minimal financial support and obvious violations of the requirements of Title IX, Coach Collins had successfully built a competitive team.

Lisa and her teammates resented the preferential treatment given the baseball team and other men's sports. They asked Coach Collins for help, but she said she would lose her job if she complained or requested more financial support. So the players, led by Lisa, asked Athletic Director Riddick for funding for more grants-in-aid, a full-time coach, better facilities, access to athletic trainers and weight-training facilities, and an expanded competitive schedule. Mr. Riddick adamantly refused. He then threatened the elimination of the softball team if these requests were brought up again. Undeterred, the team asked President Whitmire to intervene once again. He attempted to placate Lisa and her teammates by citing all the progress made at SCC for women's athletics in recent years. Also, he stated that budgetary constraints precluded providing any additional funding for the softball team.

Dismayed by the unresponsiveness of President Whitmire to their plight, the mother of one of the softball team members filed a discrimination suit based on Title IX against SCC. A furious Mr. Riddick immediately fired Coach Collins and canceled the softball team's schedule, claiming a financial crisis. No other team was eliminated.

1. What are the moral values in this case?
2. What, if any, ethical issues led to Lisa's forced exit from baseball?
3. What are the moral bases for equity in high school sports for both genders?
4. What ethical principles, if any, were violated by SCC's refusal to treat female athletes equitably?
5. What values or principles did Mr. Riddick violate by eliminating the softball team?
6. Was Lisa correct in what she did? Why?
7. If you were Lisa, how would you feel?
8. What could have been Mr. Riddick's justification for his actions?

9. What would you have done if you had been in each person's position?
10. What underlying values were used by each person in making his or her decisions?

◆ ◆ ◆

CASE 10-2

Sally learned to run by chasing her older brothers. She could never catch them, but it certainly was not for lack of effort. To channel her daughter's high energy and love of running, Mrs. Ramsey arranged for Sally to join the community-based Junior Striders Track Club. She quickly established herself as the fastest 12-year-old in the club—girl or boy—at short distances. Sally continued to decrease her times as she grew, matured, and trained under the expert coaching of a retired former college coach, Bob Jonas. In age-group competitions locally and throughout the state, she repeatedly won 100-meter, 220-meter, and 440-meter races. Sally was eager to run for Central High School.

Sally's world changed dramatically just before she entered the 10th grade, when her mother's company transferred her. After settling into their new house and enrolling in school, Sally learned that Stegall High School did not have a girls' track team. She was told that girls were not interested in this sport, although there were basketball and softball teams for the few athletic girls in the school. The boys competed in eight sports, including track.

Determined to continue her running, Sally asked Coach Hudson if she could train with the boys' track team. Only after her relentless persistence did he acquiesce, thinking she would quit after a couple of tough practices. Sally handled all of his challenges and endured the snide comments she received from classmates and track team members. Grudgingly, the boys accepted her as a dedicated athlete, but always added that they surely would not want to race against her, lest they be beaten.

After numerous attempts to get the athletic director, principal, and school board to add a girls' track team, Mrs. Ramsey filed a lawsuit against Stegall High School and the Capital Area Conference to permit Sally to compete on the boys' team. She based the complaint on Title IX, stating that females at Stegall and in the conference were denied equal opportunity in sport. Rather than fight this case, the Stegall School Board ruled that Sally must be allowed to compete on the boys' track team. The conference teams threatened to cancel their scheduled track meets with Stegall.

1. What moral principles, if any, are being violated?
2. What moral values, if any, were displayed by Coach Jonas?

3. What were the moral values of the people of Stegall that placed females in supportive, rather than participative, roles in sport?

4. What were the ethical issues, if any, why Coach Hudson initially resisted and subsequently allowed Sally to train with the boys' track team?

5. Why did Mrs. Ramsey sue Stegall High School, and what was the basis of the lawsuit?

6. Why did the School Board allow Sally to compete? Was this decision a morally reasoned one?

7. What were Sally's moral and legal rights in this situation?

◆ ◆ ◆

CASE 10-3

When Southwestern State University (SSU) merged its men's and women's athletic programs in 1990, Marilyn Graham's title changed from women's athletic director to assistant athletic director for women's athletics. Instead of having administrative authority over the eight women's sport teams, she now reported to Hugh Knowles, the athletic director. Although she was pleased with the increase in program support for the women athletes, she realized that they were not treated equitably.

Budgets for men's basketball and football far exceeded those for any other of the men's sports and all of the women's sports. Throughout the 1990s, she expressed concern that the women's percentage of the athletic budget had reached 25 percent but stayed there despite the fact that females comprised 51 percent of the student body. Whenever she raised questions, the response was always that the two men's revenue sports financed all the other sports. If these were not preferentially treated, then every team would lose support or possibly risk elimination.

Another distressing fact that Marilyn Graham noted was the gradual change in who coached the women's teams. In 1990, all were coached by women because she had hired each one—all talented, committed coaches. In the subsequent decade, six of these coaches had moved to larger universities because of their success at SSU. Although during each search she had recommended qualified women candidates, only twice did Athletic Director Knowles hire a woman. For volleyball, swimming, track, and tennis, he hired men to coach.

After over a decade of trying to gain greater financial support for the women's teams and to hire women coaches, Marilyn Graham was relieved of her administration responsibilities over women's athletics. Although the only female athletic administrator at Southwestern, she was moved out of day-to-day operations and given the title of assistant director for public relations. Her former duties were reassigned to a newly hired male associate athletic director.

1. What are the moral and ethical issues in this case?
2. What are the legal issues, if any, involved in this situation?
3. Is it ethical to treat female athletes inequitably in program support because they do not play revenue-producing sports? If not, what are the unethical practices?
4. What should the financial support for athletic teams be based on: gender, ability to generate revenue, percentage of athletes involved, percentage of students at the institution, or other criteria?
5. What moral principles, if any, could have been used by Marilyn Graham in her recommendation of women for the vacant coaching positions?
6. What moral principles, if any, could have been used by Hugh Knowles in his decision to hire men to coach the four women's teams?
7. Is it ethical for women's athletic programs to be administered exclusively by men? Why or why not?
8. What recourse does Marilyn Graham have in addressing her change of responsibilities and the treatment of women's athletics at Southwestern?

◆ ◆ ◆

CASE 10-4

Northwest State University (NSU), a NCAA Division II institution, had made some progress in complying with Title IX, but university administrators acknowledged that compliance had not been achieved. There were six teams for women; the college undergraduate population consisted of 60 percent women. Male athletes on six teams received 75 percent of the grants-in-aid.

When the university committed an annual addition of $100,000 from student fees for athletics, the athletic director was asked to submit a proposal to the president for how these monies would be allocated. He proposed the following:

(a) Add a volleyball coach (thus creating two positions instead of the former volleyball/softball combination)	$40,000
(b) Add partial and full grants-in-aid for women	$40,000
(c) Add partial and full grants-in-aid for men	$20,000

This proposal would raise the percentage of grants-in-aid for women to 40 percent.

1. What requirements of Title IX were being violated by NSU prior to the new funding? Was this ethical?

2. What requirements, if any, of Title IX would be violated if the proposal of the athletic director were to be implemented? Would this be ethical?
3. What are the relationships, if any, among the number of teams, percentage of students by gender, and percentage of grants-in-aid and compliance with Title IX?
4. If you were the athletic director, what recommendation would you have made?
5. If you were the university president, what would have been your response to the athletic director's proposal?
6. What are the ethical issues associated with this situation?

◆ ◆ ◆

CASE 10-5

When the Rodriguez family moved to Greenville, they were eager to join community activities. Fernando Rodriguez immediately signed his four children up for sports with the city recreation department. He could not understand why the leagues were configured as they were. His six-year old daughter and seven-year old son were placed on T-ball teams comprised of boys and girls. His 10-year old son was assigned to a competitive boys' baseball team, while his 11-year old daughter's (Maria) only option was a recreational girls' softball team. Because Maria had shown the best athletic abilities of his children, he had always encouraged her to play baseball to challenge herself. Suddenly, she could not play baseball with the boys as she had before.

1. When Fernando Rodriguez questioned the differences in opportunities provided for his children, what rationale do you think he received from recreation department officials?
2. What are the pros and cons of dividing sports opportunities by gender?
3. Is it equitable to force boys into competitive sports leagues and girls into recreational sports leagues? Is it ethical?
4. What recourse, if any, does Mr. Rodriguez have relative to Maria's team placement?

◆ ◆ ◆

CASE 10-6

Denise began playing volleyball when she was 12 through a youth program sponsored by the United States Volleyball Association. Her aggressive style of play, outstanding leaping ability, and hard work led to her being selected for the Junior National Team. Ted Anderson, the highly successful coach of this team, helped Denise further develop her volleyball skills. Denise and her parents really appreciated how quickly and significantly she had grown as a player under Coach Anderson's guidance.

While at the United States Olympic Training Center with the Junior National Team during the summer prior to her senior year in high school, Coach Anderson had asked Denise to spend more time with him working on her individual skills and studying videotapes of her performances. Denise was delighted to receive this special attention and especially enjoyed it when her coach positioned himself close by her for extended periods of time while viewing film. Because Denise really trusted her coach and increasingly enjoyed this closeness, she was surprised by but enjoyed it when he kissed her and then began to caress her arms and legs while he told her about what a great future she had in volleyball and how he could help her achieve her goals.

That summer the relationship between Denise and Coach Anderson became sexually intimate. Denise became emotionally tied to her coach on and off the court. His role as coach and lover initially helped Denise's play but later led to problems when team members became aware of their relationship. They questioned whether Denise's ability or her relationship with the coach led to her playing time and status as captain.

1. How were Coach Anderson's actions toward Denise appropriate or inappropriate?
2. Was Coach Anderson guilty of sexual harassment? If so, in what ways?
3. What was right or wrong about Denise's actions?
4. What ethical responsibility does Coach Anderson owe to all members of the Junior National Team?
5. What action, if any, should be taken by the governing body of the Junior National Team?

◆ ◆ ◆

CASE 10-7

Joan was well liked and respected by her teammates. Although she was not the most talented player on the women's basketball team, she was definitely the hardest working and was a likely starter as a junior at State University. Prior to the beginning of practice, Joan met with her coach, Mark Barnes, and told him that she and her partner, Sally Cunningham, who was one of the team managers, were going public with their relationship by telling team members and the media. Joan shared that Joan's and Sally's parents knew of their intimate relationship and were very supportive of them.

Coach Barnes went ballistic when he heard of Joan's relationship and her plans. Coach Barnes shouted at Joan that he would never let a homosexual play on his team because it would destroy team chemistry and ruin recruiting. Coach Barnes threatened Joan by stating that if anyone on the team or in the media was told about this relationship that Joan would lose her grant-in-aid because Coach Barnes would refuse to allow her to be on the team. Coach Barnes added that he would see that Sally would never get admitted into physical therapy school, a career she had dreamed of pursuing for years.

Joan and Sally talked for hours after Joan shared Coach Barnes's tirade. Joan knew that without a grant-in-aid, she would never be able to attend the university given her father's huge medical bills, her mother's meager salary as a teacher, and the needs of her siblings. Sally would not be able to major in physical therapy because her parents could not afford to send her to a private school or an out-of-state institution that offered this major. Although Joan and Sally wanted to be true to themselves and open about their relationship, they finally decided that the risks from the threats of Coach Barnes were too high; so they "remained in the closet" about their relationship.

Joan completed her junior and senior years on the team but never earned a starting position. Because Sally was told on the first day of practice that she could no longer serve as a team manager, she concentrated on her studies in physical therapy. Joan and Sally were convinced that things would have been so much better if Joan had never told Coach Barnes about their relationship. They felt confident, however, that he would have carried out his threats had they gone public. Joan and Sally also were disappointed that during their college years they had been forced to remain silent about their relationship.

1. How was the plan that Joan and Sally had to publicly share their relationship ethical or unethical?
2. What values did Coach Barnes model for his team through his words and actions relative to Joan and Sally?
3. What values did Joan and Sally demonstrate through their actions?
4. What would you have done if you had been Coach Barnes? Joan? Sally?

REFERENCE

Acosta, R.V., and L.J. Carpenter. 2000. *Women in intercollegiate sport: A longitudinal study: Twenty-three year update 1977–2000.* (available from the authors, P.O. Box 42, West Brookfield, MA 01585).

Gavora, J. 2001. *Tilting the Playing fields: Schools, sports, sex and Title IX.* San Francisco: Encounter Books.

Sommers, C. H. (2000) *The war against boys: How misguided feminism is harming our young men.* New York: Simon & Schuster.

ADDITIONAL READINGS

Boxill, J. 1993–1994. Title IX and gender equity. *Journal of the Philosophy of Sport* 20–21: 23–31.

Cahn, S. K. 1995. *Coming on strong: Gender & sexuality in twentieth-century women's sports.* Cambridge: Harvard University Press.

Francis, L. P. 1993–1994. Title IX: Equality for women's sports? *Journal of the Philosophy of Sport* 20–21: 32–47.

Gavora, J. 2001. *Tilting the playing field: Schools, sports, sex and Title IX.* San Francisco: Encounter Books.

Green, L. E. 1998. *A level playing field: The athletic administrator's guide to Title IX, gender equity in sports and OCR investigations.* Baldwin, KS: Sports Law Publishing.

Greenberg, J. E. 1997. *Getting into the game: Women and sports.* Danbury: Franklin Watts.

Lumpkin, A. 1998. Title IX Update. In H. Appenzeller (ed.), *Risk management in sport: Issues and strategies* (pp. 313–320). Durham, NC: Carolina Academic Press.

McMillen, J. D. 2000. *Title IX compliance and implementation.* North Chelmsford, MA: Courier Custom Publishing.

Powe-Allred, A., and M. Powe. 1998. *The quiet storm: A celebration of women in sports.* Indianapolis: Masters Press.

Priest, L., and L. M. Summerfield. 1995. Promoting gender equity in middle level and secondary school sports programs. *NASSP Bulletin* 79(575) (December): 52–56.

White, K. A. 1997. 25 years after Title IX, sexual bias in K–12 sports still sidelines girls. *Education Week* 16 (June 18): 1, 20+.

Wilde, T. J. 1995. Seeking equitable distribution of opportunities for intercollegiate athletic participation between the sexes. *Journal of Sport Management* 9: 300–16.

Application of Moral Reasoning in Other Physical Activity Settings

Ergogenic Aids for Sport Performance

- ◆ What are the effects of the use of stimulants on athletes' performances in sport?
- ◆ What are the effects of the use of depressants on athletes' performances in sport?
- ◆ What are the effects of the use of anabolic steroids on athletes' performances in sport?
- ◆ What is blood doping, and why are athletes in the Olympic Games banned from using it?
- ◆ Should the use of legal drugs be allowed in sport?
- ◆ Should sport governing organizations or the legal system be responsible for penalizing the use in sport of illegally obtained drugs?
- ◆ What are the legal and moral issues surrounding drug testing?
- ◆ What are the health issues associated with taking ergogenic aids?

Most people in sport enjoy competition; they strive to win. Competition is an integral part of our market-driven, capitalistic society. We seek to outperform the store next door in sales, a company across the country in product line, and an international corporation in our market niche. We strive to graduate at the top of our class, own the biggest house in the neighborhood, and join the most prestigious social club or organization. Seemingly, our self-concept or status in society is based on these numerous extrinsic achievements.

Similarly, sport in America has been heavily influenced by this motive to succeed, to get ahead of everyone else, and to attain status and prestige. The result in sport has been a disproportionate emphasis on outcome or the nonmoral value of winning, rather than on developing skill and having fun. Because of fame and fortune, or at least hero and heroine status and special benefits, athletes realize early in their sport experiences that only winners re-

ceive multimillion dollar contracts, endorsements, grants-in-aid, and free sports equipment and clothing. Hence, the drive to win often dominates. When the importance placed on winning supersedes all else, athletes may take drugs to enhance their performances and gain unfair advantages over their opponents.

This chapter provides an examination of how the use of ergogenic aids raises ethical issues for athletes and sport in general. It is suggested that the use of stimulants, depressants, anabolic steroids, and non-drug artificial substances is morally questionable because it provides the user with unfair physical advantages (see Box 11-1). The legal and moral issues surrounding drug testing challenge the reader to determine whether such tests should be banned, optional, or mandated. Questions also will be raised about the appropriateness of legislating morality through sanctions associated with drug use in sport. This chapter, however, does not suggest that

THREE ETHICAL QUESTIONS ASSOCIATED WITH DRUG USE

"To use or not to use drugs" is a question often asked, especially when in many sports so many athletes use drugs to gain competitive advantages. That is, if an athlete believes that everybody else in a particular sport uses drugs so to be competitive they believe they must also. This argument, however, rests on the premise that ethical principles are guided by what others do. A parallel perspective would be that rules must be followed only if others comply. Chapter 1 showed that ethical rules should be valued without regard to others because moral principles are inherently right. The first ethical question emerging is: (1) Is it right to justify the use of drugs because everyone else uses them?

A second ethical dilemma is the question of promise keeping. When people enter competitions, they give their word whether explicitly or implicitly that they will follow the constitutive, proscriptive, and sportsmanship rules governing the sport. Therefore, the second ethical question emerges: (2) Do athletes have an obligation to keep their promises?

Third is the question of responsibility. As members of a team, athletes must accept the responsibility of following game rules that will benefit all competitors. Considering that ergogenic aids place individuals in physical jeopardy, the question becomes: (3) Do athletes have the responsibility to not intentionally harm their bodies?

---

legitimate performance enhancements are unethical. For example, athletes who replace lost fluids during competition or eat balanced and nutritious diets positively impact their performance. Gaining advantage through non-drug-assisted weight training, aerobic conditioning, taking vitamin supplements, and using various rehabilitation techniques are permissible within sport rules and not questionable ethically.

USE OF ERGOGENIC AIDS

Increasingly, athletes appear to seek ways to gain competitive advantages, often because obtaining the rewards of winning becomes paramount. One way is through the use of **ergogenic aids,** any aid, supplement, or ingested substance that is prohibited by the letter or the spirit of the rules but is used to garner an advantage in the sport experience. Depending on the drug, substance, or means chosen, enhanced endurance, strength, skill, and self-confidence actually may result. In other cases, ergogenic aids alter athletes' perceptions so that they see themselves competing at superior levels,

when in reality their performances may remain the same or even erode.

Besides the real or perceived improvement in performance that may lead athletes to use drugs, there remains the drive to win, sometimes at all costs. Because winners are rewarded so highly in our society, athletes may succumb to the temptation to use artificial means to gain advantages. Many sport governing organizations and many athletes classify the use of ergogenic aids as cheating because of the fraudulent or deceptive behavior. Cheating through the use of ergogenic aids happens more frequently when the likelihood of it going undetected exists and when athletes value winning more than honesty, responsibility, justice, and integrity.

Stimulants

Central nervous system stimulants include amphetamines (speed), ephedrine (found in cold medications and nasal sprays), cocaine, nicotine, and caffeine. These drugs generally cause physiological and psychological responses such as increased alertness, reduced fatigue, heightened hostility and competi-

BOX 11-2

DRUG REFERENCE GUIDE FOR ATHLETES

Robert J. Fuentes and his colleagues compiled this reference book to educate athletes about drug education programs and the testing policies of the National Collegiate Athletic Association (NCAA) and the United States Olympic Committee (USOC). This reference guide lists thousands of drugs and indicates whether they are permitted or banned by the NCAA and USOC. It provides information about anabolic steroids and other ergogenic aids and their affect on athletic performance. It includes information about drug-testing procedures, the effect of alcohol on athletic performance, exercise-induced asthma, and sport nutrition.

Source: Fuentes, Robert J. ed. 1996. *Athletic drug reference '96.* Durham, NC: Clean Data, Inc.

Ergogenic aids are used by athletes to help them achieve the ultimate goal of winning.

tiveness, lessened fear and apprehension, and enhanced concentration, attention, arousal, drive, excitability, motivation, and self-confidence. Because these ergogenic aids affect the body so dramatically, the International Olympic Committee (IOC) bans more than 40 different types (see Box 11-2).

Physiologically, stimulants chemically induce the release of epinephrine, an adrenaline-like substance, into the bloodstream along with stress hormones. Amphetamines stimulate the release of epinephrine and norepinephrine from the adrenal glands and nervous system thus increasing muscle tension, heart rate, and blood pressure. Athletes who take large amounts of stimulants may become overly hostile and aggressive because of their elevated moods, experience a reduction of fear, and demonstrate increased pain tolerance. Psychologically, athletes' perception and alertness are not as good as they think.

Increased blood flow from the heart to the muscles produces more free fatty acids and makes glucose more available. This may help the body use fats for energy instead of muscle glycogen, which may have a sparing effect on valuable body stores. For a long time, endurance athletes have used caffeine and other stimulants to increase their performance levels. Gymnasts and wrestlers often choose to take amphetamines to help them lose weight because of initial appetite-suppressing effects.

A few athletes have become dependent on legally and illegally obtained dexedrine, benzedrine, and methedrine that they believe will help their performances. These drugs mask fatigue, giving the perception of endless energy. Cyclists, runners, and other endurance athletes have died of exhaustion because their bodies, under the influence of stimulants, were unable to naturally signal being overtaxed.

The IOC stripped Rick deMont of his gold medal in the 1976 Olympic Games because he tested positive for a stimulant taken through his asthma inhaler. Because of this and related incidents, the IOC allows the use of certain drugs, if approved in advance, for specific medical conditions. The ethical dilemma here, though, is not the taking of a banned drug but the intentional taking of stimulants to gain advantages after pledging to follow the rules. This makes the issue one of honor and responsibility rather than justice. Another question remains, though, Is taking a substance for medical reasons ethical if it gives a competitive advantage?

Cocaine, another stimulant drug, has become the drug of choice of some professional athletes, who typically use this drug recreationally rather than to enhance performance. From the federal drug-trafficking trials that implicated players from several Major League Baseball teams in the 1980s to the highly publicized death of basketball star Len Bias, sports fans have learned of the popularity of cocaine with some athletes. (Because of their salaries and star status, professional athletes can easily obtain cocaine, an expensive, illegal drug.) As an illegal substance, can cocaine be condoned if one agrees to obey the law? Does its use violate moral principles if it gives the athlete a perceived or real competitive advantage? Gary McLain, who led Villanova University to the NCAA basketball championship in 1984, played most games his senior year on a cocaine high, obtaining this drug illegally and playing without being penalized.

The ethical questions associated with the use of stimulants relate to whether drugs that enhance performance through various physiological parameters, reduce or mask fatigue, or provide psychological advantages, are morally defensible. If it is agreed that athletes competing against athletes is the essence of sport, is it honest or just to create an imbalance artificially by ingesting one of these stimulants? Because several sport organizations have banned the use of many stimulants, existing rules make the use of prohibited drugs unethical. What is the moral reasoning process that an athlete uses to decide to use or not to use banned drugs? If an athlete chooses to use a prohibited stimulant, is this action fair or beneficent? Is an athlete who must compete against an opponent who takes stimulants justified in using a similar drug to level the playing field? What penalty, if any, should be assessed against the athlete who takes stimulants?

Depressants

Although the intake of depressants impairs performance, athletes often consume alcohol as the drug of choice. Professional athletes openly drink postgame alcoholic beverages during interviews with representatives from the media. These athletes and many younger ones relax with their favorite alcoholic drinks as they recover from the intense pressures and adrenaline flow brought on by competition. Some athletes have become dependent on drugs to cope with their demanding lifestyles. For example, a professional football player may drink several bottles of beer in the postgame celebration or drown his sorrows after a tough loss. These drinks may be followed by a few more alcoholic beverages at a restaurant during dinner or at home with friends as he seeks to unwind from the game or to numb his aches and pains. A sleeping pill or tranquilizer may also be needed to permit him to rest. The combination of these depressants and tough practices may leave him tired by midweek. So, in preparation for Sunday's game, he begins to take stimulants to offset the effect of the downers. By kickoff time, he may be so pumped up with uppers that all he wants to do is hit somebody aggressively, even viciously. This cycle may repeat itself throughout the season. What moral responsibilities do athletic leagues and organizations have relative to issues such as drug use and drug dependency in sport?

Depressants typically are taken to calm feelings and to dull one's sense of problems, but continued use may lead to rapid psychological and physiological addiction. Not only does the mind crave these drugs in increasing amounts, but so does the body. What ethical issues are associated with the use of depressants by athletes?

Anabolic Steroids

The male hormone testosterone contributes to the development of secondary sex characteristics, including muscular strength. Many athletes ingest synthetic varieties of testosterone called **anabolic steroids.** When taken in large dosages before intensive weight-training sessions, such artificial hormones cause males and females to achieve significant gains in muscular strength and bulk. Not only are there appearance changes, but performance im-

Anabolic steroids are used by some athletes to help build muscle bulk.

provements linked directly to the extent of drug usage have been documented. Ben Johnson's muscular definition and his remarkable speed in the 1988 Olympic Games illustrated this vividly. His appearance and athleticism, however, did not prevent the IOC from stripping Johnson of his gold medal in the 100-meter dash because he tested positive for a banned anabolic steroid.

Even though anabolic steroids can lead to increases in muscular strength, numerous adverse side effects accompany their excessive use. Individuals who take 50 to 100 times the clinical dosage (as many athletes do) frequently experience life-threatening problems such as extreme psychoses, heart disease, liver and kidney damage, and cancer. Female users risk masculinization and abnormal menstrual cy-

cles. Adolescents using anabolic steroids experience severe facial and body acne and premature closure of the growth centers in the long bones, causing stunted growth.

Many trace the introduction of anabolic steroids in sport to the Soviets, who discovered that Nazi storm troopers had taken these drugs to heighten their aggression. Subsequently, medal-winning performances by Eastern Bloc athletes led to a proliferation in the popularity of anabolic steroid use. The practice of taking anabolic steroids, however, was not restricted to any nation. Some athletes from the United States used anabolic steroids, too.

Coaches, trainers, and athletes have mixed different types of anabolic steroids to enhance their effectiveness. Others ingeniously discovered alternative ways to use these drugs, such as ingesting equine or rhesus monkey testosterone to gain performance advantages. Some use epitestosterone to mask the addition of these nonnatural hormones, despite associated kidney and heart problems.

Even corticosteroids, medically used to reduce inflammatory conditions and pain, must be regulated because athletes have attempted to enhance performance through their use. The IOC, for example, bans orally, rectally, intramuscularly, or intravenously administered corticosteroids but permits physicians to prescribe them topically, through inhalation therapy, or intra-articularly.

Weight lifters, track and field athletes, football players, bodybuilders, swimmers, and other athletes of all ages have swallowed or injected increasing amounts of anabolic steroids. With the perception that "if a little is good, a lot must be better," many athletes have taken megadoses, thus increasing the health risks. For most athletes, performance improves until some of the side effects develop. What are the moral issues surrounding the use of performance-enhancing anabolic steroids in sport? Is it ethical to become bigger, stronger, and more aggressive through artificial drugs? What moral issues surface when athletes risk everything, including their lives and health, for winning and its associated fame and fortune? (See Box 11-3.)

NCAA STUDY OF SUBSTANCE USE HABITS
OF COLLEGE STUDENT–ATHLETES

This is the fifth in a series, which began in 1985, provided by the NCAA to report on substance-use patterns of students–athletes. These are some of the major findings of this study.

1. The use of amphetamines, anabolic steroids, and ephedrine among the entire group of student–athletes has increased since 1997. Amphetamine use and ephedrine use in Division I are up significantly. Anabolic steroids is the only ergogenic drug category whose use has increased across all divisions.

2. Cocaine is up slightly from 1997 in Division I and Division III.

3. All racial/ethnic groups report an increase in use of ergogenic drugs since 1997. African Americans report the lowest rates of drug usage in both ergogenic and social drugs, with the exception of anabolic steroids, which for the first time in the history of the study is slightly higher than for Caucasians.

4. Use of ephedrine among women's teams has increased significantly since 1997.

5. Most ergogenic substance use starts in high school. Ephedrine use, which began after college for the majority of student–athletes in 1997, now appears to start prior to college. Overall, nutritional supplement use begins mostly in high school.

6. The majority of users of anabolic steroids say they use them to improve athletic perfor-

mance. More than half the users in 1997 stated they use anabolic steroids for injuries, but those numbers have decreased significantly according to this study. Many users are now stating they use anabolic steroids to improve appearance.

7. Use of amphetamines to improve athletic performance appears to be up significantly from the 1997 study, with use primarily for social or personal reasons. The main reason stated for using ephedrine is to improve athletic performance, followed by using it for weight loss.

8. Student–athletes who use amphetamines or anabolic steroids most often obtain them through a friend or relative. Nutritional supplements are mainly purchased in a retail store.

9. Almost 60 percent of the student–athletes believe that their use of alcoholic beverages has no effect on their athletic performance or on their general health. However, almost one-third of these student–athletes stated that one or more times they performed poorly in practice or a game because of drinking or drug use.

10. Over 50 percent of the respondents believe that the NCAA and their institutions should drug-test student–athletes. Over half of the respondents believe that drug testing by the NCAA has deterred college athletes from using drugs.

Source: National Collegiate Athletic Association. June 2001.

Human Growth Hormone

When sport governing organizations banned the use of anabolic steroids, some physicians, pharmacologists, trainers, and athletes searched for new drugs that would not be detected in drug tests. They found that the naturally occurring human growth hormone (HGH) affects the body in a man-

ner similar to testosterone. The body produces a limited quantity of HGH and since there are so many demands for it medically, it can be obtained only by prescription.

Serious side effects occur from the use of HGH; most destructive are those associated with acromegalia (enlargement of the peripheral body appendages), gigantism (larger physical stature), and organomegaly, which can cause an increase in heart size leading to congestive heart failure. These irreversible changes may result in premature death, even though athletes have been led to believe that use of HGH causes no side effects. Should an athlete take a drug to grow bigger and stronger even if it is not banned? What moral issues exist when athletic accomplishments become more important than personal health?

Blood Doping

Blood doping involves reinfusing one's own red blood cells, which carry oxygen, just before a competition. Athletes who practice blood doping have previously had blood withdrawn (six to eight weeks before the competition). The reinfusion of red blood cells, sometimes called **blood packing,** increases the number of red blood cells per volume of fluid, thereby delivering more oxygen to exercising muscles to enhance performance. Some athletes have injected erythropoietin, the glucoprotein hormone produced by the kidney that stimulates the bone marrow to produce more red blood cells. Athletes believe that the reintroduction of packed cells plus their own increased production improves their endurance and, hence, performance. This procedure leads to high risk, however, because if the percentage of red blood cells (hematocrit) overshoots what is physiologically tolerable, heart failure, pulmonary edema, and even death may result.

Although not a drug, blood doping has been used to gain a competitive advantage, which led to the IOC and the United States Olympic Committee prohibiting it. Is blood doping or blood packing unethical? Should it be? Why did the IOC ban its use?

Beta-Blockers

Beta-blockers dilate the blood vessels, resulting in relaxation of the nonvascular smooth muscle of the bronchioles and the intestinal track. Beta-1 receptors affect the heart, kidneys, and adipose tissue, whereas beta-2 receptors specifically influence the

arteries, liver, and bronchi. By blocking a specific type of receptor, a beta-blocker can decrease anxiety, heart rate, nervousness, and tachycardia. Beta-blockers have been used by athletes in biathlon, bobsled, luge, ski jumping, archery, diving, equestrian events, fencing, gymnastics, modern pentathlon, sailing, and shooting. The use of ergogenic aids in sport raises questions such as those in Box 11-4.

The use of stimulants, depressants, anabolic steroids, human growth hormones, blood doping,

---

BOX 11-4

QUESTIONS REGARDING THE USE OF ERGOGENIC AIDS IN SPORT

1. Should athletes ever be allowed to use a drug obtained illegally to gain an advantage in sport?
2. If an athlete becomes stronger, faster, or more skilled in any way through the use of an ergogenic aid, should the drug, the athlete, or both be banned from competition?
3. If an athlete gains a psychological advantage by using a drug, is there cause for banning its use?
4. Should athletes be allowed to use drugs to relieve the pressures and demands of their sports?
5. Does the risk of negative side effects impact whether athletes should be allowed to use a drug?
6. Should the rules governing drug use vary depending on the level—youth, interscholastic, intercollegiate, elite amateur, or professional—of competition?
7. Should the use of human growth hormone, blood doping, or beta-blockers be permitted in sport? Why or why not?
8. Is the statement, "It is my own body, and what I take is my own business," morally suspect? Why or why not?
9. What are the legal and moral issues surrounding drug testing?

Athletes competing in NCAA competition are subject to regular and random drug testing. (Photo courtesy of the University of Kansas Department of Intercollegiate Athletics.)

and beta-blockers has led sport governing organizations to legislate against these. Rules have been enacted to prevent athletes from gaining physiological and psychological advantages. To ensure that athletes complied with rules prohibiting the use of banned ergogenic aids, drug testing began.

THE DILEMMAS OF DRUG TESTING

As athletes increasingly pursue peak levels of performance and the nonmoral value of winning, they frequently turn to ergogenic aids in search of a competitive edge. Some elite amateur, professional, intercollegiate competitors, and even younger athletes use stimulants, depressants, anabolic steroids, or other substances that they believe will improve their performances in pursuit of victories. Contrastingly, sport leaders suggest that the use of drugs undermines the equity of athletic competitions.

Drug testing was enacted to help prevent artificially enhanced performances. Drug testing gives college coaches greater control over their athletes and helps deter drug-abuse situations that can lead to bad publicity for a college. The IOC, international and national sport governing bodies, intercollegiate athletic organizations, and high school sport associations have banned performance-enhancing ergogenic aids and often mandated drug tests of winners and randomly selected competitors.

Opposition to Drug Testing

Many student-athletes have opposed mandatory drug testing on the basis of constitutional law. Under the equal-protection guarantee of the Fourteenth Amendment of the United States Constitution, athletes argue that they are being singled out for drug testing from among the general student body, whose members do not have to be tested for drug use. A college, if challenged in court for its mandatory drug testing program, must establish a rational basis or compelling state interest for testing (for example, using equity in competition and protection of athletes from harmful side effects can be used as a defense).

On the basis of the Fourth Amendment, which secures the rights of individuals against unreasonable searches, others claim that taking an athlete's urine constitutes a search. Again, the institution or sport governing organization, if challenged, must show a compelling state interest for the search. Many intercollegiate athletes and athletes in international competitions are required to submit to drug testing as a prerequisite to competing, thus waiving their Fourth Amendment protection.

A third justification for resisting drug testing involves the issue of invasion of privacy. Some question the degree of intrusiveness that occurs when the urine sample is obtained. Because most expect personal privacy during urination, this right must be balanced against the importance of securing a sample from the competing athlete, not a substitute's urine.

Do athletes believe that mandatory drug testing violates their moral values? Do the procedures used humiliate athletes, impugn their motives, or show disrespect for their human dignity? For example, athletes are often dehydrated from their competitions and may not be able to urinate on demand. After hours of consuming fluids and then finally producing the required sample, these athletes may have lost the opportunity to celebrate their victories with teammates and families. Because a few deviant drug users have substituted others' urine through creative methods or diluted their samples, sport governing organizations usually require that athletes are monitored when they urinate.

Many individuals resent being assumed guilty because of their status as athletes and strongly disagree with the indignities associated with the drug testing process. They also state that drug testing largely remains an ineffective deterrent without drug education. Still, most athletes readily relinquish their constitutional rights because otherwise they cannot compete.

Thwarting Drug Testing

Drug tests are able to detect only the specific, banned chemical compounds sought. To avoid being caught, ingenious athletes know how to cycle on and off banned substances without being detected. Even heavy drug users can taper off before competitions and not test positive. Some athletes have learned to take drugs that mask banned ergogenic aids known to enhance performance. By the time these drugs have been identified, banned, and tested for, athletes have started taking other ergogenic aids. So, even though drug testing has been touted as the way to impose ethical behavior

on athletes (that is, to prevent them from gaining unfair performance advantages), reality indicates that drug testing may deter only those athletes not clever enough to cycle-off or mask banned drugs before getting caught. Is drug testing the way to teach moral principles, or does it perpetuate a failure to educate about moral reasoning?

Justifications for Drug Testing

Some individuals justify drug testing on the basis of the harm principle. The harm principle, a form of paternalism, states that the organization or authority, because of its knowledge, goodwill, and good intentions, knows what is best for others and for society. These organizations say banned drugs undoubtedly place athletes at risk presently or in the future. Since athletes can be pressured by social conditions to make poor choices, especially when young, the sport leader has an obligation and a moral responsibility to make good decisions for the athlete. Thus, drug testing removes the burden from athletes of having to choose whether or not to use drugs. Therefore, when using the harm principle to justify drug testing, society obligates the governing authority to keep athletes from harming themselves.

Another justification for drug testing is to equalize competition. This rationale assumes that only by banning ergogenic aids will competitions match athletes versus each other on a level playing field. Does this imposition of a rule eliminate the use of moral reasoning by athletes to decide whether or not it is ethical to use ergogenic aids in sport? Is drug testing a violation of an athlete's ethical prerogatives?

Educating against Drug Use in Sport

Moral education may provide the key to a fair and just playing field as athletes, coaches, and sport managers discuss what is good and bad. People involved in sport should examine their beliefs and values through cognitive dissonance. Just talking about the physiological and psychological side effects fails to preclude drug use because young people believe in their invincibility and will readily take risks. Many elite athletes today would likely respond in the affirmative, as they did in the 1980s, to this question: "Would you take a drug that was guaranteed to kill you within five years if it would help you win a gold medal today?"

Education potentially can convince athletes about the reality of the health risks associated with drug use. However, it should be noted that some athletes with medical conditions, such as allergies, must use prescription drugs whether or not they are athletes. Is it fair and just for the IOC to ban an athlete from the Olympic Games for taking allergy medicine prescribed by a physician? Are athletes who use drugs for medical purposes cheating? Are athletes who use ergogenic aids to enhance performance cheating? Should society reward or ignore the use of performance-enhancing drugs in sport?

OTHER RELATED ISSUES
Taking Ergogenic Aids that May Cause Health Problems

The concept that coaches and sport administrators should teach values is certainly associated with the question about whether athletes should be permitted to use drugs known to be harmful to them. To some athletes, taking an amphetamine, anabolic steroid, or other ergogenic aid, even though these drugs might cause heart problems, sterility, or even death, is worth the risk because financial benefits and/or celebrity status are more highly valued.

Young athletes, and sadly even some of their parents, may discount future health risks because these have not been definitely proven, sometimes because of the recent use of these drugs in sport or the dearth of research addressing whether or not these drugs can be taken safely. Older athletes may rationalize that any potential dangers will affect others, not them. The glamour of athletic stardom may overshadow for a brief time the long-term harm. For example, many highly successful Eastern Bloc athletes have expressed outrage regarding the drugs

Some athletes believe that if they take drugs such as androstenedione ("andro") or ephedrine, they will improve their physical skills and performance.

they were forced to ingest but also concern about how these drugs have affected and may in the future affect their health.

Another related issue is when athletes are encouraged by their coaches and trainers to take ergogenic aids that may enhance their performance even though the risks associated with many of these substances have not yet been identified. What role does moral reasoning serve when athletes have to decide whether or not to take these drugs? Do athletes act responsibly toward themselves when they ingest drugs without knowing with some degree of certainty if any risks are involved? Just because a drug is not banned does not mean that taking it is fair, just, responsible, or beneficent in a sporting context.

Some female athletes may struggle to deal with an- orexia, amenorrhea, and osteoporosis as they work to achieve their optimal athletic performance. (Photo courtesy of the University of Kansas Department of Intercollegiate Athletics.)

Using Ergogenic Aids for Weight Gain and Loss

Many athletes are expected to gain or lose weight according to the demands of their coaches. Football players, for example, must add bulk and strength in order to gain starting positions or play- ing time and to be successful against strong oppo- nents. Stories abound about seniors (in high school and college) who use their weight gains of 10 to 50 pounds to bench press and squat over 100 pounds

more than they did as freshmen. Unfortunately, these large weight gains tax the heart and joints leading to health problems then and in later years, as does the increased potential for obesity and weight fluctuations.

In contrast, many wrestlers are pressured to com- pete in weight classifications below their develop- mentally appropriate weights. As a result, these ath- letes exercise in rubber suits or layers of clothing, risk dehydration by refusing to drink fluids, and eat little or nothing prior to weigh-ins. Immediately thereafter, these athletes eat and drink to regain their ability to wrestle. This cycle of under- and overeating continues throughout the season.

Gymnasts are expected to reduce their caloric in- take to ensure that they maintain the petite size thought essential to optimal performance. For some females, this means a near-starvation diet. Too often, these and other female athletes who are pressured by their coaches to lose weight for com- petitive as well as aesthetic reasons battle anorexia, bulimia, and other eating disorders trying to achieve this expectation. A related problem is that maintaining an abnormally smaller intake of food leads to amenorrhea and injuries associated with in- adequate calcium intake that may lead to osteo- porosis in later years. The female athletic triad of anorexia, amenorrhea, and osteoporosis form an interrelated set of medical concerns that have ad- versely affected performance and even led to deadly health problems.

Sadly, athletes often resort to taking drugs to help them lose or gain weight. Diuretics and stim- ulants are favored choices for eliminating fluids and reducing appetites respectively.

Possible Changes in How Drugs Are Viewed in Sport

Some ergogenic aids used illegally by athletes in the United States are legal in Europe. This adds to the debate about whether such drugs should be de- criminalized thus potentially increasing the likeli- hood of their use by athletes to enhance their per- formance. For example, if a professional athlete chooses to smoke marijuana after having previously been caught in this violation of the league's drug policy, the athlete may be suspended or banned, something that would not occur in many European nations. So, possibly, drugs that are currently banned in sport may one day be permitted, regardless of their impact on performance.

There also is the issue of athletes using drugs to enhance their performances that are not, or not yet, on the banned lists of the governing organizations of sports at various levels. Whenever a new elite-level athlete emerges victorious, some members of the media immediately question what ergogenic aids this person must have taken to suddenly win a gold medal or championship. Some have argued that already sports have become contests between pharmacologists instead of between athletes.

Given genome and stem cell studies, the issue of genetically engineering a superior athlete becomes more likely. What are the ethical issues, if any, associated with breeding bigger, stronger, faster athletes? Integral to the concept of sport is the equitable competition between opponents to determine who is superior. Is a contest fair if one or more of the athletes has been bred to have a higher ability level, thus providing an artificial (or is it?) advantage?

SUMMARY

The use of ergogenic aids threatens equity, or the concept of a fair and just playing field in sport. Because athletes believe that they can become bigger, stronger, faster, and more skilled, and then relax and recover from aggressive highs and the pressures

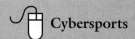

Cybersports

www.nata.org/main.htm

The National Athletic Trainers' Association provides certification standards for individuals responsible for the prevention, care, and rehabilitation of athletes from injuries. In adhering to its standards, athletic trainers are precluded from providing illegal ergogenic aids to athletes.

www.acsm.org

The American College of Sports Medicine promotes scientific research and application of sports medicine and exercise science to enhance physical performance, fitness, and health. It publishes position statements in areas such as the effect of ephedrine or creatine supplementation on performance.

www.ncsa-lift.org/menu.asp

The National Strength and Conditioning Association advocates for the physical development of athletes based on safe and effective training programs exclusive of drugs.

www.drugfreesport.com/home.htm

The National Center for Drug Free Sport, Inc., seeks to help high schools, colleges, and other organizations sponsoring sport competitions to ensure drug-free environments for their athletes. The NCAA on its website (http://www.ncaa.org) provides extensive information about its drug-testing program.

www.wada-ama.org/asiakas/003/ wada_english.nsf/Home?OpenPage

Through the initiative of the International Olympic Committee, the World Anti-Doping Agency was established to help safeguard the ideals of integrity for drug-free sport.

www.sportrec.qld.gov.au/infopaper/drugsinf.html

This site provides information about the use of prohibited substances in sport to gain an unfair advantage over opponents. It includes information about why athletes choose to use drugs and how drug tests are conducted.

of competition, they may elect to use banned drugs or abuse legally obtained drugs. In search of ever-improving performances and victories accompanied by media attention, awards, and monetary rewards, athletes may risk their current and future health. Drug testing and the risk of losing competitive opportunities have deterred some athletes from using banned drugs. Yet, many question the legal and moral basis for drug testing. Athletes, coaches, and trainers need to examine their personal beliefs and values and determine what actions are fair, just, honest, and beneficent. Making drug testing mandatory should be the final, not the initial, step in a responsible educational system. Sport leaders have the obligation to educate themselves and their athletes morally and not to abdicate this responsibility to a governing body that may only mandate drug testing, not educate morally. The use of ergogenic aids remains a question of responsibility and honor, rather than only justice.

 # ISSUES AND DILEMMAS

CASE 11-1

Carlos began swimming at the local club at age 10. After beginner lessons, he joined the local swimming team and started competing in club meets, first in the summer and then year-round. For the first few years, he never won a race, even though he entered more events than most boys because he liked all the strokes.

The summer he turned sixteen, Carlos began to question whether he wanted to keep swimming. Although he had always been the skinniest kid on the team, it never bothered him until his teammates, six most noticeably, seemed to grow bigger and stronger remarkably fast. When Carlos questioned them, they invited him to lift weights with the guys at the gym. Because he never enjoyed this activity, Carlos had always declined. This time, however, he accepted so he could see whether weight training would increase his commitment to and success in swimming.

Carlos pledged to work hard in the weight room all summer. Although he saw some strength gains after three months, he seemed to be falling farther behind his teammates and opponents in swimming races.

When Carlos asked why his efforts did not appear to result in as much size, bulk, and strength improvements as his six teammates achieved, the initial answer given was that he was not working hard enough. Carlos refused to accept this because he knew he was training as hard as his teammates. Later, Carlos cornered one of these teammates and begged to know their secret. Tom refused to tell him unless Carlos promised to join the program; Carlos agreed immediately. Tom informed Carlos that for months, the six team members had been taking Dianabol, an anabolic steroid. They were convinced that this drug, combined with their training, had improved their physiques and swimming performances. Tom explained how and where the guys bought the Dianabol tablets. Tom told Carlos where to meet the guys the next day to make a purchase.

1. Why was Carlos interested in weight training, and did this extend to taking anabolic steroids?
2. What are the moral dilemmas facing Carlos?
3. What are the legal issues or interpersonal relationship ramifications in this situation?
4. Were Carlos' teammates gaining unfair advantages through the use of these drugs, and what would others think if they found out about the use of an anabolic steroid?
5. If no rules prohibit the use of anabolic steroids in age group or interscholastic sports, is their use ethical? Why or why not?
6. What are the potential physiological side effects of adolescents using anabolic steroids?

◆ ◆ ◆

CASE 11-2

Titusville State College had a long history of successful women's volleyball teams, having won two National Association of Intercollegiate Athletics championships and the Western Conference title seven of the last nine years. Coach Whitehead was a successful yet demanding coach. His players respected, but also feared, him.

Cathy Carter, a powerful hitter from the local high school, was eager to become the next star for the Bears. Although Cathy was excited about volleyball and practiced her hardest, she also was concerned about her academic work. An average student in high school, she realized that she would have to study long and hard to remain eligible in college.

The one thing she had not anticipated when she joined the team, however, was Coach Whitehead's fixation with his players' weights. He demanded that his team look trim and attractive in their uniforms. This meant that Cathy and three teammates had to lose between 10 and 20 pounds, or they would not get to suit up with the team.

Teammates recommended that these four players take diuretics. Cathy, more so than the others, took them frequently, especially when she found that their stimulant qualities enhanced her on-the-court performance. Cathy also found that the antidoze pills she took to help her stay awake to study, when combined with diuretics, really gave her an adrenaline high. The second time she combined these drugs, her spikes were unstoppable and her serves fierce. Coach Whitehead complimented her improved aggressiveness and performance. Even after Cathy lost the required weight and earned a starting position, she continued to use a combination of diuretics and antidoze pills to psyche herself up for matches. After her matches, though, Cathy had to sleep a lot, was somewhat depressed, or popped another duo.

1. What outside pressures contributed to Cathy's decision to use stimulants?
2. Because the drugs Cathy used were obtained legally, should their use be allowed in sport?
3. What are the health risks, if any, associated with Cathy's use of these drugs?
4. How did Coach Whitehead's demands contribute to Cathy's use of drugs? Were his demands morally sound?
5. Are there any moral justifications for what Cathy did? Are there any moral justifications for Coach Whitehead's demands? Why or why not?

◆ ◆ ◆

CASE 11-3

The image of professional sports has been marred by numerous cases of athletes using drugs. From the death of All-America Len Bias from crack cocaine to suspensions of several National Football League athletes for repeated violations of the drug policy, the professional leagues have attempted to use fines, suspensions, and banishment to rid their ranks of athletes who use banned drugs. In 1998, however, questions were raised about whether the National Basketball Association (NBA) should add marijuana to its list of forbidden drugs, with penalties levied against players who used it. At issue was whether this illegal drug should be treated like other illegal drugs, such as cocaine and heroin. In the National Hockey League, controversy surrounded a legal drug, Sudafed, that was being abused by athletes because of its stimulating effects on the central nervous system. Controversy surrounded Mark McGwire's use of androstenedione, a natural substance that raised the testosterone level.

1. Should the use of marijuana be added to the NBA's list of banned drugs? Why or why not?
2. Should the use of all illegal drugs be banned by the professional leagues? Why or why not?
3. What drugs should professional athletes be allowed to use?
4. What drugs should professional athletes be banned from using?
5. What is the responsibility of professional sport league rules regarding drug use by their athletes?
6. What is the responsibility of each professional athlete relative to drug use in his or her sport?

◆ ◆ ◆

CASE 11-4

Kisha often dreamed of being an outstanding runner and jumper as she stared at the life-size poster of Jackie Joyner–Kersee in her bedroom. By her senior year in high school, Kisha had already won numerous races and long jump events and had been called "little Jackie" by the media. Everyone predicted that she would make the next Olympic team. As she read the hundreds of recruiting letters from college coaches who praised her athletic talents as well as her 3.5 GPA, she was troubled by a new drug testing program that Middlebrook High School (MHS) had just started. Even though she had never used or even considered using anabolic steroids or amphetamines, she knew of some girls on opposing teams who had. She was upset because two boys on the football team had been caught using these drugs and now the integrity of every MHS athlete was being questioned.

Because Kisha believed that mandatory drug testing was an invasion of privacy and a violation of her rights, she felt that she could not agree to a drug test. As her father patiently explained to her, if she refused to be tested, then she could not compete during her senior year. This would jeopardize her getting an athletic grant-in-aid at a major university. Even if she was fortunate enough to get recruited, she would face drug testing at that institution or in a NCAA tournament.

1. What are the pros and cons of mandatory drug testing?
2. Should drug testing be mandatory at any level of sport? Why or why not?
3. Is mandatory drug testing legal or illegal in high school, college, and professional sports and why?
4. Does mandatory drug testing violate any moral principles? If so, which ones?
5. What recourse would Kisha have if she refused to take a drug test?

◆ ◆ ◆

CASE 11-5

The National Football League drafted Randall in the first round as top running back on the basis of his All-America status as a collegian. Anticipation was high for his rookie season that abruptly ended when he suffered a tear in the medial collateral ligament of his right knee during a preseason game. Although he faithfully completed all of the rehabilitation prescribed by the team trainer during the next several months, Randall had difficulty returning to full speed; he seemed tentative on his cuts as a result of some residual pain. The team physician in an effort to reassure him suggested that Randall take a cortisone shot in his knee before the opening game of the season. Although reluctant, Randall finally agreed because he wanted to play and justify his multimillion-dollar contract. When he was able to make his cuts without pain, Randall was convinced that the cortisone shot had made this possible. Despite difficulty walking during the week and pain during his limited practice time, every Sunday Randall got a pain-blocking shot and ran with abandon. Although he ran for over 1,500 yards and won the league rushing title, by the end of the season the cortisone shot did not block out all of the pain. During the off-season, Randall found out that he had done permanent damage to his knee and that his NFL career was over.

1. What are the ethical issues associated with the physician's prescription of the initial and subsequent cortisone shots?
2. What do you think was the moral reasoning process used by Randall in making his decision to take the initial and subsequent cortisone shots?
3. What moral obligation did Randall's team owe him before and following his injury?

◆ ◆ ◆

CASE 11-6

Cycling, and especially the grueling Tour de France, has been shrouded for years with the alleged and actual use and abuse of stimulants. At least since the 1960s, cyclists have used stimulants of various types to extend their endurance capacities. Despite deaths and the banning of athletes who tested positive for drug use, this sport is tainted by allegations of widespread abuse. Some athletes have eluded detection even though they take performance-enhancing drugs. Athletes who are successful are suspected of drug abuse, even though they have never used drugs to enhance their performances.

1. Upon what moral basis, if any, can cyclists defend their use of drugs?
2. What are the moral issues associated with drug use in cycling?
3. How could or should the governing associations of cycling deal with the real and perceived use of drugs in cycling?

◆ ◆ ◆

CASE 11-7

For years, athletes competing in sports where strength was an essential component for success, such as weight lifting and field events like the shot put, have used drugs. Although anabolic steroids have probably been the predominant drugs of choice, other ergogenic aids that helped increase muscle bulk and strength have gained in popularity and use. Often called nutritional supplements, many of these are available in health stores, through mail order, or via the Web. The perceived or real extent of this drug use has resulted in drug-free competitions in which the athletes pledge to compete on the basis of their individual abilities without artificial aids.

1. What is the moral basis for the organization of drug-free sports competitions?
2. Why would an athlete choose to compete in a drug-free contest that is a lesser-known alternative to a nationally or internationally acclaimed competition?
3. Describe why an athlete might choose to avoid the use of performance-enhancing drugs.

◆ ◆ ◆

CASE 11-8

Many times athletic administrators and coaches fail to realize that the most popular drug of choice that athletes abuse is alcohol. Professional athletes who frequently and routinely consume alcohol in locker rooms model the acceptability of alcohol consumption. Although of age legally, when younger athletes are not, these athletes seem to legitimize that elite athletes can consume alcohol without any decrement in their athletic prowess. Many athletes, such as Dwight Gooden and Daryl Strawberry, have discovered the hard way that abuse of alcohol can adversely affect their performance and shorten their careers.

Regardless of how often athletes believe that alcohol will not hurt them, this drug remains a depressant and a highly addictive one. Several athletes have combined the consumption of alcohol with fast cars only to learn too late that this combination is a killer—of themselves and others. Abuse of alcohol has often been associated with collegiate athletes who while drunk assault their girlfriends and wives or get into barroom brawls. Sometimes even high school students drink illegally and then destroy their futures in automobile accidents or illegal behaviors.

1. What is the affect of the consumption of alcohol on athletic performance?
2. Upon what basis do athletes reason that the consumption of alcohol is compatible with their athletic performances?
3. What is the moral responsibility of the athlete relative to the consumption of alcohol?

4. What is the moral responsibility of the coach relative to the consumption of alcohol by his or her athletes?
5. What is the moral responsibility of the athletic administrator relative to the consumption of alcohol by athletes within his or her jurisdiction?
6. If governing organizations for sports decide to establish rules governing consumption of alcohol by athletes, what should these rules be?

ADDITIONAL READINGS

Beals, K. A. 2000. Subclinical eating disorders in female athletes. *Journal of Physical Education, Recreation and Dance* 71(7) (September): 23–29.

Black, T., and A. Pape. 1997. The ban on drugs in sports: The solution or the problem? *Journal of Sport & Social Issues* 21(1) (February): 83–92.

Browne, A., V. Lachance, and A. L. Pipe. 1999. The ethics of blood testing as an element of doping control in sport. *Medicine and Science in Sports and Exercise* 31(4) (April): 497–501.

Bucci, L. R. 1999. *Nutrients as ergogenic aids for sports and exercise.* 2nd ed. Boca Raton, FL: CRC Press.

Catlin, D. H., and T. H. Murray. 1996. Performance-enhancing drugs, fair competition, and Olympic sport. *JAMA: The Journal of the American Medical Association* 276(3) (July 17): 231–37.

Eichner, E. R. 1997. What athletes are using—and why. *Physician & Sportsmedicine* 25(4) (April): 70–83.

Fuentes, R. J. 1996. *Athletic drug reference '96.* Durham, NC: Clean Data, Inc.

Kiningham, R. B., and D. W. Gorenflo. 2001. Weight loss methods of high school wrestlers. *Medicine and Science in Sports and Exercise* 33(5) (May): 810–13.

Maron, B. J., R. W. Brown, and C. A. McGrew. 1994. Ethical, legal, and practical considerations impacting medical decision making in competitive athletes. *Medicine and Science in Sports and Exercise* (Supplement) 26 (October): S230–7.

NCAA study of substance use habits of college student–athletes. June 2001. Indianapolis, IN: National Collegiate Athletic Association.

Nutter, J., and B. J. Rauhe. 1997. Preventing anabolic steroid use: Guidelines and activities. *Journal of Health Education* 28 (November–December): 364–69.

Paterson E. R. ed. 1998. *Anabolic steroids and sports and drug testing, 1991–1997: An annotated bibliography.* Albany, NY: Whitston Publishing Company.

The physiological and health effects of oral creatine supplementation. 2000. *Medicine and Science in Sports and Exercise* 32(3) (March): 706–17.

Pipe, A. L. 1993. Sport, science, and society: Ethics in sports medicine. *Medicine and Science in Sports and Exercise* 25 (August): 888–900.

Stanley, D. 2000. *Understanding sports and eating disorders.* New York: Rosen Publishing Group.

Tricker, R. 2000. Painkilling drugs in collegiate athletics: Knowledge, attitudes, and use of student athletes. *Journal of Drug Education* 30(3): 13–24.

Tricker, R., and D. Connolly. 1997. Drugs and the college athlete: An analysis of the attitudes of student athletes at risk. *Journal of Drug Education* 27(2): 105–19.

Verducci, T. 2002. Totally juiced. *Sports Illustrated* 96(23): 34–40; 42; 44; 46; 48.

Videman, T., and K. Forsythe. 2000. The ethics of not testing in athletic competition. *Medicine and Science in Sports and Exercise* 32(7) (July): 1361–62.

Yesalis, C. E. 2000. *Anabolic steroids in sport and exercise.* 2nd ed. Champaign, IL: Human Kinetics Publishers.

Ethical Considerations of Technology in Sport

- ◆ What changes in sport have occurred because of technology and advanced materials?
- ◆ How has technology compromised the sport experience?
- ◆ What benefits occur through technology and advanced materials?
- ◆ What are possible solutions or guidelines to follow with the use of advanced materials?
- ◆ What are common scenarios that address ethical issues in technology?

Jim and Fred have been friends for over 40 years and enjoy a good competitive game of golf every Saturday morning. Jim is on a limited retirement budget, whereas Fred has enjoyed some good investments. Both Jim and Fred are below-average players, but they like to compete and love to hassle each other about skill and game outcome. They even wager lunch on the day's competition. Jim has always been better skilled and poor Fred has bought most of the lunches. Fred learns about advanced materials in golf clubs and balls that will improve his game markedly. In fact, when he tries the new clubs, his drives increase by about 25 yards, and with the addition of new composite balls, he picks up accuracy. He decides that all is fair in love, war, baseball, and golf, and never divulges his secret to Jim. He invests big bucks and gets the best equipment on the market. For the rest of the summer, Fred is highly successful, Jim is amazed at his improvement, Fred gets to razz Jim a bit, and Jim now buys the majority of lunches. Fred has enjoyed a competitive edge brought to him by the advantages of a full pocketbook—advanced materials in sport equipment design.[1]

The Freds of the world, as long as they have the money, no longer have to be the goats. They no longer have to be losers or less successful than their peers. They now can drop their scores significantly without a whole lot of skill or fitness. Advanced material design in sport equipment technology has changed the sporting experience to one in which many can succeed without much talent or training. That is, advanced materials can help people win. However, the question behind all of this is: Is the purpose of sport about gaining advantages and getting even, or is the purpose of sport about people participating, enjoying, and improving their motor skill, their physical fitness, and their overall health and wellness?

Herein lies the ethical rub. What role does "gaining" an advantage play in competing fairly and

---

[1]An earlier version of this scenario and selected parts of this chapter and an accompanying article were published by *USA Today* magazine. The article was an invited paper concerning a university core course that is taught at the University of Idaho: Moral Reasoning in a Technological Competitive Society. Permission granted by authors.

seeking excellence? Philosophically, this may seem a bit idealistic. The reality of the sporting world today is about competitive edge and gaining advantage, is it not? And should we not want to win?

Yes, one should want to win; if not, why play games in which the score is kept? However, wanting to win is not the issue, rather it's what the competitor is willing to do or, for that matter, is willing to sacrifice to gain that win.

It could be argued that the rise in technological advances in sport are directly driven by this need to win. It is doubtful that the extremes in advanced material design would have occurred if there was not a need to compete more efficiently and effectively. This in itself is not the dilemma. The advances have brought about "good" and have been revolutionary for the equipment industry. Equipment materials evolved from wood, to plastics, to steel and aluminum, to now composite materials. These engineered, composite materials known as advanced materials have "mechanical and physical characteristics that are well in excess of those exhibited by conventional high-volume materials such as steels and aluminum alloys."[2] Advanced materials contribute significantly to how well an athlete and even a recreational player can perform. That is, the sport equipment is stronger, tougher, stiffer, and more resilient.

What does this mean for the amateur tennis player? No longer does one need to spend hours developing skills or fitness. Unlike today, the traditional tennis racquet was originally made of wood, with a somewhat awkward and clumsy feel. The racquet head was small, and when the ball made contact, there often was a resounding resonance through the racquet to the player's forearm. The ball would not rebound off the racquet, but instead would pitch left or right with a decided loss of movement and return rate. In order to be effective or to hit the ball with a wooden racquet, every once in a while, one had to have a certain level of fitness to get to the ball and a certain motor skill level to actually contact the ball. Such was the case until advanced materials and all of that has changed for the novice or recreational player. "New technology use piezoelectric fibers to convert mechanical energy into electrical energy for sensing ball impact and microchip control circuits that react to the ball by stiffening the racquet and dampening vibrations. What results is a counterforce in the throat of the racquet within the first millisecond of ball impact. This provides more power than a conventional racquet that bends and vibrates upon impact, or, as the manufacturers say, the racquet hits the ball and the player is just along for the ride."[3] Players need less skill and even less fitness to play a respectable game. Instead one can compete and play a somewhat respectable game, which again emphasizes that the use and purpose of these materials is not about human improvement but about "competition as results" and a need to win.

Advanced materials have revolutionized the composition of skateboards, surfboards, skis, snowboards, javelins, golf clubs, golf balls, tennis racquets, football helmets, playing surfaces, baseball and softball bats, ad infinitum. In all of these cases the development of sport equipment is addressing the participants "competition as results" and the drive to win. If results and the win are the goal, advanced materials are a key to fulfilling the goal, in any sport. The carbon-fiber vaulting pole permits the pole-vaulter to soar up to 18 feet. Javelins with spiral tips permit the javelin thrower to reach dazzling distances in excess of 104 meters. Diving boards are now springier and provide

---

[2]Prisbey, K., S. Stoll, and S. Froes. 2001. *The ethics of the use of advanced materials in sport equipment.* Published Proceedings. Materials and Science in Sports Conference, San Diego, California. Permission granted by authors.

[3]This information comes from Sam Froes, director of Metallurgical Engineering at the University of Idaho, and was published in K. Prisbey, S. Stoll, and S. Froes. 2001. *The ethics of the use of advanced materials in sport equipment.* Published Proceedings. Materials and Science in Sports Conference, San Diego, California. Permission granted by authors.

a 15 percent more lift than those of the boards 40 years ago. They feature no-skid surfaces and a light weight and resilient board that weighs less than 10 pounds, which minimizes injuries especially if a head happens to meet the board. The new materials have made possible dives at the 1-meter board that were only possible on the 3-meter board before. Archery bows are lighter and more stable than wood-core bows. The bows shoot better and have a speed boost. Bow strings and arrows are transformed. They are now about 20 feet per second faster than the aluminum arrows that were standard until the 1980s. Such changes have sent "winning" scores upward. In competition, archers shoot a total of 144 arrows for a possible perfect score of 1,440. Before advanced materials, a winning score at major tournaments would be in the 1,100s, today those scores are in the 1,300s.

The particulars are endless. Golf balls with special dimple patterns and core design improve loft and spin so even a novice player can hit at least 400 yards. Stiffer carbon-fiber rackets reduce arm vibration and larger heads increase surface area in tennis, squash, and racquetball. Bicycles with new types of wheels, sit design, composite and reengineered frames can increase speeds up to 60 miles per hour. Discuses with weight distributed as close as possible to the perimeter permits the thrower to increase accuracy and distance.

A SPORTING CHALLENGE

If the goal of sport is "competition as results" and winning, advanced materials will continue to improve the game so that less efficiency, fitness, and skill are necessary to play. Let us first consider how advanced materials affect the human being as he or she participates in sport.

How should we as "competitors" view these new materials? Should we cling to old technology and "old" science and play the game that Sam Snead played in golf, Rod Laver played in tennis, or should we skate like Sonya Henie on unstable

steel?[4] Perhaps not. Advanced materials bring many, many benefits to participants. Athletes are able to enjoy improved performance and ease of skill acquisition with these new materials. Any athlete or recreational player can attest that advanced materials make motor skill acquisition easier and safer to accomplish, with the added benefit of being a lot more fun. There is no greater thrill than realizing that a difficult skill that appears to be beyond attaining, can be conquered with a little help from advanced materials. However, as in all issues of ethics and moral reasoning we need to realize that something that appears to be very good and helpful, may result in some harm and bad consequences. We should examine the use of advanced technology in relation to the total experience and reflect on what advanced technology has done and will do to the "humanness" of that participant. To address this issue, we have various questions to ask: (1) What help or harm comes with technology to the competitor or recreational player? (2) What is good or valuable about the activity? And, (3) how can we distribute that good or value to others?

In most cases, good or valuable refers to qualities that are not harmful or destructive to the individual who does the activity. Rather the activity should be helpful in some sense and in these cases of advanced materials, sport should help people improve their motor skills, their physical fitness, their general health, and even their inner spirit and joy of the activity. In the case of advanced materials and technology, the end result appears to be driving its application to sport equipment and even to the sporting experience. Yes, competition is good but should "competition as results" be the ultimate goal?

As we have discussed throughout this text, winning and a focus on results can drive participants to do more harm than good to themselves, to the opponent, and to the game itself. If competition and

---

[4]Sammie Snead, Rod Laver. For good on line biographies of these athletes from an earlier period and a review of the differences in technology, see on line biographies. http://www.info-please.com/ipsa/A0774467.html

winning are the goals, it is not too far-fetched to see that in some place in the future sport will ultimately mutate to "equipment" playing the game, with humans as the mere operators. What is good for humans becomes the basic ethical question. If sport is considered "good" participation for humans and is played with simple considerations of justice (fair play) and beneficence (doing good), then technology and advanced materials would enhance both the thrill and fun of competition (Jim and Fred) as well as the level of safety. However, such a perspective appears not to be the driving force today.

For all performers, the bottom line of ethics in sport is directed toward helping the performer improve fitness, skills, and health, rather than results. The value lies in performing well and not about the end results. But questions of harm do arise if the goal is to win, and the benefit for the performer is completely ignored. The good is minimized if no fitness, skill, or health considerations are prerequisites for participation. For example, harm can result to participants who have not trained in physical fitness or motor skill before performing the sport. And what happens when the end result is the only target and only aim? "Consider also the effects to the sport if technology is used only for the win. It would not be long before the introduction of electronically guided darts, heat-seeking missiles for grouse-shooting (provided the grouse is still edible), solar-energy-enhanced bicycles, and golf balls with terrain-following mechanisms that automatically find the lowest local elevation on a putting surface—the bottom of the hole."[5]

AN ALTERNATIVE ARGUMENT

However, some might argue that we have missed the point here. Do not advanced materials offer competitive opportunities to millions of individuals who have a physical challenge that would not let them participate without the aid of advanced materials? And, is it not true, that athletes with severe handicaps now can efficiently and effectively participate in numerous activities never available before to them because of these advanced materials? Yes, advanced materials have made a profound and beneficial difference. Wheelchair-bound individuals can now play basketball, participate in marathon racing, climb mountains, get into pools and swim, and numerous other activities never available before advanced, composition materials. If we assume our argument against advanced materials is faulty, and that results or wins are the ultimate and best purpose for advanced sporting materials, then should not the ultimate goal of results and wins be spread to as many as possible? That is, should not all individuals have the opportunity to use advanced material technology?

However, such is not the case. "Just distribution" is threatened by the high cost of advanced materials in sporting equipment. New designs in any sport are more expensive than the older designs and advanced composite materials are not available to individuals throughout the entire world. In fact, many of the designs are limited to countries with economic advantages, which obviously limits "good" distribution of results. Even in economically competitive countries, technology is so pricey that many individuals must seek sponsors to partake in the "good." And these individuals are ultimately the most athletic and the youngest and healthiest.

Therefore what occurs? Although advanced materials in sporting equipment provide a great measure of good for physically challenged athletes, the materials are costly and therefore are only available to the wealthy. For example, advanced material design of wheelchairs has grown to include a chair for each sport: basketball, racing, and even tennis. Tennis chairs are built with sharply slanted back wheels so the athlete can move quickly from side to side. In basketball, forwards have high seats, whereas guards have more slant in their chairs in order to turn quickly. Bikelike wheels, the use of aerospace carbon fibers and titanium, and computer-

[5]Prisbey, K., S. Stoll, and S. Froes. 2001. *The ethics of the use of advanced materials in sport equipment.* Published Proceedings. Materials and Science in Sports Conference, San Diego, California. Permission granted by authors.

aided design of the suspension are expensive. Top wheelchairs cost approximately $2,000 to $3,300 each. Also, the costs of the prosthetic devices used by elite paraplegic runners that allow them to be catapulted forward more efficiently than two human feet cost up to $7,000. Participation for these athletes is good, but limited to those who have the resources.[6]

Direct Harm

Another consideration of help or harm is the potential physical danger the equipment built with advanced materials may pose to the players or spectators. Take, for example, the javelin. From the ancient Olympic games to the modern era, the purpose of throwing a wooden javelin was about fitness—skill as measured by accuracy. During the modern era, the javelin composition changed to make it lighter and more aerodynamic. Finesse was still required to make it float correctly. However, in 1984, advanced javelin design changed this perspective in such a way that potential harm could occur at the elite level. In the manufacturers' quest for higher and further, no one seemed to understand how an elite athlete might affect the distance with this new composite material javelin. When Uwe Hohn of East Germany smashed the existing javelin throw with a distance of 104.80 meters at the 1984 Olympic game, the javelin became a danger to spectators and other athletes "safely" warming up on the far side of the stadium.[7] The new javelin had a nasty habit of veering left or right if thrown improperly. The ruling body, International Amateur Athletic, took little time in banning the new design. The banning may have been a result of poor staging of events, that is, officials not being prepared for this new technology. However, the

ethical issue arises in that Hohn did not inform the meet directors or his competitors of what would happen with this newly engineered piece of equipment. The meet officials were not prepared for what would happen and responded with the banning. When this occurred the distance dropped dramatically by 20 meters, which then led to an increase in the number of power throwers rather than finesse throwers. In this case we see an example of how advanced materials decide who will compete and who will not.

Similar problems have occurred in softball, baseball, and golf. In softball and baseball, the composite bats were thought to be the saviors of the game. Some had argued that the game of baseball, in particular, was too slow. The new composite bats sped up the game with faster exit speeds when the ball contacted the bat. Coaches appeared to agree that this was a good thing and the use of these new bats became standard operating procedures. Unfortunately, harm to the players was not originally taken into consideration. Add to the mix, bigger and stronger players who can increase the amount of force placed in swing. Combine the new balls with the new baseball bat composition and the result becomes exit speeds of balls contacting bats in excess of 130 miles per hour. Result: pitchers, especially, plus short stops, and third basemen have no time to respond, and injury becomes a rather important issue.[8] Interestingly, professional baseball never bought into this change. Their rules state the bat must still be made of wood and the specifics on the ball are the same as before technology changes. No advanced materials are acceptable. Such is not the case with the NCAA which is still studying the problem of the new technology. Much controversy surrounds the NCAA's choice to accept certain technology on bat design. It is

---

[6]Prisbey, K., S. Stoll, and S. Froes. 2001. *The ethics of the use of advanced materials in sport equipment.* Published Proceedings. Materials and Science in Sports Conference, San Diego, California. Permission granted by authors.

[7]Bjerklie, David. 1991. High-tech olympians. *Technology Review* 96 (Issue 1): 22.

[8]The NCAA and professional baseball studied the issue. Professional baseball chose wooden bats with specific dimensions to control the game, preserve the game's history, and protect its million-dollar players. The NCAA has reviewed the issue and voted to slow down the ball with specifics to make the ball less lively, though composite bats are still being tested.

argued that politics and not concern for the safety of the athlete is driving the NCAA's decision-making process.[9]

The issue of harm extends throughout sporting competition. The new technology permits the athlete to extend athleticism to newer heights. Enter now extreme sports with extreme risks that were not possible before. Bicyclists can slipstream behind a semi at 60 miles per hour and enjoy and savor the speed of the moment. Of course, a little problem exists if the cyclist falls. No matter how good the bike, the human body cannot withstand the consequences of a 60-mile-per-hour crash and bike helmets are not engineered to protect the head from a 60-mile-an-hour crash. Such is the case with most extreme sports, the technology permits dazzling thrills but the consequences are often final and debilitating.

Technology in a Bottle

The issue of help and harm does not end with advanced materials, it extends to what is available to train and condition the athlete. Performance enhancement through drugs is based on the premise that athletes are machines and a machine can be tended, maintained, and serviced to do better.[10] However, regardless of how we describe a human being, we are not machines and asking a human being to function as one is short sighted, insensitive, and unethical. Humans have limits, physical, emotional, and psychological. However, the new world of technology appears to argue that the sky is the limit and the athlete must develop the "sport ethic" to meet the challenge.[11] Unfor-

tunately, the bottom line of this sort of a mentality is physical harm to the athlete and performer with a direct effect on quality of life as the athlete ages. Life is longer than 30 years and those years beyond youth should be full of movement experiences. Consider the number of former athletes who now have extreme cases of osteoarthritis, debilitated knees, walk with limps, have loss of feeling in their extremities, and so on. The athletic badge of courage should not be a middle age full of aches and pains and loss of vitality.[12]

SUMMARY: THE FINE LINE

So how do we apply all of this to the real world? Let us return to the case of Fred and the golf game. What harm was done and what help could have occurred? What possibly could have been harmful about Fred gaining an advantage and winning a few games from his old buddy Jim. After all, Jim won most of the games before.

The issue of harm and help in Fred and Jim's case is not that technology is unethical. Rather, technology is marvelous. It offers new opportunities for many people to participate and play. However, technology also has a burden, in that when we choose to use technology we want to remember to use it to support the purposes of fair play for all people. We have to remember that technology must be used fairly and wisely for good participation. In Fred and Jim's case the issue was about

---

[9]Researchers have argued that the NCAA is being pressured by manufacturers of advanced material bats to delay a decision on ball exit speed to allow the manufacturers time to sell their bats. The manufacturer argues that they engineered the bats because the NCAA asked for them; now the manufacturer is stuck with oversupplies and a huge capital outlay and overhead costs.

[10]Chapter 11 of our text reviews the problems with doping to a greater detail.

[11]See Jay Coakley (2001). Coakley argues that there are four core beliefs to the sport ethic in which athletes make sacrifices and strive for distinction; an athlete accepts risks and plays through pain, and an athlete accepts no limits in their pursuit of possibilities. Anything is possible if the athlete will ignore external limits (p. 146–147).

[12]See also, Jan Rintala (February 1995) excellent article on "human questions." Rintala reviews the important ethical questions that should be addressed with the rise of technology and the effects on the humanness of the participant. John Charles (1998) also offers a "view of the body through the lens of science and technology," which illuminates this issue from another point of view.

gaining an advantage through unethical conduct. Fred lied to his friend. The golf game had been about Fred and Jim playing a game on the basis of their physical skill with comparable golf equipment. Fred never told Jim what he was doing and let Jim assume that Fred's improvement was due to Fred's improved play. Fred would have been better served had he taken the money for the "new" clubs and spent it on losing a few pounds, taking some lessons from a pro, enrolling in a fitness program, and rethinking the value of telling the truth. As it was, he lied to his friend, swindled him out of his lunch money, and supported a hoax for the summer. Of course, one could argue that Jim could have purchased advanced material clubs too. With advanced clubs, he too could be overweight, unfit, less skilled, and deceptive. Such is the art of moral justification.

What is the purpose of sport? Hopefully, that purpose is about people participating, enjoying, and improving their motor skill, their physical fitness, and their overall health and wellness. What is good and valuable about sport, how it can be distributed to the most people, how unfair advantages and physical harm can be minimized by new designs and materials must be continually asked as technology advances. Advanced technology for sport equipment and for human performance does not have to be harmful. We choose it to be. These materials and the science that supports them are value-neutral. We decide if they can help or harm. The vision and purpose should also be about people performing and their humanness through the experience. We should be "better" people not better athletes. The potential of technology lies in our creative ability to use it wisely and effectively for the good of humans, not the benefit of producing materials and making money.

Larissa is a ranked golfer and has an excellent tournament record. Her caddy for many years becomes

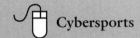

Cybersports

www-white.media.mit.edu/~intille/sports-technology.html

This page contains links and documents describing systems and research that apply computer technology and other advanced technologies to sports and the sports industry. Site contains lists of references, papers, and technology in sport conferences.

www.dmu.ac.uk/ln/fast

International organization for technology in sport. Forum consists of numerous sport philosophers. Special consideration toward innovation, technological advances, and practice of sport such as genetic technologies in sport, innovation of sports equipment, and performance-enhancing drugs.

www.ausport.gov.au/info/clothing.htm

The site is designed to assist students to locate information on the history, design, and technology of sports clothing and equipment. The organizations section provides information on companies in the sporting goods industry.

www-white.media.mit.edu/~intille/st/has_science_improved_sport.html

An article discussing the ideal of what sport should be, how equipment has changed sport, the influence of nutrition, rehabilitation, and training techniques, as well as advancements in facilities.

www.shef.ac.uk/staff/newsletter/vol25no1/index.php?name=000010

This article discusses the impact of technology as assessed by Dr. Steve Haake, head of the Sports Engineering Research Group. Specifically, this article discusses advances in equipment such as the pole vault and javelin.

ISSUES AND DILEMMAS

CASE 12-1

ill with a severe bout of flu. One of Larissa's friends volunteers to caddy for today's tournament. Larissa agrees knowing that Joan will do a good job. Joan in the meantime is so excited to be part of a greater drama: high-level athletic competition. Joan's father is a salesperson for a major golf equipment supplier and tells Joan about new golf balls that have amazing properties to improve performance. Without Larissa's knowledge, Joan substitutes balls, thinking that she is helping Larissa and not realizing the balls are considered illegal by the governing body. Larissa is leading throughout the tournament and is about to win the tournament on the last hole, when she notices Joan fumbling through the golf bag. It is then that Larissa learns that Joan has been substituting the balls. Golf is a game of self-governance. Should Larissa report the illegal ball which means she will forfeit, or should she ignore what happened because Joan had no intention of doing any harm?

◆ ◆ ◆

CASE 12-2

Coach Johnson is under great pressure to produce a winning golf team. Rumors persist that Coach Johnson must win the remaining three matches to keep her job. Despite being on the hot seat, Coach Johnson is well liked by her players and they have played hard for her all season. Many players consider Coach Johnson to be a second mother. Before the game, Coach Johnson tells the team that she is in jeopardy of losing her job. She says, we must win the three remaining games or she will be fired. Do whatever you have to do to win. Even if it means bending the rules. The players have access to illegal golf balls and decide to use the balls to help their coach and gain an advantage. Acceptable or not? Why?

◆ ◆ ◆

CASE 12-3

In 1984 at the Olympic Scientific Congress in Eugene, Oregon, an official of the East German Sport Federation was confronted with the issue that it was suspected that athletics in the Soviet Bloc were using illegal and even unknown technology to gain an unfair advantage. The official responded, "You Americans make me sick. You are wealthy. You have all the technological advances, yet you cry, 'unfair' when someone else seeks to gain an advantage. What is the difference between a knee brace, advanced material composition in bob sledding, or using a drug to improve performance. It's all about the same thing." If you were there, how would you have responded? Is there a difference? Why or why not? And, what ethical issues are involved?

◆ ◆ ◆

CASE 12-4

Mildred and Macey are playing a game of table tennis, when Mildred decides to pull out her "terminator" paddle. She had her friend Susan, an excellent woodworking artisan, develop a table tennis paddle that was twice the size of the normal paddle. Is it acceptable to use the terminator or not, and why?

◆ ◆ ◆

CASE 12-5

Coach Jones and his team A are playing a bowl game in December against team B at a Northwest U football site that is known to Coach Jones but not known to the other team. In fact, Coach Jones and team A have played at this site several times; team B, from the South, has no knowledge of the new technologically advanced playing surface. Coach Jones realizes an advantage might be gained in this bit of knowledge— he knows the playing turf and team B does not. Coach Jones orders a special shoe that has been shown to be effective on the turf during the cold, frozen conditions that are expected. Coach Jones does not ask his team to put on the shoes, until halftime when he realizes that his team can't compete against team B. Even under the poor turf conditions, team B is winning by 10. The shoes appear to make a big difference. Team A, which was predicted to lose by 10, actually wins by 20. Team B was not prepared for the weather conditions, and the shoes they had selected were not effective for the turf conditions. Was Coach Jones's action acceptable? Yes or No and why?

REFERENCES

Arthur, B. 1997. Technological Innovations. *Scientific American* 276(2) (February): 105–106.

Bjerklie, D. 1993. Sporting Goods—Technological Innovations. *Technology Review* 96(1) (January): 22–31.

Charles, J. 1998. Technology and the body of knowledge. *Quest* 50: 370–88.

Coakley, J. J. (2001) Sport in Society: Issues and Controversies. (8th) Dubuque, IA: McGraw-Hill.

Prisbey, K., Stoll, S., Froes, S. 2001. The Ethics of the Use of Advanced Materials in Sport Equipment. Published Proceedings. Materials and Science in Sports Conference, San Diego, California.

Rintala, J. 1995. Sport and Technology: Human Questions in a World of Machines. *Journal of Sport & Social Issues,* 19(1) (February): 62–76.

Stoll, S.K, Prisbey, K., Froes, S. (Accepted for publication). Advanced Materials: An Advantage or an Ethical Challenge. *USA Today (Magazine).*

Stoll, S.K., Froes, S., Prisbey, K. (Accepted for publication). Advanced Materials—Any Ethical Questions? The Development of an Undergraduate Course. *International Journal of Engineering Education.*

Sport Science, Physical Education, and Research

CHAPTER 13

- ◆ What is moral responsibility?
- ◆ How does moral responsibility relate to being a sport scientist, physical educator, or research scientist?
- ◆ How is professional responsibility related to collegiality and loyalty?
- ◆ How do we use codes of conduct and codes of ethics to address moral issues in sport science and physical education?
- ◆ In sport science fitness centers, how do we responsibly market and promote healthful living in a capitalistic venture?
- ◆ What is considered good research practice?
- ◆ Why is ethical conduct imperative in research?
- ◆ What is an ethical code in research? What is the purpose of human subject's review boards and informed consent letters and why are they important?

In the previous chapters we have focused on issues directly related to the sporting experience. However, the purpose of this chapter is to take the concept of fair play, with its implied nature of respect, honesty, and fairness and show how it should be inclusive of the total professional environment. If we define fair play in this manner, it serves as a guide in our professional lives. Fair play is what we should strive for in our professional relationships; it is thus our responsibility as professionals to treat others professionally, that is, to treat others fairly and with a sense of respect, honesty, and responsibility. This chapter will discuss "moral responsibility" as sport science, physical education, and research professionals. In this case, moral responsibility has to do with our motives, intentions, and actions as they are directed toward, impinge upon, or affect others, whether that be in schools, fitness clubs, and/or college settings.

PROFESSIONAL RESPONSIBILITY IN THE WORKPLACE

As discussed in earlier chapters, in a nonmoral sense, responsibility means one is reliable or has a certain leadership capability. Remember that nonmoral values are based on extrinsic and intrinsic values rather than on people, intentions, motives, deeds, or traits of character that affect other persons. Thus, it is possible that one could be a highly responsible leader, yet very immoral while doing it. For example, we might have a department supervisor who is highly reliable in getting the job done. This supervisor can be counted on to have all the right equipment for the job, show up on time for work, and know how to competently do the job. Yet, this individual takes materials from the company for personal use without paying for them, spends time surfing the net on company time, and uses sick days to go skiing or hiking. This supervisor's reliability, in this case responsibility as a leader, is directed toward immoral ends—stealing—which violates other human beings. Stealing in this case involves not only materials, but time. Thus one could be considered a true leader and highly responsible in a particular leadership position because one is accountable for doing the job at hand, yet one may be totally immoral in other actions within the company.

The term "responsibility" also has a decidedly moral focus. History is replete with examples of individuals who developed good working relationships with employees, customers, and the public, and who could delegate jobs and meet the needs of producing a good product, yet violate others in the process.

Now, you might be asking what this discussion has to do with us as sport science, physical education, and research professionals?

PROFESSIONAL RESPONSIBILITY AS PART OF OUR SOCIAL AND ETHICAL RESPONSIBILITIES TO SOCIETY

Professional responsibility is one part of our greater social and ethical responsibility to ourselves, our peers, our families, our clients, and our communities. This professional responsibility is an outward behavior that comes from our inner beliefs and values. Professional responsibility and how we apply it in our professional lives is related to our personal moral self, our moral values and beliefs that we discussed and developed in Chapters 1 to 3. To gain a visual perspective of this notion, see Figure 13-1. This paradigm is our perception of how professional responsibility applies to our daily lives.

The top is our personal moral self, with each of the sides being social and professional responsibil-

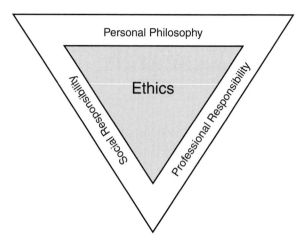

FIGURE 13-1 The personal, social, and professional responsibility triangle. What we value in a personal philosophy should be consistent with our social and professional responsibilities.

ity. To answer any question concerning professional responsibility requires that we first understand our personal moral values and beliefs (our personal moral self). Remember, finding our personal moral values requires that we ask important "self" questions such as: Who am I? What do I believe? What values do I believe are important to being a positive member of society? How do I want to be treated and how will I treat others? How we answer these questions determines the basis of our personal morality and is thus a reflection of the specific moral values in which we believe, all of which make up our personal moral system.

As you can see from the triangle, what we believe about fair play, honesty, responsibility, and justice directly influences our professional and social relationships. In other words, our personal morality reflects how we treat others in the workplace (professional responsibility) and even how we treat others around us (social responsibility). Thus, before we can be professionally or socially responsible, we must first know and understand our personal values and beliefs. For the most part, this chapter is limited to the professional side of the triangle.

UNDERSTANDING PROFESSIONAL RESPONSIBILITY

Professional responsibility is the obligation that we have to apply our personal moral values to the workplace. This, of course, is premised on the fact that we have examined our personal moral system and then looked at it in light of the values of our profession and professional position. We believe that we must examine the values of the business or educational setting in which we work and see that these values are consistent with what we personally believe. If these value systems are not compatible, then we have some serious decisions to make. (Remember that interaction among the personal, professional, and social is imperative.) However, one major problem today is that far too few people actually reflect on their values and beliefs and then examine those relative to the professional position they take. Many argue that what one believes personally has nothing to do with what one does professionally (relativism). As such, many people let themselves be put into a position that compromises their personal moral self in relation to the goals of their current workplace. Unfortunately, today it seems that the concept of professional responsibility has either become a lost art or is disregarded altogether.

Given our discussion of professional responsibility, let us examine a common issue of professional responsibility in the sport science profession. How would you resolve the professional dilemma that occurs when professional responsibility is either ignored or abrogated?

Sport Science Example

Terry, the owner and operator of a large fitness/wellness club, has a thriving business that offers many different programs and classes in fitness, wellness, and how to lead a healthy lifestyle. She has contracts with various major businesses in her area to offer their employees membership discounts if they enroll in her programs and use her facilities and staff consultants. Her business has the latest in high-tech equipment, and she hires only staff who have a sport science, physical education, and/or nutrition degree.

She fully believes in fitness and wellness which can be attested to by her personal lifestyle. She is dedicated to exercising daily, and for a 50-year-old, is extremely physically fit. She participates in a variety of aerobic activities as well as an anaerobic strength-training program on a daily basis. Additionally, she can be seen consuming fruits and vegetables in healthy amounts and drinking a variety of fruit juices and water. She regularly counsels clients in healthy behaviors and how to develop a physically active lifestyle.

Shawn, who holds a master's degree in exercise physiology, is Terry's wellness director whose responsibility it is to hire staff and oversee the various functions of the club including the pro shop and beverage and food machines (which do a healthy business for the club). Terry hired him five years ago because of his many academic qualifications; because of his personal dedication to living and modeling a healthy, active lifestyle; and because she has known him for many years and knows that they hold similar values. In other words, she believes she can trust him with the business side of things. After working for a month, Shawn decides to raise some concerns he has with Terry about the beverages and snacks that are offered for sale at the club. Although there are a couple of beverage machines that sell fruit juices, there are far more soda pop machines. The food machines all have candy, chips, and cookies, whereas the pro shop sells the latest fad in weight reduction pills and other questionable "nutritional" supplements. Shawn is concerned that the club professionals are (1) sending inconsistent messages to their clients (in that the club's mission is to promote an active, healthy lifestyle, yet it offers and sells predominantly junk food and questionable supplements) and (2) being professionally irresponsible (in that as sport science professionals they are obligated to educate and promote a healthy lifestyle).

When Shawn questions Terry, she states that this is a business and as a business it must make money to survive. It is an economic venture, and these items are what people want. Nutritional supplements make a tremendous amount of money for the business and help support the ongoing programs and purchases of equipment. Furthermore, she states that if she did not offer these products she might lose clients to the club across town that does offer these things. Shawn is frustrated because it sounds like the club is all about the "mighty buck" and not so much about education toward a healthy lifestyle or looking out for clients' best interests. What would you do if you were Shawn?

1. Because Terry is the boss, he should follow her lead and continue ordering and selling these products.
2. Because he can't support Terry's business philosophy, he should quit and find another job that is more compatible with his values and beliefs.
3. Because the club is supposedly about education, he should try to find some alternative products that are more consistent with living a healthy lifestyle.
4. Because he believes that the club should be about education, he should provide educational seminars to the club's clients in healthy alternatives to use of supplements.
5. Because he cannot change Terry's views at this point, he should provide clients with an informative newsletter and post it close to the machines and supplements.

Discussion

This is a common problem within the fitness industry. Because one goal of business is to make money, one thus needs to stay one step ahead of the competition. The fitness industry is no exception. One need only turn on the television or listen to the radio any hour of the day to find advertised the latest weight loss supplement, the latest high-tech piece of equipment, or the latest weight loss diet that will guarantee a person will lose 10 to 20 pounds in a month with little to no physical effort expended. Of course, as sport science professionals, we know that these claims are not true, but people tend to take the path of least resistance and in the case of the fitness industry it means that a lot of money can be made selling these products to an unsuspecting public.

The issue at hand is about professional responsibility—each of us has a duty or obligation to fulfill our promise to our professional values, beliefs, and knowledges. Shawn was hired to do a specific job: run the business side of the club. He has a responsibility to fulfill the duties of that position to his fullest. Rationalizing that Terry must sell these questionable products because her clients want them and its what makes money for her, is relativism at its best and professionally irresponsible. Although making money is imperative to keeping a business afloat, abrogating professional responsibility in the name of making money is unacceptable. Fair play should exist in the business of fitness just as in sport. Both Terry and Shawn have professional responsibility to the situation at hand. Shawn has an obligation to fulfill his contract and carry out his duties. Yet, both Terry and Shawn have an obligation to help clients become nutritionally literate. Thus, they should sell products that have been found through research to be nutritionally sound. Terry and Shawn are in the positions of being role models. Because they both tout this through their lifestyles, and the business has a stated goal of educating for health lifestyles, they have a professional obligation to run the business consistent with this value and belief structure.

Even though Shawn is in the right, he has a professional responsibility to be respectful to Terry. "Being right" is not his only professional obligation. As a professional, he has many duties to his clients, his professional peers, and to himself. In this role, he must convince Terry that "doing what you have to do to get ahead in business" is unfair to the clients, unfair to him, and finally unfair to her. Terry might argue that (1) she, as the owner for 20 years, has a better understanding of what works and sells in the business world; (2) the bottom line is making money because money pays salaries and upgrades equipment; and (3) she attends the latest fitness industry shows and everyone is selling and buying these supplements.

Perhaps in the end, Shawn's arguments would still fail. In this case Shawn would need to rethink whether he would remain in the business or look for a position that is more compatible with his personal and professional values and beliefs.

A Question of Professional Loyalty

The dilemma that Shawn faced in the previous discussion may be further exacerbated by his loyalty to Terry and the program. And as such, it may be difficult if not impossible for him to leave even though he believes that there are some major professional responsibility issues. Oftentimes, people placed in a dilemma such as Shawn's abrogate their professional responsibility in the name of loyalty to the individual or organization.

In discussing professional ethics and responsibility with members of different sporting organizations, businesses, teachers, administrators, and the military, we have found that the dominant moral value for them is loyalty (Beller and Stoll 1999). When it comes to these professionals, it appears that loyalty is the most important value from which honesty, responsibility, and justice derive. Most professionals will argue that loyalty to the group, team, organization, or business is imperative, without which they cannot be successful. Businesses and organizations in a capitalistic society are thus predicated on loyalty. We want people who are loyal to the goals, purposes, and people of an organization.

However, loyalty as a moral value is tenuous; in other words, it is not a prime moral value that can stand by itself. As such, loyalty must be combined with a "first principle" such as honesty, responsibility, or justice. Loyalty without being tempered with honesty, for example, can lead to immoral behavior. The problem is when individuals become confused as to whether they are loyal to an individual, organization, or group. For example, a person can be a highly dedicated, motivated, and loyal thief.

Loyalty is defined as "the willing and practical and thorough going devotion of a person to a cause" (Royce 1924: 17). His definition is based on an "ideal:" Loyalty is ". . . a cause beyond your private self, greater than you are . . . impersonal and super personal" (Royce 1924: 19–20). He basically argues that people have a duty to principles that is above any duty to particular individuals, organizations, or groups. In other words, if we are loyal to principles, our principles are also operative on us. They are not principles in the abstract as they contribute to the contours of our personalities" (Fletcher 1993: 9). In other words, loyalty to friends, groups, organizations, our country, and so forth, helps define who we are.

Furthermore, "the question of loyalty doesn't arise in the abstract but only in the context of a particular relationship. These ties generate partialities in loyalties, loves and hates, and dispositions to distrust and trust" (Fletcher 1993: 7). In other words, loyalty involves shared experiences. Thus, people outside the group, with no personal relationships to the group, cannot claim a part or equal treatment within the group. Within this context, "[o]ur loyalties are relational and partial" (Fletcher 1993: 8), and the "[m]ore purely personal characteristics of [loyalty], such as kindness, courage, amiability, honesty, or spirituality cannot serve as grounds for loyalty" (Ladd 1967: 97–98). Thus, loyalty is strengthened through shared experiences. Athletes are intensely loyal to one another, and this loyalty develops because of the strong bonds that are developed from living, eating, traveling, sweating, and working together. They have this common historical bond of teamwork, dedication, and sacrifice to the goals and tasks at hand. This intense bond becomes so strong that it is generally impenetrable. Many businesses and organizations share these same traits with sport as individuals associated with them become intensely loyal to one another and the organization.

However, because so few people today actually examine their personal or professional values, this intense loyalty leads to questionable moral behavior at the least and immoral behavior at the worst. And it generally happens because individuals have not realized the problems associated with a total and complete loyalty to the group or cause. Typically this loyalty to a group or individual has ended in either immoral behavior or professional irresponsibility, for example, Nixon and Watergate, and the *Challenger* "O-ring" disaster.

In the previous scenario, Shawn is caught in a quandary between professional responsibility and loyalty to Terry and the organization. If he remains working for Terry in the name of loyalty and does nothing to help change the situation, he is being professionally irresponsible. Yet, as a professional, he must have the courage to take a stand. He must reflect on where his loyalty lies and realize that loyalty in this case must be tempered with responsibility. If he tempers loyalty with moral responsibility, his loyalty should be to a set of principles first rather than to Terry.

BEING A PROFESSIONAL AND ITS RELATIONSHIP TO PROFESSIONAL ETHICS

We have discussed being a professional, but have not defined what it is to be a professional and what it means to be part of a profession. A professional in the sense of being a member of a profession means that (1) there is access and control of the particular knowledge base, (2) they perform a service to society, (3) they are autonomous, and (4) they have prestige, respect, and social status. Although many "professionals" may perform their duties full-time, for pay, and with considerable expertise, or as a hobby or diversion, many professionals do not belong to a profession. For example, professional athletes are considered professionals, yet they do not fall into the category of being professionals in the sense of what we just described. Our discussion here will be limited to being a member of a particular profession that satisfies the criterion listed previously. Typical professions in this sense would be teaching, athletic training, cardiac rehabilitation specialist, and working as a fitness/wellness instructor/consultant to name a few. Remember,

Sport scientists, physical educators, and athletic trainers are guided by codes of ethics which help them understand what it means to be professionals within their organizations and/or business as well as the ethical principles deemed important.

though, that just because one works in the fitness industry does not make one a professional. Unfortunately, the fitness industry is not guided by mandatory standards and anyone with a little money and a "shingle" can open a fitness center and "claim" professional status with the public.

Yet you are probably wondering what does being a member of a profession have to do with our discussion of professional ethics? Typically, professions are guided by a "code of ethics" and sometimes this code of ethics is called a code of conduct. Most of our professional organizations, such as the National Athletic Trainers Association and the National Association for Sport and Physical Education, have a code of ethics.

CODES OF ETHICS

A code has some very specific purposes: It (1) is regulative, (2) protects public interest and the interests of those it serves, (3) is not self-serving, (4) is specific and honest, and (5) must be both policeable and policed. A code of ethics is typically written by an association or organization to make the professional membership aware of principles of ethical behavior that should be followed in the practice of that particular profession. In athletic training for instance, "The primary goal of the Code is the assurance of high quality health care" (www.nata.org/publications/brochures/ethics.htm). A code in this sense represents standards of behavior to which all members should strive. As in our fair play discussions, the principles within this code cannot cover all possible situations or dilemmas, but rather should be taken in light of the "spirit" of rules and how professionals should make decisions.

For a professional organization, a code of ethics forces large numbers of people to think through their mission and the important obligations they as a group and as individuals have to the organization, each other, and their clients. Once adopted, the code itself can be used to generate continuing discussion of how to improve and make the code more workable. For instance, the NATA Code of Ethics states, "[t]he guidelines set forth in this Code are subject to continual review and revision as the athletic training profession develops and changes" (www.nata.org/publications/brochures/ethics.htm). In other words, a code of ethics, while a standard for professionals to strive toward in their actions, intentions, and motives, requires that it be revisited, reevaluated, and continually checked against the mission and goals of the organization and/or business.

Additionally, a code should help inculcate in new employees or members their responsibility to develop professional virtues. However, a code is only as good as the education surrounding it. The American Bar Association, while having a very strong code of ethics with questions that candidates must pass during their bar examination, requires its members to enroll in continuing legal units specifically in ethics every three years. The goal is to keep the view of ethics and ethical behavior in the forefront of professional practice. Interestingly, many professionals in other organizations know little of their codes of ethics and little if any education accompanies membership. Oftentimes, many of the problems happening in the workplace can be solved

using a code of ethics. For example, if the code of ethics holds that one must uphold the highest quality of health care, then certain practices, such as returning an obviously injured player to the game or promoting and selling certain supplements, would be deemed in violation of the code.

Yet, knowledge of the code typically occurs when a supposed violation or questionable behavior occurs. However, the strength of the code is only as good as the education and the regulation of it. Furthermore, a code acts as a ready guide to help make decisions. For example, the NATA Code, states, "[th]e principles are written generally and the circumstances of a situation will determine the interpretation and application of a given principle and of the Code as a whole" (www.nata.org/publications/brochures/ethics.htm). The code can also be used to reassure customers and the public that a touchstone to measure ethical actions exists within the organization or business. Even though ethics is the overriding umbrella for action, most codes state that if a conflict arises between the code and legal questions, the individual must follow the law. Finally, the code must have a provision for the reporting of violations and due process for the individual(s) in question. In the typical code, members within the organization itself police the organization's members, adjudicate, and then make sanctions if applicable.

Most codes have similar broad statements about the behavior of members. Generally, there is an overall preamble that broadly defines the purpose in an ideal sense of the particular code. Then, a series of principles or statements are listed that cover how they should (1) treat clients, patients, and/or students; (2) follow the laws and regulations that govern that particular business or profession; (3) make responsible, reasoned, and sound judgments; (4) maintain high standards of professional practice; and (5) not engage in conduct that is a conflict of interest with their professional duties and obligations. The conclusion of the code generally has a series of statements about the responsibility of the membership to police itself as well as how and where to report potential violations of the code.

Codes of Ethics in Physical Education

Physical educators have codes of ethics that are generally set by the state department of education in which they work. Codes of ethics in teaching are generally focused toward competency, service, integrity, and the welfare, fulfillment, and potential of each student. Generally these codes have a variety of main principles that concern (1) professional ethical conduct, (2) professional practices and performances, (3) ethical conduct toward colleagues, (4) ethical conduct toward students, and (5) ethical conduct toward parents and the community. These codes state that educators shall exemplify the highest standards of professional commitment, comply with standard teaching practices (commonly accepted practices by the teaching industry), and conduct themselves in a respectful, honest, just, and responsible manner toward students, professional colleagues, school officials, parents, and members of the community.

Professional ethical conduct involves principles that specify that teachers are obligated to keep their personal values and beliefs and political agendas separate from their professional duties, with the goal to help teachers avoid using their professional positions as platforms to influence impressionable minds. Principles also state that educators should not take money outside their teaching duties to tutor their students, or accept gratuities, gifts, or favors that impair professional judgment.

Professional practices and performance principles involve statements about the manner in which educators should carry out their teaching responsibilities. These statements hold that one should (1) organize instruction that seeks to accomplish objectives related to learning; (2) comply with school board policies, state regulations, and other state and federal laws; and (3) continue professional growth through courses, workshops, and membership in professional societies.

Finally, principles that address ethical conduct toward colleagues, ethical conduct toward students, parents, and the community address how one should avoid (1) making false statements; (2) coercing, harassing, or discriminating against another based on race, color, religion, national origin, age, sex, disability, or family status; and (3) revealing confidential information concerning students unless disclosure serves lawful professional purposes or is required by law. Additionally, these principles provide teachers with academic freedom to teach as a professional privilege and obligate them to act as role models in the classroom and community.

Codes of Ethics in Sport Science and Research

The study of sport science is about research and its application of research and theory to practice. The practice of research within this discipline is also governed by a series of codes. Sport scientists read and analyze research as well as conduct studies about the human adaptation to movement and exercise under a variety of conditions. Because sport science research most often involves the study of human adaptation to sport and exercise, an element of ethical concern exists. The conduct of sport science research is replete with many ethical issues, such as bias in research (i.e., sexism and racism), conflicts of interest, intellectual property rights, and unjustified risk to human participants.

Codes of ethics typically state that educators shall exemplify the highest standards of professional commitment, as well as conduct themselves in a respectful, honest, just, and responsible manner toward students, professional colleagues, school officials, parents, and members of the community.

Although codes of ethics exist in most major professional organizations, those who conduct research are also bound by codes of ethics. These codes help define what is considered acceptable research practice and proper ethical conduct, as well as how human subjects should be treated and should expose those individuals who are responsible for unacceptable conduct in research. It is important for those considering or engaged in the different sport science disciplines to become aware of these codes and how these codes are inherent within these individuals' professional responsibilities.

However, many argue that conducting research in an ethical manner is intuitive and that everyone knows how to be ethical; however, that has not always been the case. Until the 1960s and 1970s when a series of scandals broke (the Milgrim studies, Tuskeegee prison studies, and atomic bomb studies to name a few) about fabrication of experiments and deception of research subjects, few scientists wrote about or raised questions concerning research ethics. Because of the blatant violation of the rights of human subjects and the unethical scientific practices in these studies, the federal government in 1974 required all institutions receiving federal research grants to have research ethics committees typically called "human subjects review boards," "human subjects assurances committees," or "institutional review boards" (Shrader-Frechette 1994). The purpose of these committees is to oversee research design and ethical concerns in studies; in other words, a major component to the review is how human subjects (animals as well, although in the sport science and physical education setting most research is conducted with humans, thus our discussion will center around human research) are treated within the research setting.

HUMAN SUBJECTS REVIEW BOARDS IN RESEARCH

Scientists, like other professionals, have a duty and obligation to perform research in an ethical manner. Even though scientists are governed by their individual societies and their specific codes of ethics, there are five general guiding principles in order to conduct ethical research: (1) "Scientists ought not do research that causes unjustified risks to people;" (2) "Scientists ought not do research that violates norms of free informed consent;" (3) "Scientists ought not do research that unjustly converts public resources to private profits;" (4) "Scientists ought not do research that seriously jeopardizes environmental welfare;" and (5) "Scientists ought not do biased research" (Shrader-Frechette 1994: 26). The goal of ethical research is to weigh the obligation and duty to the client, profession, and society with the knowledge that can be gained to further the aforementioned.

The conduct of ethical research is premised on the fact that individual scientists and researchers bear the primary responsibility for the conduct of their research. The National Science Foundation as well as the National Institutes for Health and other federal organizations state that an institution's faculty, staff, researchers, and graduate students as well as sponsoring organizations have a shared responsibility in setting the environment and implementing consistent research practices that promote and foster integrity of the research process. Because of the diverse nature, commonly held practices, and standards and expectations of each discipline, these organizations believe that research scientists bear the primary responsibility to systematically communicate to their research scientists, trainees, graduate students, and others acceptable research practices, standards, traditions, and customs. They further state that communication, education, mentoring, discussions (both formal and informal), seminars, and colloquia will foster an environment that helps individuals within the research process come to value, know, and respect integrity in research.

Before studies involving humans can take place, these boards review each study's purpose, methods, the degree of risk to the study participant (physical, mental, or emotional), each subject's rights, and provisions for informed consent (Thomas and Nelson 2000). The goal of the committee is to assure, given the information presented, that human subjects are treated fairly, safely, and with dignity.

Scientists have a duty and an obligation to perform research in an ethical manner. Human subjects review boards, professional societies as well as scientific integrity and misconduct in research manuals provide guidelines for scientists in ethical practice in science.

Informed Consent in Research

Because research involves potential risk as well as benefit, individuals should have the right to exercise free consent to participate or not participate in the study. Thus a part of the human subjects review considers how the human subject must be informed about the study and how he or she will be treated as an individual while a part of the study. Therefore, these boards examine the study to see that researchers are concerned about any potential harm to the participant. Harm should be interpreted to mean [how the study might] "frighten, embarrass, or negatively affect the subjects" (Tuckman 1978). The goal is to balance the degree of risk against the subject's rights (Thomas and Nelson, 2000). The researcher is obligated to protect the well-being of participants in his or her study. The U.S. Department of Health and Human Services has regulations (45 CFR 46.101) that state specifically how risks are to be minimized and the well-being of the participant maximized. What the committee examines besides the scientific methods is the "informed consent letter" that all participants in the study must read and sign.

Letters of informed consent explain to the subjects how they will be treated in the study as well as their rights as participants. An informed consent letter has some typical components: (1) a statement as to the right to privacy or nonparticipation, (2) the right to remain anonymous, (3) the right to confidentiality, (4) the right to expect experimenter responsibility, (5) the right to drop out of the study without reprisal at any time, (6) a description of the potential discomforts and/or risks, (7) a description of the benefits to be expected, (8) a fair explanation of the study procedures, and (9) an offer to answer any questions about study procedures (Thomas and Nelson 2000).

However, as we mentioned in our discussion of codes of ethics, many research scientists are out of touch with their professional codes and fail to take into account research ethics. "[S]ome scientists fail to take into account . . . research ethics and, as a consequence, endanger the health and welfare of the public, research subjects, and the environment. We also argue that flawed research may push society 'out of joint' by creating biased studies, by helping to justify questionable policy decisions, and by emphasizing profit rather than justice in the quest for knowledge" (Shrader-Frechette 1994: 23). Although research is important because it leads to development and improvement of a discipline's knowledge base and addresses many important societal issues and problems, not all research should be conducted.

Whereas the Human Subjects Assurance Committee evaluates prospective studies for particular information concerning informed consent, ethical conduct, and proper research methods within the study, each institution has an overriding code or manual that governs how the institution addresses proper research practices, ethical conduct, allegations of misconduct in research, and adjudication of said misconduct. This code is sometimes called the "Scientific Integrity and Misconduct in Research Manual" and all institutions receiving federal funds must develop and implement these policies and procedures for their scientists. These manuals are founded on the philosophies of what constitutes good research practice and ethical conduct in scientific research that we have discussed previously.

The purpose of this "Scientific Integrity and Misconduct in Research Manual" is to provide researchers with a general framework concerning individual and institutional rights, responsibilities, and obligations for (1) education about acceptable research practices, standards, ethics, traditions, and customs; (2) guidelines to bring forth allegations of scientific misconduct in research; (3) protection of individuals bringing forth allegations of scientific misconduct (a whistle-blower statement); (4) assurance of the rights of those being investigated; and (5) methods of reporting findings to external sponsoring organizations and agencies.

All in all, the goal of such manuals is to articulate how researchers within a particular institution believe, promote, and maintain research integrity. Although the manuals articulate specific practices, scientists within the institutions typically hold that research integrity is an ongoing, shared responsibility that goes beyond specific guidelines and practices, and all research scientists, associate researchers, graduate students, and those involved in research must emphasize responsible scientific practices and articulate a sound and consistent research philosophy.

Fair play is predicated on the belief that scientists should integrate into the curriculum educational programs that foster faculty, graduate student, and research assistant awareness of concerns related to the integrity of the research process. As with the codes of ethics in organizations, each department, college, and research unit should have formal guidelines that can provide scientists with the ability to clarify the nature of responsible research practices. Moreover, because scientists know the specific matters and customs relevant to their respective work, the development of guidelines, as with professional codes of ethics, should be ongoing and modified as experience dictates and the profession evolves.

SUMMARY

Professional responsibility is key to ethical behavior in the practices of sport science, physical education, and research. This outward behavior, fair play, is imperative to our greater social and ethical responsibility to ourselves, our peers, our families, our clients, our students, and our communities. To understand and practice professional responsibility requires that individuals first understand their personal values and beliefs and then develop professional behavior consistent with these personal values and beliefs.

The notion of fair play is imperative in sport, as well as physical education, sport science, and the research practice. Most organizations and many businesses have codes of ethics for members that basically address fair play in the workplace/organization by providing guidelines for accepted professional and ethical behavior. The knowing, valuing, doing triangle of morality discussed earlier in this chapter applies to codes of ethics as well. Individuals involved in the physical education and sport science disciplines must discuss and must be educated in the meanings of their codes of ethics so that they will value the codes enough to practice them responsibly.

ISSUES AND DILEMMAS

CASE 13-1

Tyrone is an athletic trainer at a large midwestern university. He has passed the NATA exam and is thus certified. He loves his job and is highly motivated in his profession to do the best job he can. He arrives to work on time, carries out all duties assigned to him, works well with the other training staff, and is well liked by the players because he treats these individuals with decency and respect. In his spare time, Tyrone enjoys working out in the athletic department's weight room. At different times, other trainers also join him in their workouts. One evening while Tyrone was working out, he noticed that Bob (another certified athletic trainer) is in the corner, and it looks like he is buying some drugs from one of the "known" suppliers of different performance-enhancing drugs. It is hard for Tyrone to see exactly what Bob is buying and figures it is none of his business so he decides to shrug it off and continue in his weight lifting routine. Several days later after a late Saturday night game, Bob invites Tyrone over to his apartment for pizza. Tyrone noticed that Bob has a bulletin board on the wall next to his phone that has a series of used hypodermic needles stuck in it. Jokingly, Tyrone mentions to Bob that he has a "real interesting dart board." Bob, though, states that it is not a dart board but a place for him to keep his needles where they can be found easily. When asked what they were for, Bob says that he is using anabolic steroids and that amazingly his squats and presses have increased significantly and that Tyrone ought to try some—he knows where they can be bought cheaply. Tyrone tactfully declines; however, now he is in a difficult position. Tyrone can think of at least two of the principles in the NATA's Code of Ethics that Bob is violating: "Members shall avoid substance abuse and, when necessary, seek rehabilitation for chemical dependency" and "Members shall comply with applicable local, state, and federal laws and institutional guidelines" (http://www.nata.org/publications/brochures/ethics.htm). Tyrone is torn between loyalty to his friend and fellow athletic trainer (with whom he has spent many hours in the training room) and NATA's Code of Ethics.

1. If you were a member of NATA and knew its Code of Ethics, how would you react?
2. Given the NATA Code of Ethics, what are your professional responsibilities? (Remember the triangle of personal and professional responsibility in light of the code of ethics.)

◆ ◆ ◆

CASE 13-2

Brad is a graduate student in exercise physiology. He works for Dr. Smith conducting various research studies in the exercise physiology lab. Currently, he and Dr. Smith are beginning a study on the effects of creatine on football linemen's strength. Dr. Smith has a good working relationship with Coach Nelson and knows he will have no difficulty getting players to be a part of the study. Between Coach Nelson and Dr. Smith, they figure that they can easily get 30 players to be a part of the study.

In order to determine if the effects of the drug truly improve linemen's strength, Dr. Smith discusses with Brad the need for a strong experimental design, the better the design, the better the study. Players will be randomly selected into one of three groups. Group one will receive a high dosage of the drug, group two a moderate level, and group three a placebo. They decide to do a double-blind study so as researchers they do not know exactly who is getting what dosage.

Brad remembers from his introduction to research class that a variety of things must be done to gain approval for the study. First, they must gain *human subject approval* from the University Human Assurances Committee, and second they must obtain an *informed consent* from each of the players agreeing to be a part of the study. Brad talks with Dr. Smith about both forms so they can get the process moving inasmuch as they are on a deadline to conduct the study. Dr. Smith tells Brad not to worry about the paperwork. He says that because players are a part of the athletic department and have signed consents to play, they do not need to have special paperwork for this study. Second, he says that the Human Assurances Committee will unnecessarily "get in the way" of good, important, and timely research. And, because this study is between the athletic department and the lab, and the drug is not illegal to use (whereas steroids are), there is no reason to go to the committee. Two days later the study began and no human subject approval was granted and no players signed an informed consent. Brad is torn—Dr. Smith is a full professor, a highly respected researcher on campus, and his major professor. He does not want to "bite the hand that feeds him" and he is not sure that anyone would listen to what he had to say because he is only a "lowly graduate student."

1. What is the moral dilemma that Brad faces?
2. What is he professionally obligated to do?
3. What safeguards exist in guidelines for scientific research that would help support Brad in making a good, principled decision?

4. What are the ramifications for Brad, Dr. Smith, and the university if human subjects approval is not gained, the study commences, and the improper practices are reported to university personnel?

5. What would you do in this situation? Are your decisions consistent with your personal and professional values and beliefs?

REFERENCES

Beller, J. M., and S. K. Stoll. 1999. *Loyalty . . . a philosophic examination in sport.* Paper presented to the International Association of the Philosophy of Sport. Bedford, England. Available from Authors Center for Ethics, Univ. of Idaho, Moscow, Idaho.

Fletcher, G. P. 1993. Loyalty: An essay on the morality of relationships. New York: Oxford University Press.

Ladd, J. 1967. Loyalty. *Encyclopedia of Philosophy.* New York: Macmillan, pp. 97–98.

National Athletic Trainers Association: http://www.nata.org/publications/brochures/ethics.htm.

Royce, J. 1924. *The philosophy of loyalty.* Macmillian Co. Pub. New York: New York.

Shrader-Frechette, K. 1994. *Ethics of scientific research.* Lanham: MD: Rowman & Littlefield.

Thomas, J. R., and J. K. Nelson. 2000. *Research methods in physical activity.* 4th ed. Champaign, IL: Human Kinetics Press.

Tuckman, B. W. 1978. *Conducting educational research.* 2nd ed. New York: Harcourt Brace Jovanovich.

ADDITIONAL READINGS

Angell, M., and A. S. Relman. 1988. Fraud in biomedical research: A time for congressional restraint. *The New England Journal of Medicine* (June 2), 318(22), pp. 1462–1463.

Clark, R. W., and A. D. Lattal. 1993. *Workplace ethics: Winning the integrity revolution.* Lanham, MD: Littlefield Adams.

DeGeorge, R. T. 1990. *Business ethics.* 3rd ed. New York: Macmillan.

Engler, R. L., J. W. Covell, P. J. Friedman, P. S. Kitcher, and R. M. Peters. 1987. Misrepresentation and responsibility in medical research. *The New England Journal of Medicine* (November 26), 317(22), pp. 1383–1390.

Erwin, E., S. Gendin, and L. Kleinman. 1994. *Ethical issues in scientific research: An anthology.* New York: Garland.

National Academy of Sciences. 1992. Responsible science: Ensuring the integrity of research process. Volume I. Washington, DC: National Academy Press.

National Academy of Sciences. 1992. Responsible science: Ensuring the integrity of research process. Volume II. Washington, DC: National Academy Press.

Pensler, R. L. 1995. *Research ethics: Cases and materials.* Bloomington: Indiana University Press.

Solomon, R. C. 1994. *The new world of business: Ethics and free enterprise in the global 1990s.* Lanham, MD: Littlefield Adams.

Thomas, J. R., and J. K. Nelson. 2001. *Research methods in physical activity.* 4th ed. Champaign, IL: Human Kinetics Press.

U.S. Department of Health and Human Services, PHS. 1995. *Integrity and misconduct in research.* Report of the Commission on Research Integrity. Washington, DC: U.S. Government Printing Office.

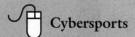 Cybersports

www.nata.org/publications/brochures/ethics.htm

This site provides an example of an organization's code of ethics.

http://www.hhs.gov/topics/humanresearch.html

This site provides information on the US Dept. of Health and Human Services Topics and Policies concerning Human Research

Protections. Provides links to the HHS Office of Human Research Protections, the FDA Office of Human Reserach Trials, The NIH Office of Human Subjects' Research, The HHS National Human Research Protections Advisory Committee, and the White House National Bioethics Advisory Commission.

Epilogue: Morality in Sport

This text describes how moral reasoning can address moral issues in sport. Ethical dilemmas surface daily in our personal and sporting lives. Addressing these issues requires good critical examination, which, in turn (1) makes us more tolerant of others' views, (2) gives us intellectual independence, and (3) frees us from dogmatic beliefs. The less reasoned and more dogmatic our thinking, the easier we fall prey to the obstacles and fallacies that impede moral reasoning. The more morally reasoned our view, the more consistent with our beliefs and values are our actions.

Moral reasoning predicated on a system of personal values and beliefs calls for a consistent application of these values, beliefs, and practices within sport. We must take the time to examine our personal values and beliefs, as well as their consistency, and have the courage to take a stand for what we value. Because we do not live, play, and work in isolation, we must have the courage to challenge common beliefs such as, "I have no right to judge someone else's values," "Everyone has the right to their own beliefs," "Everyone else is doing it," and

"That is just the way things are." Yet, if we all "did our own thing" without taking into consideration the effects of our views and actions on others, chaos would assuredly result and violations against others would occur.

Challenging others' beliefs may help us (1) better understand our personal values as they relate to our relationships with others, (2) become stronger and more consistent in our beliefs, and (3) better understand our beliefs relative to the whole. In this sense, the whole relates to sport, school, community, the nation, and in other settings. Consequently, moral reasoning allows us to develop our own value and belief system, while requiring that it be compatible with the whole: the societies in which we live, work, *and* play.

MORAL REASONING: A REVIEW

Moral reasoning, a systematic, logical, and rational process whereby we identify issues, examine opposing views, and attempt solutions, is predicated on our abilities to be impartial, consistent, and reflective. Impartiality requires that we consider others' views when making decisions. Although difficult because we see and perceive the world through our own eyes and may hold biases and stereotypes, becoming impartial requires that we deliberately seek to correct our sometimes narrow and distorted perceptions. Inherent within impartiality is the concept of fairness in which we are free from bias, fraud, or injustice and we do not make decisions based on "what's in it for me" or to take advantage of another. Consistency requires ensurance that our actions are consistent with what we value and believe relative to the past and present and universality principles. Reflective thinking, based on a clear understanding of moral and nonmoral values, helps us make careful judgments or observations about an issue. Reflection may also lead to several viable, alternative views. We may not find a correct answer; however, the reasoning process may free us from our own prejudices, help us discard false beliefs, and enable us to better understand opposing views.

MORAL AND NONMORAL VALUES: A REVIEW

Germane to our discussion of moral reasoning are values, both moral and nonmoral. Nonmoral values, things such as money, fame, power, and winning, do not include people, their intentions, motives, deeds, or character traits. In contrast, moral values, the relative worth that we place on some virtuous behaviors, are internal, subjective, and immeasurable in an objective sense. Moral values are traits or dispositions that we hope to portray and support. In order, in this text, to address moral issues, we chose as basic moral values justice, honesty, responsibility, and beneficence. We chose these because they are universally understood. The importance lies not in the particular value chosen but in our respective efforts to (1) rank these values by their relative importance and (2) be consistent in using our designated primary value to address our individual moral issues and dilemmas. Principles, universal guides or universal rules of conduct that govern our lives, are directly related to the moral values we hold. Examples of universal principles in-

Gender equity is but one issue about which we must develop and practice good moral reasoning.

clude respect for self and others, respect for others' property, and respect for the truth. Although some issues such as gender and racial equity inherently involve the value of justice and the principle "Do not be unfair," we may choose the value of responsibility with the principle "Do not be irresponsible" and come to a similarly reasoned perspective.

In the process of ranking our moral values and developing principles by which to guide day-to-day action, we also must examine these principles and identify ahead of time any exceptions we may have to the rule. In other words, there may be a very few instances in which we might violate one of our principles in favor of another principle. For example, let us say that you have ranked honesty as your number one value. It is WWII. You are harboring people in your attic, people who are wanted by the Nazis. A

Nazi storm trooper comes to your door and says, "Are you harboring any people in your attic?" If you value honesty and hold the principle of "Do not lie, cheat, or steal" you are obligated to say "Yes, I have people in my attic." However, most prudent, morally sensitive individuals would lie and say "no." In this case, you probably made your decision based on another value, such as justice, or beneficence. With exceptions though, we must be careful with how many exceptions we have for any given principle and that the exception is made in relation to another moral value, not a nonmoral value.

The relationship of nonmoral values to moral values is paramount to our moral actions. Essentially, nonmoral values drive our moral actions. What we value nonmorally, such as winning or money, affects our moral actions. If we value winning or money to a greater extent than we value justice, honesty, responsibility, and beneficence, it becomes easier for us to violate others to get what we want.

The approach suggested in this text challenges each of us to examine what we value and believe and then to rationally scrutinize these values and beliefs relative to the issues. Some of you may find the approach of this text uncomfortable; it is a value/principle-based approach. Our purpose is not to moralize, or tell you what to believe, what to value, or how to act; our purpose is to challenge you to discover for yourself values in relation to universal values, principles, and reversibility (the ability to treat others as you want to be treated). Finding the truth and the most reasonable view becomes the goal. Not unlike a physical skill, moral reasoning must be practiced constantly for it to improve.

MORAL REASONING IN RELATION TO SPORT AND SOCIAL ISSUES: A REVIEW

Throughout this text, we have challenged you to develop and practice moral reasoning with common, yet seemingly difficult moral issues in sport, such as gender and racial equity, elimination from sport, gamesmanship and intimidation, ergogenic aids, eligibility, violence, and commercialization. These issues are but a few of those that we en-

counter daily in sport. Whereas many of the issues have existed throughout the history of sport, others have surfaced and become more prevalent only recently. Essentially, because sport involves participation among and between people, moral issues continually surface and persist. The issues come and go and may change with the seasons, but the reasoning process remains the same. Moral reasoning, the constant in the moral equation, challenges us to examine what is of relative importance to us before an issue or dilemma occurs. Once the dilemma surfaces, it becomes more difficult to sift through the issues as we face emotionalism, controversy, and our personal biases. Thus, we must constantly challenge ourselves through the reasoning process.

Moral issues surface in our personal lives and may or may not involve the same potential conflicts as those in sport. Of importance, then, is that we examine and debate each dilemma, ensure consistency in our beliefs and actions whether they involve social, personal, or sport settings, and find solutions workable for each of us. Solutions to moral issues are not easy to come by because of the involvement of emotions, opinions, circumstances, and personal histories. Each multifaceted issue involves a multitude of questions. Violence in sport, for example, raises several moral questions, such as how important is winning relative to our moral values and principles and how do we view the concept of gamesmanship relative to sportsmanship. If we value the nonmoral value of winning more than our moral values and principles, it becomes easier to harm an opponent, bend the rules, and take advantage of another person.

Moreover, while the advent of advanced material design has revolutionized the equipment industry, the role these new designs play in gaining an advantage and fairly seeking excellence in sport raises moral questions. These advanced materials have contributed greatly to how athletes and recreational players perform in that the equipment is stronger, tougher, stiffer, and more resilient, thus increasing distance and accuracy. If results and the win are the primary goals for sport, then advanced materials are the key to fulfilling these goals in any sport. If competition is about results, advanced materials will continue to improve the game so that less efficiency, fitness, and skill are necessary. However, in all issues of ethics and moral reasoning, some things that appear to be good and beneficial, might actually result in harm and bad consequences. From a moral perspective we have asked three basic questions: (1) What help or harm comes with technology to the competitor or recreational player? (2) What is good or valuable about the activity? and (3) How can we distribute that good or value to others? Throughout the text we have shown how a focus on winning and results can drive participants to do harm to themselves and to the sport. If sport is considered "good," participation should occur with consideration for justice (fair play) and beneficence (doing good). In the ideal sense, technology and advanced materials should enhance the thrill and fun of competition. And, if the activity is good for the competitor, advanced materials should help people improve their motor skills, their physical fitness, their general health, and perhaps their inner spirit and joy of the activity. Advanced materials and the science that supports them are value-neutral, thus we decide if they can help or harm. The vision and purpose, therefore, should be about people performing and their humanness through the experience and our creative ability to use technology and advanced materials effectively and wisely for the good of humans and the good of sport.

Moral reasoning opens the door and helps us identify issues, see opposing points of view, take a stand, and attempt solutions. We may not always agree and our beliefs may not withstand rational scrutiny; another position may be more defensible. To withstand rational scrutiny, our values and beliefs must be universal and hold true for all people at all times. They must also be reversible in that we treat others as we would hope to be treated. Relative to issues of gender or racial equality, if our beliefs and actions were equitable, universal, and reversible, we would feel comfortable and satisfied taking the other person's position. For example, this position would hold that coaches or athletes in a men's program would be happy and satisfied taking the budgets, facilities, practice times, or other support services of the women's program (and vice versa).

Adopting a moral reasoning approach is not easy, though, because we must examine what we value and what we believe. Through this process, we learn to listen and examine carefully all views, and all inaccuracies and half-truths, and take a stand based on our beliefs no matter how popular or unpopular. We may find that what we believe and value is not shared by the entire group. It takes courage to take a stand, because we may be challenging the status quo, with others in strong opposition, or we may be the only one holding this belief. Moreover, through debate and dialogue, we may come to the realization that our beliefs are based on false or inaccurate information. Thus, we must have humility. We must realize that we may be wrong and we must reevaluate our beliefs and our position.

MORAL REASONING IN RELATION TO THE SPORT SCIENCE DISCIPLINE: A REVIEW

Once we have a strong understanding of our personal values and beliefs, we have a professional responsibility and obligation to apply our personal moral values to the workplace, whether that be as sport scientists, fitness professionals, teachers, athletics trainers, and/or researchers. This professional responsibility as in other moral principles, requires that we examine our personal moral system in light of the values of our profession and professional position. Remember that the professional responsibility paradigm triangle (with the top as our personal moral self and the sides social and professional responsibilities) is our perception of how professional responsibility applies to our daily lives and is one part of our greater social and ethical responsibility to ourselves, our peers, our families, our clients, and our communities. Thus it is our responsibility as professionals to examine our motives, intentions, and actions as they are directed toward, impinge upon, or affect others in the schools, fitness clubs, and/or college settings. Oftentimes, however, people abrogate their professional responsibility in the name of loyalty to the individual or organization thus leading to questionable moral acts. The problem is when individuals become confused as to whether they are loyal to an individual, organization, or group and forget that loyalty as a moral value, is tenuous and must be tempered with a prime moral value such as responsibility.

Inherent within this notion of professional responsibility is the concept of being a professional and thus an active member of a professional organization such as the National Association for Sport and Physical Education, The National Athletic Trainers Association, and the American College of Sports Medicine. Professions, and thus the professional members are typically guided by a code of ethics which may be called a code of conduct. These codes have very specific purposes in that they (1) are regulative for members, (2) protect public interest and the interests of those they serve, (3) are not self-serving, (4) are specific and honest, and (5) must be both policeable and policed. These codes of ethics are typically written by members of an association or organization to make the professional membership aware of principles of ethical behavior that should be followed in the practice of that particular profession. As such, a code acts as a ready guide to help professionals make good ethical decisions.

Besides codes of ethics from their professional organizations, sport scientist researchers are also held accountable to the standards set forth in their institution's "Scientific Integrity and Misconduct in Research Manual." The purpose of this manual is to provide researchers a general framework concerning individual and institutional rights and obligations concerning ethics in research as well as how researchers within a particular institution believe in, promote, and maintain research integrity.

Having reviewed the processes of how to reason morally as well as how to tie our personal values and beliefs to professional practice, let us examine a real situation with issues and dilemmas and use moral reasoning to see how far we have come. As with most moral dilemmas, we are given little warning and little time to prepare our response. However, we have learned that if we understand our values and beliefs and have examined these beliefs relative to universal principles (such as respect for the self and others, honesty, reversibility, and universality), making a reasoned decision, taking a stand, and acting on that stand becomes easier—and our actions are more consistent.

 # ISSUES AND DILEMMAS

Keith has just completed his junior year as a grant-in-aid student–athlete. He has been successful this year, not only on the golf team as the number-two man on a 10-member roster, but also in the classroom, where last semester he earned a 4.0 grade-point average, resulting in a cumulative grade-point average of 3.87. He believes in justice, honesty, and responsibility and attempts to guide his life by the concomitant principles. He qualified for and played in all but one tournament during the season; he chose to not qualify for the one tournament, giving priority to two academic projects due during the tournament dates. Keith, respected by all team members for his dedication, loyalty, and integrity, was voted team cocaptain.

Despite Keith's success in the classroom and on the golf course, he has experienced a difficult year working with his coach. As Keith talks with his team members, he finds that they all share similar concerns such as: (1) The coach calls practices but tells only a select few about the time and place (despite Keith's position as cocaptain, he is not told); (2) the coach works with only a select few and is belligerent toward the others; (3) he finds the negative in everything, yelling, screaming, and swearing at players; (4) he seldom coaches, encourages, or works with players on the course, either during practice or matches; and (5) a written qualification process does not exist for selection to the tournament-travel team. Essentially, the coach changes the process on a whim. He has regularly stated, "I do not care what anyone else says, I can choose any five players I want."

Keith and his teammates decide to talk with the coach about their concerns. Keith, with the support of his teammates, shares their concerns, but these are met with hostile responses from the coach. Unfortunately, practices and coaching do not improve. Rather, quite the opposite occurs. The coach's verbal assaults and negativity increase, with Keith becoming the focus of the coach's wrath. Things become so bad that the team talks in confidence with the assistant athletic director, explains the problems, gives a list of possible solutions, and asks for help and advice. The assistant athletic director assures the team that the discussion will be held in confidence, the problems will be examined, and the team will be notified of results. However, within a half hour of the team's leaving the assistant athletic director's office, the coach knows about the discussion and Keith again receives verbal abuse. In desperation, Keith and his team talk to the athletic director and are again assured that the complaints will be examined.

Two months pass with no change and no response from the athletic director or athletic department personnel. Keith and his teammates leave for summer break, believing they still have their grants-in-aid for the following year. However, on June 30, Keith receives a letter stating that his athletic grant-in-aid has not been renewed. The letter states, "After review, the university athletic department has decided to not renew your academic year athletic grant-in-aid. If you have any questions, you may request a hearing. If you wish to transfer universities, we will assist in any way we can." The letter was signed by the athletic director, the coach, and the director of financial aid.

The letter gives no reason for not renewing Keith's grant-in-aid. At the end of the academic year, the coach gave no indication to Keith that he was considering not renewing his grant-in-aid. Now, in the middle of his summer vacation, Keith has limited opportunities to earn sufficient funds to finance his senior year. He understands that his grant-in-aid can be rescinded at any time without a particular reason. He also believes that there are usually three general reasons why athletes do not have their grants-in-aid renewed: academic, athletic, and attitudinal. Keith knows that his loss of a grant-in-aid cannot be because of grades—he is an exemplary student. He knows that it cannot be because of performance—he is second on the 10-roster, plus he qualified for all but one tournament and has the second lowest scoring average for the team. Only one plausible reason exists; he is a troublemaker in the eyes of the athletic department and coach. Keith is mad, upset, and frustrated and does not know what to do. He comes to you and says, "I took a stand on what I thought was right and look what happened. I thought that the purpose of higher education was to support critical thinking. It does not pay to take a stand when no one else believes in treating someone fairly!"

The following questions, which are guidelines to help you begin reasoning, are not exhaustive, nor do they give a complete picture of the issues and dilemmas. As you examine these issues and look for alternatives and reasoned perspectives, be sure to use systematic and logical approaches.

1. What issues are involved in this scenario?
2. What moral questions are raised?
3. What moral values are involved?
4. What principles may have been violated?
5. What nonmoral values may have been involved in the decision to ignore the athletes' concerns?
6. In the coach's decision to not renew Keith's grant-in-aid, what rights, if any, have been violated?
7. If athletes sign grant-in-aid contracts renewable on a year-by-year basis, what rights, if any, do they have regarding due process?
8. Knowing that those who ask questions are often thought of as troublemakers and that whistle-blowers are usually expunged from the system, what would you do if you felt the treatment of Keith was morally unacceptable?
9. Suppose that you are a young administrator with some training and a desire to approach issues through moral reasoning. What would be your recommendations to Keith? To the coach? To the athletic director? To the assistant athletic director?
10. If you were in Keith's position, what would you do?

From this scenario, several issues and moral questions arise—some obvious, others hidden. These questions listed above challenge you to examine the issues and your nonmoral and moral values and their concomitant principles, as well as your consistency and impartiality.

Keith chose a certain path to address his concerns; the coach and athletic department took another. As you examine the issues, think about what you value. We know that a morally reasoned approach may result in several equally viable alternatives. What possible alternatives exist for Keith, the coach, and the athletic director? It may be easy to identify the principles violated, but do your views or solutions change depending on whether you have job security? Do you change your position if your colleague or best friend is the administrator in charge?

A LOOK TO THE FUTURE

Today, we in sport and the sport science and physical education disciplines face ethical questions concerning gender and racial equity, commercialization, gamesmanship, athletes' and coaches' rights, drug use and abuse, as well as the use of advanced materials and technology, issues of loyalty versus moral principles, and what is considered good professional and ethical conduct. The questions may be of a moral nature, but more often than not people do not intentionally violate others. Rather, actions may occur as a result of the desire to do what one *feels* is right, rather than what may be *truly* right. Oftentimes, though, actions and responses are based on faulty or dogmatic thinking, generally as a result of poor or nonexistent moral reasoning skills.

We also know that our value systems and the foundations of moral character develop at a very young age and are shaped by diverse factors, most involving environment, modeling, and education. Generally, those environments in which we spend the greatest time have the most impact on our values and beliefs. Because athletes spend much time immersed in the culture of sport and many hours practicing and developing their sport skills, the values and beliefs they hold are often shaped by those with whom they work and the environment in which they play and train. Similarly, modeling, either positively or negatively, powerfully impacts our actions and what we may hold as true and right. Nowhere is this more apparent than in the sport milieu. One need only to watch the corner playground to find children mimicking their favorite sport stars' moves or wearing their favorite teams' jackets, shirts, and hats. For the past forty years, a comprehensive, concentrated moral education curriculum, though, has been practically nonexistent in most schools, colleges, and universities. Although many coaches and administrators state that they stress ethical play, research finds that little or no concentrated moral education exists in sport.

Nor has research been favorable concerning the development of moral character through sport, even though this is universally expressed as a primary purpose of sport. For many years, the belief has existed that sport builds character and promotes moral growth. This belief stems from the nineteenth-century English public school system justification for the development of sport programs based on sport's supposedly inherent ethical values. Most sport and physical education texts, teachings, and programs for the past 150 years have supported this belief. A strong body of qualitative and quantitative research exists, however, supporting that the longer athletes participate in sport, the more their moral reasoning is adversely affected by the competitive experience. Moreover, athletes' reasoning skills are significantly lower than those of their nonathletic peers. It would appear from the research that sport does not model, challenge, support, or teach the critical reasoning skills paramount to making good moral decisions.

Yet, all is not lost for sport. Research has found that a very specific teaching methodology, based on a morally reasoned approach, can significantly affect moral reasoning and moral development. As advocated in this text, participants must be challenged to examine their beliefs and actions, consider others' views, and take a stand relative to universality and reversibility concepts. They are challenged by peers and others to defend their points of view. The process results in what Kohlberg (1981) called cognitive dissonance, a state where we begin to question whether our beliefs and views are the most reasoned for us. Kohlberg and other cognitive development theorists believe that cognitive dissonance is essential to the reasoning process and improvement of moral development.

Currently, few sport organizations, teams, or programs teach athletes sport ethics or moral reasoning. Although athletes may be taught about the dangers of alcohol and drug use and racism, seldom do we challenge them to examine themselves, their beliefs, and their actions. With these issues, rarely do they experience cognitive dissonance.

Similarly, few professional organizations in the sport disciplines teach about their respective codes of ethics and challenge professionals to develop a personal value and belief structure that is consistent with their professional beliefs and goals. As with athletic programs, few coaching certification programs teach sport ethics or moral reasoning, with the National Youth Sport Coaches Association possibly being the only organization to date with specific sport ethics competency requirements in its coaching certification program. Although some see little reason for such programs, some interesting questions arise. Because of the importance of the situation or setting, what happens to an athlete who reasons from a more developed perspective but must participate in an environment that does not support moral reasoning? If the longer people participate in sport the lower their moral reasoning, and if coaches have been involved in sport for many years, what perspectives do they hold? How do their perspectives affect their athletes' moral reasoning? What role do coaches have in moral education? Finally, can moral reasoning exist in sport if the environment does not value the basic premises of a reasoned perspective? Most research shows that we will have limited success in matching what we know and value to prosocial actions if the environment does not embrace and value the moral reasoning process.

Consequently, if we value the institution of sport and the sport discipline professions, and are concerned about the development of honor and integrity through sport, the sport disciplines, and sport science research, we should use moral reasoning to debate, discuss, and encourage critical inquiry. Moral reasoning must be taught from the moment children enter sport throughout their competitive experiences. We should make a concerted effort to develop moral reasoning skills to the same extent and effort as we do motor skills, strategy, and tactics. The society of sport should value and support ethics, integrity, and honor as the foundation from which all aspects of sport and the sport science and physical education disciplines emerge.

Moreover, those of us involved in sport, sport science, physical education, and sport science research should support an open and honest environment that encourages (1) individuality, (2) the worth of the individuals as they participate in sport and physical education, and (3) the use of critical inquiry to examine and address the many moral issues that surface daily in our personal, sport, and professional lives. Finally, would it not be wonderful if we valued and developed moral reasoning and critical thinking skills in our athletic populations to the same magnitude and extent as we do motor skills, strategy, and tactics? A start in this direction would involve nothing more than treating others with dignity, respect, and common decency. If we use common decency as a beginning, the future of sport as a vehicle to support and foster ethical and moral practices becomes brighter.

REFERENCE

Kohlberg, Lawrence. 1981. *The philosophy of moral development: Moral stages and the idea of justice.* New York: Harper and Row.

ADDITIONAL READINGS

Beller, J. M., and S. K. Stoll. 1992. A moral reasoning intervention program for Division I athletes. *Academic Athletic Journal* (Spring). 43–57.

Beller, J. M., S. K. Stoll, B. Burwell, and J. Cole. 1996. The relationship of competition and christian liberal arts education on moral reasoning of college student athletes, research on christian higher education, 3, pp. 99–114.

Beller, J. M., and S. K. Stoll. 1995. Moral reasoning of high school student athletes and general students: Empirical study versus personal testimony, pediatric exercise science, 7(4), pp. 352–363.

Berkowitz, L. 1972. Sport competition and aggression. In *Fourth Canadian Symposium on Psychology of Motor Learning and Sport*, edited by I. Williams and L. Wankel. Ottawa: University of Ottawa Press.

Bredemeier, B. J. 1984. Sport, gender, and moral growth. In *Psychological foundations of sport*, edited by John M. Silva and R. S. Weinberg. Champaign, IL: Human Kinetics Press. 400–413.

Bredemeier, B. J., and D. Shields. 1986. Moral growth among athletes and nonathletes: A comparative analysis. *J Genet Psychol* 147(1):718.

Bredemeier, B. J., M. Weiss, and D. Shields, B. Cooper, n.d. Young sport involvement and children's moral growth and aggression tendencies. Unpublished manuscript. Minneapolis: University of Minnesota.

Fraleigh, W. P. 1982. Why the good foul is not good. *JOPERD* 51(1): (January):41–42.

Hahm, C. H. 1989. Moral reasoning and development among general students, physical education majors, and student athletes. Ph.D. dissertation, University of Idaho.

Hall, E. 1981. Moral development levels of athletes in sport specific and general social situations. Ph.D. dissertation, Texas Women's University.

Kretchmar, R. S. 1993. Fair play: who committed the robbery? *Strategies* (May):23–24.

Martens, R. 1978. Kids sports: Den of iniquity or land of promise. In *Children in sport: A contemporary anthology,* edited by R. A. Magill, M. J. Ash, and F. L. Smoll. Champaign, IL: Human Kinetics.

Rudd, A. May 1998. Sports perceived ability to build character. Unpublished doctoral dissertation, Univeristy of Idaho, Moscow, Idaho.

Simon, R. L. 1991. *Fair play: Sports, values, and society.* Boulder, CO: Westview Press.

Stoll, S. K., and J. M. Beller. 1998. The SBH ethical standard: A methodology and curriculum text (2nd ed). Contor for ethics, Moscow, Idaho.

Stoll, S. K. and J. M. Beller. 2000. Do sports build charactor? J. R. Gerdy (Ed). Sports in school. New York: Teachers College Press, pp. 18–30.

Stoll, S. K., J. M. Beller, and S. M. Durrant. 1993. A bill of right for athletes: A novel idea or blasphemy? *For the Record* (July).

Stoll, S. K. 1999. 2nd ed. *Who says this is cheating? Anybody's sport ethics.* Dubuque, IA: Kendall/Hunt.

Glossary

A

Aesthetic A philosophic term applied when something is "pleasing to the senses," whatever the sense might be—sight, sound, touch, feel, movement, taste, or smell.

Amoral An ethical position meaning one is not able to make a judgment. Such actions are outside the realm of morality.

Anabolic steroid A drug that resembles male testosterone; a controlled substance used for body building or increasing strength.

Applied ethics The practical application of ethical theory directed toward issues in life and certain professions, such as, medical ethics, sport ethics, business ethics, and law ethics.

Athletics The competitive experience of sport, whereby coaching is essential, spectators are present, and specific constitutive, proscriptive, and sportsmanship rules are highly developed within an organized structure.

Autonomy A philosophic term meaning self-governance, whereby one has the right, power, or condition of self-governance. The individual has self-determinism and freedom from external control or coercion.

Axiology The branch of philosophy dedicated to the study of values.

B

Beneficence The ethical position whereby one attempts and is actually obligated to do no harm, but rather to remove harm, prevent harm, and actually do good.

Bias The position whereby an individual shows partiality and prejudice, slanting an opinion in one direction only.

C

Character A moral demeanor that refers to one's outward demeanor as judged by society. Positive moral character refers to one's ability to know the right and to have the courage to follow the right. Character refers to one's virtue or how one lives by a set of moral values. A person of character is known to be just, honest, fair, and decent to others, as well as being a person of honor and integrity.

Choice One of the necessary stipulations (value, principle, obligation, and choice) to determine whether a moral issue is being presented. A moral dilemma does not exist if one does not have a choice. Coercion, manipulation, or other excusing conditions usually abrogate moral responsibility.

Code of ethics Moral guidelines written for a professional body to follow. These guidelines are always developed by the professional body, monitored by that body, and enforced by that body.

Cognitive dissonance The cognitive process whereby an individual's values and beliefs are challenged. The challenging process is necessary in moral reasoning to wrestle with moral dilemmas.

Commercialized sport This type of sport is comprised of organized competitions that are advertised and promoted for entertainment value and for which the outcome has significance financially and leads to status within the sport context.

Consequential ethics   A theory based on utilitarian philosophy; right and wrong are based on the greater amount of good resulting. The consequences of action play a major role in deciding the greater amount of good. Major philosophers include John Stuart Mill and Jeremy Bentham, both of whom espoused utilitarian ethics.

Consistency   Requires ensuring that our actions are consistent with what we value and believe relative to the past and present and universality principles.

Constitutive rules   The specific game rules that guide play in a sport. Constitutive rules may have unsportsmanlike conduct explicitly described and violations specifically written to punish such behavior.

Corticosteroids   Steroids developed particularly to reduce inflammation, especially that brought on by overuse syndrome. Corticosteroids do not cause anabolic effects, and they are the only legal form of steroid ingestion or injection presently acceptable.

D

Deductive reasoning   Philosophic reasoning in which the argument moves from the general perspective to the specific.

Deontic ethics (nonconsequential)   Ethical theory based on the ideal that we can perceive rightness apart from any consequences. This perspective believes that there is an inherent right that must be followed, regardless of any extraneous factors. Right and wrong are based on the ideal of what should be. Major philosophies include Kantian ethics, the ethical theory of Immanuel Kant.

Determinism   Every event, including human choice and volition, is caused by other events and is an effect or result of these other events.

Discriminatory practices   Prejudical actions that result in inequitable treatment of others.

Dogmatism   The argumentative position based on opinion that is not supported by fact.

Due process   The act of the right to refute accusations or actions and give individuals a just accounting.

E

Educational sport   This type of sport is comprised of competitions between individuals enrolled in schools and colleges that are of interest mostly to the athletes, friends, and family because the outcome, although valued, is secondary to the sporting experience as characterized by behaviors such as fair play, teamwork, and cooperation.

Epistemology   One of the philosophic branches of philosophy. The epistemologist studies knowledge, particularly addressing such questions as, "Can we know?" "What do we know?" "How do we come to know?"

Ergogenic aids   Any aid, supplement, or ingested material that is prohibited by the letter or the spirit of the rules; used to garner an advantage in the sport experience.

Ethics   The theoretical study of morality. Ethics is also the standard of morality that a profession should follow.

Excusing conditions   An ethical position in which outside factors beyond an individual's control excuse the individual from moral action. That is, if the moral action places one in undue jeopardy, if one cannot readily affect the outcome, or if one is ignorant of the conditions, one is excused from acting.

Extrinsic value   The relative worth that an individual places on objects, things, or actions that have an objective worth. For example, an athlete or others in the athletic community might place much value on an article like a letter jacket, which is a symbol awarded for work done.

F

False obstruction   A reasoning obstacle that does not permit an individual to morally reason through a dilemma. Usually this obstacle is permitting a bias or perception to cloud one's thinking.

Free choice   The philosophic position that individuals have the freedom to choose their moral actions without intimidation, coercion, or manipulation being a factor. Free choice in contrast to determinism supports the concept of autonomy. One can make choices based on values, outside of determinism.

G

Gamesmanship The perspective of pushing the rules to the limit without getting caught, using whatever dubious methods necessary to achieve a win.

H

Honesty The quality of trustworthiness in which an individual can be depended on to "not lie, cheat, or steal."

Honor A virtue or distinguishable characteristic of an individual that implies the individual is obligated to follow a specific set of written or unwritten moral guidelines. Honor implies that individuals have given their word as a guarantee of future moral performance.

I

Immoral A moral perspective in which the individual knows the good, right, and proper course of action but instead chooses to do wrong.

Impartiality Requires that we consider others' views when making decisions.

Inductive reasoning Reasoning from particular facts to a general conclusion.

Integrity A moral virtue or distinguishable character trait in which an individual is free from corruption. That is, the individual has been shown to have certain positive moral character traits and, even when challenged and tempted to do wrong, will choose the good, right, and proper.

Intimidation An intentional act done to frighten or inhibit others or render them unable to do certain behaviors.

Intrinsic value A nonmoral value in which relative worth of an event, object, or experience is placed on some internal, personal satisfaction. An intrinsic nonmoral value in sport might be the internal, personal joy of playing, the joy of success, or the joy of experience.

J

Justice A universal moral value in which the essential nature of fairness and equity should be applied to all people. Justice in sport refers to "making a level playing field" either in constitutive rules or for past inadequacies, social injustices, or physical or mental handicaps.

L

Logic The philosophic branch of philosophy that focuses on the study of language.

M

Materialism The doctrine that everything in the world, including thought, can be explained only in terms of matter; the individual tendency to be more concerned with material objects than with spiritual or intellectual values.

Meta-ethics The specific philosophic study of ethics in which the formal academic inquiry is toward the analytical.

Metaphysics The philosophic branch of philosophy in which study is directed toward questioning the nature of reality; divided into several different directions such as cosmology (What is the nature of the universe?) or ontology (What is the nature of man?). In sport a metaphysician might ask the question, "Why do we play"?

Moral The moral perspective in which one knows the good, proper, and right. The moral perspective is played out through one's motives, intentions, and actions as they impinge on or affect other human beings.

Moral development The evolving growth process by which one learns to take the welfare of others into consideration when making moral decisions. Moral development is usually considered to occur through six different stages in three different levels, from a lower reasoned perspective to a greater reasoned perspective.

Morality The motives, intentions, and actions of an individual as they are directed toward others and how these are judged by the greater society.

Moral judgment The ability to form an opinion based on moral issues.

Moral reasoning The ability to systematically think through a moral problem, taking into consideration one's own values and beliefs while weighing them against what others value and believe.

Moral value The worth each individual places on specific nonmoral values that affect and impinge on others, such as winning. Moral values are usually highly specific—for example, justice, honesty, responsibility, and beneficence.

Motivation The psychological condition that moves an individual to action.

N

Nonmoral value The perspective taken toward an issue in which good and bad are determined on the basis of nonmoral issues. The question is based on intrinsic or extrinsic values.

Normative ethics The theoretical study or position of morality in which rightness and wrongness are analyzed and reviewed with a decision specifically stated. For example, that is the wrong thing to do.

O

Objectivity The philosophic position in which one is without bias or prejudice. The position is concerned with reality rather than perceptions or feelings.

Obligation One of the four stipulations that must be met to equate an event to a moral dilemma. Obligation implies that one "should" and even "must" follow one's principles based on one's moral values.

P

Paradox An apparent illogical statement that at first appears to be contradictory but may be true or false.

Paternalism The practice of governing or monitoring adults in a manner that suggests a father–child relationship. The practice ethically violates an adult's status as an autonomous moral agent.

Pedagogy The educational study that is directed toward the art and science of teaching.

Philosophy The deliberate and rational attempt to understand the whole and the sum of one's objective and subjective experiences with a view for effective living.

Pragmatism The practice of testing validity of all concepts by their practical results.

Prejudice A preconceived, usually unfavorable, idea or opinion that is biased and often intolerant.

Principle An affirmation of one's values. Always stated in the negative, a principle says what one will not do based on what one morally values. If one values honesty, the principle becomes, "Do not lie, cheat, or steal." Principles do have exceptions or qualifiers. For example, if a principle violates another principle, qualifiers may exist. "Do not lie, cheat, or steal, unless failing to do so places another human being in personal jeopardy."

Proscriptive rules Game rules that expressly forbid specific actions.

R

Recreational sport This type of sport, which should include youth sport, is comprised of competitions between noncompensated individuals of any age who play sport for fun, skill development, social interaction, and value development.

Reflective thinking Process of making careful judgments or observations based on a clear understanding of moral and nonmoral values.

Relative worth The individual importance placed on some intrinsic or extrinsic object, experience, or person.

Relativism The popular position that states either that (1) there is no standard of right and wrong, (2) no one has the right to make moral judgments, (3) right and wrong are unknowable because of different societies and cultures, or (4) no one should judge others concerning right and wrong.

Respect The moral value in which one holds someone or something in high regard.

Responsibility The moral value in which one is answerable, accountable, and possibly liable for actions in the past, present, and future; a statement of character that one is trustworthy to carry out deeds.

Reversibility The moral perspective of placing the burden on oneself or the ability to treat others as we would hope to be treated. It is asking the question, "What would it feel like if this were done to me?" Reversibility in common usage is the Golden Rule.

Rules Individual day-to-day moral guidelines, written or unwritten. Rules are usually based on specific First Rules or principles. Rules are divided into three different types—constitutive, proscriptive, and sportsmanship. Constitutive rules guide play within a specific game. Proscriptive rules expressly forbid specific actions. Sportsmanship rules are to be followed while in the game and out of the game.

S

Situational ethics The position that every ethical or moral decision is made on the spot and no consistency is shown between individual decisions.

Skepticism The doctrine that the truth of all knowledge must always be in question or doubt.

Spirit of a rule Usually refers to the intent of a sportsmanship rule or what was intended by the rule. No rule can take into consideration all possibilities, hence the spirit of a rule is to cover the possibilities.

Sports Games and activities directed toward the play experience in which organization and rules play a significant role.

Sportsmanship The quality inherent in playing a game in which one is honor-bound to follow the spirit and letter of the rules. Sportsmanship rules are rules of conduct explicitly written or implicitly believed that adhere to this principle.

Syllogism Reasoning in which a logical conclusion is drawn from two premises.

T

Teleologic ethics (consequential) Matters of right and wrong are decided on the issue of the greater amount of good.

Trust To have confidence in someone or something.

U

Universality An ethical perspective in which decisions are based on whether the decision can be applied across all societies and cultures in every instance.

Utilitarianism John Stuart Mill's perspective on teleologic ethics in which ethical questions are decided on the amount of good generated by the decision; usually stated as, "The greatest amount of measurable good for the greatest number of people."

V

Validity A measurement of sound reasoning whereby consistent, impartial, and reflective logic is the standard.

Value Individual relative worth placed on some intrinsic or extrinsic object, experience, or persons.

Violence Physical force exerted to injure another.

Virtue The quality of living by one's stated moral values. Persons have virtue if they are fair, honest, responsible, and beneficent.

Index